Daniel Eggers
The Language of Desire

Ideen & Argumente

Edited by
Wilfried Hinsch and Thomas Schmidt

Daniel Eggers

The Language of Desire

Expressivism and the Psychology of Moral Judgement

DE GRUYTER

ISBN 978-3-11-112218-2
e-ISBN (PDF) 978-3-11-073369-3
e-ISBN (EPUB) 978-3-11-073374-7
ISSN 1862-1147

Library of Congress Control Number: 2021935287

Bibliografic information published by the Deutsche Nationalbibliothek
The Deutsche Nationalbibliothek lists this publication in the Deutsche Nationalbibliografie;
detailed bibliografic data are available on the internet at http://dnb.dnb.de.

© 2022 Walter de Gruyter GmbH, Berlin/Boston
This volume is text- and page-identical with the hardback published in 2021.
Cover design: Martin Zech, Bremen
Cover concept: +malsy, Willich
Printing and binding: CPI books GmbH, Leck

www.degruyter.com

Contents

Foreword —— VII

Introduction —— 1

Metaethics: Moral language and beyond —— 12
1   First order and second order questions about morality —— 12
2   Contemporary metaethics: The 'ontological turn' and the 'psychological turn' —— 15
3   Summary —— 20

Expressivism – a moving target? —— 22
1   Expressivism and truth —— 23
2   Moral facts and moral properties —— 28
3   The standard definition: *Mentalism* and *sentimentalism about moral expression* —— 30
4   A note on terminology —— 36
5   Summary —— 41

A brief history of classic expressivism —— 44
1   Alfred J. Ayer —— 45
2   Charles L. Stevenson —— 48
3   Richard M. Hare —— 51
4   Simon Blackburn —— 57
5   Allan Gibbard —— 58
6   Summary —— 62

Quasi-realism and the problem of creeping minimalism —— 65
1   Metaethical analysis: Conservative or revisionary? —— 65
2   The classic expressivists revisited: Methodology —— 72
3   Quasi-realist expressivism, non-quasi-realist expressivism and the error theory —— 87
4   Creeping minimalism: The case of belief —— 91
5   Summary —— 97

Further complications: Hybrid expressivism, relational expressivism, neo-expressivism —— 100
1   Hybrid expressivism and the standard definition —— 100

2	Hybrid expressivism and the 'Frege-Geach problem' —— **104**	
3	Hybridism in Stevenson and Hare —— **109**	
4	Speaker-relative accounts of descriptive meaning —— **114**	
5	Non-speaker-relative accounts of descriptive meaning —— **124**	
6	Descriptive meaning and *de dicto* beliefs —— **137**	
7	Does pure expressivism collapse into a hybrid variant of speaker subjectivism? —— **143**	
8	Relational expressivism and neo-expressivism —— **155**	
9	Summary —— **159**	

The moral attitude problem and the expression relation —— 164

1	The specification challenge and the open question argument —— **164**
2	The expression relation (I): The causal account and its place in classic expressivism —— **177**
3	The expression relation (II): Alternatives to the causal account —— **190**
4	Summary —— **205**

Against independence: Expressivism and (empirical) moral psychology —— 207

1	The independence thesis —— **207**
2	Modern expressivists and the psychology of moral judgement —— **210**
3	Why expressivists ought to be sentimentalists about moral judgement —— **214**
4	Philosophical moral psychology, empirical moral psychology and experimental philosophy: A note on methodology —— **221**
5	Summary —— **229**

Conclusion —— 232

References —— 234

Index of names —— 248

Index of subjects —— 252

Foreword

This book is a slightly revised version of Part I of my *habilitation thesis* 'The language of desire. Expressivism, sentimentalism and the role of reason in moral judgement' which was submitted to the Faculty of Philosophy of the University of Cologne in June 2019. The remaining parts of the thesis, in which I provide an in-depth examination of the classic sentimentalism/rationalism debate of the 18th century (Part II) and develop and defend my own version of moral rationalism (Parts III and IV) are intended to be published as separate books in the future.

In working on my thesis, I have been supported by numerous people, many of whom have made an important impact on my understanding of metaethics in general and expressivism in particular. The person I am most indebted to in this context is Wilfried Hinsch who accompanied the writing of the thesis from the very beginning and provided invaluable comments and suggestions over the years. As my employer at the universities of Aachen and Cologne, he has always provided me with great working conditions, helping me to secure third party funding for the project and striving to arrange my other obligations in a way that allowed me sufficient time for my research work. Last, but not least, he functioned as one of the four reviewers of my thesis and made helpful comments with regard to matters of publication. I am therefore especially pleased that this book is published in the *de Gruyter* series *Ideen&Argumente* which is co-edited by him.

I would also like to express my gratitude to the second co-editor, Thomas Schmidt, who agreed to include my book in the series and acted as an external reviewer for my *habilitation* thesis, as well as to Christine Chwaszcza and Jürgen Richter who kindly provided the two remaining reviews. Jürgen Richter, who holds a professorship in paleolithic prehistory at the University of Cologne, contributed the non-departmental review that is demanded by the *habilitation* regulations of the Faculty of Philosophy, agreeing to assess a manuscript of over 800 pages dealing in matters outside his subject area. I am particularly indebted to him.

Another special thanks goes to Markus Stepanians who sparked my interest in expressivism and is responsible for the fact that I awarded it such a prominent place in my *habilitation* project. Although this book is probably quite different from the one Markus would have wanted me to write, I would never have written it without his help and encouragement. Moreover, especially in the early stages, my examination and discussion of the semantic and logical aspects of expressivism would have frequently gone astray without his valuable comments.

As far as the many other helpful suggestions are concerned which I received over the years, I will restrict myself to those colleagues and friends who specifically commented on Part I of my thesis and leave other due acknowledgements for future occasions. Some of my initial ideas on expressivism were presented at the Graz Research Seminar in Practical Philosophy in 2010 and the *Habilitandenkolloquium* at the Department of Philosophy of the University of Cologne in 2013. I am grateful to all participants for their comments and criticism. In particular, I would like to thank Lukas Meyer, Peter Koller, Thomas Grundmann, Andreas Hüttemann and my colleagues Tanja Munk and Sven Nyholm. Parts of chapter 5 were originally written for the workshop *Normativity and Meaning*, which took place at the Universität des Saarlandes in Saarbrücken in 2014. I would like to thank the organizer, Stephan Padel, for inviting me and for commenting on my paper. I am also grateful to other participants who provided helpful suggestions, in particular to Michael Ridge, Jan Gertken and Christoph Fehige. My work on expressivism has also greatly benefited from conversations at other conferences and workshops over the years, including conversations with Michael Smith in Gothenburg and Bielefeld, with David Enoch and Gerhard Ernst in Freiburg, with Oliver Hallich in Münster, and with Neil Roughley, Markus Rüther and Sebastian Muders in Delmenhorst.

I am grateful to *de Gruyter* for accepting my manuscript for publication and to Marcus Böhm and Mara Weber for providing important help in the process of preparing the manuscript. I would also like to thank an anonymous reviewer for the series *Ideen&Argumente* for recommending the manuscript for publication and providing helpful comments on how to improve it. Parts of Chapter 5 of this book have previously been published under the name "Nothing new in Ecumenia? Hare, hybrid expressivism and de dicto beliefs", in *Ethical Theory and Moral Practice*, 19, 2016, pp. 831–847. I would like thank the publisher Springer and the editors for allowing me to include the relevant parts and two anonymous reviewers for providing insightful suggestions.

The first draft of this book was written during my time as a *Junior Research Fellow* at the *Centre for Advanced Studies in Bioethics* at the University of Münster in 2015 and 2016. I would like to thank all the persons involved, especially Ruth Langer, Stefan Klatt and Kurt Bayertz, for providing me with such excellent working conditions. Also, I would like to express my gratitude to the *Deutsche Forschungsgemeinschaft* (German Research Foundation) for funding the *habilitation* project from which this book has emerged (HI 376/6–1).

Last, but not least, I am grateful to my wife Anna, for taking up the Sisyphean task of improving my English, for expressing profound philosophical and methodological worries with regard to the entire metaethical enterprise, and, most of all, for the world's two greatest children, Ella and Jonas.

Introduction

The metaethical theory commonly referred to as expressivism has dominated much of the metaethical debate of the past 30 years. According to the standard definition, expressivism is the view that moral terms and moral utterances express desire-like states of mind rather than beliefs. When Allan Gibbard and Simon Blackburn established the term 'expressivism' for this metaethical view in the early 1990s, they took it to equally apply to Alfred Ayer's and Charles Stevenson's 'emotivism' and Richard Hare's 'prescriptivism' as to their own versions of 'quasi-realism'. Since then, many reformulations and advancements of the basic idea have been forwarded. At the same time, the term has come to be applied in a slightly broader fashion, having been used to also describe theories that depart some way from the standard definition. As a result, the metaethical landscape now contains destinations such as "pure expressivism"[1], "hybrid expressivism"[2], "ecumenical expressivism"[3], "cognitivist expressivism"[4], "realist-expressivism"[5], "neo-expressivism"[6], "relational expressivism"[7], "tempered expressivism"[8], "attitudinal expressivism"[9] and "global expressivism"[10] – to name only a few.

While the expressivist theory in its various guises has received a huge amount of attention, there are some important issues which have been neglected and rarely addressed in a systematic fashion. One of those issues is the historical development of expressivism and the question of how exactly the views of the 'classic' expressivists relate to one another. There is a consensus that the history of expressivism more narrowly construed begins with the publication of Ayer's book *Language, truth and logic* in 1936, and there is also considerable agreement that Ayer, Stevenson, Hare, Blackburn and Gibbard are the key proponents and most influential endorsers of the expressivist idea. However, one striking fact about the previous debate is that the expressivist status of almost all these 'classic' expressivists has been challenged. While scepticism may have been particu-

---

1 Toppinen 2015a.
2 Schroeder 2009.
3 Ridge 2006a.
4 Horgan/Timmons 2006b.
5 Copp 2001.
6 Bar-On/Chrisman 2009.
7 Toppinen 2015b.
8 Schroeder 2013.
9 Chrisman 2014.
10 Price 2015.

larly prominent in the case of Richard Hare,[11] similar reservations have been expressed with regard to Stevenson,[12] Blackburn[13] and Gibbard.[14]

Where the status of modern proponents of hybrid expressivism or cognitivist expressivism such as Stephen Barker, Daniel Boisvert, David Copp or Terry Horgan and Mark Timmons is concerned, there is even less of an agreement to begin with. Thus, Michael Ridge classifies the approaches of Copp, Boisvert and Barker as cognitivist rather than expressivist,[15] in spite of the fact that Copp and Boisvert themselves consider their positions to be genuine examples of expressivism. As though to make things even more complicated, Neil Sinclair has argued that Barker is indeed an expressivist, but that neither Copp nor Boisvert are.[16] Moreover, as far as Horgan and Timmons are concerned, the problem of appropriately classifying their theory is nicely illustrated by Horgan and Timmons's own difficulties in finding a proper label for their position.[17] Given this surprising uncertainty as to who can count as a genuine expressivist and what makes a theory a true variant of expressivism, it seems valuable to revisit the question of what expressivism is really all about and to show what the approaches of the classic expressivists have in common and where and to what extent they differ from one another.

The only author whose status as an expressivist seems uncontroversial among metaethicists is Ayer. Yet, in his case, a further problem of the previous debate becomes pertinent. In the more recent discussion of expressivism, which is strongly influenced by Blackburn's and Gibbard's attempts to develop quasi-realist versions of expressivism that can do justice to the surface structure of moral discourse and the role of rational discussion and argument, Ayer is almost exclusively referenced as a cautionary tale, as an example for 'how not to be an expressivist'. An analysis and discussion of Ayer's views in their own right is hardly ever attempted any more, his theory being dismissed as "notoriously crude"[18] even by fellow expressivists. As a result, important aspects and, in particular, important developments of his theory are not sufficiently appreciated.

---

[11] See, for example, Czaniera 2001, 93 ff.; and Joyce 2009, 31 and 34. See also Schulte 2010, 150 f.
[12] See Gibbard 2003, 6 f.
[13] See Thomson 2006, 244.
[14] See Barker 2006, 299; and Cuneo 2006, 37. See also Blackburn/Sinclair 2006, 705.
[15] See Ridge 2006a, 308; and Ridge 2014, 83–85.
[16] See Sinclair 2009, 138.
[17] Instead of describing their theory as 'cognitivist expressivism', Horgan and Timmons have also referred to it as 'nondescriptivist cognitivism' (Horgan/Timmons 2000) and 'assertoric nondescriptivism' (Timmons 1999).
[18] Ridge 2006a, 310.

One example for the somewhat unsatisfactory approach to Ayer's theory is that he is indiscriminately credited with a naïve, causal interpretation of the expression relation, without any real attempt being made to back up this reading with robust textual evidence. To achieve a more balanced and charitable understanding of Ayer's relevant position not only appears to be a demand of exegetical fairness. It can also contribute to a better understanding of the problems faced by alternative conceptions of the expression relation, such as the ones forwarded by Gibbard, Mark Schroeder, Michael Ridge or Peter Schulte.

A further issue that has not been given due attention in the past is whether expressivism is a conservative or a revisionary doctrine, which issue is linked to the question of how exactly expressivism relates to John Mackie's error theory (or, for that matter, to modern derivatives of his theory, including variants of moral fictionalism). In the more recent literature, it is usually claimed that expressivism is a conservative, non-revisionary theory which is concerned with how we *actually* use moral language, not with how we *ought* to use it. What remains unclear, however, is whether this is meant to apply to all major forms of expressivism or only to the quasi-realist variants developed in the wake of Blackburn and Gibbard. Similarly, there is a routine distinction between expressivism and the error theory which draws upon the idea that, for Mackie, moral utterances express (false) beliefs rather than desire-like states of mind, which would render him a peculiar sort of metaethical non-naturalist. However, not only does Mackie himself abstain from characterizing his theory in these terms. The references in question often display certain inconsistencies that have not been taken up by commentators so far. As already indicated, expressivism is typically viewed as an alternative to, and contender of, the error theory, and Blackburn has placed much emphasis on the fact that expressivism is not itself a version of the error theory. At the same time, however, Blackburn explicitly refers to Mackie as an expressivist in his own right,[19] and other writers have seen important affinities between the two approaches as well. Now one way of resolving these inconsistencies might be to attribute to Mackie a non-expressivist conception of moral language, but an expressivist conception of moral thought. Yet, it is by no means obvious that Mackie can be interpreted in this way, nor is it obvious whether the suggested combination presents a stable overall position.

The distinction between moral language and moral thought appealed to above already points to a final and more general problem of the previous debate. The more recent discussion of expressivism prompted by the writings of Blackburn and Gibbard has been accompanied by a growing discussion of issues in

---

19 See Blackburn 2006, 154.

moral psychology to which not only social and developmental psychologists and neuroscientists such as Jonathan Haidt, Joshua Greene, Adina Roskies or Fiery Cushman have made their contributions but also numerous metaethicists. In virtue of these contributions, modern metaethics has experienced something akin to a 'psychological turn' since the 1990s which has superseded the ontological turn initiated by Mackie and Gilbert Harman in the late 1970s, and it does not seem far-fetched to claim that this psychological turn has been facilitated, if not caused, by the increasing importance of the expressivist approach.

Yet, the question of how exactly the expressivist approach to moral language connects with issues in the philosophy of mind and the philosophy of action has rarely been addressed head-on. Many commentators just seem to take it for granted that expressivism has a psychological side to it or that it at least has certain psychological commitments in tow.[20] Something like this might also be taken to be indicated by the fact that many writers describe expressivism as a variant of moral sentimentalism.[21] However, this latter kind of evidence is by no means unambiguous, given that there is no agreed upon definition of the term 'sentimentalism', it being used to refer to quite different psychological, epistemological and ontological views. Moreover, some commentators, most notably Richard Joyce, explicitly *deny* that there is any interesting link between expressivism as a linguistic claim on the one hand and sentimentalist approaches in moral psychology on the other.[22] What lends *prima facie* plausibility to this denial is that the existing versions of expressivism seem to stand in different proximity to classic versions of moral sentimentalism such as the one defended by David Hume. While Blackburn is a self-professed "card-carrying Humean"[23] and something similar may be true of Ayer, the Humean credentials of Gibbard and Hare are much more precarious. On the other hand, it might be for exactly this reason that some metaethicists have reservations against viewing Hare and Gibbard as full-fledged expressivists to begin with – which would again suggest that there *is* an important link between the primary linguistic analysis on the one hand and more substantial commitments in the philosophy of mind and action on the other.

The psychological implications of expressivism therefore not only merit a systematic discussion in their own right. Their examination can be expected to

---

20 See, for instance, Dunn 2004.
21 See, for example, d'Arms/Jacobson 2000a, 70; Svavarsdottír 2001, 18; Nichols 2004, 83; Slote 2010, 3; Parfit 2011, 379 f; Kauppinen 2014b, 3; and Prinz 2015, 70 f.
22 See Joyce 2008; and Joyce 2009.
23 See Blackburn's unpublished commentary on Marc Hauser's Princeton Lecture, delivered in 2008.

importantly contribute to a better understanding of the strengths and weaknesses of expressivism as a metaethical theory. In fact, trying to settle the question of whether, and how, metaethical expressivism relates to questions regarding the psychological nature of moral judgement will provide ample opportunity for addressing the other neglected issues mentioned above, given that they are all, in one way or the other, connected to the psychological issue. Although the guiding idea of this book then is to critically discuss Joyce's 'independence thesis' and to demonstrate that and why expressivists should be sentimentalists about moral judgement, its overall aspiration extends further than this. Rather than just helping to unearth a systematic link between the linguistic and the psychological enterprise, the purpose of the book is to tie together some loose ends of the previous debate over metaethical expressivism and to sharpen our conception of what expressivism is really all about.

Given that the intention behind this book is to address some crucial problems raised by the expressivist approach, it seems important to point out that, and why, I will not offer a lengthy treatment of what is typically considered to provide the main obstacle for an expressivist analysis of moral language: the problem of accounting for uses of moral predicates in embedded and unasserted contexts, commonly referred to as the 'Frege-Geach problem'. There are two main reasons for not engaging with this latter problem in more detail. The first is that it is not intimately related to the psychological aspects of expressivism that are my main concern. Rather than entering into a detailed discussion of whether, and how, expressivists can solve the 'Frege-Geach problem', I shall therefore focus on problems that bear such an intimate relation, such as the problem of 'creeping minimalism', the 'moral attitude problem' or the problem of providing a plausible account of the 'expression relation'.

The second reason is that the problem does not seem to have been neglected in the previous debate over expressivism at all, having in fact provided the debate's primary focus. In accordance with this, the historical influence exerted by the problem is widely acknowledged. What has motivated the move to 'quasi-realist' versions of expressivism in the 1980s and 1990s is the ambition to better account for the propositional surface of moral language, and within this enterprise, solving the 'Frege-Geach problem' is one if not the key objective. Although I will be concerned with the historical development of expressivism and the differences between earlier and later articulations of the basic expressivist idea, my emphasis will not be on this developmental stage because the important role played by Blackburn and Gibbard is well-established. As far as the history of expressivism and the relationship between different expressivist theories are concerned, the shortcomings of the previous debate do not consist in having failed to acknowledge important differences between Blackburn's and Gibbard's quasi-realism and the emotivism of Ayer and Stevenson. If anything, they consist in having *overstated* these differences and been insensitive to important continuities between the earlier and the later approaches. Rather than adding to the orthodoxy regarding the 'Frege-Geach problem' and its place in the history of expressivism, therefore, my aim will be to qualify the orthodox view and gain a more nuanced picture of the historical development, by emphasizing what quasi-realist and non-quasi-realist versions of expressivism have in common. In the course of doing so, however, I will also offer a positive proposal for how to conceive of their differences. Moreover, I will explicitly introduce and address the 'Frege-Geach problem', if somewhat briefly, in my discussion of hybrid expressivism.

The main objective of this book is to defend the idea that there is an intimate link between expressivist accounts of moral utterances and sentimentalist accounts of moral judgement and that, by subscribing to an expressivist interpretation of ordinary moral discourse, one incurs substantial commitments in the philosophy of mind. The argument developed in support of this claim will touch upon a number of other issues which have been neglected in the previous debate and seem worthy of discussion in their own right.

I start with a brief general characterization of the metaethical enterprise in Chapter 1, entitled 'Metaethics: Moral language and beyond'. After introducing the distinction between first order and second order questions about morality and the related distinction between the 'internal' and 'external' moral perspective (section 1), I briefly describe how metaethics has evolved over the years, turning from a more narrow debate over the meaning of moral terms into a much broader field of philosophical research that extends to linguistic, epistemological and ontological as well as to psychological issues (section 2).

The aim of Chapter 2, 'Expressivism – a moving target?' – is to provide an adequate definition of expressivism, which task is somewhat complicated by the fact that the expressivist approach has been subjected to certain revisions and shifts of emphasis in the past. After rejecting the idea that expressivism should be defined in terms of the denial of moral truth, moral facts or moral properties (sections 1 and 2), I introduce what has become the standard definition of expressivism, i.e. the thesis that moral utterances express desire-like states of mind rather than beliefs, and distinguish two central elements of this claim: the idea that we ought to analyse the meaning of utterances in terms of the mental states they express (to which idea I refer by the name *mentalism*), and the idea that what is expressed by moral utterances are non-cognitive rather than cognitive mental states (to which idea I refer by the name *sentimentalism about moral expression*) (section 3). Moreover, I briefly explain my reasons for choosing the relevant designations and for avoiding others, such as 'noncognitivism' or 'projectivism' (section 4).

Chapter 3 – 'A brief history of classic expressivism' – is devoted to the origins of the expressivist approach and the writings of the 'classic' expressivists. My main interest in sections 1 to 5 is to demonstrate that the view we find in many publications on expressivism, namely that Alfred Ayer, Charles Stevenson, Richard Hare, Simon Blackburn and Allan Gibbard are the key proponents of expressivism, is fully justified. Though the expressivist status of almost all of these writers has been challenged in the past, we can legitimately ascribe to all of them the two claims characteristic of the expressivist approach, be it because they explicitly endorse them or because we can plausibly re-interpret their statements in these terms.

While the contribution of the first three chapters is mainly expositional, Chapter 4, entitled 'Quasi-realism and the problem of creeping minimalism', leads over to a more critical discussion of the expressivist thesis. The purpose of the chapter is to discuss the methodological status of the expressivist analysis and to inquire whether Blackburn's and Gibbard's aspirations of developing a 'quasi-realist' version of expressivism that can accommodate the role of rational argument and the propositional surface of ordinary moral discourse threatens to undermine the general expressivist idea that moral utterances are expressions of desires. The claim I will ultimately defend is that quasi-realist expressivists can only avoid undermining their own position in this way if they the conceive of the fundamental distinction between beliefs and desires in non-linguistic, robustly psychological terms.

I start by discussing the question whether expressivism is a conservative or a revisionary doctrine, and whether quasi-realist and non-quasi-realist versions of expressivism differ with regard to this question. After introducing the issue and questioning a hard-and-fast distinction between conservative and revisionary analyses of moral language (section 1), I show that all classic expressivists think of their theories as accounts of the actual usage of moral words while admitting, at the same time, that these accounts make certain revisions to how some ordinary speakers speak (section 2). Moreover, the review of the relevant passages in the works of the classic expressivists reveals that the arguments by which the five key proponents support their expressivist analysis are rarely, if ever, linguistic in nature. Rather, Ayer, Stevenson, Hare, Blackburn and Gibbard rely on epistemological, metaphysical and psychological arguments, and the two latter writers positively suggest that, given the propositional surface of ordinary moral discourse, there is no way to successfully defend expressivism in terms of a specifically linguistic argument. After discussing what these findings imply with regard to the distinction between quasi-realist and non-quasi-realist expressivism and their relation to Mackie's error theory (section 3), I take up the question of whether their recent sympathy for minimalist conceptions of truth, facts and properties deprives quasi-realists like Blackburn and Gibbard of the fundamental idea that moral utterances do *not* express beliefs, given that minimalism also suggests a minimalist understanding for beliefs according to which a belief is merely what is expressed by a declarative sentence (section 4). As already indicated, my conclusion is that the expressivist can solve this problem of 'creeping minimalism', but only if he embraces a genuinely psychological conception of beliefs and desires.

Chapter 5 – 'Further complications: Hybrid expressivism, relational expressivism, neo-expressivism' – is devoted to a view which has dominated the more recent discussion of expressivism and is commonly referred to under the name 'hybrid expressivism': the view that moral utterances express *both* desires *and* beliefs. The reason why this view has become increasingly popular is that it promises to provide the 'best of both worlds', and the overall purpose of the chapter is to examine whether this promise holds true. My ultimate conclusion is that hybrid expressivism fails because hybrid expressivists are unable to account for the descriptive meaning of moral utterances while, at the same time, remaining faithful to the general expressivist spirit of their analysis.

I start with a discussion of whether hybrid expressivism is plausibly viewed as a version of expressivism in the first place, showing why and how we can reconcile hybridism with the standard definition of expressivism (section 1). I will then attend what is usually taken to be the main virtue of hybrid expressivism, namely that it provides a solution to the 'Frege-Geach problem' (section 2). Following Mark Schroeder, I emphasize that hybrid expressivism's potential for solving this problem is dependent upon some further crucial features. The purpose of section 3 is to reject the view that hybrid expressivism is a recent invention, by showing that we may legitimately interpret both Stevenson and Hare as hybrid expressivists.

My more substantial critique of hybrid expressivism is then developed in sections 4 to 6 where I discuss the problems faced by both the existing speaker-relative accounts of descriptive meaning (Ridge, Barker, Stevenson, Hare) and the existing non-speaker-relative accounts (Hallich). One crucial claim defended in the course of the relevant discussion is that, even if the hybrid expressivist might succeed in identifying a plausible non-speaker-relative belief that is conventionally expressed by moral utterances, he thereby loses an important part of his leverage against naturalist analyses because the appeal to Moore's 'open question argument' becomes problematic.

Section 7 takes up a challenge against expressivism raised by Frank Jackson and Philip Pettit, namely that any expressivist account of moral language must ultimately collapse into a (hybrid) variant of 'speaker subjectivism'. After arguing that defenders of a 'pure' (as opposed to a 'hybrid') version of expressivism can overcome Jackson and Pettit's challenge, I take a brief look at two other approaches that have recently been forwarded under the name 'expressivism', namely relational expressivism (as defended by Teemu Toppinen and Michael Ridge) and neo-expressivism (as defended by Matthew Chrisman, Dorit Bar-On and James Sias), if only to argue that neither approach straightforwardly qualifies as a version of expressivism and that the relationalist approach in particular gives rise to a variety of so far unresolved issues. The conclusion suggested by the discussion of Chapter 5, then, is that the only way for the expressivist to go is to defend a version of pure expressivism, which is why the subsequent discussion very much focuses on this variant.

The aim of Chapter 6, entitled 'The moral attitude problem and the expression relation', is to take up two of the main objections against the existing expressivist accounts of moral language: the claim that expressivists have not provided an appropriate specification of the particular desire(s) or attitude(s) supposedly expressed by moral utterances (and might in fact be unable to ever do so), and the claim that expressivists have not provided us with an appropriate analysis of the 'expression relation', leaving it unclear what it actually means to say that an utterance 'expresses' a particular state of mind. In introducing the former issue, i.e. the 'moral attitude problem', in section 1, I first describe the dilemma some critics take expressivists to find themselves in: the dilemma of having to either characterize the desire(s) expressed by moral utterances in purely descriptivist terms, thereby becoming vulnerable to some version of the 'open question argument', or characterize it in specifically moral or normative terms, thereby becoming vulnerable to some variant of Mackie's 'argument from queerness' or at least to a charge of circularity or emptiness. Relying on considerations forwarded by Sebastian Köhler and others, I provide a tentative argument to the effect that there really is no dilemma for the expressivist. However, I emphasize that any specification of the relevant desire(s) comes at a cost because it will inevitably deprive the expressivist of some of his supposed dialectical advantages over the naturalist or the non-naturalist.

At the beginning of section 2, I first sketch the worries about the insufficient treatment of the 'expression relation' that have been expressed by Mark Schroeder and others. I then elaborate on the issue by reconstructing their views about why a purely causal account of the expression relation, which they take to be suggested by the early emotivist theories of Ayer and Stevenson, is inappropriate. While I concur in the negative assessment of the purely causal account, I demonstrate, against Schroeder and the other commentators, that neither Ayer's nor Stevenson's views are captured by the purely causal account in the first place. In section 3, I then consider the alternative to the causal account that has been forwarded by Allan Gibbard and the more recent accounts of Schroeder, Ridge and Schulte which all aspire to overcome certain problems with Gibbard's account. In doing so, I shall remain largely agnostic about how best to ultimately conceive of the expression relation. My aim is, rather, to show that any plausible conception of the expression relation must posit *some* kind of frequent causal connection between the moral utterances that supposedly express certain mental states and the relevant mental states themselves. That the purely causal account of the expression relation is inappropriate, on this view, should not mislead us into thinking that the states of mind users of moral language are actually in do not at all bear on the question of which states they can express by way of linguistic convention.

The aim of the Chapter 7 is to more systematically address the question of whether and how the expressivist approach to moral utterances depends on a particular view about the psychology of moral judgement. Tying together the relevant results of Chapters 4 to 6, I reject the 'independence thesis' suggested by Richard Joyce. According to Joyce, the linguistic and the psychological enterprises are entirely separate from one another which is why the view that psychological theory and empirical psychological evidence bear on the plausibility of expressivism is fundamentally misguided. After reconstructing Joyce's relevant arguments (section 1), I first emphasize that, contrary to what might be taken to be suggested by Joyce, modern expressivists such as Blackburn and Gibbard do in fact conceive of their theories as theories about *both* moral language *and* moral thought and actually appeal to psychological evidence and other empirical considerations in making their cases (section 2). If nothing else, therefore, Joyce's independence thesis fails to provide an accurate description of the reality of modern expressivism.

However, the stronger claim I shall defend in section 3 is that this is not just a contingent fact about modern expressivism, since versions of expressivism that do *not* take a stand on whether moral judgements are constituted by desire-like states (or even explicitly concede that they are not) are seriously unstable. In making this point, I crucially draw on the main conclusions of the previous chapters: the conclusion that expressivism can only solve the problem of creeping minimalism by relying on a genuinely psychological account of the belief-desire distinction; the conclusion that there really is no specifically linguistic case to be made for expressivism because the propositional surface of ordinary moral discourse is *prima facie* at odds with the expressivist analysis; the conclusion that the expressivist needs to actually specify the desire-like states that are supposedly expressed by moral utterances and assign them a plausible place in the overall picture of our mental set up as human agents; and the conclusion that any plausible account of the expression relation needs to make room for the idea that, when expressing desire-like states of mind by way of moral utterances, we are typically in those very states as a matter of empirical psychological fact. Moreover, against the background of my rejection of Joyce's independence thesis, I finally address some more general methodological issues and further characterize the overall approach of the thesis as an example of what is now usually referred to as philosophical psychology.

The overall conclusion emerging from the analysis, then, is that there is no way to defend metaethical expressivism without, at the same time, embracing a particular version of moral sentimentalism. Investigations into the plausibility of moral sentimentalism therefore not only make a contribution to the question of whether or not morality has some kind of rational foundation, but *a fortiori* to the assessment of expressivism as well. Moreover, given that many of the considerations forwarded in support of modern expressivism as a theory of both moral language and moral thought are either themselves of a psychological nature or at least bear on the psychological issue in one way or the other, something like the reverse holds as well: any discussion of moral sentimentalism will importantly benefit from the arguments and conceptual distinctions introduced by modern quasi-realist expressivists.

Metaethics: Moral language and beyond

1 First order and second order questions about morality

It is widely agreed that the emergence of metaethics as an autonomous philosophical (sub-) discipline is marked off by the publication of G. E. Moore's *Principia Ethica* in 1903. Though we find considerations we would now describe as metaethical in the works of virtually all major moral thinkers, especially perhaps in Aristotle, Hume, Kant, Mill and Sidgwick, it is only with Moore's systematic discussion of the meaning of the word 'good' that metaethics is established as an independent philosophical enterprise.

In order to describe the distinctive aim of metaethics (as opposed to normative ethics), we can draw on a distinction that has become customary in contemporary moral philosophy: the distinction between first order moral questions and second order moral questions.[1] First order moral questions are the province of normative ethics. Examples include specific questions such as 'is abortion morally wrong?' or 'should I donate to famine relief?' as well as the more general questions underlying those specific questions: 'what is (morally) right/wrong?', 'what ought I (morally) to do?' or 'what is (morally) good/bad?'. In contrast, second order questions, which are the province of metaethics, are questions *about* these first order moral questions, and the question which mainly preoccupied Moore, namely 'what does 'good' (as in 'what is (morally) good?') mean?' clearly falls into this category.

Of course, exactly *how* independent metaethical questions really are from normative moral questions is a matter of on-going dispute. Moore not only suggests the above distinction between moral questions and questions about moral questions, but seems to have taken the view that conceptual first order questions can and should be treated independently from substantive normative questions. Thus, in his introductory remarks in the preface to the *Principia Ethica*, Moore claims that the crucial mistake of traditional ethicists is "the attempt to answer questions, without first discovering *what* question it is which you desire to answer", and he predicts, perhaps overly optimistic in hindsight, that many difficulties in moral philosophy would simply disappear once philosophers "would *try* to discover what question they were asking, before they set out to answer

---

[1] For uses of the distinction between first order and second order questions, see, for instance, Mackie 1977, 9; Blackburn 1993b, 153 und 164f.; Smith 1994a, 2; Gibbard 2003, 6; Miller 2003, 1f.; Scarano 2006, 27; Ernst 2008, 9f.; Hallich 2008, 30; and Chrisman 2016, 1. See also the related distinction between 'internal' and 'external' questions (e.g., Blackburn 1993c, 172f.)

https://doi.org/10.1515/9783110733693-003

it"[2]. Moore leaves hardly any doubt, however, that the ultimate value of discussing conceptual first order questions lies in what such a discussion can contribute to answering the normative questions. As we have just seen, Moore's proposal is that we should "first" (hence not exclusively) concern ourselves with the relevant first order questions. Moreover, he explicitly refers to his metaethical theory as "Prolegomena to any future Ethics that can possibly pretend to be scientific"[3] and accordingly goes on to address more substantial ethical questions in the final two chapters of *Principia Ethica*.[4]

Some of Moore's metaethical successors have taken a more extreme view with regard to the relationship of metaethics and normative ethics. Alfred Ayer, for instance, accepts and, in fact, reinforces the distinction between different classes of questions or statements with "ethical content"[5] and, in doing so, puts particular emphasis on distinguishing between definitions of moral terms on the one hand and "actual ethical judgements"[6] on the other. Yet, far from viewing the enterprise of defining moral terms as a kind of *prolegomena* for making and justifying actual ethical judgements, Ayer claims that the latter judgements have no place whatsoever in moral philosophy properly understood, which he takes to be exclusively concerned with the enterprise of providing definitions of moral terms and arguments in favour of those definitions.[7] At the other end of the spectrum, we find writers such as Ronald Dworkin who question the distinction between first and second order questions in the first place. Dworkin not only doubts the normative neutrality of metaethics, but goes as far as to intimate that the entire metaethical projects rests on a mistake because metaethical questions are really just first order moral questions in disguise.[8] A middle view is taken by those who consider the distinction between first order and second order question to be viable and useful, but question whether metaethics is fully normatively neutral.[9] According to these authors, holding certain metaeth-

---

2 Moore 1903/1993, 33.
3 Moore 1903/1993, 35.
4 See Moore 1903/1993, 192 ff.
5 Ayer 1936/1967, 103.
6 Ayer 1936/1967, 103.
7 See Ayer 1936/1967, 103 f. and 112. See also Ayer 1954, 235.
8 See Dworkin 2011, 10 f., 25 f., 37 and 67. See also Dworkin 1996, 112. That the distinction between metaethics and normative ethics needs to be abandoned is also Gilbert Harman's view (see Harman 1977, VIII).
9 The view that metaethics is normatively neutral has traditionally been defended by Ayer, Hare and Mackie (see Ayer 1954, 246 f.; Hare 1963, 88 f. and 192; and Mackie 1977, 16).

ical positions may commit us to particular normative conclusions, without these metaethical positions therefore being second order positions in their own right.[10]

No matter how exactly we conceive of the relation between metaethics and normative ethics, and whether or not we subscribe to Moore's suggestion that the function of the former is to set the stage for the latter, there can be no doubt that metaethics has come quite a long way since Moore's *Principia Ethica*. One impressive but, at the same time, ambivalent piece of evidence for the development of metaethics into a vast and complex field of philosophical research are the numerous '-isms' that abound in the contemporary metaethical debate. While Moore largely contented himself with the labels 'naturalism' and 'non-naturalism' (and was much more hesitant than his critics to use the label 'intuitionism' for his own position)[11], modern metaethicists happily appeal to a multitude of designations: subjectivism, emotivism, intuitionism, prescriptivism, expressivism, cognitivism, non-cognitivism, realism, anti-realism, irrealism, quasi-realism, fictionalism, contextualism, quietism – to name only a few. While the function of these designations may originally have been to provide some orientation within the potentially confusing array of different metaethical positions, it is hard to deny that, by now, they have added more to the confusion than they have helped to resolve it. The reason is, of course, that there is no agreement on how exactly to employ the relevant terms and sometimes not even an agreement about the more general *type* of systematic question – semantic, ontological or other? – to which they refer.

It may be for this reason that many recent introductions to metaethics refrain from mapping the metaethical field with the help of such labels and responding flow charts. Instead, there is a tendency to characterize metaethics and the current metaethical debate in terms of the different systematic questions to which the various metaethical positions try to provide an answer. In what follows, I will give a brief overview of the relevant questions and indicate how they relate to one another.

---

10 See, for example, Czaniera 2001; Radtke 2009, 20; and Enoch 2011, 41 ff. Notice, however, that Czaniera explicitly distinguishes between 'input-neutrality' and 'output-neutrality' and accepts the view that metaethics is normatively neutral in the former sense. See also Blackburn who strongly rejects Dworkin's view and emphasizes the distinction between internal and external moral questions (see Blackburn 1998, 295 ff.), but concedes that certain metaethical views, in particular certain interpretations of the function of morality, may be hard to square with certain deontological approaches in normative ethics and criticizes Mackie for happily engaging in first order theorizing in spite of his own error theory (see Blackburn 1993b, 164 f.).
11 See Moore 1903/1993, 35.

2 Contemporary metaethics: The 'ontological turn' and the 'psychological turn'

The most important point to notice with regard to the current metaethical debate is that metaethics is now rarely defined as an inquiry into moral language, although most commentators still seem to agree that semantic questions provide the primary focus of metaethics. Rather, metaethics is usually characterized in terms of four distinct, though inter-related, kinds of questions:

a) *semantic* questions, e.g. 'what does (morally) 'good' mean?' and 'are moral judgements truth-apt?'
b) *epistemological* questions, e.g. 'is there such a thing as moral knowledge?' and 'by what faculty do we acquire such knowledge?'
c) *ontological* or *metaphysical* questions, e.g. 'are there any moral facts?' and 'are there any moral properties?' and 'are moral properties natural or non-natural properties?'
d) *psychological* questions, e.g. 'what kind of mental state or event constitutes a moral judgement?' or 'are moral judgements motivationally efficacious?'

Though there are still some writers who endorse the traditional narrow conception of metaethics,[12] the vast majority has come to characterize it in these broader terms,[13] and, contrary to what Oliver Hallich has recently suggested, there seems nothing wrong with doing so. Hallich argues that, under the broader notion, metaethics becomes shapeless and virtually collapses into philosophical ethics.[14] Yet, as the widespread distinction between first and second order questions demonstrates, the primary aspect about metaethics is that it essentially differs from normative ethics (which is also a sub-discipline of philosophical ethics after all). Defining metaethics in terms of the questions listed above, however, does not threaten this distinction at all, since what all these kinds of questions have in common is that they focus on morality from a descriptive point of view. If, on the other hand, we go as far as to challenge the distinction between first

---

[12] See Gibbard 2003, 6; Hallich 2008, 29; and Gibbard 2014, 7f. Gibbard explicitly concedes, however, that his use of the term 'metaethics' may not do justice to how the term is now being employed (see Gibbard 2014, 7). See also Radtke whose list of metaethical questions only includes semantic and epistemological examples (Radtke 2009, 19f.).
[13] See, for example, Scarano 2001, 11–14; Miller 2003, 2; Smith 2005, 6; Scarano 2006, 27; Ernst 2008, 76; Schroeder 2008a, 6f.; Tarkian 2009, 11; Sayre-McCord 2012, 1; Rüther 2013, 14; Kauppinen 2014a, 281f; and Chrisman 2016, 1. For an explicit rejection of narrower definitions of current metaethics, see also Miller 2003, 2f.; and Ernst 2008, 76f.
[14] See Hallich 2008, 30.

order and second order questions and follow Dworkin into thinking that metaethical questions are themselves normative questions, then there is no need for a distinct notion of metaethics in the first place.

The coexistence of such distinct issues in the current metaethical debate is the result of a more recent development. In its early stages, metaethics was almost primarily devoted to the meaning of moral terms or moral sentences and hence to the linguistic aspects of morality. This applies, for example, to G. E. Moore, Alfred Ayer and Charles Stevenson as well as to the early work of Richard Hare, whose 1952 book title *The language of morals* provides a summary for this kind of metaethical enterprise. Thus, much in agreement with Moore, Stevenson describes the aim of his theory as that of "making ethical questions clear"[15], which aim he equates with the task of clarifying the meaning of ethical terms.[16] Similarly, Hare introduces his early theory as a "study of the chief moral words"[17], even though he puts additional emphasis on the connection between the meaning of moral words and their "logical properties"[18].

This interest in moral semantics was usually connected with epistemological questions, though, in particular with the question of whether and how it is possible to provide justifications for moral judgements. Moore explicitly professes an interest into the evidence by which ethical propositions "can be proved or disproved, confirmed or rendered doubtful"[19], while Ayer forwards the negative claim that, given the true nature of moral judgements, there can be "no way of determining the validity of any ethical system"[20] whatsoever. Again, Stevenson's view of the matter is close to Moore's in that he conceives of the clarification of the meaning of moral terms as only a "preliminary step"[21] and takes the second task to consist in the characterization of "the general methods by which ethical judgments can be proved or supported"[22]. Finally, in Hare's case, the preoccupation with moral justification becomes most visible in his attempt to pro-

---

15 Stevenson 1963c, 10.
16 See Stevenson 1944, 1.
17 Hare 1963, V.
18 Hare 1963, V. See also Hare 1999a, 1. A further difference between the two is that Stevenson presents this kind of theoretical project as comprising only a "narrowly specialized part" (Stevenson 1944, 1) of ethics, whereas Hare, not unlike Ayer, tends to equate the "logical study of the language of morals" (Hare 1952, III) with the whole of ethics or moral philosophy (see Hare 1952, III; and Hare 1999a, 39 and 43f.).
19 Moore 1903/1993, 34.
20 Ayer 1936/1967, 112.
21 Stevenson 1963c, 10.
22 Stevenson 1944, 1.

vide an account of the logic of moral reasoning that can help to improve our moral thinking.[23]

Whereas ontological and psychological considerations certainly lingered in the background of the semantic and epistemological analyses and often provided important, albeit usually unelaborated motivations for the particular approaches defended in these areas, they have become an integral part of metaethics only in the course of the last four decades.[24] The increasing interest in ontological or metaphysical aspects of morality primarily emerged from the discussion of John Mackie's book *Ethics. Inventing right and wrong* and, to a lesser extent, from the discussion of Gilbert Harman's *The nature of morality*, both published in 1977.[25] As far as purely linguistic questions are concerned, Mackie's error theory does not differ much from Moore's non-naturalism. Mackie agrees that moral terms such as 'good' or 'right' refer to some kind of non-natural, *sui generis* property and that the sentences in which they appear are assessable in terms of truth and falsity. However, Mackie thinks that there is no such thing as moral knowledge and no way of justifying moral judgements because the properties to which moral terms refer, i.e. objective values, do not exist. It is, therefore, a specifically ontological assumption that leads Mackie to his peculiar disagreement with important strands of the metaethical tradition:

> If second order ethics were confined, then, to linguistic and conceptual analysis, it ought to conclude that moral values at least are objective: that they are so is part of what our ordinary moral statements mean [...]. But it is precisely for this reason that linguistic and conceptual analysis is not enough. The claim to objectivity, however ingrained in our language and thought, is not self-validating. It can and should be questioned.[26]

In the wake of Mackie's error theory, ontological questions have temporarily dominated the discussion of second order moral questions, so much so that some commentators refer to the development in the late 1970s as an 'ontological turn' in metaethics. If we accept this view, however, then we seem to have good reason to conceive of the current state of metaethics as the result of another turn, namely a 'psychological turn', in the late 1980s and early 1990s which largely replaced

---

[23] See, for instance, Hare 1963, V; and Hare 1999a, 1 and 39.
[24] Note that the view that metaethics is concerned with two kinds of questions, namely questions of meaning and questions of justification, still has its firm place in introductions and ethics textbooks of the 1950s and 60s. See, for example, Brandt 1959, 8f.; and Frankena 1963, 78f.
[25] For this view, see also Hallich 2008, 153. The same suggestion is made by Scarano (see Scarano 2006, 32).
[26] Mackie 1977, 35.

the discussion of ontological questions with a discussion of the mental and motivational aspects of moral life.[27]

The reasons for this 'psychological turn' are manifold. It is clearly associated with the strong interest in the foundations of morality shown by evolutionary biologists, social and developmental psychologists and neuroscientists. Relevant examples include Frans de Waal, Antonio Damasio, Marc Hauser and Jonathan Haidt as well as philosophers like Stephen Stich, Joshua Greene, John Doris, Shaun Nichols or Jesse Prinz who advocate the use of empirical methods in philosophy and have set examples with their own research projects. A second factor is arguably the philosophical and empirical-psychological debate over the human emotions which has long dominated the contemporary philosophy of mind and is associated with the works of Peter Goldie, Ronald de Sousa and others. Yet, a third and at least equally important influence came from within metaethics itself, namely from the theories of Simon Blackburn and Allan Gibbard who simultaneously developed their versions of metaethical expressivism in the 1980s.

Blackburn's and Gibbard's quasi-realist versions of expressivism, which arguably represent the dominating metaethical paradigm of the past three decades, follow the path laid by emotivist and prescriptivist theories of moral language. As I will demonstrate in the subsequent chapter, the approaches of Ayer, Stevenson, Hare, Blackburn and Gibbard can all be seen as articulations of the same basic idea, namely that moral utterances and moral terms express desire-like states of mind – which is also why all five writers are equally being classified as expressivists nowadays. However, while Blackburn and Gibbard may share Ayer's, Stevenson's and Hare's interest in the linguistic aspects of morality and their view that the meaning of moral language is best analysed in terms of the expression of non-cognitive states of mind, they have shown a much stronger and more explicit interest in the psychological underpinnings of morality. As a result, Blackburn and Gibbard have helped to bring aspects into the focus of the metaethical debate that previously lingered in the background.

Yet, although discussions of expressivism, and the current metaethical debate more generally, are strongly characterized by the appeal to psychological issues, such as the nature of moral judgement and the connection of moral judgement and motivation: the question of how exactly these issues relate to

---

[27] The tendency of metaethicists to more strongly invoke psychological questions is also emphasized by Michael Smith and Jay Wallace (see Smith 2005, 9f.; and Wallace 2005, 87). It is also implicitly confirmed by Ernst who argues against the extreme view that psychological questions or, as he refers to them, questions in the philosophy of action, (should) form the centre of the metaethical discussion (see Ernst 2008, 77).

the semantic, epistemological or ontological questions and to what extent the different types of questions depend upon each other has not systematically been investigated. The purpose of this book is to contribute to such an investigation by examining whether or not expressivists commit themselves to any substantial claims in the philosophy of mind. My point of reference will be provided by Richard Joyce's recent publications on the subject.[28] Joyce vehemently denies that there is any interesting link between expressivism's primary linguistic thesis and more substantial claims in moral psychology. The key goal of the subsequent discussion is to critically evaluate and ultimately reject this view, to which I will refer as the 'independence thesis', and to show that and why expressivists should subscribe to a particular view about the nature of moral judgement, namely to a view I call *sentimentalism about moral judgement*.

Gaining a better understanding of the psychological commitments that attach to the basic expressivist idea not only seems a valuable enterprise in its own right. The psychological issue is intimately related to a number of further relevant questions that have been neglected in the previous debate as well. Due to the emergence of Blackburn's and Gibbard's 'quasi-realism' and the introduction of even further modifications of the basic expressivist idea, such as hybrid expressivism, neo-expressivism or relational expressivism, the debate about expressivism has become increasingly complex in recent years. As a result, there now seems to be a certain unclarity as to what the characteristic idea of expressivism really is and which authors we may legitimately classify as expressivists. In spite of this unclarity, however, only few attempts have been made to more systematically examine how the relevant theories relate to each other and to what extent they are captured by the different definitions of expressivism that have been proposed over the years. For example, Blackburn's und Gibbard's theories are often treated as if they were basically identical. Yet, as Gibbard himself has recently emphasized, he and Blackburn seem to have quite a different understanding of the type of mental state that is expressed by moral utterances, and there are similar differences and discontinuities between the various versions of hybrid expressivism as well as between the emotivist theories of Ayer and Stevenson.

With regard to the latter, a further and related problem of the current discussion deserves to be mentioned, namely that there is no real interest in, and appreciation for, the history of expressivism. Earlier expressivist approaches, most notably Ayer's theory but also Stevenson's, are usually dismissed as naïve and simplistic formulations of the basic expressivist idea. As a result, the questions

---

28 See Joyce 2008; and Joyce 2009.

of what these theories have to offer and where they anticipate moves of the contemporary debate have not been given the amount of attention they deserve. This can be seen, for example, in the recent discussion of how best to conceive of the 'expression relation', which some commentators consider to be one of the main challenges and unresolved issues faced by modern expressivists.

As far as other systematic issues are concerned, one important omission is that the questions of whether expressivism is conservative or a revisionary doctrine and how exactly it relates to Mackie's error theory have insufficiently been addressed in the past, which seems all the more unfortunate in view of the fact that this question refers us to questions about the methodological status of the entire metaethical enterprise which deserve closer attention in their own right. Our examination of the 'independence thesis' will provide us with an opportunity to address or revisit this question and the others mentioned above since they all bear – in one way or the other – on the psychological issue. Though the *leitmotif* of the discussion is provided by Joyce's 'independence thesis' and the underlying psychological issue, therefore, the overall aim of the following chapters is to is to provide a systematic analysis of metaethical expressivism, to describe its most important developments and challenges, and to thereby help to sharpen our understanding of what expressivism is really all about.

3 Summary

The purpose of this chapter was to provide an initial characterization of the metaethical enterprise as well as a rough sketch of the metaethical landscape and the way in which the objective of this book relates to the current state of the debate. Starting from the common distinction between first order and second order moral questions, I indicated how metaethics has turned from an inquiry into the meaning of moral terms and utterances into a vast research field devoted to quite different linguistic, epistemological, ontological and psychological issues.

Moreover, taking up on the idea that the works of John Mackie and Gilbert Harman effected something like an 'ontological turn' in metaethics in the late 1970s, I argued that the more recent metaethical discussion is the upshot of a 'psychological turn'. I also intimated that the latter has been caused by numerous empirical inquiries into the psychological aspects of morality led by social and developmental psychologists, neuroscientists and evolutionary biologists, but also by metaethical theories that crucially appeal to psychological concepts and ideas, most notably Simon Blackburn's and Allan Gibbard's 'quasi-realist expressivism'.

As I emphasized, however, although the interdependencies between the metaethical and the more specifically psychological debate are hard to deny, the exact relationship between both kinds of approaches has rarely been addressed in a systematic fashion. In particular, the question of how expressivism relates to substantial questions in the philosophy of mind and the philosophy of action has been neglected in the previous discussion of the expressivist approach. The aim set for the subsequent discussion was to redress this omission and to use the discussion of the psychological commitments of the metaethical expressivist to address other neglected aspects of expressivism as well.

Expressivism – a moving target?

There are arguably easier tasks in metaethics than to define expressivism. One reason why it is difficult to provide a definition that can expect general acceptance is that the term 'expressivism' is now mostly being used as a generic term that extends across a family of quite disparate metaethical positions. In the 1980s and the first half of the 1990s, it was quite customary to treat expressivism as a position *distinct* from emotivism and prescriptivism. Thus, the term 'expressivism' – introduced into the metaethical discussion by Allan Gibbard – was mainly being used to refer to Gibbard's 'norm-expressivism' and then extended to the theory of Simon Blackburn, which before had mostly been described as a version of 'projectivism'. Yet, it is now the dominant practice to treat emotivism and prescriptivism not merely as precursors, but as *examples* of expressivism. As a result, the task of defining expressivism has become the task of finding a definition that summarizes what is the common theme of all these different positions and can do equal justice to the positions of Ayer, Stevenson, Hare, Blackburn, Gibbard and quite a number of other writers.

To be sure, Mark van Roojen has recently suggested that the terminological trend runs into the opposite direction. According to van Roojen, the term 'expressivism' was initially applied to emotivist 'boo-hurrah' theories of moral language as well, but has now come to be used in a more restrictive sense.[1] Van Roojen's reading, however, does not withstand scrutiny. To begin with, virtually all leading expressivists still use the term 'expressivism' so as to include not only the modern theories of Blackburn, Gibbard, Terry Horgan and Mark Timmons or Michael Ridge, but also the theories of Ayer, Stevenson or Hare.[2] Likewise, the broad use of 'expressivism' has been dominating the discussion in the secondary literature since the mid-1990s and continues to do so.[3] Two of the few authors who prefer a more restrictive use of the term are Matthew Chrisman and Mark

---

[1] See van Roojen 2014, 10 f.
[2] Two fairly recent examples of this are Gibbard 2014, 19; and Ridge 2014, 193 f. For other relatively recent uses, see Blackburn 2006, 149; Gibbard 2003, 6; Horgan/Timmons 2006a, 73; Ridge 2006a, 309 f.; and Ridge 2006c, 633 f. As far as I can see, there is no positive evidence that Blackburn or Horgan/Timmons have more recently resorted to a narrower application of the term.
[3] For instance, see Sinnott-Armstrong 1993, 297; d'Arms/Jacobson 1994, 739; Smith 1994a, 12 f. and 16; Dreier 1996, 29 f.; Kölbel 1997, 4–6; Jackson/Pettit 1998, 239; Copp 2001, 2 f.; Joyce 2002, 337; Shafer-Landau 2003, 20; Smith 2005, 4; Barker 2006, 299; Cuneo 2006, 37; Wedgwood 2007, 37; Boisvert 2008, 170; Harth 2008, 38 f.; Joyce 2009, 31 and 34; Radtke 2009, 67 f.; Tarkian 2009, 160; Parfit 2011, 384 and 411; Kauppinen 2014b, 21; Boisvert 2015, 38; and Price 2015, 134 f.

Schroeder.⁴ Yet, Chrisman explicitly concedes that the broader use of 'expressivism' is much more common and has used the term in a similar way himself, describing emotivists such as Ayer or Stevenson either as expressivists,⁵ or at least as 'proto-expressivists'.⁶ Similarly, Schroeder has employed the term 'expressivism' more loosely in other publications.⁷ There is little support, then, for the diagnosis that the discussion of expressivism has recently shifted towards a more narrow understanding of what the label signifies.

The second reason why metaethicists have struggled with a definition of expressivism in the past is that at least some of the positions subsumed under this heading have been subjected to certain revisions over the years. This has given rise to complaints that expressivism is a "slippery fish"⁸ or a moving target. What these complaints suggest is that the advocates of expressivism did not stick to their initial positions but readjusted them so as to evade the most damaging criticism, while nevertheless sticking to the label 'expressivism' and perhaps even suggesting that their positions had not really changed at all. Without attempting to pass a final judgement on this issue here, it seems undeniable that the way in which expressivists now set up their positions has changed as a result of the past debate and that some characterizations of expressivism which were once widespread no longer seem appropriate. On the other hand, however, it deserves to be emphasized that at least some familiar characterizations of expressivism were never well suited to capture the essence of expressivism in the first place, and it is those characterizations to which I shall turn first.

1 Expressivism and truth

One example of the latter kind is the view that, according to expressivism, moral sentences are not assessable in terms of truth and falsity.⁹ Of all the writers usu-

---

4 See Chrisman 2014, 133 f.; Schroeder 2008a, IX and 3; and Schroeder 2008b, 704.
5 See Bar-On/Chrisman 2009, 135.
6 See Bar-On/Chrisman/Sias 2015, 223; and Chrisman 2016, 5
7 See, for example, Schroeder 2010, 65 and 74.
8 Smith 2001, 94. Even some expressivists, such as Michael Ridge, admit that it has recently become quite difficult to safely identify expressivists (see Ridge 2006c, 633 f.).
9 For characterizations of expressivism (or of non-cognitivism as comprising expressivism) in these terms, see Horwich 1993, 67 f.; Jackson/Oppy/Smith 1994, 287; Smith 1994b, 3; Divers/Miller 1995, 37; Wedgwood 1997, 73; Jackson/Pettit 1998, 239; Schaber/Wolf 1998, 130; Czaniera 2001, 75; Jackson/Pettit 2003, 86; Shafer-Landau 2003, 19 f.; Schnall 2004, 587; Smith 2004b, 182; Smith 2004f, 319; Schmidt 2006, 49 and 52; Sayre-McCord 2008, 403; Radtke 2009, 67; Parfit 2011, 265 and 380; and Van Roojen 2014, 1. Jackson and Pettit explicitly claim that it is by denying

ally assorted to the expressivist camp, it is only Ayer to whom we may safely attribute the claim in question. Ayer explicitly emphasizes that, like aesthetic statements, ethical statements such as 'Stealing money is wrong' do not express any propositions and can therefore be neither true nor false. In fact, it is for this reason that Ayer thinks that there is no way to determine the validity of ethical judgements and excludes actual ethical judgements from the sphere of ethical theory properly understood:

> We can now see why it is impossible to find a criterion for determining the validity of ethical judgements. It is [...] because they have no objective validity whatsoever. If a sentence makes no statement at all, there is obviously no sense in asking whether what it says is true or false. And we have seen that sentences which simply express moral judgements do not say anything. They are pure expressions of feeling and as such do not come under the category of truth and falsehood. They are unverifiable for the same reason as a cry of pain or a word of command is unverifiable – because they do not express genuine propositions.[10]

However, this radical view concerning the truth-assessability of moral sentences is already rejected by Stevenson in his book *Ethics and language*, published a mere eight years after Ayer's *Language, truth and logic*. Stevenson characterizes Ayer's contention that ethical judgements are neither true nor false as "paradoxical" and "wholly misleading"[11]. He claims that, in addition to their emotive meaning, moral terms also have descriptive meaning, and that insofar as the latter kind of meaning is concerned, moral judgements "may be true or false in the ordinary way"[12]. It is arguably in response to these claims that, in the introduction to the second edition of *Language, truth and logic* published in 1967, Ayer admits that "a great many ethical statements contain, as a factual element,

---

the truth-assessability of moral judgements that expressivists arrive at their distinctive position. Schaber and Wolf claim that, all their differences aside, the denial of the truth-assessability of moral judgements marks the common ground between the theories of Ayer, Stevenson, Hare, Blackburn and Gibbard. For commentators who initially define expressivism in terms of the denial of truth-assessability, but add some qualifications to their initial characterization, see Gert 2002, 292f.; Ernst 2008, 81f.; and Harth 2008, 40ff. There are also commentators who employ a distinction between a 'robust' or 'strict' notion of truth and a broader notion of truth and claim that expressivists deny at least that moral judgements can be true in the former sense. See, for instance, Schaber 1997, 15f.; Lenman 2003, 32; and Gert 2006, 459. For commentators who view the denial of truth-assessability as a characteristic feature of 'classical noncognitivism' (which presumably includes the theories of both Ayer and Stevenson) or 'emotivism' only, see Brink 1997, 11; Miller 1998, 103; and d'Arms/Jacobson 2000b, 730.
10 Ayer 1936/1967, 108f. See also Ayer 1936/1967, 102f. and 107.
11 Stevenson 1944, 267.
12 Stevenson 1944, 154.

some description of the action, or the situation, to which the ethical term in question is being applied"[13]. However, he still defends the idea that in many ethical statements, moral terms are used in a purely normative or emotive way and that for such statements, the question of truth and falsity simply does not arise.

In addition to claiming that moral utterances are truth assessible in virtue of their descriptive meaning, Stevenson emphasizes that there is also a broader use of 'true', as when we respond to somebody's 'Stealing is wrong' by saying 'Yes, that's true'. According to Stevenson, this use of the truth predicate does not refer to the descriptive meaning of 'Stealing is wrong', but to the attitude that is being expressed. For Stevenson, this second notion of truth is not only legitimate, but quite useful in ethics, even though it needs to be strictly distinguished from the notion of validity.[14] Again, the broader use of 'true' is subsequently acknowledged by Ayer. In his 1949 article *On the analysis of moral judgement*, Ayer even goes as far as to concede that, given the actual usage of English, his own claim that ethical statements cannot be either true or false is "in an obvious sense incorrect"[15]. Rather than viewing the broad use of 'true' as harmless or even useful in ethics, however, Ayer describes it as "logically misleading"[16] and suggests that we should better avoid it.

We find a similar position to that of Stevenson in Richard Hare. Hare adopts Stevenson's distinction between descriptive and evaluative meaning and claims, quite similar to Stevenson, that the question of whether moral statements can be true or false is misleading and does not provide a suitable criterion for distinguishing his own theory or other non-descriptivist approaches from their naturalist or non-naturalist rivals.[17] On Hare's account, what distinguishes moral statements from non-moral statements is not that they do not have any truth-conditions, but that their truth-conditions do not wholly determine their meaning, not even in conjunction with the statement's syntactical features.[18] It is compatible with Hare's universal prescriptivism, then, to say that moral statements can be true or false and that we can know some of them to be true.

The most extensive discussion of the place of the truth predicate within an expressivist framework has been provided by Blackburn, whose position has notably shifted over the years. In one of the earliest formulations of his theory, in the 1971 paper *Moral realism*, Blackburn already emphasizes that we may legit-

---

[13] Ayer 1936/1967, 21.
[14] See Stevenson 1944, 169 f.
[15] Ayer 1954, 231.
[16] Ayer 1954, 232.
[17] See Hare 1999a, 47 f. and 56.
[18] See Hare 1999a, 51.

imately attribute truth to moral judgements. He only suggests that the sense in which moral judgements can be said to be true differs importantly from the sense in which ordinary descriptive judgements can be said to be true, which latter sense he describes in terms of the correspondence with facts or states of affairs.[19] Yet, Blackburn quickly gives up on this qualification. According to his 1981 paper *Rule-following and moral realism*, for instance, the expressivist may earn the right to invoke the notion of correspondence with the facts or the world. This is a central part of what Blackburn calls the quasi-realist programme. What he emphasizes is only that the expressivist does not award to moral facts or moral states of affairs the same explanatory role as the moral realist, most importantly the role of *causing* moral judgements.[20] As a result of his move to quasi-realism, therefore, Blackburn comes to consider the question of whether moral judgements can be true in exactly the same sense as non-moral judgements to be a question that should be ignored.[21]

The most recent act in Blackburn's treatment of moral truth is his explicit adoption of truth minimalism. According to truth minimalism, the predicate 'true' does not denominate any robust property, such as correspondence with the facts. To claim that 'p is true' is just to claim that 'p', not to ascribe any additional property to it. The only thing to be said about the truth of the claim 'snow is white', then, is that the claim is true just in case snow is white. The function of the truth predicate, according to this view, is only to allow us to form generalizations such as 'Everything I said is true' and to thereby avoid having to make this claim and similar ones in the form of potentially infinite conjunctions.[22]

As already noted above, in his 1984 *Spreading the word* Blackburn rejects the question of whether moral truth differs in any significant way from non-moral truth, which may already be interpreted as an indication of his minimalist leanings. However, it is only in his later works that Blackburn explicitly embraces truth minimalism.[23] In *Securing the nots*, for example, published in 1996, Black-

---

19 See Blackburn 1993e, 111f. and 129.
20 See Blackburn 1981, 185f.
21 See, for instance, Blackburn 1984, 257.
22 For a recent overview of the central ideas of truth minimalism (sometimes also referred to as 'deflationism', the 'deflationary theory of truth', 'disquotationalism' or the 'redundancy theory of truth'), see Stoljar/Damnjanovic 2010. Truth minimalism can be traced back to the works of Gottlob Frege and Frank Ramsey (see Frege 1918; and Ramsey 1927). Two of the most important contemporary proponents are Hartry Field and Paul Horwich (see, for instance, Field 2001; and Horwich 1998). For an attempt to disentangle the different claims which are usually lumped together under the above labels, as well as for a detailed critical discussion, see Künne 2003.
23 That Blackburn's move towards truth minimalism takes place between the publication of *Spreading the word* in 1984 and the publication of *Ruling passions* in 1998 is also indicated

burn adopts the minimalist attitude to truth and treats ethical commitments "as strictly and literally true"[24]. While this endorsement is presented by Blackburn as somewhat provisional, his sympathy with the position is clearly expressed in the claim that the history of attempts to identify the extra content that distinguishes robust truth from non-robust forms of truth is "not at all encouraging"[25]. We find a similar position in *Ruling passions*, where Blackburn officially remains agnostic about whether there is any way of defending the idea of truth as a robust property, but proposes the adoption of a more minimalist conception of truth as the best strategy for dealing with moral truth.[26] In his more recent publications, Blackburn seems to have even given up on his official agnosticism and appears as an unambiguous supporter of the idea of truth minimalism.[27]

There has been some discussion about whether expressivists should welcome and embrace truth minimalism because it allows them to defend a notion of moral truth (as Blackburn suggests), or whether a minimalist conception of truth rather creates unwanted and potentially damaging problems for expressivism.[28] What ought to be noted in this context is that, somewhat ironically, we find Ayer among the early proponents of truth minimalism. According to Ayer's view, truth and falsehood "are not genuine concepts"[29]. Rather, the terms 'true' and 'false' function "merely as assertion and negation signs"[30]. The reason why Ayer nevertheless denies that ethical judgements can be true or false is that he re-interprets the question which theories of truth attempt to answer as the question of how propositions can be validated. And, as we have just seen, Ayer denies that ethical judgements, which he takes not to express any proper propositions at all, can be validated in any way.[31]

---

by Jackson (see Jackson 2001, 12). Moreover, Blackburn himself has explicitly accepted Jackson's account (see Blackburn 2001b, 30 f.).
24 Blackburn 1996, 86.
25 Blackburn 1996, 86.
26 See Blackburn 1998, 318.
27 See, for example, Blackburn's recent paper *Truth, beauty and goodness*, where he makes heavy use of the central ideas of the deflationary theory of truth and even tries to transfer some of these ideas to the predicate good in a more direct manner (see Blackburn 2010c, 35 ff.). See also Blackburn 2001b, 30 f.; Blackburn 2002, 134; and Blackburn 2006, 160 f.
28 See, for instance, Divers/Miller 1994; Jackson/Oppy/Smith 1994; Smith 1994b; Divers/Miller 1995; and Cuneo 2013.
29 Ayer 1935, 29.
30 Ayer 1935, 28. See also Ayer 1936/1967, 87 ff.
31 I do not, therefore, agree with Dreier's suggestion that Ayer's denial of moral truths is incompatible with his own views on truth (see Dreier 2004a, 23 f.).

In Gibbard's work, we find a somewhat stronger development with regard to the question of whether moral judgements are assessable in terms of truth and falsity than in Blackburn's work. Gibbard starts with an outright denial of the truth-assessability of both moral judgements and judgements about rationality (which are Gibbard's prime concern). Up to the publication of *Wise choices, apt feelings* in 1990, Gibbard repeatedly claims that to call something rational is not to state a matter of fact or to ascribe a property to it, "either truly or falsely"[32]. However, Gibbard at times qualifies his claim by merely denying that such judgements are true or false "[i]n a strict sense"[33]: suggesting something like Stevenson's broader notion of truth, Gibbard concedes that anyone who shares the state of mind being expressed by the judgements will consider them true and that anyone who does not share this state of mind will consider them false. By the time of the publication of his second book, *Thinking how to live*, however, Gibbard officially turns "non-committal"[34], accepting a minimalist understanding of 'true' and leaving it an open question whether or not a more demanding sense of 'true' can be defended.[35] According to Gibbard's new view, we may legitimately describe moral judgements and judgements about rationality as true or false,[36] and Gibbard also joins Stevenson, Hare and Blackburn in emphasizing that the question of truth-assessability does not provide a criterion by which we can usefully describe what is distinctive about the expressivist approach.[37]

2 Moral facts and moral properties

It appears, then, that definitions of expressivism should not place much weight on the notion of truth. Yet, very much the same seems to be true of the notions of fact and property.[38] The reason is that both notions are commonly viewed as

---

32 Gibbard 1990a, 8. See also Gibbard 1983, 199; Gibbard 1985a, 41; and Gibbard 1985b, 6.
33 Gibbard 1986a, 473.
34 Gibbard 2003, X.
35 See Gibbard 2003, 18. Nevertheless, some commentators take Gibbard, just like Blackburn, to positively endorse truth minimalism (see, for instance, Chrisman 2008, 341)
36 See also Gibbard 2006b, 198.
37 Gibbard 2003, 62f.
38 For characterizations of expressivism (or noncognitivism) in terms of the denial of moral properties or moral facts, see Urmson 1968, 15; Horwich 1993, 67; Copp 2001, 6; Czaniera 2001, 75; Shafer-Landau 2003, 19f.; Cuneo 2006, 37; Prinz 2007, 107; Chrisman 2008, 336; and Van Roojen 2014, 1. That these characterizations fail to do any more justice to modern versions of expressivism than characterizations in terms of truth-assessability is also emphasized by Dreier, Ridge and Kauppinen (see Dreier 2004a, 24f.; Ridge 2009, 183; and Kauppinen 2014b, 22).

being so intimately related to the notion of truth that modern expressivists usually extend their acceptance of truth minimalism to minimalism about facts and minimalism about properties. Even Hare, in emphasizing that the criterion by which we may distinguish non-descriptivist from descriptivist theories should not be provided by the truth-assessability of moral judgements, points out that pretty much the same applies to the question of "whether moral facts or properties exist in the world"[39], because there are perfectly good senses in which the non-descriptivist can allow talk of such facts and properties.

A more fundamental argument against characterizing expressivism via the denial of moral facts and moral properties is provided by Blackburn. Blackburn rejects what he refers to as the 'substantive way' of thinking about properties and proposes to conceive of properties merely "as the semantic shadows of predicates, not as self-standing objects of investigation"[40]. Under this view, which Blackburn applies in about the same way to facts, the expressivist simply inherits the justification for talking of moral properties and facts once the justification for talking of moral truth is in place. Moreover, given the minimalist nature of this justification, there remains no basis for distinguishing between 'robust' moral properties or facts on the one hand and 'non-robust' moral properties or facts on the other: just as there is only one (minimal) notion of moral truth, there is only one (minimal) notion of moral properties and moral facts.[41]

Again, a similar view has been taken by Gibbard in his more recent writings. Gibbard explicitly extends his non-committal attitude about whether there is truth in any non-minimalist sense to the question of whether there are facts in any non-minimalist sense.[42] As a result, Gibbard uses 'fact' only in a minimalist sense, namely as synonymous with 'true thought',[43] in which sense it can straightforwardly be applied to moral judgements. In its current form, therefore, Gibbard's expressivist theory does not extend to any denial of moral facts, and in much the same vein, Gibbard has given up his earlier denial of moral properties.[44]

---

39 Hare 1999a, 47 f.
40 Blackburn 1993f, 262. In fact, Hare suggests a similar view by claiming that there is no clear way of formulating the supposedly ontological dispute about whether there are moral facts or moral properties without translating it into a dispute about moral words and their meaning (see Hare 1999a, 44 f.).
41 That Blackburn's current position is still sympathetic to the distinction between properties or facts in a minimal sense and properties or facts in a non-minimal sense is suggested, falsely in my view, by Scanlon (see Scanlon 2014, 45).
42 See Gibbard 2003, X and 18.
43 See Gibbard 2003, 182
44 See, for instance, Gibbard 2006b, 198.

It deserves to be noted, however, that Gibbard's talk of moral facts and moral properties is facilitated by the concept-property distinction which Gibbard introduces to his work shortly before the publication of *Thinking how to live*. According to Gibbard's distinction, we may view certain *concepts*, such as the concept of being the thing to do, as genuinely and irreducibly normative, but nevertheless claim that the *properties* to which such concepts refer, such as the property of being the thing to do, are constituted by ordinary natural properties.[45] In virtue of the distinction, Gibbard can freely talk about moral facts and moral properties and still hold to his view that the expressivist theory has no need to allow for any non-natural normative properties or states of affairs.[46]

3 The standard definition: *Mentalism* and *sentimentalism* about moral expression

In order to define the key idea of metaethical expressivism and characterize the common theme of Ayer, Stevenson, Hare, Blackburn, Gibbard and others, therefore, we should better avoid any direct reference to moral truths, moral facts or moral properties. In fact, this is what the majority of commentators has striven to do for the past two decades. As a result, the following characterization has been established as the standard definition of metaethical expressivism:

> *Expressivism:* Moral utterances express desires (or desire-like states of mind) rather than beliefs.[47]

---

45 See Gibbard 2002a, 153 ff. See also Gibbard 2003, XII, 7 and 31 ff.
46 See Gibbard 2003, 181.
47 For identical or similar characterizations of expressivism, see Smith 1994a, 12 f. and 16; Dreier 1999, 567; Baldwin 2001, 3; Harcourt 2005, 251 und 254; Sinclair 2006, 249–251; Boisvert 2008, 170; Ernst 2008, 82; Harth 2008, 38; Merli 2008, 25; Railton 2008, 44; Schroeder 2008a, 177; Copp 2009, 167 f.; Sinclair 2009, 136; Dunaway 2010, 356; Strandberg 2012, 90; Cuneo 2013, 234 f.; Köhler 2013, 480; Toppinen 2013, 252 f.; Kauppinen 2014b, 3; Jenkins 2015, 64 f.; Toppinen 2015a, 151; and Chrisman 2016, 9. For related characterizations of noncognitivism (as comprising expressivism), see Hill 1992, 958; Alm 2000, 355; Smith 2001, 93; Audi 2004, 151; Joyce 2002, 336 f.; Smith 2004e, 298; Smith 2005, 4; Joyce 2008, 373 f.; Joyce 2009, 31; Schroeder 2009, 257 and 260. Definitions that do not appeal to the belief-desire formula at all have become quite rare in the current metaethical discussion (see, however, Gill 2008, 387; and Loeb 2008, 356). Most rival definitions consist of more complex characterizations that *include* the belief-desire definition but add further aspects, such as the claim that moral judgements are conceived of as non-truth-assessable or the claim that there are no moral facts and moral properties. See, for instance, Horwich 1994, 20; Smith 1994c, 26; Sayre-McCord 1997, 57; Jackson/Pettit 1998, 239 f.; Miller 1998, 103; Sinnott-Armstrong 2000, 678; Unwin 2001, 60; Gert 2002, 292 f.; Lenman 2003,

If understood in this way, expressivism consists of two proposals. The first is to explain the meaning of utterances in terms of the mental states they express, a proposal that is often referred to under the heading *mentalism*.[48] The second is to conceive of the states of mind from which moral utterances derive their distinctive meaning as non-cognitive or conative states rather than cognitive ones, a proposal to which I will subsequently refer as *sentimentalism about moral expression*.

The idea that we can explain linguistic meaning in terms of the mental states that are conventionally being expressed by a speaker's utterance is usually traced back to John Locke, even though the proponent of mentalism to whom we may attribute the biggest impact on the modern metaethical debate is Herbert Paul Grice.[49] There is some disagreement, however, regarding the exact relationship of expressivism and mentalism. While some authors suggest that the mentalist programme is an element of modern expressivism only, i.e. of the theories of Blackburn and Gibbard,[50] most treat it as a view that we may also attribute to earlier expressivists such as Ayer, Stevenson and Hare. Also, while some authors suggest that mentalism is only a contingent aspect of expressivism and that one could in principle endorse the latter without embracing the former,[51] others emphasize that expressivists are, in one way or the other, committed to the mentalist programme.[52] Given that the standard definition of expressivism at least im-

---

32; Miller 2003, 6f.; Schnall 2004, 587; Gert 2006, 459f.; Wedgwood 2007, 4; Kennett/Fine 2008, 190; Tarkian 2009, 12f.; Parfit 2011, 384f. and 391; Van Roojen 2014, 1; and Ridge 2015, 143. For reasons I will discuss below (see chapters 4 and 5), some authors try to provide somewhat narrower characterizations of expressivism, by further qualifying the 'beliefs' in question as a 'moral', 'representational', 'ordinary' or 'descriptive' beliefs (see, for example, van Roojen 1996, 311; Unwin 1999, 337; Dreier 2002, 136; Harcourt 2005, 250f.; Horgan/Timmons 2006a, 73; Sinclair 2007, 343f.; Schroeder 2008a, 3; Cuneo 2013, 234f.; Schroeder 2013, 283; Chrisman 2014, 117; Eriksson 2015a, 149.

48 See Schroeder 2008a, 23f.; and Schroeder 2008c, 96. See also Cuneo 2013, 225; and Boisvert 2015, 23. Other labels that are currently being used are "psychologistic semantics" (Rosen 1998, 387; see also Wedgwood 2007, 35), "psychologism" (Kauppinen 2014b, 21; see also Chrisman 2008, 339) and "ideationalism" (Ridge 2014, 107; see also Chrisman 2014, 120; and Bar-On/Chrisman/Sias 2015, 223f.).

49 We find Locke's mentalist account of meaning book III of the *Essay concerning human understanding*, entitled 'Of Words', where Locke develops his crucial claim that "words, in their primary or immediate signification, stand for nothing but the ideas in the mind of him that uses them" (Locke 1689/1975, 406). For Grice's much more elaborate account, see Grice 1989. For a more recent mentalist theory along Gricean lines, see Davis 2002.

50 See Kauppinen 2014b, 21; and Boisvert 2015, 23f. See also Chrisman 2008, 336ff.

51 See, for instance, Ridge 2014, 79f. See also Chrisman 2014; and Chrisman 2016, 6.

52 See Schroeder 2008a, 23; and Schroeder 2008c, 96.

plicitly appeals to the mentalist approach to meaning, my view is that we should include writers such as Ayer, Stevenson and Hare among the proponents of expressivism only if we can at least reasonably re-interpret their theories in terms of the mentalist programme. One purpose of the brief history of expressivism following in the next section is to show that this is indeed the case. In accordance with this, I am sceptical with regard to the view that mentalism is not a necessary component of expressivism, but has only standardly been embraced by expressivists because it provides the "most natural home"[53] for their theories. Though it is certainly possible to develop non-mentalist metaethical theories that have important affinities to expressivism as we know it, it is not at all obvious why we should classify these theories as examples of expressivism in their own right, at least as long as we take the standard definition seriously.

The slight disagreement over the exact relationship of expressivism and mentalism notwithstanding, it must be stressed that characterizations of expressivism that appeal to *speech act theoretic notions* of 'expression' fail to do justice to the current status of the debate. According to such characterizations, the distinctive claim of expressivism is that moral utterances are expressive speech acts (as opposed to assertive or constative speech acts), or that moral utterances have an expressive function (as opposed to a descriptive or assertive function).[54] As we will see in the following section, some of the early expressivists made use of such distinctions, and we even find traces of them in the early works of Blackburn and Gibbard. However, as the implicit appeal to mentalism in the standard definition of expressivism suggests, the debate over expressivism and its rival positions is not conceived of in these terms anymore, since the speech act paradigm has largely been superseded by general mentalist terminology. In fact, Mark Schroeder has argued that the "parity thesis"[55], according to which moral utterances bear the same expressive relation to desire-like attitudes as ordinary descriptive sentences bear to beliefs, is not only a necessary ingredient of

---

53 Ridge 2009, 198; and Ridge 2014, 107.
54 See, for instance, Scarano 2001, 148; Halbig 2007, 196; Ernst 2008, 78 f.; Hallich 2008, 111; Rüther 2013, 36 ff.; and Boisvert 2015, 38. See also Cuneo's description of the linguistic element of expressivism as "the expressivist's speech act thesis" (Cuneo 2006, 37). Note, however, that Cuneo now seems to prefer to characterize expressivism in terms of mentalism (see Cuneo 2013, 225) and that Boisvert explicitly concedes that both Blackburn and Gibbard would not categorize themselves in terms of his speech act theoretic proposal (see Boisvert 2015, 38). For an explicit rejection of this way of contrasting expressivism with its rival positions, see also Schulte 2010, 199 f.
55 Schroeder 2008c, 89.

any plausible version of expressivism, but an important part of what makes expressivism attractive in the first place.⁵⁶

What is more important at this point than to settle the exact relationship of expressivism and mentalism is to emphasize that mentalism is not, by itself, sufficient to turn a metaethical position into a variant of expressivism. Since it is the first of the two proposals that introduces the talk of 'expression', it is sometimes suggested that any theory that approaches the meaning of moral language from a mentalist perspective is expressivistic. In fact, in his book *Thinking how to live*, Gibbard himself feeds this impression, by introducing the key idea of expressivism in the following manner:

> The term 'expressivism' I mean to cover any account of meanings that follows that indirect path: to explain the meaning of a term, explain what states of mind the term can be used to express.⁵⁷

However, it is only by adding the second proposal that the expressivist arrives at the distinctive position that is commonly attributed to him,⁵⁸ and – as we will see in the subsequent chapter – Gibbard is fully aware of this fact. As long as the expressivist allows that the mental state expressed by a moral utterance is an ordinary belief, there is *prima facie* no reason for viewing him as endorsing anything other than a mentalist variant of naturalism or non-naturalism.

Let us turn to the second proposal then. The background for the second proposal is traditionally provided by a broadly Humean philosophy of mind and, in particular, by the view that beliefs and desires are 'distinct existences'.⁵⁹ This is usually explicated by saying that belief and desires are modally separable or that there is no necessary connection between beliefs and desires: for any belief and any desire a person may have, we can imagine her having the belief but not the desire. What is meant to be ruled out by this is the possibility of 'besires': single unitary mental states that are, at the same time, beliefs and desires.⁶⁰ The general idea behind the second proposal, then, is that any single state of mind that might be expressed by moral utterances must be either a belief or a desire. Moreover, the 'beliefs' in question are commonly specified as representational states

---

56 See Schroeder 2008c, 89 ff.
57 Gibbard 2003, 7. See also Toppinen 2013, 252.
58 For similar points, see Horwich 1993, 77; Sinnott-Armstrong 1993, 298; Rosen 1998, 388 f.; Blackburn 2006, 149; Chrisman 2008, 339; Sinclair 2009, 136; and Parfit 2011, 401 ff.
59 See also Smith 1994a, 12 f.; Smith 2004c, 363; Ridge 2006a, 304; Ridge 2006d, 53; Tarkian 2009, 21; Chrisman 2014, 119 f.; Railton 2015, 210; and Ridge 2015, 142 f. For my subsequent development of the idea, cf. Smith 1994a, 119; Smith 2004a, 156 ff.; and Smith 2010a, 155 ff.
60 For the term 'besire', see Altham 1986, 284 f.

of mind. Accordingly, 'desire' is given a broad interpretation under which the term refers to *all* non-representational states of mind. The most popular way of drawing the distinction between beliefs and desires, or between representational and non-representational mental states, is in terms of their respective 'direction of fit': what characterizes beliefs as representational states is that they possess a 'mind-to-world direction fit' because their point is to fit the world; what characterizes desires is that they possess a 'world-to-mind direction of fit' because their point is to have the world fit them.[61]

It is important to note, however, that, as it stands, the proposal I have introduced as *sentimentalism about moral expression* is itself a linguistic rather than a psychological claim: though it appeals to a distinction between two types of mental states, it is meant to only provide a specification for the general mentalist proposal and thus remains within the linguistic context of providing an account of the meaning of moral utterances.[62] To distinguish *sentimentalism about moral expression* from substantive claims in the philosophy of mind is important because authors such as Richard Joyce have not only emphasized that expressivism is first and foremost a thesis in the philosophy of language, but even suggested that the metaethical expressivist does not incur any substantial commitments in the philosophy of mind at all.[63] As I have already indicated in the previous chapter, I consider this view to be false, and one key purpose of the subsequent chapters is to demonstrate *why* it is false. However, given that the psychological commitments of expressivism have not yet been discussed with the appropriate amount of detail and that at least some authors deny that there are *any* such commitments, it would be unfortunate to write genuine psychological claims into the very definition of expressivism or to feed the impression that *sentimentalism about moral expression* is a claim of this kind.

For this reason, I did not follow authors such as Peter Schulte and Markus Rüther into adding a further, purely psychological clause to my initial characterization of expressivism, either.[64] The problem is not that it seems ultimately un-

---

[61] See also Smith 1987, 51 ff.; Dreier 2002, 136; Ridge 2003, 568; Dreier 2004a, 26; Harcourt 2005, 250 ff.; Chrisman 2008, 339 f.; Schroeder 2013, 283; Toppinen 2013, 253; Chrisman 2014, 120; Ridge 2015, 143; and Toppinen 2015a, 151. The 'direction of fit' metaphor is usually traced back to Elizabeth Anscombe (see Anscombe 1957). As Ridge emphasizes, however, cashing out the metaphor in a satisfactory way has proven quite difficult (see Ridge 2003, 568). The most influential proposal in this regard has been made by Michael Smith (see Smith 1987, 54).
[62] Things would be different if the notion of expression to which the general mentalist proposal appeals were to be understood in terms of a causal relation. However, as we will see in chapter 6, this way of interpreting the expression relation is commonly rejected.
[63] See, for example, Joyce 2008, 375 f.; and Joyce 2009, 34.
[64] See Schulte 2010, 142 f.; and Rüther 2013, 41.

3 The standard definition: *Mentalism* and *sentimentalism about moral expression* — 35

justified to link such a genuinely psychological claim to expressivism properly understood. It is that, given the disagreement over the psychological commitments of expressivism, any such attribution needs to first be justified. However, there is no such justification, and not even an explicit discussion of the problem, in either Schulte's or Rüther's book. For similar reasons, I think that we should also reject characterizations of expressivism which concede (or even emphasize) that expressivism is first and foremost a thesis in the philosophy of language but refer to the expression claim as a *psychological* claim.[65]

By saying that expressivism is first and foremost a thesis in the philosophy of language and by referring to both *mentalism* and *sentimentalism about moral expression* as linguistic claims, or as claims concerning the meaning of moral language, I have so far left aside more specific classifications and evaded the question of whether we should conceive of expressivism as a semantic, metasemantic or pragmatic thesis. This question has only recently been raised and has been answered differently by some key contributors to the debate over expressivism.

The view that expressivism's distinctive claim is a pragmatic one clearly has the least following. That we should understand expressivism as a pragmatic thesis has explicitly been argued by Matthew Kramer recently,[66] and Scarano has at least suggested that expressivism *makes* a pragmatic claim and that this claim is the *primary* one.[67] However, Scarano himself emphasizes that the pragmatic aspect cannot wholly be separated from the semantic aspect. Similarly, Sinnott-Armstrong has described expressivism as consisting of three claims, two of which are pragmatic in nature. According to Sinnott-Armstrong, expressivism's semantic claim is that "evaluative language is not used to assert propositions with truth values", while the pragmatic side of expressivism consists in the negative claim "that evaluative assertions do not describe the world" and the positive claim that "evaluative assertions do express emotions or other non-cognitive states, such as attitudes or desires"[68]. Finally, Richard Joyce has explicitly distinguished a pragmatic version of expressivism from a semantic one without, however, taking a clear stand on which of these interpretations he considers to be more appropriate.[69]

The main reason why pragmatic interpretations of expressivism are unpopular is arguably that the epistemological, ontological and psychological assumptions which traditionally motivate the expressivist approach, and which I will

---

[65] See, for instance, Jackson 2001, 10; Tarkian 2009, 21; and Van Roojen 2014, 3.
[66] See Kramer 2017, 186.
[67] See Scarano 2001, 42 and 148 ff.
[68] Sinnott-Armstrong 2000, 678.
[69] See Joyce 2008, 374.

further discuss in chapter 4, are not sufficiently preserved in a pragmatic version of expressivism since the pragmatic expressivist seems committed to interpreting the primary semantic content of moral utterances in a naturalist or non-naturalist fashion. Traditionally, therefore, expressivism has been understood as a *semantic* thesis that attempts to analyse the primary content of moral utterances in non-truth-conditional terms.[70]

Matthew Chrisman and Michael Ridge have recently argued that we should understand expressivism *neither* as a pragmatic *nor* as a semantic but as a metasemantic thesis. According to them, expressivism is best thought of as a thesis about the way in which moral utterances *acquire* their semantic meaning rather than as a thesis about this meaning itself.[71] The relevant debate has only just begun and we should probably not expect it to be decided anytime soon. Since this book will be mainly concerned with the psychological implications of expressivism, the question of whether expressivism's primary claim is a semantic or a metasemantic one is only of subordinate importance, which is why I will subsequently remain agnostic on this issue.

4 A note on terminology

Before I move on, I would like to comment on the terminology that I have been using so far and will continue to use in the subsequent chapters of this book. To begin with, I would like to give my reasons for referring to the second proposal as *sentimentalism* about moral expression and not as *noncognitivism* about moral expression. There are two main reasons for doing so and for generally avoiding the terms 'noncognitivism' and 'cognitivism' in this book. The first derives from the self-description of modern expressivists. While it is still extremely common in the secondary literature to refer to expressivism as a species of noncognitivism or to describe the proponents of expressivism as noncognitivists,[72] several expres-

---

70 For explicit characterizations to this effect, see, for instance, Rosen 1998, 387; Smith 2004f, 319; Finlay 2005, 1; Wedgwood 2007, 35; Harth 2008, 39; Schroeder 2008a, XI; Schroeder 2008b, 704; Sinclair 2009, 136; Dworkin 2011, 56; Van Roojen 2014, 10f.; and Boisvert 2015, 23f. For the view that expressivism is traditionally conceived of as a semantic thesis, see also Bar-On/Chrisman/Sias 2015, 223.
71 See Chrisman 2012, 325; Chrisman 2014, 123 ff.; and Ridge 2014, 8 f. and 105. See also Sepielli 2012, 192; Silk 2013, 217 f.; and Charlow 2014, 661. That we should adopt the metasemantic interpretation has also been suggested by Kauppinen and, recently, Allan Gibbard who, however, do not explicitly discuss the issue (see Kauppinen 2014b, 21; and Gibbard 2014, 169).
72 See, for example, Hale 1986, 69; Hill 1992, 957f.; Brink 1997, 6; Kölbel 1997, 3; Schaber/Wolf 1998, 130; Smith 1998, 86; Alm 2000, 355; d'Arms/Jacobson 2000b, 724; Czaniera 2001, 76; Joyce

sivists, most notably Hare and Blackburn, have explicitly rejected these labels in the past.[73] Moreover, Gibbard, who long consistently described his position as noncognitivistic,[74] has more recently expressed doubts as to whether noncognitivism is an appropriate label for his theory and since then avoided the term.[75] It is mainly Stevenson, then, who accepts the label noncognitivism (even though he does not use it much himself), given that Ayer, as far as I can see, does not comment on it at all.[76]

The second reason is that the term 'noncognitivism' is used so diversely that even commentators who agree that expressivism is a variant of noncognitivism have widely differing views about what the noncognitivism of expressivists such as Ayer, Stevenson, Hare, Blackburn or Gibbard actually consists in. There are at least three different understandings of the noncognitivist thesis. Some commentators treat noncognitivism as the *epistemological* thesis that there is no such thing as moral knowledge,[77] some treat it as the *psychological* thesis that moral judgements are constituted by desires (or desire-like states)

2002, 336f.; Miller 2003, 6f. and 26; Ridge 2003, 563; Shafer-Landau 2003, 19f.; Schmidt 2004, 131; Smith 2004b, 182; Smith 2004d, 260f.; Smith 2004e, 298f.; Smith 2005, 4; d'Arms/Jacobson 2006, 192; Dancy 2006, 122; Schmidt 2006, 52; Halbig 2007, 196f.; Wedgwood 2007, 3f. and 37; Ernst 2008, 81; Kennett/Fine 2008, 190; Schroeder 2008a, 3; Schroeder 2008b, 703; Joyce 2009, 31; Tarkian 2009, 160; Kauppinen 2010, 238; Schroeder 2010, 12f.; Schulte 2010, 141f.; Skorupski 2010, 436; Parfit 2011, 384 and 411; Sayre-McCord 2012, 14 and 32; Rüther 2013, 88; Van Roojen 2014, 7; Kauppinen 2014b, 20; Ridge 2014, 5f.; and Scanlon 2014, 56f.
73 For Hare's rejection of the term, see Hare 1995, 67f.; and Hare 1999a, 56. That 'noncognitivism' is not an appropriate description for Hare's position has also repeatedly been stressed by Hallich (see Hallich 2000, 30; and Hallich 2008, 117). Though Blackburn has at times provisionally, if half-heartedly, used the term 'noncognitivism' for his own position (see Blackburn 1998, 119), his reservations concerning the term date back as far as his earliest publications (see, for instance, Blackburn 1981, 178f.; and Blackburn 1986, 122). Moreover, in more recent publications, Blackburn has gone beyond describing the term as "unfortunate" (Blackburn 1986, 122; and Blackburn 1998, 85), by explicitly 'disowning' it (see Blackburn 2010a, 294).
74 See, for instance, Gibbard 1982, 43; Gibbard 1983, 199; Gibbard 1985a, 41; Gibbard 1985b, 6; Gibbard 1986a, 472f.; Gibbard 1990a, 8; Gibbard 1992a, 202; and Gibbard 1994, 98.
75 See Gibbard 2003, 184f.
76 For Stevenson's acceptance of the term, see his 1962 paper *Relativism and nonrelativism in the theory of value* in which he refers to a simplified version of his theory as the "noncognitive view" (Stevenson 1963d, 79).
77 See, for example, Blackburn 1981, 178f.; Hare 1995, 67f.; Blackburn 1996, 82f.; Hare 1999a, 56; Hallich 2000, 21 and 30f.; Scarano 2001, 27f.; Ernst 2008, 77f.; Hallich 2008, 71; and Radtke 2009, 61.

rather than beliefs,[78] and some treat it as a broadly *semantic* (or *metasemantic*) thesis, concerned with the properties of moral utterances or statements.[79]

Once we look at the ways in which some of these latter commentators try to specify this broadly semantic (or metasemantic) thesis, we stumble upon further differences: while some commentators use the term 'noncognitivism' to refer to the claim that moral utterances express desire-like states rather than beliefs (and hence largely synonymous with the standard definition of 'expressivism'),[80] others use it to refer to the claim that moral sentences are not assessable in terms of truth and falsity,[81] or the claims that moral utterances are not assertions, statements of fact or ascriptions of properties.[82] It should be pretty obvious, therefore, that when it comes to clarifying the central ideas and implications of expressivism, the term 'noncognitivism' does not provide much assistance but tends to create confusion in its own right.

The term 'sentimentalism' fares much better in this regard. Though the term has only recently come to be applied more frequently in the modern metaethical discussion, there is wide agreement that expressivism is a variant of sentimentalism.[83] Also, as far as I can see, no leading expressivist has so far objected to this kind of classification, and Blackburn has even made heavy use of the ter-

---

[78] See, for instance, d'Arms/Jacobson 2006, 192; Kauppinen 2010, 236f.; Kauppinen 2014b, 17; Ridge 2014, 5f.; and Sinhababu 2017, 5f.

[79] See Brandt 1959, 152; Frankena 1963; Ridge 2003, 563; Halbig 2007, 196; Gill 2008, 387; and Copp 2009, 171.

[80] See, for instance, Blackburn 1993d, 185; Brink 1997, 6; Sayre-McCord 1997, 52; Alm 2000, 355; Smith 2001, 93; Joyce 2002, 336; Miller 2003, 3; Smith 2005, 4; Kennett/Fine 2008, 190; Sayre-McCord 2008, 403; Joyce 2009, 31; Tarkian 2009, 24; and Sayre-McCord 2012, 11. This use of the term is also acknowledged by Ernst (see Ernst 2008, 78). See also Horgan and Timmons who describe expressivism as "a close cousin of (if not identical to)" noncognitivism (Horgan/Timmons 2006a, 73).

[81] See, for instance, Wedgwood 1997, 73; Schaber/Wolf 1998, 130; Miller 2003, 6; Schmidt 2006, 49; and Parfit 2011, 265. Note also that Hare and Hallich take this to be a second element of the noncognitivist thesis (see Hare 1995, 67f.; Hare 1999a, 56; Hallich 2000, 21; and Hallich 2008, 71).

[82] See, for instance, Gibbard 1983, 199; Gibbard 1985a, 41; Jackson 2001, 8; and Skorupski 2010, 3.

[83] For descriptions of expressivist theories as instances of sentimentalism or 'neo-sentimentalism', see d'Arms/Jacobson 2000a, 70; d'Arms/Jacobson 2000b, 724; Svavarsdóttir 2001, 18; Nichols 2004, 83; d'Arms/Jacobson 2006, 190 and 214; Slote 2006, 220; Nichols 2008, 258; Slote 2010, 3; Debes 2011, 2; Parfit 2011, 379f.; Kauppinen 2014b, 3 and 17ff.; and Prinz 2015, 70f. See also Sauer who refers to expressivism as a version of 'emotionism' and admits that 'sentimentalism' is the traditional label for emotionist theories (Sauer 2017, 4). Note also that many commentators explicitly relate expressivism to David Hume as one of the major proponents of moral sentimentalism (see Baldwin 2001, 3; Nichols 2004, 66; Halbig 2007, 38; and Railton 2015, 210f.).

minology himself.[84] Moreover, though there is certainly no agreed upon definition of 'sentimentalism', there is one aspect which the relevant uses of the term have in common, namely that the term is taken to refer to the psychological rather than the semantic or epistemological side of things. The term provides a much better a denomination of the psychological aspect of the expression claim, then, than the term 'noncognitivism'. It also provides the better label for the substantive psychological claim that moral judgements or states of mind are constituted by desires (or desire-like states) rather than beliefs which I will later introduce as *sentimentalism about moral judgement*.

The second term I want to comment on is the term 'projectivism'. While the term has mostly been applied to the theory of Simon Blackburn, it is quite clearly intended as a label for his more general kind of approach, and there can be no doubt that Blackburn himself has used the term in exactly this sense. According to Blackburn's definition in his 1984 book *Spreading the word*, the term refers to "the philosophy of evaluation which says that evaluative properties are projections of our own sentiments (emotions, reactions, attitudes, commendations)"[85].

There are three reasons why I will avoid talk of 'projectivism' in what follows. The first is that Blackburn is the only modern expressivist who has described himself in this way: neither Ayer, nor Stevenson, nor Hare, nor Gibbard, nor Terry Horgan and Mark Timmons nor Michael Ridge have labelled their theories 'projectivist' or 'projective' in the past.[86] Secondly, even Blackburn has now

---

84 See, for example, Blackburn 1998, 248f., 269 and 279; Blackburn 2001a, 1; Blackburn 2005a, 144; and Blackburn 2006, 146. Blackburn has also frequently emphasized the Humean credentials of his theory (see Blackburn 1981, 181; Blackburn 1995, 36; Blackburn 2001a, 1), going as far as to describe himself as a "Humean expressivist" (Blackburn 2010c, 26) and, in an unpublished commentary on Marc Hauser delivered in 2008, as a "long-time, card-carrying Humean". Though we do not find such self-descriptions in the case of other expressivists, Ayer, Stevenson and Gibbard do explicitly link their theory to Hume's moral philosophy (see Ayer 2000, 104; Stevenson 1944, 273; and Gibbard 2003, 184). Note also that Ayer describes ethical utterances as expressions of "moral sentiments" (Ayer 1936/1967, 107f.) and refers to the kind of metaethical theory he strives to refute by the term 'rationalism' (see Ayer 1936/1967, 114). Gibbard's characterization of the meaning of moral judgements also relies heavily on the notion of moral sentiments (see, for instance, Gibbard 1990a, 255f.; Gibbard 1992a, 200; Gibbard 1992c, 33).

85 Blackburn 1984, 180. Blackburn names Hume and Mackie as further proponents of projectivism (see Blackburn 1981, 163f.; Blackburn 1984, 180; and Blackburn 1993b, 152) and describes Ayer's emotivism and Hare's universal prescriptivism as "immediate ancestors" (Blackburn 1993c, 167). For similar broad uses of the term 'projectivism', see Miller 2003, 38f.; and d'Arms/Jacobson 2006, 188f.

86 Gibbard explicitly rejects this way of characterizing expressivism (see Gibbard 1996, 332), though he has recently conceded that the talk of projection could be innocuous if understood somewhat differently (see Gibbard 2015, 180ff.).

explicitly distanced himself from the term and striven to avoid it.[87] Thirdly, the relation between projectivism on the one hand and expressivism as defined above on the other is not one of perfect identity. Though we might want to claim that all expressivist theories are projectivist theories in the sense originally intended by Blackburn, the reverse claim is most certainly false, as is demonstrated by the fact that Mackie's error theory, which is widely regarded as an example of projectivism, is not usually considered to be an example of expressivism.[88] To describe the theories of Hare, Gibbard and others as 'projectivist theories', therefore, not only seems historically inaccurate. It also invites the misunderstanding that error theories instantiate the kind of expressivism with which I will subsequently be concerned.

With the third and last term, the term 'quasi-realism', the case is slightly different. That the term will not have any significant role to play in what follows is not due to the fact that I consider the application of the term misleading. Describing expressivist theories as instances of 'quasi-realism' is unproblematic as long as we confine the term to the theories of Blackburn and Gibbard (or additionally include those modern expressivists that have directly been influenced by Blackburn and Gibbard), and as long as we treat 'quasi-realism' not as a synonym for 'expressivism', but as a designation for the additional programme of justifying the 'propositional surface' of moral discourse on an expressivist basis. The reason why, with the exception of chapter 4, I will not greatly discuss

---

[87] Blackburn consistently described his position as projectivist up to the late 1980s (note, however, that in *Spreading the word*, he also refers to projectivist theories as "expressive theories" (Blackburn 1984, 167), thereby somewhat anticipating his later turn to the term 'expressivism'). In several works published between 1988 and 1998, 'projectivism' and 'expressivism' are explicitly introduced as synonyms, but the latter term is then used almost exclusively within the discussion (see, for example, Blackburn 1993d, 185; Blackburn 1996, 83; and Blackburn 1998, 88). As far as I see, there have hardly been any uses of the term 'projectivism' in Blackburn's works since then. In his 1995 article *The flight to reality*, Blackburn concedes that the projection metaphor is somewhat unfortunate (see Blackburn 1995, 36), and in his 2010 article *Truth, beauty and goodness*, Blackburn states that it is better to avoid talk of 'projection' altogether (see Blackburn 2010c, 33).

[88] For classifications of Mackie as a projectivist, see Brighouse 1990, 225f.; and d'Arms/Jacobson 2006, 189; as well as the works of Blackburn already mentioned. Some commentators even argue that *only* Mackie's error theory is a proper example of projectivism and question whether Blackburn's quasi-realist version of expressivism is compatible with projectivism at all (see Joyce 2002, 376; and Lewis 2005, 315f.). The differences between Mackie's error theory and expressivism are highlighted, for instance, in Joyce 2001, 9; Shafer-Landau 2003, 19f.; Harcourt 2005, 249; d'Arms/Jacobson 2006, 197; Halbig 2007, 197f.; Tarkian 2009, 24f.; Dworkin 2011, 32; Parfit 2011, 265 and 384; Van Roojen 2014, 1; Jenkins 2015, 66; and Price 2015, 136f. For a more detailed discussion of this point, see also chapter 4.

quasi-realism in this book is simply that the quasi-realist programme is mainly devoted to the linguistic and epistemological aspects of expressivism, not to those psychological aspects with which I will mostly be concerned.

After having provided in this section an initial characterization of the central idea of expressivism, the purpose of the next section will be to ensure that this central idea is indeed one we can legitimately attribute to Ayer, Stevenson, Hare, Blackburn and Gibbard. Though the vast majority of commentators agrees that these five authors are proponents of expressivism in the sense described by the standard definition, their expressivist status has also been challenged in the past, with Ayer providing the only exception.[89] It seems important, therefore, not to rest with having shown that most commentators of expressivism accept the standard definition of expressivism as articulated above, but to also show that this definition captures what the main proponents of expressivism do in fact endorse. Following from the way in which I have explicated the standard definition the resulting task will be twofold: first, to demonstrate that Ayer, Stevenson, Hare, Blackburn and Gibbard subscribe to the general mentalist programme (or that their approaches can at least sensibly be interpreted in this way); and, secondly, to show that the states of mind which, according to these writers, are expressed by moral utterances are non-cognitive attitudes which we may describe as 'desires' in a broad sense of this term.

5 Summary

The purpose of this chapter was to get a firm grip on what the basic idea behind metaethical expressivism is, something which seemed all the more important given that there have been certain shifts over the years in how leading expressivists have defined or presented their approaches. It could be shown that, these shifts notwithstanding, definitions which appeal to the notion of moral truth were never suited to capture the essence of expressivism in the first place: though it is still common to describe expressivism as the view that moral utter-

---

[89] The author whose status as an expressivist is questioned most often is Richard Hare (see, for example, Czaniera 2001, 93ff.; and Joyce 2009, 31 and 34; see also Schulte 2010, 150f.). For the view that the early Stevenson is not an expressivist, see Gibbard 2003, 6f. For doubts as to whether Gibbard himself deserves to be called an expressivist, see Barker 2006, 299; and Cuneo 2006, 37. Blackburn and Neil Sinclair raise the more specific question of whether the theory defended in *Thinking how to live* is still expressivistic (see Blackburn/Sinclair 2006, 705). The view that Blackburn is an expressivist is challenged by Judith Thomson (see Thomson 2006, 244).

ances are not assessable in terms of truth and falsity, a closer look at the writings of the classic expressivists reveals that – apart from the early Ayer – all classic expressivists explicitly allow for the truth-assessability of moral utterances and deny that the notion of moral truth provides a proper criterion for distinguishing expressivist from non-expressivist approaches to moral language. It could also be shown that the appeal to moral facts or moral properties does not fare much better in this regard, since Blackburn and Gibbard have come to be as sceptical with regard to such an appeal as they are with regard to the appeal to moral truth, their relevant considerations already being foreshadowed in the writings of Hare.

Rather than in terms of the denial of moral truths, moral facts or moral properties, then, expressivism ought better to be defined in other terms, namely as the view that moral utterances express desires (or desire-like states of mind) rather than beliefs, which is what has more recently become the standard definition of expressivism. If defined in this way, expressivism consists of two proposals. According to the first proposal, to which I have referred to as *mentalism*, we ought to explain the meaning of utterances in terms of the mental states they express. According to the second proposal, to which I have referred to as *sentimentalism about moral expression*, we ought to conceive of the states specifically expressed by moral utterances as non-cognitive or conative rather than cognitive states of mind.

By conceiving of this latter proposal as a claim about moral *expression* rather than moral judgement, I tried to do justice to the fact that expressivism is first and foremost a linguistic thesis and not itself a psychological one. With regard to the further question of whether this linguistic thesis is best thought of as a semantic, metasemantic or pragmatic one, I remained partly agnostic, ruling out only the pragmatic reading and emphasizing that the differences between the semantic and the metasemantic reading do not crucially bear on the questions this book is meant to answer.

Finally, in section 4, I explained my reasons for avoiding other terms that are quite well-established in the literature on expressivism, such as 'noncognitivism', 'projectivism' and 'quasi-realism'. One important reason for avoiding the two former terms is that some of the classic expressivists themselves have explicitly rejected the relevant labels in the past. A second reason, especially for dispensing with the term 'noncognitivism', is that the terms are employed in such different ways in the metaethical discussion that they are bound to create unwanted confusion, even more unwanted confusion, that is, than the term 'sentimentalism' which has at least consistently been used to refer to the *psychological* aspects of morality, which are my ultimate concern. The reason for largely avoiding the term 'quasi-realism' is that it does not even purport to describe these psychological aspects, referring instead to Blackburn's and Gibbard's strategy for justifying the propositional surface of moral discourse on an expressivist basis. Accordingly, I shall mainly rely on the notion in chapter 4 where I shall discuss implications and possible problems of this very strategy.

A brief history of classic expressivism

Given the formative influence of David Hume's moral philosophy on both early and contemporary versions of expressivism, it might seem appropriate to start a history of expressivism with Hume's *Treatise of human nature* (1739/40) or his *Enquiry concerning the principles of morals* (1751). However, although Hume is clearly an important ancestor of expressivism, there are at least two reasons why we should not include him among the expressivists himself. The first is that Hume's obvious interest in moral psychology is not accompanied by the systematic interest in the linguistics of morality that we find in the expressivists of the 20th and 21st century. Though we may classify Hume's discussion of morality as largely metaethical in character – as long as we subscribe to the broader interpretation of the issues and purposes of metaethics introduced above –, he does not offer us the kind of explicit theory on the meaning of moral language that is the key element of modern expressivism. The second reason is that, as a result, it is simply not clear whether Hume would accept the linguistic part of expressivism or whether he would rather opt for one of expressivism's rival theories, such as subjectivism, Mackie's error theory or some kind of ideal observer or ideal advisor theory.

In accordance with this, we find quite different interpretations of Hume in both the metaethical literature and Hume scholarship more narrowly construed. That Hume is an expressivist (or emotivist) is suggested, for example, by Ayer and Blackburn as well as by Páll Árdal, Francis Snare and Huw Price.[1] However, this interpretation has explicitly been challenged by John Sweigart, W. D. Falk and Rachel Cohon as well as by David Wiggins who argues that we should view Hume as a subjectivist instead.[2] The expressivist interpretation has also been questioned by Joyce who claims that there are pieces of evidence in Hume's writings that speak in favour of subjectivism, moral scepticism or an ideal observer theory.[3] That Hume holds some kind of ideal observer or ideal advisor theory is claimed by John Rawls and Gilbert Harman, and this interpretation is also suggested by Charlotte Brown who describes of Hume's overall theory as a 'spectator theory'.[4] That Hume's theory amounts to some kind of error theo-

---

[1] See Árdal 1966, 198; Ayer 2000, 104; Blackburn 1981, 164; Snare 1991, 24; Blackburn 1993c, 167; and Price 2015, 134f.
[2] See Sweigart 1964, 229; Falk 1975, 1; Wiggins 1991, 181 and 188; Cohon 1997, 251 and 256ff.; Wiggins 1998, 214f.; and Cohon 2008, 11ff. For a different kind of subjectivist interpretation, see also Broad 1930/2009, 84f.
[3] See Joyce 2008, 374; and Joyce 2009, 30.
[4] See Rawls 1971, 184; Harman 1986, 1; and Brown 1994, 20f.

ry is intimated by Mackie himself, but, in turn, questioned by Árdal.[5] Lastly, the problem of safely attributing *any* of these views to Hume is emphasized by Joyce, Jonathan Harrison and John Bricke.[6]

It may be for this reason that histories of expressivism usually start with the emotivist theories of the early 20th century. The common view is that emotivism was first articulated by C. K. Ogden and I. A. Richards in their book *The meaning of meaning*, published in 1923.[7] However, in his Axel Hägerström lectures held at the university of Uppsala in 1991, Hare draws attention to the fact that we find a similar account of moral language in works of the Swedish philosopher Axel Hägerström, published around 1910.[8] Other early proponents of expressivism, whose positions are, however, sometimes described not with the help of the term 'emotivism' but with the help of the terms 'prescriptivism' or 'imperative theory',[9] include W. H. F. Barnes, A. S. Duncan-Jones, Rudolf Carnap and Bertrand Russell.[10] Yet, although these authors are routinely mentioned as early proponents of expressivism, their theories do not really provide any reference points for the current metaethical debate. The first expressivist whose work can be said to still be relevant in this sense is Alfred Ayer.

1 Alfred J. Ayer

While there is wide agreement that Ayer embraces a version of expressivism, his theory is now mostly being introduced as an example for 'how not to be an expressivist'. The common opinion is that Ayer's theory provides an unacceptably crude and revisionary account of moral language and that it is only in virtue of the more sophisticated theories of Stevenson and Hare and the modern quasi-realist theories of Blackburn and Gibbard that expressivism becomes a respectable doctrine in the first place.

---

5 See Mackie 1980, 72 and 145; and Árdal 1977, 416 f.
6 See Harrison 1976, 110 ff.; Bricke 1996, 2; Joyce 2008, 374; and Joyce 2009, 30.
7 See, in particular, Ogden/Richards 1923/1930, 124 ff. and 149 ff.
8 See Hare 1999a, 103. The text Hare refers to is Hägerström's inaugural lecture, entitled *Om moraliska förestallningars sanning*, which was held at the university of Uppsala in 1911. A translated version was published under the name *On the Truth of Moral Propositions* in a volume edited by R. T. Sandin in 1964 (see Hägerström 1964).
9 See, for instance, Hare 1952, 15 f; Toulmin 1970, 51; Joyce 2002, 336 f.; Van Roojen 2014, 7 f.; and Chrisman 2014, 133 f.
10 For the relevant claims of these authors, see, for instance, Barnes 1934, 45; Carnap 1935, 22–26; Russell 1935/56, 229 ff. Duncan-Jones's position is summarized by C. D. Broad in his 1934 article *Is 'goodness' the name of a simple non-natural quality?* (see Broad 1934, 250–54).

Yet, many of the reservations against Ayer's theory seem to be due, not to his expressivist analysis itself, but rather to his further conclusions which are mediated by his logical positivism and his verificationism, namely that moral concepts are mere "pseudo-concepts"[11] and that moral sentences cannot be said to have any proper meaning at all.[12] Given that, in the preface to the second edition of *Language, truth and logic*, Ayer himself claims his emotive theory to be logically independent of his positivism and valid and valuable in its own right,[13] it seems important to assess Ayer's expressivist analysis of moral language independently of the further assumptions that one may, or may not, derive from it.

The fundamental claim developed in chapter 6 of Ayer's *Language, truth and logic* is that ethical utterances such as 'Stealing is wrong' are not statements of fact because they do not express propositions. Rather, they serve to express "feelings"[14] of disapproval, to which feelings Ayer also refers as "sentiments"[15] or "emotions"[16]. According to this view, the function of 'wrong' and other normative ethical predicates in typical moral utterances is purely emotive, where this emotive function not only includes the expression of certain feelings on the part of the speaker but also the attempt to arouse particular feelings in the hearer.[17]

Regarding our key question of whether we may legitimately attribute to Ayer the standard definition of expressivism, the first thing to emphasize is that there is no lack of talk of 'expression' in the relevant passages. This, however, is part of the problem. Ayer's use of 'to express' or 'expression' is by no means confined to the expression of mental states. While Ayer most frequently refers to utterances as expressing those states of minds already mentioned, i.e. feelings, sentiments and emotions, he also refers to utterances as expressing 'judgements', 'statements', 'propositions', 'sentences' and 'commands'.[18] To be sure, given the way in which Ayer describes the expression of non-cognitive states of mind as the distinctive function of moral utterances, there is no problem with ascribing to him the proposal I have referred to as *sentimentalism about moral expression*.

---

11 Ayer 1936/1967, 107.
12 See, in particular, Ayer's claims that 'statements of value' "are not in the literal sense significant" (Ayer 1936/1967, 102), that a moral predicate such as 'wrong' "adds nothing to the literal meaning of the sentence" (Ayer 1936/1967, 107) and that sentences expressing moral judgements "do not say anything" (Ayer 1936/1967, 108).
13 See Ayer 1936/67, 20.
14 Ayer 1936/1967, 107.
15 Ayer 1936/1967, 107.
16 Ayer 1936/1967, 102.
17 See Ayer 1936/1967, 108.
18 See Ayer 1936/1967, 21f., 103, 105 and 108f.

What is less clear, however, is whether we can equally attribute to him the first proposal and credit him with a general mentalist approach to language.

There are two reasons why we cannot straightforwardly assign this part of the standard definition to Ayer. The first is that Ayer does not explicitly describe non-moral utterances as expressing beliefs or, as a matter of fact, as expressing mental states at all. Rather than applying a general mentalist framework, Ayer tends to distinguish between utterances which express mental states on the one hand and utterances which express statements of fact or propositions on the other. The second reason is that, as I have already indicated, Ayer denies that moral utterances have any proper meaning at all. The only exception is provided by the meaning that is introduced by those factual statements that may be part of a moral utterance, such as the statement 'You stole that money' which Ayer takes to be expressed by the utterance 'You acted wrongly in stealing that money'.[19] If, therefore, we understand the mentalist approach as a way of explaining linguistic meaning, it may seem that we cannot even attribute to Ayer a mentalist analysis of *moral* utterances, given that his reliance on mentalist terminology only serves to *deny* the existence of any distinctly moral meaning.

However, I do not think that what we need to conclude from this is that the common conception of Ayer as an expressivist is mistaken. Although Ayer does not speak of non-moral utterances as expressing beliefs, he does come quite close to the general view of utterances as expressing mental states when he describes them as expressions of *judgements*. In view of Ayer's references to "ordinary judgements" and "perceptual judgements" in chapter 5 of *Language, truth and logic*, there can be no doubt that, for him, there can be both moral and non-moral judgements.[20] Moreover, his treatment suggests that he conceives of judgements as mental events rather than public utterances, especially where he criticizes the focus on 'judgements' rather than 'propositions' in traditional treatments of logic. Ayer's critique is premised on the view that the former term refers to psychological phenomena, which is why he takes the focus on 'judgements' rather than 'propositions' to inappropriately suggests that logic is concerned with the "laws of thought"[21].

The question, then, is what kind of mental state, according to Ayer, becomes manifest in non-moral judgements, and it seems that the only plausible answer is: a belief. In fact, that Ayer accepts this link between beliefs and non-moral judgements is positively suggested by some further passages in chapter 5

---

19 See Ayer 1936/1967, 107.
20 Ayer 1936/1967, 92.
21 Ayer 1936/1967, 80.

where he discusses propositions as the real bearers of truth and presents them as the possible object of *both* judgements *and* beliefs.²² By viewing utterances as expressing various kinds of judgements, therefore, Ayer seems to equally commit himself to the view that moral utterances express non-cognitive states of mind, such as feelings, emotions or sentiments, as to the view that non-moral utterances express beliefs (or perhaps other cognitive states of mind), and this is all it takes for allowing us to interpret his theory in terms of the standard definition.

Moreover, it does not seem that Ayer's remarks on meaning really present an obstacle to this kind of interpretation, either. In the preface to the second edition of *Language, truth and logic*, Ayer explicitly concedes that there is a broader sense of 'meaning' which is applicable to moral utterances or moral predicates. While Ayer is still keen to reserve the terms 'proposition' and 'truth' and, as a result, the terms 'statements of fact' and 'literal meaning' to non-moral utterances, he takes a far less critical view on describing moral utterances in terms of 'statements' or 'meaning' altogether.²³ In fact, it seems that this is the only plausible position to take, given that Ayer can hardly deny that moral utterances, which he likens to exclamations such as 'Ouch' or 'Hurrah', serve a communicative function and hence transfer *some* kind of information from speaker to hearer. In accordance with this, where aesthetic utterances are concerned, Ayer explicitly describes the expression of emotion as an act of communicating an emotion to another person.²⁴ The more qualified claim concerning meaning we should then ascribe Ayer, namely that moral utterances do not have 'literal meaning' or 'meaning in the strict sense', does not stand in the way of re-interpreting Ayer's account of moral language in terms of a mentalist approach at all.

2 Charles L. Stevenson

With Stevenson, the case is ultimately similar albeit for different reasons. Where Ayer's talks much of expression but rarely links this kind of talk to general questions about meaning, Stevenson devotes most of his discussion to meaning but rarely employs the terminology of expression, at least in his *magnum opus*, *Ethics and Language* and in his early paper *The emotive meaning of ethical terms*,

---

22 See Ayer 1936/1967, 88.
23 See Ayer 1936/1967, 15 f. For the diverging treatment of the terms 'proposition' and 'statement', see also Ayer 1936/1967, 8 f.
24 See Ayer 1936/1967, 113 f.

originally published in 1937. In the end, however, his position turns out not to be fundamentally different from Ayer's and to be just as interpretable in term of the two expressivist proposals as his.

Stevenson agrees with Ayer that one characteristic function of moral utterances is to influence the feelings, interests or behaviour of the hearer (what Stevenson describes as the "dynamic use"[25] of language), and he also agrees with him that moral utterances characteristically possess emotive meaning.[26] Unlike Ayer, however, who presents the two aspects as somewhat independent from one another, Stevenson links them together by *explaining* the function of moral utterances *in terms of* their emotive meaning: what allows speakers to influence others by making moral utterances, and allows them to influence them in a much more subtle way than by issuing commands or imperatives,[27] is that moral terms such as 'good' and 'wrong' carry emotive meaning and thus implicitly appeal to the feelings and interests of the hearer.

Though Stevenson takes pains not to simply identify the dynamic purpose of language with the emotive meaning of words,[28] he emphasizes the "intimate relation"[29] between the two, claiming that certain words "become suited, on account of their emotive meaning, to a certain kind of usage – so well suited, in fact, that the hearer is likely to be misled when we use them in any other way"[30]. For Stevenson, the word 'good' is such a word: it "simply does *lead* to dynamic usage"[31].

A second difference between Stevenson and Ayer is that the former explicitly emphasizes that moral utterances typically have descriptive meaning as well, a point we will have to revisit when discussing versions of hybrid expressivism in chapter 5. Again, however, the disagreement between Ayer and Stevenson does not run very deep here, although their theories are often presented in this way. Stevenson not only concedes that the emotive meaning of utterances can be independent of their descriptive meaning, but sometimes suggests that there are purely emotive usages of moral language.[32] Ayer, on the other hand, not only acknowledges, in the preface to the second edition of *Language, truth and logic*, that "a great many ethical statements contain, as a factual element, some de-

---

25 Stevenson 1963c, 19. See also Stevenson 1944, 36.
26 See Stevenson 1944, 33; and Stevenson 1963c, 24.
27 See Stevenson 1963c, 25; and Stevenson 1944, 32.
28 See, for instance, Stevenson 1963c, 22.
29 Stevenson 1963c, 21.
30 Stevenson 1963c, 22.
31 Stevenson 1963c, 24.
32 See Stevenson 1944, 72f. and 267. See, however, Stevenson 1963b, 9.

scription of the action, or the situation, to which the ethical term in question is being applied"[33], but even admits that there are cases in which ethical terms themselves are to be understood descriptively.[34]

It is with Stevenson's attempt to present a general definition of emotive meaning that the idea of utterances expressing mental states comes into play. In the definition provided in *The emotive meaning of ethical terms*, this idea is only suggested. According to the definition, "[t]he emotive meaning of a word is a tendency of a word, arising through the history of its usage, to produce (*result from*) *affective* responses in people."[35]. Moreover, we find a second and somewhat clearer reference to the expression of feelings in Stevenson's characterization of the dynamic use of language.[36] More importantly, however, the definition provided in *Ethics and Language* explicitly links the emotive meaning of words to the expression of non-cognitive attitudes: the emotive meaning of a word, we are being told, "is the power that a word acquires, on account of its history in emotional situations, to *express attitudes*, as distinct from describing or designating them"[37].

As in the case of Ayer, then, there is no problem with attributing to Stevenson the position referred to as *sentimentalism about moral expression:* to express non-cognitive or desire-like attitudes is a characteristic feature of moral utterances, and it is because of this feature that descriptivistic accounts of moral language are misleading. In contrast to Ayer, however, there is also less of a problem with attributing to Stevenson a general mentalist approach to meaning: just as he analyses emotive meaning in terms of the expression of attitudes, Stevenson explicitly analyses descriptive meaning in terms of the expression of beliefs. Again, the parallel mentalist treatment of emotive and descriptive meaning is suggested rather than fully developed in *The emotive meaning of ethical terms*, where Stevenson claims that ethical disagreements are cases of disagreement in interest rather than cases of disagreement in belief,[38] and where he characterizes the descriptive purpose of language (as opposed to the dynamic purpose) by saying that, when we subject words to a descriptive use, we use them "to record,

---

33 Ayer 1936/1967, 21.
34 See Ayer 1936/1967, 21.
35 See Stevenson 1963c, 21. (first emphasis added)
36 See Stevenson 1963c, 18, where Stevenson describes one of the functions subsumed under the dynamic use of language as "to give vent to our feelings".
37 Stevenson 1944, 33. (my emphasis). See also Stevenson 1944, 207. For a definition of emotive meaning that likewise appeals to the expression of attitudes, see Stevenson 1963a, 63 f.
38 See Stevenson 1963c, 26.

classify, and communicate *beliefs*"[39]. In *Ethics and Language*, however, Stevenson emphasizes the descriptive aspect of moral utterances by explicitly characterizing them as expressing beliefs in addition to attitudes,[40] and in Stevenson's later works, this becomes his standard way of explaining descriptive meaning in general.[41]

3 Richard M. Hare

The picture we find in Hare's writings is, to some extent, a mixture of the tendencies we find in Ayer and Stevenson. On the one hand, reminiscent of Stevenson, Hare makes much of the distinction between descriptive and emotive or, as Hare prefers to call it, "evaluative"[42] meaning. On the other hand, reminiscent of Ayer, Hare provides us with a somewhat inflationary talk of 'expression' in which the term is simultaneously applied to various linguistic and psychological phenomena.

To start with the former aspect: Hare fully agrees with Stevenson that the characteristic feature of moral utterances is that they possess evaluative meaning, even though, for Hare as for Stevenson, they typically possess descriptive meaning, too. For Hare, the main function of moral utterances is to "commend"[43] a person or character or "prescribe"[44] a way of behaviour, and it is because of this essentially practical function that the evaluative meaning of moral utterances is usually primary.[45] Exceptions are presented by what is now commonly referred to as 'thick moral predicates', such as 'tidy' and 'industrious'.[46] In the case of these words, the commendatory force, though still present, is overshadowed by specific and fixed references to certain descriptive properties of the objects that are being evaluated. Moreover, Hare concedes that under certain circum-

---

39 Stevenson 1963c, 18.
40 See Stevenson 1944, 34.
41 See, for instance, Stevenson 1993b, 9; and Stevenson 1963d, 79f. The parallelism is further emphasized by the fact that Stevenson reframes his distinction between disagreement in interest and disagreement in belief as the distinction between disagreement in *attitude* and disagreement in belief (see Stevenson 1963b, 3).
42 Hare 1952, 135.
43 Hare 1952, 85.
44 Hare 1952, 29.
45 See Hare 1952, 118f. See also Hare 1952, 146 and 149ff.; and Hare 1999a, 70.
46 See Hare 1952, 121.

stances, moral terms can lose their evaluative meaning altogether and come to be used purely descriptively.[47]

Given that Hare takes moral utterances to be not only prescriptive but also "universalizable"[48], he emphasizes that the evaluative meaning of moral utterances is, strictly speaking, not related to individual objects, such as particular persons or actions in a given situation, but to objects *as being of a certain kind:* to make a moral utterance is to commend or prescribe something *in so far as* it has certain descriptive characteristics and, in this sense, to subscribe to a more general standard or principle.[49]

It is important not to overlook the important similarities between Hare's analysis of moral utterances and the accounts of both Stevenson and Ayer in the face of Hare's explicit rejection of emotivism. Even in his early, and perhaps most critical, discussion of emotivism in *The language of morals*, Hare emphasizes that we need to distinguish the fundamental idea of emotivism from the further conclusions drawn from it, and from those drawn by Ayer in particular.[50] While Hare, as we have seen, views the idea that moral statements cannot be true or false as misleading and also opposes Ayer's view that moral utterances do not have proper meaning,[51] he seems much more sympathetic to the initial emotivist analysis of moral language. The only part of this analysis which Hare straightforwardly rejects is the way in which both Ayer and Stevenson interpret moral utterances as attempts to influence people by inculcating certain feelings or interests in them: although Hare does not deny that it is part of the typical function of moral utterances to influence people's behaviour – in fact, this is one of the main ideas behind Hare's prescriptivism –, he insists on the distinction between the illocutionary force of an utterance and its perlocutionary effects or, as he also puts it, between 'telling somebody to do something' and 'getting somebody to do something'.[52] For Hare, the changes in the behaviour or emotional constitution of the hearer, which we may want to bring about by making moral utterances, are not, strictly speaking, part of the meaning of the

---

47 See Hare 1952, 120 and 124.
48 Hare 1963, 17.
49 See, for instance, Hare 1952, 129, 135f. and 145f. See also Hare 1981, 216ff.
50 See, for example, Hare 1952, 9, where Hare distinguishes the "substance" of Ayer's theory, which he takes to consist in the idea that moral judgements do not ordinarily function in the same way as ordinary statements of fact, from Ayer's unfortunate way of stating his position and his tendency to assimilate moral judgements to other "quite distinct" types of non-factual sentences. For Hare, the "storms of protest" raised by Ayer's theory are, therefore, not reducible to the substantial part of it, which is why he describes them as "needless".
51 See Hare 1952, 8f.
52 See Hare 1952, 15f.; and Hare 1999a, 16f.

utterance, and it is here that Hare takes Ayer's and Stevenson's accounts – which present, after all, attempts to analyse meaning rather than do sociology – to go astray.

In contrast, Hare seems to accept that part of Ayer's and Stevenson's conception of emotive meaning which is most relevant with regard to the standard definition of expressivism, even if he may not put this aspect in terms of 'expression' as unambiguously as they do. As already indicated, Hare makes frequent use of the expression terminology. The problem is that he applies it even more indiscriminately than Ayer. Moreover, unlike in Stevenson, it is not the explicit purpose of his application to define or further characterize the notion of evaluative (and descriptive) meaning. According to Hare's use of the term, utterances or sentences can express such disparate things as 'judgements', 'statements', 'wishes', 'opinions', 'beliefs', 'desires', 'relations', 'feelings' (such as anger and joy), 'approval' and 'disapproval', 'attitudes', 'commands', 'prescriptions', 'ideals', the 'acceptance of standards', 'choices', 'resolves', 'prayers', 'thoughts', 'states of mind', 'duties', 'preferences', 'concepts' and 'speech acts'.[53] Yet, these examples also demonstrate that Hare, though not explicitly introducing talk of 'expression' in order to elaborate on his understanding of evaluative and descriptive meaning, provides the material for doing just that. Among the things that, in Hare's view, can be expressed by utterances are states of mind such as beliefs and desires. The only thing to be done in order to attribute to Hare the standard definition of expressivism, therefore, is to plausibly link the belief/desire terminology to the way in which Hare associates statements of fact with descriptive meaning and prescriptions with evaluative meaning.

In trying to do so, we can actually draw on further material provided by Hare himself. Hare explicitly relates prescriptions, which he conceives of as a linguistic or logical phenomenon rather than a psychological phenomenon, to preferences: to have a preference, according to Hare, is to accept a prescription,[54] and to utter a prescription is to linguistically express a preference.[55] Moreover, Hare suggests that preferences are themselves motivational states, and hence *mental* states, or at least intimately related to them,[56] and this may be the reason why Hare at times replaces the term 'preference' with the term 'desire'. Consequently, Hare explicitly, if rarely, describes prescriptions as linguistic expressions of de-

---

53 See Hare 1952, 4, 8–11, 79 and 129; Hare 1963, V, 71, 76, 99f. and 152; Hare 1981, 107, 152f., 185 and 215; and Hare 1999a, 8, 50 and 105f.
54 See Hare 1981, 91.
55 See Hare 1981, 107, 185 and 220.
56 See Hare 1981, 107.

sires (in a wide sense of that word), and he analogously, if even more rarely, describes statements of fact as linguistic expressions of beliefs.[57]

The only remaining problem is that Hare not only seems hesitant to relate the relevant discussion to the aspect of meaning, but even explicitly questions the benefit of explaining meaning in terms of the expression of states of mind. There are two examples of this, one in his early *The language of morals* and one in *Sorting out ethics*, published in 1999. In both passages, Hare concedes that, in one sense of that word, there is nothing wrong with saying that moral utterances 'express' desires, wishes or attitudes.[58] Given that 'expression' is also used as a synonym for 'word' or 'term', the terminology of expression can harmlessly be applied to language in general. Moreover, it may be harmless to refer to words or utterances as expressing something else, as long as this something else is itself understood in a broadly linguistic way. According to Hare, a non-moral example for this kind of case is the claim that the term 'not' expresses negation. In Hare's view, however, the emotivists are using 'express' in a quite different sense, and to say that moral utterances 'express' desires, wishes or attitudes in this latter sense is misleading.

Hare seems to have two main reservations against making this latter kind of claim. The first is that Ayer uses 'express' as synonymous to 'evince' and thereby suggests that when we make moral utterances, "we have welling up inside us a kind of longing"[59] or a "peculiar warm feeling"[60], to which we "give vent"[61] or which we "show"[62] to others by uttering a sentence. To Hare, this way of putting things is philosophically misleading, given that we can, and usually do, make moral utterances in a calm state of mind as well, without this affecting the meaning of our utterances.

However, we need to be absolutely clear about what Hare is really rejecting with these claims. Hare does *not* reject the idea that utterances express mental states, and he does *not* explicitly reject the possibility of explaining or reconstructing meaning in terms of the expression of mental states, either. What he rejects is the kind of simple *causal* understanding of the expression relation that he attributes to Ayer: the view that moral utterances 'express' desires and feelings in the sense that they are directly caused by some occurrent desire or feeling of the speaker and make this desire or feeling visible (or audible). Yet,

---

57 See Hare 1981, 107.
58 See Hare 1952, 9 ff. See also Hare 1999a, 105.
59 Hare 1952, 10.
60 Hare 1952, 10.
61 Hare 1952, 10.
62 Hare 1999a, 105.

the view that moral utterances are necessarily connected to desires or feelings in this way and express them in about the sense in which we linguistically display pain by saying 'ouch' is one that virtually all modern expressivists would reject as well. By itself, then, Hare's position does not put him into contradiction with expressivism's general mentalist framework at all.

Hare's second reservation is that explaining linguistic meaning in terms of the expression of desires, attitudes or feelings of approval faces the general problem of how to characterize the mental states in question without relying on the linguistic meaning that is to be explained in the first place. According to Hare, it is fine to think that 'never hit a man when he is down' expresses a negative attitude to ever hitting a man when he is down. However, once we try to specify what attitude exactly it is that we express with the utterance, we have no way of doing so that would be intelligible to anyone who does not already understand the meaning of 'never his a man when he is down'.[63] Hare's quite drastic conclusion in *The language of morals* is that it would be "perverse"[64] to use the notion of approval or the "comparatively complex notions"[65] of desire and attitude in order to explain the meaning of moral utterances which we learn to make and to respond to long before we learn the meaning of 'approval', 'desire' or 'attitude'.

It should be obvious that the passage in question provides the strongest evidence against interpreting Hare in terms of the standard definition of expressivism. However, it ought to also be noted that, by the time of *Sorting out ethics*, Hare has somewhat relaxed his opposition and seems to be much more optimistic about the prospect of explaining moral approval and disapproval in terms of psychological attitudes (which he interprets as behavioural dispositions). In fact, Hare's treatment suggests that *only* an appeal to psychological or even causative aspects will ultimately help us to explain the meaning of moral utterances because trying to explain approval or disapproval in terms of other linguistic operations, such as speech acts, will not get us anywhere.[66]

Hare's move to a more lenient position does not come as much of a surprise, given that in the passage in *The language of morals*, Hare is clearly overstating his case. As a matter of fact, Hare even seems to be involved in some kind of category mistake: understanding the meaning and the implications of the terms 'desire', 'attitude' and 'approval' is not the same thing as understanding what it means to be in the state of desiring or approving, and it seems that only the lat-

---

63 See Hare 1952, 10f.
64 Hare 1952, 12.
65 Hare 1952, 12.
66 See Hare 1999a, 106f.

ter, psychological understanding is required for somebody to be able to understand the meaning of moral utterances by reference to the mental states that are being expressed. Furthermore, the presupposition that a speaker who makes or responds to a moral utterance understands the meaning of the utterance by himself consciously viewing it as an expression of certain mental states is a presupposition expressivists need not accept. For one thing, if we take expressivism to be a metasemantic thesis about why or how moral utterances acquire the kind of semantic meaning they have, it seems that expressivism need not appeal to the conscious understanding of users at all. At best, this kind of appeal seems relevant for a decidedly semantic version of expressivism. Yet, it seems that even such a semantic version need not postulate that the complete meaning of moral utterances or the exact nature of the mental states which conventionally find their expression in those utterances must be fully transparent to each and every individual who successfully makes and responds to moral utterances all the time.

Given the gist and the vehemence of the passages discussed above, it is not surprising that Hare is the metaethicist whose status as an expressivist is challenged most often. However, we should not yield to these challenges, but follow the majority of commentators into including Hare among the endorsers of the standard definition. In light of the previous discussion, we can distinguish three reasons why the textual evidence from Hare's works does not force us to do otherwise. First, it is hard to interpret Hare's own characterization of evaluative and descriptive meaning in terms of prescriptions and statements of fact, and his further characterization of prescriptions and statements of fact in terms of the expression of desires and beliefs, as anything other than a mentalist account of meaning. Secondly, the true object of Hare's criticism of the talk of 'expression' in the emotivism of Ayer and Stevenson is not the general idea of explaining meaning in terms of the expression of mental states, but a naïve causal understanding of the expression relation which is not a necessary part of the expressivist proposal and is, in fact, commonly rejected by modern expressivists. Thirdly, the suggestion that there is no plausible way of explaining moral utterances in terms of the expression of desires or feelings (because it is harder to explain and understand the nature of these desires or feelings than to understand the meaning of moral utterances) appears somewhat misguided and does not seem to apply to most modern versions of expressivism, either.

4 Simon Blackburn

In comparison to settling the status of Hare's theory of universal prescriptivism, attributing the standard definition to Blackburn and Gibbard is an easy task. Ever since his earliest publications on morality and moral language, Blackburn has put much emphasis on the distinction between two types of mental states, or as the early Blackburn preferred to call them, 'commitments': ordinary, representational beliefs on the one hand and desire-like or conative attitudes on the other. According to Blackburn, the key idea of projectivism or expressivism is that moral judgements are commitments of the latter kind: to think, for instance, that an action is wrong is not to believe something about the action but to take a certain stance towards it; it is not to hold a representational belief but to concur in an attitude.[67]

As the relevant examples show, Blackburn's initial focus, even in his 1984 book *Spreading the word* which mainly deals with issues in the philosophy of language, is on the psychological side of things: the central idea of expressive or projectivist theories is introduced, not so much as a claim about the meaning of moral terms or utterances, but as a claim about the nature of moral thought. However, Blackburn leaves no doubt that he simultaneously subscribes to the specifically linguistic claim that moral utterances acquire their distinctive meaning by *expressing* the very desire-like or conative attitudes he identifies with moral judgements or 'commitments'.[68]

In fact, it seems that in the course of the 1990s, Blackburn has even come to largely reserve the term 'expressivism' for the linguistic part of the programme. While in *Securing the nots* (1996) and *Ruling Passions* (1998), he uses the terms 'projectivism' and 'expressivism' to describe the package deal of both psychological and linguistic claim,[69] he later suggests that the term 'expressivism' refers only to the linguistic part.[70] In accordance with this, he rarely applies the term 'expressivism' to the psychological claim in his more recent publications: although this claim is undoubtedly still part of his overall theory, the expressivist

---

[67] See, for example, Blackburn 1984, 167 and 187f.; Blackburn 1986, 122; Blackburn 1993c, 168; Blackburn 1993d, 184; Blackburn 1993e, 129; Blackburn 1993a, 365; Blackburn 1995, 36 and 50; Blackburn 1996, 83; Blackburn 1998, 50; Blackburn 2001a, 1; Blackburn 2002, 122–24; and Blackburn 2005b, 323.
[68] See, for example, Blackburn 1981, 163; Blackburn 1984, 167 and 170; Blackburn 1986, 122; Blackburn 1993d, 184f.; Blackburn 1996, 83; Blackburn 1998, 50f.; Blackburn 2005a, 146; Blackburn 2005b, 323; and Blackburn 2006, 149f.
[69] See Blackburn 1996, 83; and Blackburn 1998, 50f.
[70] See, for example, Blackburn 2001a, 1.

terminology is mainly applied where the aspect of linguistic expression is concerned.[71]

Even though Blackburn avoids to explicitly and systematically commit himself to a general mentalist approach of meaning, there is no problem in interpreting his account in these terms. His treatment may sometimes suggest that he wants to confine the idea of explaining meaning in terms of the expression of mental states to specific types of discourse, such as morality, normativity, modality or probability, and that with regard to other types of discourse, he takes truth-conditional approaches to be more appropriate. Also, there are a few instances where he opposes the expression of attitudes distinctive of moral utterances with "the speech-act [...] of asserting that some state of affairs obtains"[72] rather than with the expression of beliefs. However, from Blackburn's earliest publications onwards, we find a parallel treatment of moral utterances as expressions of attitudes and (certain types of) non-moral utterances as expressions of beliefs.[73] Moreover, it is this fundamental distinction which is used by him to make the distinction between expressive and descriptive utterances (or between expressive and assertive speech-acts) intelligible in the first place. According to Blackburn, we use language to express our attitudes "in the same way"[74] in which we use it to express ordinary beliefs, and even where this fundamental contrast is not explicitly introduced by him, it is understood to provide the background for his expressivist analysis of moral utterances.[75]

5 Allan Gibbard

In some of Gibbard's works, we find an asymmetrical treatment of the meaning of normative and non-normative utterances which seems to explain the former but not the latter in terms of expression. Just as the early Gibbard claims that normative utterances are not attributions of properties or statements of fact and that they are neither true nor false, he at times tends to give the impression that what is distinctive about moral or other normative utterances is that they express state of minds, whereas non-moral or non-normative utterances do

---

71 See, for example, Blackburn 2006, 149 f.
72 Blackburn 1984, 184. See also passages in which Blackburn contrasts the 'expressive' function of moral language with the 'descriptive' function of (certain types of) non-moral language, Blackburn 1984, 170; and Blackburn 1998, 50;
73 See, for example, Blackburn 1981, 185; and Blackburn 1998, 50 f.
74 Blackburn 1981, 185.
75 See, for example, Blackburn 1993d, 184 f.

something entirely different, namely state facts, assert truths or describe properties. One clear example of this is provided by the following passage in which Gibbard characterizes his own approach as noncognitivistic:

> The analysis is *non-cognitivistic*, in that according to it, to call something rational is not to ascribe a property to it, but to do something else. It is to express a state of mind: one's acceptance of norms that permits that thing.[76]

However, even in these earlier works, we find passages which suggest that a psychologistic interpretation of meaning can be, and perhaps should be, applied across the board.[77] Moreover, and most importantly, in Gibbard's later writings, we not only find a clear commitment to the standard definition of expressivism, but, in fact, the most explicit commitment to a general mentalist approach to meaning that we find in any of the five 'classic' expressivists.

That the meaning of moral and other normative utterances should be explained in terms of the states of mind they express, and that these states of mind should not be conceived of as beliefs (at least not initially), but rather as non-cognitive states, becomes the standard characterization of Gibbard's expressivist position with the publication of *Wise choices, apt feelings* in 1990.[78] By putting the (im)possibility of normative utterances expressing factual or representational beliefs to the fore, Gibbard implicitly suggests, in a much stronger way than before, that the meaning of factual statements or property ascriptions can be explained in terms of the expression of states of mind as well. However, far from only implicitly suggesting this kind of general mentalist approach to meaning, Gibbard explicitly provides a parallel treatment of normative and non-normative utterances in mentalist terms.[79] As part of this treatment, and

---

76 Gibbard 1985a, 41. See also Gibbard 1985b, 6 and 11; Gibbard 1986a, 473; and Gibbard 1990a, 7f.
77 See, for instance, Gibbard 1983, 208.
78 See Gibbard 1990a, 84f.; Gibbard 1992c, 34; Gibbard 1993a, 67f.; Gibbard 1993b, 316 and 318; Gibbard 1994, 98; Gibbard 2002c, 51f.; Gibbard 2003, 63, 181 and 194f; and Gibbard 2006c, 688f. It can be argued that the characterizations offered by Gibbard prior to *Wise choices, apt feelings* ultimately amount to the same thing. Gibbard equally claims that we should understand the meaning of moral and other normative utterances in terms of the states of mind they express, and he identifies this state of mind as a kind of *sui generis* non-cognitive state, the "acceptance of a system of norms" (Gibbard 1985a, 41). The only difference is that Gibbard does not as explicitly emphasize that the state in question is not a belief. However, in his 1982 paper on *Human evolution and the sense of justice*, Gibbard already argues that judgements of fairness are not representational, thereby providing the material for making this kind of claim about at least a subgroup of normative utterances. (see Gibbard 1982, 40ff.).
79 See Gibbard 1990a, 84.

reminiscent of Blackburn's related claim referred to above, Gibbard subscribes to what Schroeder refers to as the 'parity thesis':

> Just as a straightforwardly factual assertion expresses a straightforwardly factual belief, so an assertion that such-and-such is rational expresses a normative judgment. To judge something rational is to accept a system of norms that on balance permits it."[80]

Moreover, and unlike Blackburn, Gibbard provides an explicit analysis of the expression relation which is meant to equally apply to both these cases.[81]

A closer look at the works of Ayer, Stevenson, Hare, Blackburn and Gibbard, then, provides sufficient support for the common practice of citing them as the key proponents of expressivism, as characterized by the standard definition. Though there are passages in the works of all of these writers that might be taken to suggest only a partial mentalist approach to meaning, namely one confined exclusively to moral or other normative utterances, all of these writers either explicitly provide symmetrical analyses of the meaning of both normative and non-normative utterances in terms of the states of mind that they express or, as in the case of Ayer, can be legitimately re-interpreted in this way. Moreover, all writers describe the kind of mental state expressed by moral or other normative utterances as non-cognitive and explicitly contrast it with ordinary factual or representational beliefs. All of the classic expressivists, therefore, can be taken to endorse both *mentalism* and *sentimentalism about moral expression*.

There is a recent development, however, which is apt to put some pressure on the standard definition. Thus in the more recent works of Blackburn and Gibbard as well as in those of other modern expressivists, there is a tendency to allow that the state of mind expressed by moral utterances may be conceived of as a belief, at least in some sense of the word. This tendency is the result of two related factors. First, virtually all modern expressivists subscribe to some kind of quasi-realist programme and try to accommodate into their expressivist theories the ways in which we ordinarily talk about morality and moral judgements. Given that we not only say things like 'Abortion is wrong' or 'You ought to help your father', but also things like 'I believe that abortion is wrong' or 'I believe that you ought to help your father', a too literal commitment to the standard definition appears unattractive.

As far as I can see, two main strategies for dealing with this problem have emerged in the past. One strategy, which was employed by Blackburn and Gibbard quite early on, is to concede that the expressivist may *end up* talking of

---

80 Gibbard 1990a, 84.
81 Gibbard 1990a, 84 ff.

moral beliefs and even of moral utterances expressing such beliefs, but to emphasize that he starts his explanation without these notions, initially explaining the meaning of moral utterances in other terms.[82] In accordance with this strategy, some contributors to the expressivism debate treat the term 'belief' as a more general term covering both cognitive and non-cognitive mental states and explicitly allow that, according to expressivism, moral utterances express beliefs. The distinct idea meant to distinguish expressivism from rival positions is then introduced as the claim that the beliefs expressed by moral (as opposed to non-moral) utterances are themselves desire-like non-cognitive states of mind.[83] A second but related strategy, which is employed by Terry Horgan and Mark Timmons, is to attempt to develop a decidedly cognitivist or rationalist version of expressivism by explicitly distinguishing, even at the fundamental explanatory level, between descriptive beliefs and normative beliefs and by interpreting moral utterances as expressions of the latter.[84]

The second, related factor responsible for the tendency towards 'belief-friendly' characterizations of expressivism derives from the debate over expressivism and truth minimalism. As I have already indicated, defences of minimalism have not been confined to the notion of truth, but have been extended to other notions as well, such as the notions of property and fact. Yet, some writers have argued that, given the way in which our notion of belief is related to these other notions, there is no way of stopping the move towards minimalism from extending to the notion of belief. According to this view, we have no reason to think that there is any more to an utterance being the expression of a belief than for it to possess certain syntactic features. Denying that moral utterances express beliefs, then, presupposes that there is such a thing as a 'robust' belief as opposed to the kind of 'minimal' belief expressed by all declarative sentences. However, according to minimalism about belief, there just is no property by which we can distinguish between 'robust' beliefs and 'minimal' beliefs in this sense. Yet, if the expressivist accepts minimalism about belief and gives up

---

[82] See, for example, Blackburn 1993c, 168; Gibbard 1993b, 318; Blackburn 1993d, 184f.; Blackburn 1998, 82; Gibbard 2002c, 51f.; Gibbard 2003, 180f. and 194f.; and Gibbard 2006c, 688f. as well passages in Blackburn's unpublished manuscript *Social and individual expression* (3 and 6). Note, however, that even the later Blackburn sometimes expresses some unhappiness with regard to talk of moral utterances expressing moral beliefs (see Blackburn 1998, 51).
[83] See Gibbard 1982, 40; and Blackburn 1993a, 367. See also Dreier, Harcourt, Ridge, Smith, Kauppinen and Railton who present current versions of expressivism in these terms (see Dreier 2004a, 27f.; Harcourt 2005, 362; Ridge 2006c, 635; Smith 2010b, 518f.; Kauppinen 2014b, 23f.; Ridge 2014, 112; and Railton 2015, 212f.)
[84] See Horgan/Timmons 2006b, 256f.; and Horgan/Timmons 2006a, 76f.

the distinction between 'robust' beliefs and 'minimal' beliefs, it seems that he can no longer embrace the standard definition. In fact, it even seems that there might be no way for him to maintain a distinctive metaethical position at all.

Given that these challenges have emerged not so much from the original idea of expressivism but from the attempt to couple an expressivist analysis with a quasi-realist justification of the propositional surface of moral discourse, I will postpone my examination of these challenges to the more detailed discussion of quasi-realism that is the object of the following chapter. This discussion will also provide us with an opportunity for examining the common but insufficiently scrutinized view that expressivism, being a thesis about our actual moral discourse, is a conservative doctrine that does not force us to make any revisions to our ordinary understanding of morality and moral language. The discussion of some more general methodological issues that need to be addressed in this context (but which are usually neglected as well) will throw some suspicion on the view that expressivism, or in fact any plausible metaethical view, provides a fully conservative account of moral language and will suggest that the difference between expressivism and error theories is not easily captured in terms of the conservative/revisionary distinction. Moreover, it will give us an opportunity for summarizing the main arguments that the classic expressivists have put forward in support of their partially revisionary positions.

6 Summary

The purpose of this chapter was to provide a brief history of expressivism and to see whether the writers most often referred to as the leading proponents of expressivism actually embrace the basic expressivist idea as given by the standard definition. Since the earliest advocates of 'emotivism', 'prescriptivism' or the 'imperative theory', such as Hägerström, Ogden and Richards, Barnes, Duncan-Jones, Carnap and Russell, do not serve as reference points for the more substantial debate over expressivism, I restricted myself to those five major proponents previously referred to as the 'classic' expressivists, i. e. to Ayer, Stevenson, Hare, Blackburn and Gibbard.

With the exception of Ayer, the expressivist status of all these writers has been challenged. In part, this may be due to the fact that the writers revised their theories, or the way in which these were presented, over the years. It may also be due to the fact that commentators did not strictly adhere to the standard definition and conceived of expressivism in alternative terms, such as the denial of moral truth, moral facts or moral properties. Once we stick to the standard definition, however, there is no way of denying that Blackburn and Gibbard are expressivists, or at least were expressivists for the most part of the past three decades: as key passages from their writings make abundantly clear, they both embrace a general mentalist approach to linguistic meaning and the idea that the states of mind expressed by moral utterances are desire- rather than belief-like.

The true task of this chapter, therefore, was to show that the same holds for Ayer, Stevenson and Hare. Though we found a clear and unambiguous commitment to the standard definition of expressivism in neither of these writers, there was sufficient textual evidence for (re)interpreting their theories in terms of this very definition. Since both Ayer und Stevenson describe the expression of non-cognitive states of mind such as emotions, feelings and attitudes as the distinctive function of moral utterances, there was no real problem with attributing to them *sentimentalism about moral expression*. Something similar holds for Hare, even though he tends to avoid overtly sentimentalist terminology in this context. Although Hare predominantly describes moral utterances as expressing prescriptions, he does also describe them as expressing desires, and he even provides a conceptual link for these two manners of speaking, by defining prescriptions as the linguistic expressions of preferences and preferences as motivational states of mind.

As far as the endorsement of a more general mentalist framework was concerned, Stevenson could be shown to present the least problems: just as he analyses the emotive or evaluative meaning of moral utterances in terms of the expression of attitudes, Stevenson analyses the descriptive meaning of both moral and non-moral utterances in terms of the expression of beliefs. The very least we could attribute to him, therefore, was the 'parity thesis' – which is the key component of Blackburn's and Gibbard's mentalist approaches. Since Ayer does not explicitly speak of non-moral utterances as expressing beliefs, his case proved slightly more difficult. However, Ayer generally refers to linguistic utterances as expressions of *judgements*, of which he conceives as mental events, and links non-moral judgements to beliefs in about the same the way in which he links moral judgements to feelings and emotions. For this reason, Ayer's approach to meaning could plausibly be re-interpreted in terms of the 'parity thesis' as well. Moreover, Ayer's radical suggestion that moral utterances do not have any meaning at all, did not present any serious obstacle to this interpretation, either, given that Ayer retracts to a more lenient position in his later publications.

Crediting Hare with the mentalist proposal proved the most difficult, given that, in two passages from *The language of morals* (1952) and *Sorting out ethics* (1999), he seemed to explicitly question the benefit of explaining linguistic meaning in terms of the expression of mental states or events. However, Hare's reservations mostly apply to a particular interpretation of the expression relation, namely the kind of naïve causal interpretation he attributes to Ayer. Moreover, his further worry that there might not be a way to characterize the mental states that are supposedly expressed by linguistic utterances without already relying on the very meaning of these utterances could be shown to be actually disowned by him in his later work, where he suggests that *only* an appeal to psychological aspects will eventually allow us to explain the meaning of moral utterances. For this reason, it seemed ultimately legitimate to attribute the mentalist idea to Hare, and this attribution was not affected by Hare's explicit criticism of the emotivist theories of Ayer and Stevenson, either, given that this criticism relates, not to the basic expressivist approach, but to the close link the two seek to establish between the meaning of a speaker's utterances and the aim of causing certain reactions in the hearer.

The upshot of chapter 3, therefore, is that the common conception of Ayer, Stevenson, Hare, Blackburn and Gibbard as the leading proponents of expressivism is not only legitimate, but can positively be justified by relying on the standard definition. In fact, close attention to the existing textual evidence suggests that some of the oppositions we find in the metaethical literature rather tend to overstate the differences between the five writers, and the subsequent chapters will give us opportunity to further substantiate this idea. For the time being, the thing to be emphasized is that, if there are fundamental differences between the theories of the classic expressivists, they do not concern the way in which they conceive of the basic expressivist idea but must be sought elsewhere.

Quasi-realism and the problem of creeping minimalism

1 Metaethical analysis: Conservative or revisionary?

As I have emphasized above, and as is clearly demonstrated by the standard definition, expressivism is commonly regarded as a theory that is primarily concerned with the meaning of moral utterances and moral terms. Moreover, what has repeatedly been emphasized by expressivists and commentators alike is that expressivism makes a claim about our *actual* moral discourse: it is the explicit aim of expressivists, not to show how moral language *ought* to function, but to describe how it *does* in fact function.[1] This aspect of expressivism is often addressed by saying that expressivism is a "conservative"[2] or "hermeneutic"[3] doctrine as opposed to a "revisionary"[4] one. Also, it is this aspect of expressivism that frequently provides the basis for opposing expressivism and Mackie's error theory.[5]

It ought to be noted, however, that this part of the self-understanding of expressivists has also been challenged. While most commentators concede that expressivism can successfully be distinguished from the error theory, or at least from Mackie's specific variant of it, it is often urged that expressivism provides a revisionary account of moral utterances in its own right because, as the propositional surface of moral discourse is taken to indicate, ordinary speakers do not typically conceive of themselves as expressing desire-like attitudes when they are making such utterances. In forwarding his crucial claim about the

---

1 See, for example, Rosen 1998, 388; Shafer-Landau 2003, 20; Ridge 2004, 302; Cuneo 2006, 38; d'Arms/Jacobson 2006, 197; Ridge 2009, 182; and Price 2015, 136 f.
2 Harcourt 2005, 252.
3 Ridge 2009, 203.
4 Harcourt 2005, 252. See also Rosen 1998, 388; Ridge 2004, 302; Ernst 2008, 197; Ridge 2009, 203; and Tarkian 2009, 174. This latter type of doctrine is also sometimes described as 'reformative' (see Frankena 1963, 81; and d'Arms/Jacobson 2006, 197) or, following Burgess, 'revolutionary' (see Joyce 2005, 288; and Tarkian 2009, 24 f.; for Burgess's original distinction between 'hermeneutic' and 'revolutionary' doctrines, see Burgess 1983, 95 f.).
5 See, for instance, Shafer-Landau 2003, 20; Harcourt 2005, 249; Cuneo 2006, 37 f.; d'Arms/Jacobson 2006, 197; Ernst 2008, 197 f.; Ridge 2009, 184; Dworkin 2011, 32; Rüther 2013, 171; Van Roojen 2014, 1; and Jenkins 2015, 66;

meaning of moral language, therefore, the expressivist is said to veer away from how ordinary people actually understand this kind of language.[6]

In my view, modern expressivists (and commentators who accept their self-stylization) have done far too little to dispel such worries and to further specify and justify the status of expressivism's linguistic claim. This is also admitted by Ridge who is one of the few expressivists to have explicitly tackled the issue in the past.[7] What makes the omission even more striking is that a similar point has already been made by James Urmson in his 1968 book *The emotive theory of ethics*. Urmson critically remarks that Ayer, though taking pains to show that subjectivism and other ethical theories fail to appropriately account for our actual linguistic practice, does not really try to demonstrate that and how his emotivist analysis fares better in this regard.[8]

Now as far as the more recent discussion is concerned, there are several interrelated issues that deserve scrutiny. To begin with, it is not wholly clear whether the characterization of expressivism as a conservative linguistic doctrine is meant to only apply to quasi-realist versions of expressivism or to expressivism *tout court*. Some commentators, as, for example, Stephen Barker, suggest that early versions of expressivism, and Ayer's version in particular, *were* in fact revisionary and that the intention of providing a conservative account of moral language is a distinctive feature of the more sophisticated theories of modern expressivists.[9] A similar view has been taken by Tatjana Tarkian who distinguishes between a revisionist and a non-revisionist variant of expressivism and claims that emotivists such as Ayer and Carnap have done nothing to distance themselves from the revisionist position.[10] Like Barker, Tarkian argues that it is only the modern quasi-realist variant of expressivism that is unambiguously intended as a non-revisionary doctrine. A slightly more charitable interpretation has been forwarded by Justin d'Arms and Daniel Jacobson who are willing to accept that emotivism was *intended* as a conservative account, but think that the emotivists simply failed to make good on this intention.[11] This view is seconded by Huw Price who argues that it is only by subscribing to the quasi-realist pro-

---

[6] See, for example, Cuneo 2006, 35f.; Ernst 2008, 231; Radtke 2009, 100f.; Dworkin 2011, 56; and Bar-On/Chrisman/Sias 2015, 230. See also Lewis who claims that, contrary to what Blackburn himself argues, his theory is an example of moral fictionalism (see Lewis 2005, 319f.).
[7] See Ridge 2009, 182.
[8] See Urmson 1968, 19.
[9] See Barker 2006, 299.
[10] See Tarkian 2009, 174.
[11] See d'Arms/Jacobson 2006, 197f.

gramme that expressivists can provide a conservative account of our actual moral discourse in the first place.¹²

It is by no means obvious, however, that this is also the view of those commentators who do *not* explicitly qualify their characterizations in the above manner. If so, then it seems that it would be more truthful and less misleading to say that *quasi-realism* (or *quasi-realist* expressivism) is a conservative doctrine rather than to claim this about expressivism in general. Moreover, and more importantly, it is not clear how this view accords with the widespread characterization of expressivism in terms of the standard definition. If we take into account that purely causal interpretations of the expression relation are commonly rejected, then it seems that the point of defining expressivism in terms of the conjunction of *mentalism* and *sentimentalism about moral expression* must be that expressivists take moral utterances to express desires rather than beliefs *by linguistic convention*. Yet, if expressivists commit themselves to this view in virtue of embracing the standard definition, then it seems that *any* expressivist must subscribe to conservativism on pain of self-contradiction: once we become expressivists in the sense characterized by the standard definition, a wholesale revision of our linguistic practice just does not seem to be an option.

A similar problem emerges from the way in which expressivism is usually contrasted with Mackie's error theory. The vast majority of commentators tends to distinguish expressivism from Mackie's theory by appealing to the quasi-realist programme. According to this line of thinking, expressivists such as Blackburn and Gibbard can avoid attributing a fundamental error to ordinary users of moral language only by earning a right to those features of our actual moral discourse that seem hostile to the expressivist analysis: the general propositional surface of moral discourse as well as claims to objectivity and mind-independence and talk of moral truth, moral properties, moral facts and moral beliefs.

Again, however, it is not clear how this fits with the widespread claim that *expressivism*, and not *quasi-realism* or *quasi-realist* expressivism, is a conservative doctrine. Nor is it clear what to make of Mackie's rival position. What the above way of opposing expressivism and the error theory suggests is that Mackie himself is an expressivist, though not of the quasi-realist and conservative variety. In fact, at one point Blackburn himself explicitly describes Mackie in this way,¹³ and in several other writers, we at least find the claim that Mackie is a projectivist. However, if the expressivist position is characterized by the conjunction

---

12 See Price 2015, 136f.
13 See Blackburn 2006, 154.

of *mentalism* and *sentimentalism about moral expression*, then it seems quite obvious that Mackie should *not* be classified as an expressivist. The main problem is not that we cannot safely attribute to Mackie a general mentalist approach to meaning; it is that Mackie clearly does not subscribe to the view that moral utterances conventionally express desires rather than beliefs. The whole point of his theory seems to be that our ordinary conception of morality is framed by a false belief in objective moral values which is at least implicitly expressed by our moral utterances and renders them systematically untrue.

There is a certain inconsistency, then, in the way in which expressivism is now characterized, and this inconsistency provides strong reasons for paying more attention to the status of the expressivist doctrine and to the relevant statements we find in the classic expressivists. In my view, the fact that the exact relationship between expressivism and actual moral discourse has been neglected in the past is the upshot of a more general problem in contemporary metaethics: the problem of paying insufficient attention to the methodological foundations of the metaethical enterprise. A discussion of these foundations seems strongly required given that the metaethical debate is *prima facie* characterized by ambiguities or inconsistencies which are quite similar to the ones we encounter in the more specific discussion of expressivism.

One of the main purposes of modern metaethics, which is often reaffirmed by major contributors to the metaethical debate, is to explain or analyse the meaning of our ordinary moral concepts. Although this is *prima facie* an empirical matter, however, metaethicists hardly ever make any attempt to explore the meaning of moral concepts by way of empirical investigation. Moreover, without much further justification, most metaethicists seem to put up with the fact that their analyses depart from the self-understanding of competent linguistic users – although this is, again, *prima facie* at odds with the explicit purpose of the metaethical approach. Now my point is not that this necessarily renders the relevant metaethical analyses illegitimate. It is rather that we should not take their legitimacy for granted and that we should expect metaethicists to justify their approaches to linguistic meaning by addressing the relevant methodological issues and by showing how exactly they conceive of the relationship between the empirical reality of ordinary moral discourse on the one hand and their metaethical analysis on the other.

It seems helpful at this point to introduce a methodological distinction made by David Lewis in his discussion of quasi-realism and moral fictionalism. Though Lewis's distinction appeals to the different ways in which we may describe moral *thinking* rather than to the way in which we may describe moral talk, it can easily be applied to this latter aspect as well:

You might take fictionalism or quasi-realism in two alternative ways: as possible revisions of our thinking in response to the discovery of error, or as descriptions of how we are thinking already. Or there is an intermediate alternative: you might describe us – some or all of us – as being in state of confusion such that fictionalism or quasi-realism would be the minimal unconfused revision of our present state.[14]

If we apply Lewis's distinction to the question of how to characterize the status of expressivism, we can distinguish three potential claims the expressivist might want to make. The first claim (a) is that our ordinary conception of moral discourse is erroneous and that we should therefore fundamentally revise this conception and come to understand moral utterances as expressing desire-like states rather than beliefs. The second claim (b) is that we *do* already understand moral utterances as expressions of desire-like states rather than beliefs and that our ordinary way of ascribing meaning to these utterances proceeds along just those lines. The third claim (c) is that some or all ordinary speakers have a somewhat confused understanding of the meaning or the function of moral utterances so that *some* revision is required, and that the best (and most conservative) way of making this revision is if we all come to understand moral utterances as expressions of desire-like states rather than beliefs.

Before I will try to further assess these three ways of being an expressivist, it is important to introduce a further methodological and terminological distinction. As I have already indicated in the discussion of Hare's universal prescriptivism, we need to distinguish the question of whether moral language has the meaning the expressivist analysis attributes to it, or acquires its meaning in the way the expressivist analysis tells us, from the question of whether the expressivist nature of moral language is fully *transparent* to ordinary speakers.

Properly understood, expressivism is a claim about how ordinary speakers *use* moral language, not a claim about what they *know* about this language. A classic example used to illustrate this distinction is grammar. In order for a theory to provide a plausible account of grammar rules, it is not necessary – and surely not advisable – to include the claim that all speakers following the rules in question know exactly what they are doing and consciously apply abstract grammatical instructions when they formulate well-formed sentences. A claim of this kind would undoubtedly be false, and this seems to be equally true for any initially plausible account of grammar rules whatsoever. However, by conceding that the rules of grammar are not transparent to all or even to the majority of ordinary speakers, a grammatical theory by no means becomes unfaithful to its inherent purpose. The crucial claim that ordinary speakers prac-

---

14 Lewis 2005, 319.

tically *apply* the rules in question or formulate their sentences *in accordance with* these rules is simply not affected by the former concession. Nor does it commit the grammarian to the claim that ordinary speakers are confused with regard to the rules of grammar. In a similar vein, the concession that the expressive nature of moral utterances is not fully transparent to all ordinary speakers all of the time does not undermine the expressivist analysis, and it should not, by itself, be taken to amount to the claim that ordinary speakers are confused about the meaning of moral language, either.

Yet, even if we distinguish between a lack of transparency on the one hand and outright confusion on the other, it seems that, as it stands, option (b) is not really an option for the expressivist, or in fact for any metaethicist. By understanding his expressivist analysis in terms of option (b), the expressivist seems to commit himself to the view that all ordinary speakers use moral language in exactly the same way, and a uniformity claim of this kind is highly implausible, at least if we interpret the 'confusion' from which ordinary speakers might suffer to include incoherent uses of moral terms, as I think we should. Given that, as we have already seen, the error-theoretic option (a) is not an option for the expressivist, either, it follows that the only consistent and plausible way of being an expressivist is to argue along the lines of option (c). However, this still leaves us with the task of marking the difference between option (c) and option (a). It seems that option (c), by including the claim that some or all speakers are confused or incoherent in their use of moral language, attributes at least *some* kind of error to ordinary discourse. The question, therefore, is: what difference is there between option (a) and option (c) in the end?

Where Mackie is concerned, the defining feature of error theories is sometimes described by saying that error theories charge ordinary moral discourse with a *systematic* error. If we add this as a further criterion to the question of whether *all or only some* speakers are confused in their use of moral language, we end up with four possible positions:

(i) all ordinary speakers are involved in systematic errors in their use of moral language
(ii) some ordinary speakers are involved in systematic errors in their use of moral language
(iii) all ordinary speakers are involved in non-systematic errors (and *only* in non-systematic errors) in their use of moral language
(iv) some ordinary speakers are involved in non-systematic errors (and *only* in non-systematic errors) in their use of moral language

Again, it seems that by demanding that we count a theory as an error theory only if it takes *all* ordinary speakers to be involved in systematic errors, we would set the bar far too high. Mackie's insight into the supposed systematic errors underlying ordinary moral discourse would then make his own theory false or at least deprive it of its status as an error theory – since the insight itself would exonerate Mackie and his followers from the diagnosed error, and this conclusion is obviously absurd. In order for a position to count as an error theory, therefore, it should be sufficient to attribute a systematic error to the majority of ordinary speakers. Still, the distinction between options (ii) on the one hand and (iii) or (iv) on the other hand totally hinges on whether we can provide a good-enough definition of 'systematic' as opposed to 'non-systematic' errors to begin with. In my view, we have reason to expect that, in the end, we can only *gradually* distinguish the kind of errors made by ordinary speakers, which suggests that we should conceive of error theories as specific manifestations of option (c) rather than as theories of a completely different kind. If this is right, then we should locate not only expressivism but in fact any plausible metaethical position somewhere within the range provided by option (c).

This raises a further question, though. If any plausible metaethical analysis will charge some ordinary speakers with confusion and, accordingly, capture only the language use of a *sub-group* of ordinary speakers, doesn't this make the entire metaethical enterprise somewhat arbitrary? Aren't we forced to conclude then that there is really no such thing as *the* correct metaethical analysis because, given the variety of sub-groups of ordinary speakers, different analyses can be equally correct at the same time?

The only viable way to avoid this conclusion is to emphasize the further criterion that is implicit in Lewis's characterization of option (c), namely that the revision proposed by a certain metaethical analysis should be *the most minimal* revision. Of course, there are different ways of interpreting this criterion. One way, though surely not a very fruitful one, is to wholly interpret it in terms of quantity: a revision is most minimal if it requires us to charge less ordinary speakers with confusion and urge them to revise their linguistic habits than the revisions postulated by all alternative analyses. Though quantitative criteria should not be wholly discarded in metaethics in the way they usually are, they can hardly ground a metaethical analysis all by themselves. In my view, therefore, they should be seen as a kind of last resort, as potentially providing a tip of balance.

An aspect more important than quantity is whether a metaethical analysis coheres with other fundamental aspects of ordinary morality, both linguistic and non-linguistic. In fact, it seems that a plausible demand, and one that is implicit in much of the relevant metaethical literature, is that the analysis should not only be *coherent with* but *required by* these aspects in the sense that the aspects provide a basis for positive arguments in favour of it. A further distinctive criterion which I take to be important is the level of differentiation that the analysis allows, i.e. whether it provides an appropriately fine-grained framework for distinguishing different linguistic phenomena or rather forces us to lump these phenomena together under a common and unsophisticated description.

If we accept these criteria, or other criteria of this kind, we can stick to the view that there are more appropriate and less appropriate analyses of moral language without implausibly having to presuppose that ordinary moral discourse is unified in the sense that all ordinary speakers use moral terms or understand moral concepts in exactly the same way. Though we have to conceive of any plausible metaethical analysis as partly revisionary, then, we can importantly distinguish the ways in which the revisions themselves are, or are not, justifiable in terms of fundamental aspects of ordinary moral talk or common sense morality.

As we will see in what follows, there is evidence in the works of virtually all the classic expressivists that their understanding of the strength or validity of the expressivist analysis is based on considerations of a similar kind. What justifies the expressivist approach, according to this evidence, is not that each and every speaker's use of moral language cannot but be explained in terms of the standard definition. It is rather that the expressivist approach provides the account of moral language that coheres best with our overall linguistic and non-linguistic moral practice.

2 The classic expressivists revisited: Methodology

In the case of Ayer, we mainly find the relevant methodological assumptions in his widely neglected paper *On the analysis of moral judgements*. Although the discussion in *Language, truth and logic*, and Ayer's rejection of 'subjectivist' and 'utilitarian' analyses of moral concepts in particular, clearly suggests that he conceives of his own theory as an attempt to provide an account of the "conventions of our actual language"[15] and an analysis "of our existing ethical notions"[16], Ayer does not bother much to specify in which way his analysis ultimately meets this requirement. However, one consideration which we may infer from his criticism of 'subjectivism' and 'utilitarianism' is that the emotive theory is more faithful to ordinary moral talk in that it is immune to variants of Moore's open question argument.[17]

---

15 Ayer 1936/1967, 105.
16 Ayer 1936/1967, 105.
17 See Ayer 1936/1967, 104 f.

If, for example, we follow the subjectivist into thinking that to call an action wrong is to say that it is generally disapproved of, then it seems that we commit ourselves to the position that in saying something like 'X is wrong although it is generally approved of', we are contradicting ourselves. Yet, according to Ayer, we do usually not take statements of the former kind to be self-contradictory at all. Similarly, if we accept the utilitarian analysis that 'X is wrong' means something like 'X would cause, or be likely to cause, more pleasure than pain', we commit ourselves to the view that saying that it is sometimes wrong to perform the action that would cause, or is likely to cause, more pleasure than pain is self-contradictory. Again, however, this is not how Ayer takes ordinary speakers to conceive of this statement. In contrast, if we accept the emotive analysis, we do not commit ourselves to any such claim of self-contradiction which means that, in one important sense, emotivism is more faithful to our ordinary linguistic practice.

In *On the analysis of moral judgements*, Ayer explicitly takes up the objection that the emotive theory is *not* faithful to the way in which we talk about moral utterances and moral terms, attempting to at least partially defend the conservative status of his analysis, despite its *prima facie* unconventional nature. According to Ayer, endorsing the emotive theory very much amounts to recommending a new way of speaking because the old, ordinary way of speaking about morality is conceived of as "logically misleading"[18] or at least as ill-suited to sufficiently highlight the crucial aspects of moral language. Ayer explicitly concedes that, when asked, the majority of speakers would not agree that to describe moral utterances as statements of fact is in any way misleading or incorrect. However, suggesting something like our above distinction between knowing-how and knowing-what, Ayer claims that the ways in which ordinary speakers *actually use* moral utterances nonetheless suggest that moral utterances function differently from non-moral utterances and therefore ought to be classified differently, just as the emotive theory proposes.[19]

Moreover, Ayer even confronts the possible worry that analysing the meaning of moral language thereby becomes an "arbitrary procedure"[20] and subsequently tries to show that, independently of the merely verbal issue, our moral practice provides good reasons for adopting the emotive theory. One of these reasons, according to Ayer, is that we do not ordinarily take moral evaluations to simply follow from the empirical facts: two individuals can entirely agree in their description of the empirical aspects of a certain situation or action and

---

18 Ayer 1954, 232.
19 See Ayer 1954, 232f.
20 Ayer 1954, 233.

still arrive at different moral conclusions. However, as Ayer also notes, thereby suggesting a kind of supervenience thesis, our moral evaluations are not entirely independent of the empirical facts, either, but do depend in some way on the natural features of the situations or actions we evaluate. For Ayer, then, the best way to make sense of these and other aspects of morality is to think of moral evaluations as emotional responses towards these natural features.

It does not seem fully adequate, then, to characterize Ayer's position as revisionary. While Ayer concedes that his analysis stands in contrast to how the majority of ordinary speakers *talks* about moral language, it is his professed aim to analyse the meaning of moral utterances in accordance with how they actually use it, and he tries to make good on this claim (a) by distinguishing between the theoretical and the practical knowledge of ordinary speakers, and (b) by appealing to other crucial aspects of our ordinary understanding of morality, most importantly our understanding of moral deliberation and moral disagreement.

The position we find in Stevenson is not unlike Ayer's at all. To begin with, Stevenson describes his aim as that of disclosing the *actual* meaning of ethical terms rather than inventing new ones.[21] However, Stevenson does not give the impression that, in pursuing this aim, we can possibly avoid any revision whatsoever. To begin with, Stevenson explicitly concedes that it is impossible, in trying to give a definition of ethical terms such as 'good', to come up with a substitution that is strictly identical with the meaning of the original term.[22] Accordingly, Stevenson admits that all the definitions he forwards for 'X is good' can only provide approximations.[23] This holds, for example, for 'we like x' (as when used for suggestion), 'I approve of X, do so as well!' or examples of the more general schema 'This has qualities or relations X, Y, Z ...' (plus a suggestion of the favourable attitude of the speaker)

Moreover, although Stevenson seems somewhat more interested than Ayer in salvaging aspects of the way in which we ordinarily *talk* about morality, such as our practice of describing moral utterances as 'true', he seems quite clear about the fact that his analysis cannot fully capture each and every speaker's linguistic habits and will therefore be partly revisionary in the sense described above. While Stevenson questions the view that the ways in which ordinary speakers use ethical terms are "*totally* confused"[24], he admits that there is *some* confusion

---

21 See, for example Stevenson 1963c, 10.
22 See Stevenson 1963c, 10 f. and 24 f.
23 See Stevenson 1963c, 24 f.; and Stevenson 1944, 32 f. and 207.
24 Stevenson 1963e, 118.

in how ordinary speakers make and respond to moral utterances. Accordingly, the purpose of his metaethical analysis is not to describe, in a fully conservative fashion, what ordinary speakers do or mean in using moral language, but rather "to *look for* some salvageable element in their usage"[25].

Just like Ayer, then, Stevenson does not seem to be shaken by the fact that his analysis will fail to do some actual uses of ethical terms justice, and the reason why he nevertheless conceives of his analysis as an analysis of our actual moral language is that he follows Ayer into defending the analysis on the basis of fundamental assumptions implied in our ordinary understanding of morality.[26] According to Stevenson, for a definition of ethical terms to be justified, the definition must be "relevant"[27]. A definition is relevant, in Stevenson's sense, if those who understand the definition must be able to say all they want to say by using the term in the defined rather than in the original way and, therefore, "never have occasion to use it in the old, unclear sense"[28]. Stevenson concedes that in some cases, it may only be possible to provide definitions that are partially relevant, namely when words are commonly used confusedly and ambiguously. Yet, he nevertheless emphasizes that it is with the criterion of relevance that the subjectivist analysis and other analyses of ethical terms go wrong.

What makes the emotive analysis more relevant, in Stevenson's view, is that it allows us to salvage three crucial aspects of our ordinary moral practice. The first is the nature of moral disagreement, to which, as we have seen, Ayer appeals as well. Because it helps us to interpret moral disagreement as disagreement in attitude rather than belief, emotivism cannot only explain why somebody uttering the sentence 'X is good' disagrees with somebody uttering sentence 'X is not good', it can also explain why we can continue to disagree even after we have reached an agreement in our non-moral beliefs.[29]

---

25 Stevenson 1963e, 119.
26 This is not intended as a historical claim: it may well be the case that, historically speaking, it is Ayer who follows the path laid by Stevenson whose relevant publications were released before Ayer wrote his paper *On the analysis of moral judgements*.
27 Stevenson 1963c, 11.
28 Stevenson 1963c, 11.
29 For the claim that disagreement in attitude is distinctive of moral disagreement, see Stevenson 1963c, 26; and Stevenson 1963b, 3 ff. For the claim that certain variants of subjectivism, to which Stevenson refers under the label "interest theories", cannot explain moral disagreement at all, see Stevenson 1963c, 13. For the claim that moral disagreements can pertain even after a complete agreement in belief has been achieved, see Stevenson 1963c, 27 f.; and Stevenson 1963b, 5.

The second aspect of our ordinary moral practice that supposedly speaks in favour of the emotive analysis is what Stevenson refers to as the "magnetism"[30] of goodness. It is what is now usually described as the motivational or action-guiding force of moral judgements: the fact that somebody who recognizes something to be good usually or even necessarily possesses a tendency to act in its favour. Given the widespread Humean view that motivation for action cannot be explained in terms of the agents' beliefs alone, but necessarily presupposes certain desires on his behalf, emotivism can accommodate this aspect of morality in a way rival theories cannot.

The third aspect is the idea that, as Stevenson himself puts it, "the "goodness" of anything must not be verifiable solely by the use of scientific method"[31]. What is meant by this is that a plausible definition of 'good' must pay tribute to the fact that we do not ordinarily conceive of goodness as something that can be determined by empirical means. Stevenson's point, therefore, is similar to Ayer's and is supported by an even more direct appeal to Moore's open question argument. According to Stevenson, no matter what set of empirical or scientifically knowable properties an object may have, we will always take the question of whether an object with such properties is good to be an open question, and there is no reason, in Stevenson's view, to think that in taking the question in this way, we are totally confused.[32] If this is correct, however, then it seems that 'good' cannot refer to an empirically accessible property. Moreover, since Stevenson rejects Moore's non-naturalist conclusion on epistemological grounds,[33] the only plausible thing for him to do is to deny that goodness is, strictly speaking, a property at all, which is what the emotive theory suggests, by explaining goodness-claims in terms of the expression of attitudes rather than beliefs.

Hare is slightly less explicit about whether he understands his metaethical enterprise as one of giving the actual meaning of moral words or moral utterances, at least in his earlier works. However, there still is sufficient evidence that this is indeed the case. For instance, there are numerous references to the ways in which "we" use words such as 'good',[34] or to the ways in which certain moral terms are applied "by speakers of the language"[35], or even to "how people

---

30 Stevenson 1963c, 13.
31 Stevenson 1963c, 13.
32 See Stevenson 1963c, 15 and 30. See also Stevenson 1944, 109.
33 See, for instance, Stevenson 1944, 108 f.
34 See Hare 1952, 83 f.
35 Hare 1999a, 82.

use words in particular cultures"[36]. Moreover, Hare explicitly refers to the question of what moral words *mean* as the question of "what *people* mean when they utter them"[37].

Hare's focus on the ways in which ordinary speakers actually use moral language may be somewhat obscured by his strong emphasis on the logical characteristics of moral words, which one might want to conceive of as an issue largely independent of human convention. Yet, though Hare at times suggests that the logical characteristics of moral words are his primary interest,[38] he explicitly emphasizes that these logical characteristics are not detachable from the way in which words are actually being used:

> It would be a mistake to suppose that logic discovers only contingent truths about language; but it is also a mistake to think that logic is independent of the study of language. It is a necessary truth that, in one common meaning of 'all' and the other words used, if all the books on the top shelf are by Wittgenstein, and this is a book on the top shelf, then this is by Wittgenstein. But in order to establish that this is a necessary truth, we have to be assured that the words are being used and understood in the senses that make it so. Logic is, at least in part, the study of words which people use in their discourse, to ascertain which of the things they say are, as they use their words, necessary truths.[39]

We may describe Hare's purpose, therefore, as that of analysing the actual meaning of moral language with a particular emphasis on the logical properties moral terms acquire in virtue of this very meaning.

Again, Hare does not explicitly take up the issue of whether ordinary speakers are confused or incoherent in their application of moral terms, and neither does he discuss the question of whether his ultimate analysis might be in contradiction with certain aspects of ordinary moral practice. However, Hare at least concedes that moral terms are being used quite differently, and he therefore explicitly confines his analysis to the *typical* uses of the terms he examines. Given this emphasis on the complexity of the actual usage of moral words, it seems that we should also attribute to him the somewhat trivial view that there is not one typical use of moral words which we could ascribe to all speakers of the language in exactly the same way. There seems to be no problem, then, with interpreting Hare's account as partially revisionary in the way sketched above.

---

36 Hare 1999a, 1.
37 Hare 1999a, 1. (my emphasis).
38 See, for instance, Hare's characterization of theoretical ethics as a "branch of logic" (Hare 1999a, 4).
39 Hare 1999a, 3.

This brings us to the question of how Hare justifies his particular account of moral language. There are various aspects of our ordinary moral practice that Hare's analysis appeals to. First, in chapter 5 of *The language of morals*, Hare explicitly embraces Moore's question argument or, more precisely, a specific restatement of it.[40] In order to demonstrate that evaluative terms such as 'good' have evaluative in addition to descriptive meaning, Hare points out that purely descriptive definitions of 'good' are incompatible with our practice of commending things *because* they possess certain good-making characteristics. According to Hare, once we accept that the meaning of 'good' can be given in terms of a set of purely descriptive characteristics, call this set C, we are debarred from saying that a certain object is good in virtue of being C, because this claim would come out as the trivial claim that the object is C in virtue of being C. Descriptivistic analyses for moral terms fail, therefore, in Hare's view, because they deny us the possibility of "saying something we do sometimes want to say"[41] and which we "do succeed in saying meaningfully in our ordinary talk"[42].

The full argumentative import of these considerations depends on the idea that the moral, or the evaluative in general, supervenes on the non-moral or non-evaluative, which idea Hare has previously developed.[43] As Hare claims in the beginning of chapter 5, the characteristic of an object P being good logically depends on other, non-evaluative characteristics of P in a way that it would be a violation of our fundamental linguistic conventions to say that P is exactly like some other object Q in all of its non-evaluative properties and to nevertheless claim that, unlike P, Q is not good. According to Hare, therefore, the evaluative characteristics of objects *logically depend* on their non-evaluative properties, but are not *identical* with these properties, and the way to explain this particular relationship is to say that, in claiming some object to be good, we are expressing the acceptance of a certain standard which, in the end, comes down to having certain preferences or desires with regard to the descriptive properties which this object should, or should not, have.

---

40 See Hare 1952, 83 f.
41 Hare 1952, 84.
42 Hare 1952, 85 f.
43 See Hare 1952, 80 f. For the conjunction of the two points, see also Hare 1952, 145 f. Note, however, that in Hare's view, supervenience is itself a result of the practice of commendation: it is because we use moral and other evaluative terms for commending ways of behaviour and thereby guiding other people's choices that there needs to be a consistent connection between evaluations and the descriptive properties of the objects being evaluated (see Hare 1952, 134).

The second aspect that Hare's argument appeals to is the nature of agreement and disagreement. Hare justifies his claim that the evaluative meaning of terms such as 'good' is primary to their descriptive meaning by drawing attention to the fact that we can (partially) agree with other people in our moral assessment of certain ways of behaviour without agreeing about the descriptive characteristics grounding the assessment. Thus, as Hare's tale of the cannibal and the missionary is meant to illustrate,[44] we can communicate happily and successfully about morals with individuals who have moral standards different from our own, in so far as we can understand that they are using their moral vocabulary to commend certain people or certain ways of behaviour. In fact, it is this agreement in the commendatory function of moral words which allows us to teach our moral standards to other individuals, which means nothing other than getting them to apply moral words to the kind of descriptive properties to which we already apply them. Again, this aspect of our common moral practice is not well preserved in naturalist accounts of moral language: given that the cannibal and the missionary do not seem to disagree about the descriptive properties of the relevant people or ways of behaviour at all (but only about how to react to them), naturalists would have to interpret their case as a case of complete moral agreement, thereby leaving out the fact that the cannibal and the missionary disagree in their particular moral standards.

The aspect of moral disagreement is relevant for one of Hare's other arguments as well. As Stevenson before him, Hare rejects non-naturalist versions of descriptivism on epistemological grounds. According to Hare, it is not clear whether there is such a thing as a special faculty of intuition by which we can perceive non-natural properties, but it is also not clear whether the non-naturalist can do without such a faculty. Moreover, people obviously differ in their moral judgements, and the intuitionist usually fails to explain what exactly goes wrong in these cases and to offer a criterion by which we could decide which party to a moral disagreement is right and whose intuitions are at fault.[45]

A final aspect, which is not really justified by Hare, but presupposed by much of his analysis, is the motivational or practical aspect of morality which, in Hare's view, favours his own analysis over both naturalism and non-naturalism. For Hare, moral thinking is a sub-species of "practical thinking"[46], moral utterances serving an essentially practical function.[47] This is also reflected in the way in which Hare describes moral utterances as prescriptive, in his empha-

---

[44] See Hare 1952, 148 f.
[45] See Hare 1999a, 82 ff.
[46] Hare 1981, 169.
[47] See Hare 1981, 59.

sis on the commendatory role of moral utterances and in how he links moral utterances with teaching and the guiding of choices. Although Hare does not provide a full-blown argument for this view that would be independent of the arguments already reviewed, he makes an additional appeal to our moral practice in support of it. Thus, in his discussion of moral dilemmas in the early chapters of *Moral thinking*, Hare points out that we tend to experience situations in which two of our moral principles get into conflict as "tragic"[48]. Hare suggests that we can salvage this aspect of our moral practice only if we conceive of morality as essentially practical, i.e. as essentially related to motivation and action, and in his view, this is something descriptivistic analyses will not allow us to do.

In Blackburn's works, we find as explicit and extensive a discussion of the non-revisionary status of expressivism as to be found in none of the three proponents of expressivism discussed above. This discussion seems to have been prompted by Mackie's error theory, which was fully formulated only after the key works of Ayer, Stevenson and Hare had already been published.[49] Blackburn's main interest in raising the question is to dispel the impression that expressivism amounts to the kind of theory defended by Mackie, and his way of dealing with this challenge is to point to the quasi-realist enterprise, which he explicitly describes as the enterprise of showing that there is no error or mistake involved in the ordinary use of moral predicates.[50] According to Blackburn, then, it is the quasi-realism in expressivism that guarantees the conservative status of the expressivist approach, not necessarily the nature of the expressivist approach itself. We have already seen that it is hard to square this way of putting things with the standard definition of expressivism which, as we have seen, is explicitly accepted by Blackburn. We will therefore have to come back to the question of how exactly, if not in these terms, we are to conceive of the quasi-realist programme.

For the time being, the important thing is to emphasize that Blackburn's theory is not meant to apply to any fictitious moral discourse, but that he subscribes to the general aim of providing an account of how moral language is actually being used. Moreover, there is clear evidence that Blackburn does not want to go as far as claiming that the conative or sentimental foundations of moral utterances, or the reasons for adopting the propositional surface of

---

[48] Hare 1981, 32.
[49] See, however, Mackie 1946, for an early sketch of Mackie's theory.
[50] See Blackburn 1984, 171. For a discussion of the differences between Mackie's error theory and quasi-realist expressivism, see also Blackburn 1984, 195f. and 210; Blackburn 1986, 123f.; Blackburn 1993a, 366; Blackburn 1993b, 152; Blackburn 1996, 83f.; Blackburn 2005b, 323ff.; Blackburn 2006, 154.

moral discourse (which his quasi-realism attempts to reconstruct), are fully transparent to ordinary speakers.[51] Finally, Blackburn repeatedly emphasizes the complexities and variations within ordinary moral discourse and describes the purpose of his metaethical theory, not so much as proffering an *analysis* of moral terms in the strict sense of the word, but rather as giving "a description of central or paradigm cases"[52]. The most natural position to attribute to him, then, seems to be one I have attributed to Ayer, Stevenson and Hare, namely that (quasi-realist) expressivism is essentially, but not wholly conservative because it tries to give a straightforward and coherent account of what is, empirically, less coherent and sometimes confused.

This brings us to the question of how Blackburn supports his particular account of moral language. The first thing to be noted here is that Blackburn explicitly questions whether specifically linguistic evidence will help us to adjudicate between the different positions within the metaethical debate. Just because the propositional surface of moral discourse can equally be explained by realist and quasi-realist approaches, Blackburn thinks that the philosophy of language might not provide arguments to decisively favour one approach over the other.[53] In accordance with this, the arguments Blackburn appeals to are metaphysical, psychological and epistemological rather than linguistic in nature.

One reason why Blackburn takes quasi-realist expressivism to be superior to non-naturalist realism is because it is more economical with regard to both metaphysics and epistemology: whereas the non-naturalist initially needs to postulate two types of properties, natural and non-natural ones, and two types of epistemic processes, sense perception and intuition, the expressivist only appeals to natural properties and sense perception and couples this with an uncontroversial theory about certain non-cognitive patterns of human reaction.[54]

The second argument makes use of the idea of supervenience, which Blackburn employs in a much more complicated manner than Ayer or Hare.[55] Yet, Blackburn's basic point is not very different from the points of his predecessors: while naturalism conceives of moral states of affairs as identical to natural states of affairs and therefore poses too strong a connection between the two, non-naturalism offers no plausible theory for why moral states of affairs should depend on natural states of affairs at all. The expressivist approach, in contrast, occupies

---

51 See, for instance, Blackburn 1995, 54.
52 Blackburn 2001b, 28.
53 See Blackburn 1984, 210.
54 See Blackburn 1984, 182. For an explicit commitment to metaphysical naturalism, see also Blackburn 1998, 48f.
55 See Blackburn 1984, 182ff.

a kind of middle ground, claiming that moral states of affairs are, in some sense of that word, constituted by our non-cognitive reactions towards natural states of affairs and, for this reason, sensitive to changes in these states of affairs on some kind of regular basis.

Blackburn's third argument appeals to the philosophy of action and, in particular, to the motivational nature of moral commitments.[56] Following Stevenson and, more importantly, Hume, Blackburn suggests that subscribing to a positive evaluation with regard to some object *typically* implies that we "feel a pull towards promoting or choosing it, or towards wanting other people to feel the pull towards promoting or choosing it"[57]. Yet, presupposing something like the strict orthodox Humean philosophy of mind, Blackburn takes it that having any belief with regard to that object is, in principle, consistent with being completely indifferent or even hostile to it. It seems, then, that in order to explain the motivational pull of moral or other evaluative commitments, we need to explain these commitments in terms of desires or other conative states, and this is exactly what Blackburn does.

In addition to the above argumentative strategies, which Blackburn lays out in some detail, we find appeals to virtually all of the other ideas developed in the works of Ayer, Stevenson and Hare. Thus, Blackburn explicitly subscribes to Moore's open question argument against naturalism,[58] he criticizes non-naturalism for providing no criterion "for distinguishing better or worse intuitions"[59], and he claims that expressivism allows us to give the right account of moral agreement and disagreement.[60]

Gibbard's position on the issue is clearly the most complex one, which is partly due to the fact that it seems to have been subjected to certain changes over the years. It is pretty clear that in the early works, Gibbard is generally interested in explaining the actual meaning of normative terms. However, we do not yet find any explicit commitment to Blackburn's quasi-realist programme, which Gibbard adopts only some time after the publication of *Wise choices, apt feelings*.

---

56 See Blackburn 1984, 187 f.
57 Blackburn 1984, 188. The qualification is important here, given that Blackburn admits that it may be possible not to care about morality, but still make moral judgements (see Blackburn 1984, 188). For a similar qualified appeal to the practical nature of morality, see Blackburn 1996, 85 and 91. See also Blackburn 1998, 86 f. and 90 f.; and Blackburn 2006, 147 ff.
58 See Blackburn 1998, 70 and 86 f.
59 Blackburn 1998, 86.
60 See Blackburn 1984, 168.

The way to describe Gibbard's initial position, then, is in analogy to Ayer's position: as an account of actual moral language that unashamedly demands certain revisions, by rejecting, for example, ordinary talk of moral truth, moral facts and moral properties. Given that, *prima facie* at least, these two features stand in opposition to one another, it seems that we must take the early Gibbard to be conceiving of the metaethical enterprise in terms of the intermediate position I have ascribed to the other classic expressivists as well. It has to be noted, though, that certain aspects of ordinary moral practice which are sometimes thought to be incompatible with non-cognitivistic approaches are ones that even the early Gibbard explicitly tries to salvage, for example the claim to moral objectivity.[61]

Gibbard gives what is perhaps the most explicit characterization of his earlier methodological approach in his reply to Walter Sinnott-Armstrong's review of *Wise choices, apt feelings*, published in 1993. On the one hand, Gibbard emphasizes that the actual meanings of terms such as 'wrong' or 'rational' are bound to be controversial and that there is no easy way to ascertain the truth of the matter. In view of this problem, Gibbard claims that the important question "is not how our language currently works, but how to sharpen it"[62]. Similar to Ayer, then, Gibbard recommends a slightly revised way of speaking about morality and normativity. On the other hand, Gibbard emphasizes that he does not propose "a blanket reform in our normative thought and talk"[63], and he rejects the view that the expressivist analysis commits us to charging ordinary speakers with any kind of substantial error: anticipating his explicit commitment to the quasi-realist programme, Gibbard presents it as one of the chief aims of his theory to show that we can accept the expressivist analysis and still "coherently go on talking and thinking, normatively, pretty much as we do talk and think"[64].

That Gibbard's more recent position differs somewhat from the one just described is not so much due to the more explicit commitment to quasi-realism.[65] Rather, it results from the fact that Gibbard presents the slightly different account of normative language developed in *Thinking how to live* as a kind of "pos-

---

61 See, for example, Gibbard 1985a, 41 f.; Gibbard 1990a, 154 f.; and Gibbard 1992b, 971.
62 Gibbard 1993b, 320. For the suggestion that the philosophical analysis needs to somewhat depart from ordinary uses of normative terms, see also Gibbard 2006a, 740. See also Gibbard's recent reference to "the imprecise complex mess that is ordinary thinking" (Gibbard 2015, 176).
63 Gibbard 1993b, 315.
64 Gibbard 1993b, 315.
65 For Gibbard's explicit adoption of quasi-realism, see Gibbard 1996, 331; Gibbard 2002a, 153; Gibbard 2002b, 212 f.; Gibbard 2002c, 55; Gibbard 2003, XII and 18 f.; Gibbard 2006c, 687 f.; and Gibbard 2014, 232 f.

sibility proof"⁶⁶. According to Gibbard, the aim of the latter work is not to show that our actual language works in the way laid down by his revised analysis of normative utterances (which interprets such utterances as expressions of contingency plans), but to show that normative language *could* work in this way.

To be sure, Gibbard ultimately takes up the question of whether his theory also provides an appropriate account of how we do in fact talk and think about normative matters. In the end, however, his qualified conclusions pretty much amount to the kind of agnosticism he maintains with regard to truth minimalism and minimalism about facts and properties. Gibbard claims that "we do mix plan with fact"⁶⁷ in our normative language and that plan-laden concepts "have much to do"⁶⁸ with what ordinary normative terms express. However, he avoids the claim "that certain terms express plan-laden concepts, always and definitely, with no ambiguity"⁶⁹ and he now even allows that, given the looseness of ordinary talk and the indeterminacy of the presuppositions carried by certain terms, "there may be no clear fact of the matter just what a term expresses in a given use"⁷⁰.

Gibbard's current position is further complicated by the fact that, despite his explicit commitment to the quasi-realist programme, Gibbard seems to have come quite close to the concession that the ordinary understanding of morality (or of normativity in general) involves some kind of substantial error. Thus, in two articles from 2006 and 2015 in which he discusses the popular analogy between moral judgements and colour judgements, Gibbard admits that naïve moral thought is subject to certain misconceptions about moral discourse, not unlike the misconceptions contained in our ordinary thinking about colour. Accordingly, Gibbard suggests that a naïve form of moral realism might provide the appropriate account of ordinary moral thought.⁷¹ However, Gibbard implicitly appeals to the distinction between knowing-what and knowing-how, i.e. between *thinking* about moral language and *using* it, by describing the misconceptions of ordinary speakers as misconceptions about *what they themselves are doing* when they engage in moral deliberation and moral talk.⁷² Moreover, Gib-

---

66 Gibbard 2003, 5.
67 Gibbard 2003, 138.
68 Gibbard 2003, 139.
69 Gibbard 2003, 138.
70 Gibbard 2003, 138. Note, however, that, despite these worries, Gibbard has recently claimed that the kind of normative language he describes is at least "analytically equivalent" (Gibbard 2014, 194) to normative language as we know it.
71 See Gibbard 2006b, 204 ff.
72 See Gibbard 2006b, 204 f.

bard denies that the misconceptions of ordinary speakers force us to conceive of expressivism as an example of the error theory because the quasi-realist variant of expressivism allows us to vindicate the core of our ordinary judgements and practices. According to Gibbard, therefore, we do not have to conclude that moral judgements are systematically or uniformly false, even though various errors may be ingrained in common sense morality.[73]

As in *Thinking how to live*, then, Gibbard's main thesis is not so much that his expressivist theory provides the right account of how we actually think about normative matters, but that we can, in principle and somewhat charitably, interpret ordinary talk and thinking in expressivist terms. Moreover, he more positively claims that we should in fact *do* vindicate the ordinary practice in expressivist terms because the vindication provided by the expressivist is superior to the ones offered by non-expressivist approaches. In making these claims, however, Gibbard seems to suggest, not unlike Blackburn, that it is the quasi-realist strategy that allows for a vindication of ordinary moral talk, not so much the expressivist analysis itself.

The position taken by Gibbard can therefore be described as a kind of pluralism about the theoretical description of our actual moral language. In Gibbard's view, the linguistic evidence is, in principle, compatible with different theoretical approaches. Accordingly, what favours quasi-realist expressivist over other approaches is not that it provides us with a singular opportunity of explaining how we actually use moral terms. It is rather that quasi-realist expressivism allows us to salvage more of our ordinary moral practice and fits better with our non-moral assumptions about the world. Gibbard, then, seems to hold a view about the metaethical enterprise that is quite close to the one formulated by Blackburn in *Spreading the word*. According to this view, specifically linguistic arguments will not provide much help in deciding which metaethical theory is best or most appropriate to the reality of moral discourse, which means that we must go beyond the philosophy of language in order to adjudicate between rival metaethical theories.

That something like this must be Gibbard's view is also demonstrated by the particular arguments by which he tries to support his expressivist thesis and which, according to his more recent statements, are meant to prove that quasi-realist expressivism provides a better or more extensive vindication of our ordinary moral practice. In *Wise choices, apt feelings*, the main element of Gibbard's positive argument for expressivism is a speculative evolutionary story that is intended to make plausible the idea that humans have evolved

---

[73] See Gibbard 2006b, 210 f. See also Gibbard 2015, 187 f.

the special mental state of norm-acceptance that, according to Gibbard's analysis, is being expressed by normative utterances.[74]

One major aspect of this story is the link between language and motivation. Gibbard's speculative account suggests that one crucial function of language is practical, given that it is with regard to the function of coordinating and motivating human behaviour that language provides the most significant evolutionary advantages. According to Gibbard, normative language is so intimately related to these practical or directive aspects that we may conceive of coordination as the "chief biological function of normative discussion"[75]. The deficit of descriptivist approaches is that they cannot sufficiently accommodate this very fact and, in particular, cannot satisfactorily explain the element of endorsement that is contained in moral utterances or normative utterances.[76] Therefore, while Gibbard may not provide anything like the straightforward Humean motivation argument suggested by Blackburn, he crucially appeals to the connection between moral or normative utterances on the one hand and motivation for action on the other in order to argue for the superiority of expressivism over naturalism and non-naturalism.

Further important aspects of Gibbard's case for expressivism are his commitment to metaphysical naturalism, which leads him to the rejection of any non-natural reality,[77] his reference to the epistemological problems arising from the non-naturalist appeal to moral or normative intuitions,[78] and his appeal to Moore's open question argument which, not unlike Hare and Blackburn, he takes to rest on a secure foundation even if the particulars of Moore's discussion may invite certain objections.[79]

We can conclude, therefore, that the positions of all the classic expressivists can be assigned to the same general spectrum with regard to the question of whether their metaethical theories provide a conservative or revisionary account of moral language. While none of them aspires to give a wholly conservative description of the reality of moral discourse, they all express the ambition to explain or analyse our actual use of moral language or to at least provide a theory by which we can vindicate this use. Moreover, the accounts of Ayer, Stevenson, Hare, Blackburn and Gibbard are all conservative in that their positive arguments in support of the basic expressivist analysis try to appeal to fundamental

---

74 See Gibbard 1990a, 55 ff.
75 Gibbard 1990a, 76.
76 See Gibbard 1990a, 9 f. See also Gibbard 2003, 9 and 11.
77 See Gibbard 1990a, 23; Gibbard 2011, 34 f.; and Gibbard 2014, 222 f.
78 See Gibbard 2003, 268; and Gibbard 2011, 45.
79 See Gibbard 2003, 13 and 21 f.

aspects of our ordinary understanding of morality and moral language. We should reject, therefore, the widespread view that it is only in its modern, quasi-realist guise that expressivism attempts to provide a conservative account of moral discourse.

3 Quasi-realist expressivism, non-quasi-realist expressivism and the error theory

It seems that there is also a further conclusion to be drawn from the above considerations, namely that we should be quite sceptical as to whether the appeal to the revisionary/non-revisionary distinction is helpful in distinguishing expressivist theories from error theories. Since reasonable error theorists would hardly claim that each and every speaker is constantly involved in the kind of error diagnosed by their theories, it appears that, in principle, error theories are located within the same spectrum to which we have just assigned expressivism. With regard to its non-revisionary status, then, error theories might seem to be only gradually distinguished from expressivist theories, which raises the question of whether there is any systematic way of making the distinction between expressivism and error theories at all.

To answer this question, it is vital to first distinguish between two different 'errors' the error theorist might want to attribute to ordinary speakers. According to one view, ordinary moral discourse is erroneous because the truth-assessable beliefs expressed by moral utterances are all false, given they presuppose the existence of mind-independent objective moral facts or values. According to a second view, ordinary moral discourse is erroneous because ordinary speakers falsely think that their moral utterances express beliefs whereas they do in fact express desires or attitudes.

If the 'error' characteristic of error theories about moral discourse is the latter one, it seems indeed that there is not much of a difference between expressivism and error theories after all, given that the 'error' in question does not appear to be systematically different from the partial 'confusion' which the classic expressivists attribute to them. Moreover, to try to make more of the difference by claiming that the 'error' is much more widespread than the 'confusion' diagnosed by the expressivist is a strategy the error theorist should better avoid because it threatens to make his view internally unstable, at least once we admit that the kind of 'expression' we are talking about is not a purely causal notion, but one that crucially appeals to the idea of linguistic convention. If the claim that moral utterances express desires or attitudes is the claim that moral utterances express desires or attitudes *by linguistic convention*, then it is hard to see how the majority of ordinary speakers should ever come to make the kind of 'error' the error theorist would end up attributing to them: since the 'error' must consist in thinking that moral utterances express truth-assessable belief by *linguistic convention*, it can only occur if the speakers in question have fundamentally misunderstood the existing linguistic conventions, which means that they cannot be competent speakers to begin with.

The only plausible way of arguing for the second view, therefore, would be to rephrase the relevant claim as a claim about moral *judgements* rather than moral utterances. Rephrased in this sense, the view would amount to the claim that ordinary speakers falsely conceive of their moral judgements as beliefs while in truth they are desire-like states of mind. This reformulation would turn the point supposedly characteristic of the error theory into an essentially psychological claim about how ordinary people misjudge of their own moral states of mind and commit the error theorist to the claim previously referred to as *sentimentalism about moral judgement*.

It is far from being clear that error theorists, including Mackie, would accept this kind of commitment and debar themselves from defending a rationalist version of the error theory which takes moral judgements to be constituted by proper beliefs. Nevertheless, it seems that something like this view is what lies at the heart of the idea that Mackie's theory is a variant of ethical projectivism. Somewhat ironically, the only way to defend this characterization seems to be to appeal to some kind of quasi-realist justification of ordinary discourse which can serve as an intermediate link between the psychological claim and the linguistic-cum-ontological claim with which Mackie is primarily concerned. According to this line of thinking, Mackie's error theory would make the following four interrelated claims:

(i) moral judgements are desire-like states of kind (*psychological claim*),
(ii) ordinary people tend to project these desire-like states of mind onto the external world and to think that their moral judgements are truth-assessable beliefs (*psychological claim*),
(iii) our ordinary moral discourse can successfully be reconstructed in terms of the idea that moral utterances conventionally express truth-assessable beliefs about mind-independent objective moral facts or values (*linguistic claim*),
(iv) the beliefs conventionally expressed by moral utterances are all false because there are no mind-independent objective moral facts or values (*linguistic-cum-ontological claim*).

Reconstructing the error theory in terms of the above four claims has the advantage of making more obvious where (and where not) the error theorist parts company with the expressivist. Both sentimentalist error theorists and expressivists can agree upon the first two claims. Moreover, while the non-quasi-realist would reject the third claim and instead argue for something like (iiia) *moral utterances conventionally express desire-like states of mind*, the quasi-realist expressivist can even agree with the sentimentalist error theorist on the third claim: that we can successfully reconstruct ordinary moral discourse in terms of the idea that moral utterances conventionally express truth-assessable beliefs about mind-independent objective moral facts or values.

The key disagreement between the quasi-realist expressivist and the sentimentalist error theorist, therefore, seems to lie in the fact that the former would reject claim (iv) and allow that there are some true moral beliefs or some true moral utterances. Of course, being an expressivist, the quasi-realist expressivist will also emphasize that our primary description of ordinary moral discourse should be in terms of the idea that moral utterances conventionally express desire-like states of mind and thus embrace both (iiia) and (iii).

There is, then, a relevant difference between the relationship of non-quasi-realist expressivism and error theory on the one hand and quasi-realist expressivism and error theory on the other hand, and there may also be a fundamental disagreement between error theorists and expressivists in general. However, neither the two are easily captured by appealing to the distinction between conservative and revisionary accounts of moral language, since all three groups of theorists will plausibly concede that there are certain variations in how ordinary speakers conceive of moral utterances and the linguistic conventions surrounding them so that their metaethical theories must make some revisions to what ordinary people think and say.

The difference between non-quasi-realist expressivists and error theorists is that the former reject any attempt to interpret moral utterances as expressions of belief-like states of mind and therefore do not even face the question of whether the beliefs expressed by moral utterances are systematically false or not. The difference between quasi-realist expressivists and error theorists is that the former allow some of the beliefs which we may take to be expressed by moral utterances after having earned the right to talk of moral beliefs to actually be true. While one may want to argue that his denial of the truth of any moral beliefs commits the error theorist to yet another kind of revisionism, it is not obvious that this is indeed the case, and Mackie's way of engaging in first-order moral claims in spite of his own metaethical theory may serve as a case in point. Moreover, even if we were to only classify theories as error theories that ask for a wholesale abandonment of our ordinary moral talk and to describe more conservative theories as examples of moral fictionalism, this would only mean that the task of distinguishing quasi-realist expressivism and error theory reoccurs as the task of distinguishing quasi-realist expressivism and moral fictionalism and here, again, the appeal to the conservative/revisionary distinction would hardly provide much help.

Whether there is a further, more fundamental disagreement between expressivist theories and error theories obviously depends very much on how exactly the error theorist conceives of his position. In particular, it depends on whether the error theorist has any place for the idea that the primary description of ordinary moral discourse should be in terms of the idea that moral utterances conventionally express desire-like states of mind. We may expect defenders of rationalist versions of the error theory, who take moral judgements to be belief-like states of mind and accordingly reject psychological claims (i) and (ii), to have no incentive whatsoever to do so, which means that their accounts would quite fundamentally be opposed to expressivism. In contrast, defenders of sentimentalist versions of the error theory might not be committed to rejecting claim (iiia), which means that with regard to such accounts, the wholesale denial of true moral beliefs might be all there is to distinguish them from non-quasi-realist expressivism on the hand and quasi-realist expressivism on the other.

This leaves us with the question of how best to systematically distinguish quasi-realist expressivism and non-quasi-realist expressivism, without making the detour of appealing to how both positions relate to the error theory. As we have seen, both positions are partly revisionary, but, at the same time, generally concerned with the actual usage of moral terms and the actual meaning of moral utterances. My proposal is to conceive of quasi-realism as an active theoretical attempt to salvage as much of our ordinary understanding of morality as possible. 'Active' in this context means that the attempt involves some kind of explicit argument, such as an explicit reconstruction of the notion of moral truth or a defence of moral objectivity or the mind-independence of moral judgements, on an expressivist basis.

We find such elements in Blackburn and Gibbard, but not, in the same way, in Ayer or Stevenson, which is why the above characterization of the quasi-realist strategy allows us to vindicate the way in which the four writers are usually classified: given the systematic and constructive manner in which Blackburn and Gibbard address the underlying challenge and make a concerted attempt at solving the 'Frege-Geach problem', the proposed distinction supports the view that their theories represent an important departure from traditional emotivist approaches to moral language. At the same time, however, the distinction casts certain doubts on the view that Blackburn's and Gibbard's relevant publications herald an entirely new era in the history of expressivism: given that Hare explicitly confronts the 'Frege-Geach problem' in his 1970 paper *Meaning and speech* *acts*⁸⁰ and generally puts great effort into defending the rationality of moral discourse, there is a reasonable basis for conceiving of him as a quasi-realist in his own right.

4 Creeping minimalism: The case of belief

Understanding the relationship of expressivism and quasi-realism in the way developed above does not yet help the expressivist to escape the problem sketched at the end of the last section, a problem that is now commonly referred to as the problem of 'creeping minimalism'. The problem, to recapitulate, is to defend expressivism's distinctive claim in the face of the minimalist challenge, and this problem is only made more serious by the fact that most modern expressivists accept minimalism at least with regard to *some* relevant area, such as truth.

The general worry that the quasi-realist strategy might end up being too successful, undermining the fundamental idea of expressivism and its claim to distinctiveness, has been raised ever since Blackburn launched his quasi-realist programme.[81] Moreover, the dangers looming in the quasi-realist enterprise were not lost on the proponents of expressivism, either. In fact, it seems that it was Blackburn himself who pointed the critics of quasi-realism into this direction. Blackburn explicitly confronts the question as early as 1981 in his paper on *Rule-following and moral realism*, and we find further attempts to rebut the challenge in several other of his and Gibbard's works.[82]

The two specific variants of this general worry that are most relevant to our present context both relate to the question of whether the expressivist can make room for the notion of moral beliefs. The first issue here is: does the expressivist, if he decides to accommodate the common sense notion of moral belief in his theory, run the risk the undermining his own position or at least force himself to abandon the standard definition of expressivism? The obvious answer to

---

80 See Hare 1970.
81 See, for example, Wright 1985, 318f.; Sinnott-Armstrong 1993, 297; Dworkin 1996, 110; Rosen 1998, 387; Dreier 1999, 570; Harcourt 2005, 249f.; Ernst 2008, 98; Harth 2008, 47; Radtke 2009, 102; Dworkin 2011, 434f.; and Price 2015, 138ff.
82 See Blackburn 1981, 185f.; Blackburn 1984, 219f.; Blackburn 1993a, 366f.; Blackburn 1998, 77ff.; Blackburn 2005b, 323; Blackburn 2006, 160f.; Gibbard 1992b, 971; Gibbard 1993b, 317; Gibbard 2003, 18f. and 184ff.; Gibbard 2014, 218ff. See also Ridge 2006c, 635ff. Note that Crispin Wright, who is now usually cited as the first proponent of the objection in question, takes up the issue from Blackburn's own discussion in *Spreading the word*. Note also that Hare – though not a professed quasi-realist himself – tries to respond to quite a similar challenge in chapter 12 of *Moral thinking* (see Hare 1981, 218ff.).

the first part of this question is that the expressivist can maintain a distinctive position as long as he conceives of moral beliefs in a way significantly different from the one employed by his opponents. How something like this could be possible has already been indicated above. Any solution of the relevant kind will ultimately have to operate with two notions of belief: one that excludes non-cognitive mental states and one that does not. This means that, as far as the second part of the question is concerned, the standard definition of expressivism has not to be given up, but slightly modified, by including, for example, a reference to the distinction between representational and non-representational beliefs or between descriptive and moral beliefs.

The second issue is whether the expressivist needs to embrace minimalism about belief and thereby threaten the distinctiveness of his position, be it because this fits best with his overall quasi-realist approach or because a robust notion of belief is simply dubious, i.e. independently of the entire debate over expressivism and quasi-realism. One idea that is often thought to establish a link between this point and the previous one is that the concept of representation is inapt to provide a criterion for distinguishing two kinds of belief because it is itself a concept for which a minimalist understanding suggests itself.[83]

It should be obvious that it is this second issue which raises the more threatening challenge to the expressivist enterprise. In my view, however, it does not necessarily undermine either the distinctiveness of expressivism or the standard definition. The serious problem intimated by the challenge arises only if we accept a specifically linguistic conception of 'belief' according to which a belief is what is being expressed by a declarative sentence (and, in fact, nothing above and beyond than what is being expressed by declarative sentences). Yet, such a conception of belief seems quite dubious in its own right and in dire need of justification. Moreover, it is doubtful whether the appeal to folk platitudes linking the notion of belief to the notions of truth and assertion – such as the alleged platitudes that 'any truth-evaluable statement is an assertion' and that 'an assertion is the expression of a belief' – can provide a justification of this kind.[84] It seems, therefore, that we should not even accept the fundamental premise from which the objection from minimalism about belief takes its start. However, once the expressivist defines the notion of belief in other, genuinely psychological or functional terms, it seems that he can simply avoid the problem.

---

83 See, for example, Dreier 2004a, 29.
84 See Divers/Miller 1994, 14 f. See also Smith 1994b, 3 f.; Lenman 2003, 37; Dreier 2004a, 27 f.; and Chrisman 2008, 344.

If we follow this line of thinking, the challenge from minimalism about belief is not a devastating objection to the expressivist approach but rather goes to show that the plausibility of expressivism ultimately depends on the plausibility of an underlying psychological theory that can successfully distinguish between beliefs and desires, or between cognitive and non-cognitive mental states in general. That expressivism is somehow dependent upon a genuinely psychological or functional version of the belief/desire distinction has explicitly been acknowledged by leading expressivists, most notably by Blackburn and Ridge, neither of whom seems shaken by this fact but express confidence that an appropriate psychological distinction can indeed be drawn – if not in terms of representation and non-representation then in other terms.[85]

As far as the possible minimalist character of 'representation' is concerned, it is certainly right that the term itself is not very helpful when it comes to making the required psychological distinction. Not least, this is due to the fact that representation, as it is employed in this context, is a philosophical rather than a common sense concept,[86] which means that we can hardly draw on ordinary talk in trying to provide conclusive arguments for any particular understanding of representation. It is for this very reason, however, that the expressivist may legitimately stipulate a certain definition of representation and use the concept in a way that secures the distinctiveness of his theoretical position.

Given that, as we have just seen, the aim of the classic expressivists is to explain the actual meaning of moral language, one might be uncomfortable with the fact that their position depends upon an act of mere stipulation. An alternative would then be to largely dispense with the concept of representation and to instead draw on a distinction widely acknowledged to be a common sense distinction, such as the distinction between world-to-mind and mind-to-world direction of fit. As long as one at least accepts the fundamental distinction between mental states whose point is to fit the world and mental states whose point is to make the world fit them, the expressivist position (as characterized by the standard definition) seems well guarded against the challenge from minimalism about belief.

It may be, however, that this way of defending the distinctive nature of expressivism forces us to conclude that some recent approaches, which are commonly described as instances of expressivism, should not be classified in this way. One example is the cognitivist expressivism of Terry Horgan and Mark Tim-

---

85 See Blackburn 2005b, 323; and Ridge 2006c, 642. See also Blackburn 2001b, 27f. and 30f.; Blackburn 2002, 122ff.; Blackburn 2006, 160f. For a more cautious position, see Lenman 2003, 37ff.
86 For a different view, see Dreier 2004a, 29.

mons already mentioned above. Another example is Gibbard, if we take seriously his more recent agnosticism about whether moral utterances do or do not express beliefs. Yet, denying these positions their expressivist status would by no means be without precedent in the debate over expressivism. In fact, Blackburn himself suggests that we should not think of the belief-agnostic version of Gibbard's theory as an example of expressivism anymore,[87] and as far as Horgan and Timmons are concerned, the problem of appropriately classifying their theory is nicely illustrated by Horgan and Timmons's own difficulties in finding a proper label for their position.[88] However, given that Horgan and Timmons explicitly accept both the distinction between representational and non-representational mental states and the view that moral utterances express the latter, it certainly remains possible to classify their position as expressivist even if one accepts the above line of thinking. Whether or not one should view their position as expressivist, then, very much depends on the question of which particular psychological theory one takes to be ultimately adequate.

The above considerations already suggest, therefore, that in trying to maintain a distinctive metaethical position, the expressivist incurs substantial commitments in the philosophy of mind. However, before we can move on to further examine the relationship between expressivism on the one hand and folk and empirical psychology on the other, it needs to be noted that two alternative, non-psychological strategies of ensuring the distinctiveness of expressivism have been suggested in the past. The first one, which is endorsed by Gibbard and also suggested by Dreier, is sometimes referred to as the 'explanation explanation'. It amounts to the idea that what makes expressivism special, even in the face of minimalism about belief, is that it follows a distinctive order of explanation in trying to account for the meaning of moral language.[89] Instead of starting with moral beliefs or propositions, with normative truths or non-natural facts and properties, the expressivist starts with attitudinal reactions towards natural properties and goes on to explain the former elements in terms of the latter, thereby earning the right to those concepts which the non-naturalist takes for granted.

Yet, even if this may capture an important difference between quasi-realist expressivism and traditional variants of metaethical non-naturalism, it is doubt-

---

[87] See Blackburn/Sinclair 2006, 705. See also Sinclair 2009, 141.
[88] The labels tried by Horgan and Timmons include 'cognitivist expressivism' (Horgan/Timmons 2006b), 'nondescriptivist cognitivism' (Horgan/Timmons 2000) and 'assertoric nondescriptivism' (Timmons 1999).
[89] See, for example, Gibbard 1993b, 317f.; Gibbard 1996, 332; Gibbard 2003, 63; Gibbard 2014, 235ff. See also Dreier 2004a, 36ff.

ful whether the mere order of explanation, if stripped of any psychological characterization of moral judgements in terms of a more or less robust belief/desire distinction, provides a sufficient basis for systematically distinguishing quasi-realist expressivism and non-naturalism as rival metaethical positions. If quasi-realist expressivists end up with a theory that contains all the elements of the non-naturalist's toolbox,[90] then it is hard to see how the mere order of explanation, i.e. the way in which the expressivist argument arranges these elements with regard to one another, could ground the relevant systematic distinction.

The same seems true of another difference Gibbard sometimes appeals to, namely that quasi-realist expressivism provides an explanation for what non-naturalism leaves unexplained.[91] In order for this to yield a criterion for making the distinction the expressivist is after, the relevant difference must go beyond the contingent fact that actual non-naturalists, such as Moore, Scanlon or Dworkin, have not typically offered any explanation of the non-natural properties or facts their theories (implicitly) appeal to. It seems that the quasi-realist expressivist needs to make the somewhat stronger claim that the explanation offered by him is one that is not *available* to the non-naturalist in the same way. However, given that the existence of those attitudinal responses to which the quasi-realist expressivist explanation appeals is quite uncontroversial, it seems that the quasi-realist expressivist will not be able to make good on this stronger claim at all.

The upshot of the above discussion, then, is that the 'explanation explanation' can only ground a non-contingent distinction between quasi-realist expressivism and non-naturalism if it is accompanied by a systematic distinction between beliefs and desires, or representational and non-representational mental states, which awards one side of this distinction an authority with regard to morality that the non-naturalist cannot accept. That this is indeed the way in which we need to conceive of the 'explanation explanation' is also suggested by the fact that Blackburn repeatedly appeals to the specific explanatory features of expressivism as well, but still thinks that the distinction between quasi-realist expressivism and non-naturalism depends on the psychological story.[92] Emphasizing

---

90 In his more recent book *Meaning and normativity*, Gibbard makes what appears to be an even stronger claim, namely that quasi-realist expressivism and suitably refined version of non-naturalism will "end up coinciding in their theses" (Gibbard 2014, 218; see also Gibbard 2014, 229).
91 See, for instance, Gibbard 2006c, 694ff.; and Gibbard 2014, 22f.
92 For Blackburn's appeal to the aspect of explanation, see Blackburn 1981, 164f. and 185f.; Blackburn 1984, 162 and 213; and Blackburn 1991, 41f. Moreover, Blackburn himself suggests that the explanatory strategy is dependent on the psychological strategy (see Blackburn 2001b, 27f. and 30f.). For a similar suggestion, see Kauppinen 2014b, 23f.

differences in the respective explanations offered by the quasi-realist expressivist and the non-naturalist, then, will not release the expressivist from the burden of having to provide a contrastive (moral-)psychological account in terms of belief and desire.

The second strategy, which has been suggested by Matthew Chrisman, is to reformulate the opposition between expressivism and its rivals in *inferentialist* rather than representational terms. Instead of explaining the content of moral utterances in terms of the mental states these utterances conventionally express, the expressivist should, according to Chrisman, reverse the order explanation and explain the content of mental states in terms of the utterances that conventionally express these mental states – where the contents of these utterances are in turn explained in terms of their role in socially-embodied inferential practices.[93]

Without even attempting to assess the viability of the overall inferentialist programme at this point, it seems unquestionable to me that adopting the inferentialist paradigm would not so much, as Chrisman suggests, 'save' the original debate over expressivism, but rather replace it with a new one. Given that, as we have seen, the original debate was conceived of in terms of the psychological distinction between cognitive and non-cognitive mental states from the very beginning, it would be more appropriate, in moving to the inferentialist model, to also replace the traditional labels and terminological oppositions. This is also suggested by Sinclair who claims that the move to inferentialism would relocate the debate to a place where "the psychologized labels of 'expressivism' and 'descriptivism' are no longer appropriate"[94]. In fact, it seems that Chrisman himself has come to view matters in this way, given that in his 2016 book *The meaning of 'ought'*, he describes the inferentialist approach to moral language as a view "beyond descriptivism and expressivism"[95]. In addition, it should be noted that the debate over expressivism has not, so far, followed Chrisman's suggestion but rather moved into other directions. These directions, which create difficulties of their own, will be the object of the following chapter.

---

93 See Chrisman 2008, 349.
94 Sinclair 2009, 141.
95 Chrisman 2016, 16 f.

5 Summary

The purpose of this chapter was to systematically tackle the question of whether expressivism is a conservative or revisionary doctrine and how exactly it relates to Mackie's error theory, which is commonly presented as a rival to metaethical expressivism but sometimes as an expressivist theory in its own right.

I started off, in section 1, by examining how to spell out the distinction between conservative and revisionary metaethical analyses in more detail, showing that relevant proposals, such as the one forwarded by David Lewis, do not bear up against close scrutiny. Since neither the idea that a particular metaethical theory describes the actual usage of all competent speakers nor the idea that all these speakers are constantly involved in some kind of fundamental error seems attractive or even internally stable, the only plausible view for any metaethicist to take is that his analysis does justice to the linguistic habits of some speakers at the expense of others.

The question immediately arising from this was how to avoid the charge of arbitrariness: if all any metaethical analysis can plausibly claim is to provide an adequate account of the usage of some sub-group of competent speakers, how are we to avoid metaethical relativism and to make good on the idea that one such analysis is the correct or best one? In response to this possible objection, I argued that the only way to distinguish a particular metaethical analysis in the above way is by showing that it is more in equilibrium with other central aspects of morality, both linguistic and non-linguistic: in order to be able to claim that a specific theory of moral language, such as expressivism, provides us with the correct or best analysis of the meaning of moral utterances, one needs to demonstrate that the theory is capable of explaining other properties of our moral practice in a way rival conceptions cannot.

The aim of section 2 was to show that this is actually an idea which we find, at least implicitly, in all the classic expressivists and which positively guides their methodological approaches. All classic expressivists emphasize that their analyses are meant to describe how moral language is actually being used, while admitting that they require certain revisions with regard to how some speakers use and/or think about their moral utterances. The classic expressivists could therefore all be assigned to the general spectrum regarding the conservative/revisionary distinction that was outlined in section 1. Moreover, the arguments they provide in support of their primary linguistic analysis suggest that they are all aware of the resulting problem of arbitrariness and try to solve it in about the way described above. The clearest example of this was Blackburn who explicitly challenges the view that linguistic evidence or considerations from the philosophy of language more generally will allow us to adjudicate between expressivism and rival metaethical approaches. We found similar statements in Gibbard's writings who emphasizes that the available linguistic evidence is compatible with different metaethical approaches, but claims that quasi-realist expressivism fits best with our overall moral practice and our non-moral assumptions about the world.

Although Ayer, Stevenson and Hare may not as explicitly subscribe to this methodological creed, they very much conform to it, justifying their expressivist interpretation of moral utterances in ways that go some way beyond linguistic analysis. Thus, the key arguments provided by them, as by Blackburn and Gibbard, consist in appeals to the phenomenon of moral disagreement, to the supervenience of the moral on the non-moral and to the epistemological problems surrounding intuitionist versions of non-naturalism as well as in variants of Moore's open question argument and Hume's motivation argument. While none of the classic expressivists aspires to give a wholly conservative description of the reality of moral discourse, then, they all express the ambition to explain or analyse our actual use of moral language or to at least provide a theory by which we can vindicate this use. Moreover, their accounts are conservative in that their positive arguments in support of the basic expressivist analysis draw upon fundamental aspects of our ordinary understanding of morality and moral language. We should reject, therefore, the widespread view that it is only in its modern, quasi-realist guise that expressivism attempts to provide a conservative account of moral discourse.

In section 3, I revisited the question of how to systematically distinguish Mackie's error theory from expressivism, focusing more specifically on the question of how to distinguish it from quasi-realist expressivism on the one hand and non-quasi-realist expressivism on the other. Drawing on the results of the previous sections, I first argued that the appeal to the conservative/revisionary distinction does not provide a sound basis for dividing the relevant approaches, since we must expect any plausible version of the error theory to be located somewhere within the same general spectrum occupied by plausible versions of expressivism.

I then ventured to show that there are two alternative possibilities for making the relevant distinction, depending on whether the error theorist subscribes to a sentimentalist or a rationalist conception of moral judgement. Error theorists endorsing the former conception view moral judgements as being constituted by desire-like mental states which we then project unto reality. As a result, our linguistic moral practice can, and ought to, be reconstructed in terms of the expression of beliefs – which, however, are systematically false. What distinguishes the non-quasi-realist expressivist from this kind of error theorist is that he is bound to deny the reconstructibility of moral discourse in terms of beliefs. In contrast, the quasi-realist expressivist, who makes use of this very reconstructibility himself, is distinguished from the sentimentalist error theorist only because, and if, he admits that at least some of our moral beliefs are actually true. With the rationalist error theorist, however, the case is different. Since he identifies moral judgements with proper beliefs even at the fundamental psychological level, he has no incentive whatsoever to accept the link between moral utterances and desire-like states of mind that is postulated by both the quasi-realist and the non-quasi-realist expressivist, already parting company with them at a more fundamental explanatory stage.

In section 4, I took up the problem of 'creeping minimalism' introduced at the end of chapter 3. I first argued that the expressivist can incorporate the notion of moral belief into his theory as long as he operates with a double notion of belief and that, if he does so, his position can still be subsumed under the standard definition of expressivism. I then discussed the potentially more damaging objection that expressivists ought to embrace minimalism about belief, but that they would undermine their own position by doing so because it would render false their key idea that moral utterances express desires rather than beliefs. Drawing on the way in which Blackburn and Ridge have discussed the issue, and rejecting other possible ways of securing the distinctiveness of expressivism, I argued that the only viable strategy for expressivists is to resist the minimalist conception of belief, for which there do not seem to be any compelling arguments to begin with, and to subscribe to some kind of robust psychological conception of the distinction between beliefs and desires.

This chapter, then, revealed further similarities in the approaches of Ayer, Stevenson, Hare, Blackburn and Gibbard, namely with regard to their understanding of the methodological status of the expressivist approach (and of the metaethical enterprise more generally) as well as with regard to the specific arguments with which they try to defend the expressivist idea and prove its superiority over rival metaethical approaches. Moreover, it provided important evidence that expressivism, though first and foremost a thesis in the philosophy of language, is by no means independent of non-linguistic assumptions and considerations. Since the propositional surface of moral language is compatible with different metaethical approaches, and even bound to favour naturalist or non-naturalist approaches over expressivism, the case for expressivism crucially depends on epistemological, ontological or psychological considerations. Moreover, a particular importance of the latter derives from the fact that, without a robust psychological conception of the distinction between beliefs and desires, the basic expressivist thesis does not even get off the ground.

Further complications: Hybrid expressivism, relational expressivism, neo-expressivism

In discussing metaethical expressivism and its history, I have, up to this point, deliberately simplified the issue by leaving out some theoretical options that have shaped the more recent debate. In both my explicit definition of expressivism and my discussion of the implications and possible problems of this definition, I have mostly concentrated on the position that is now often referred to as 'pure expressivism'. Arguably, however, the most influential position in the more recent discussion of expressivism is what is called "ecumenical expressivism"[1] or "hybrid expressivism"[2] (which is the label I will use in what follows). In order to provide an appropriate account of the debate over expressivism, I will subsequently extend my discussion to this latter position as well as to a few other metaethical positions developed in its wake.

1 Hybrid expressivism and the standard definition

The aim of hybrid expressivism is to mediate between pure expressivist and non-expressivist theories of moral language, but to do this in a way that is quite different from (though perhaps complementary to) the strategy used by the quasi-realist. The basic idea of hybrid metaethical theories, of which hybrid expressivism is but one example,[3] is not to accept the premise that moral utterances must express *either* desire-like states *or* beliefs, but to argue that they express both. The hybrid expressivist, then, accepts the general mentalist framework of expressivism. Yet, he qualifies his acceptance of *sentimentalism about moral expression* in so far as he conceives of the mental state expressed by moral utterances as a hybrid state that consists of both a cognitive and a non-cognitive state. What is important to note, however, is that the hybrid expressivist does not thereby give up the basic distinction between beliefs and desires: while the hybrid mental state in question consists of both a belief and a desire, it is not conceived of as a 'besire', that is, one single unitary state that is both belief- and desire-like.

---

[1] Ridge 2006a, 308. See also Eriksson 2009, 8; Strandberg 2012, 90; and Toppinen 2013, 253.
[2] Schroeder 2009, 257. See also Kauppinen 2014b, 36f.; Bar-On/Chrisman/Sias 2015, 243; Boisvert 2015, 25; Eriksson 2015a, 169; and Hay 2015, 77.
[3] Other common labels for the more general approach are "mixed theory" (Sinnott-Armstrong 1993, 298; see also Gibbard 1993b, 316; and Joyce 2009, 55) or "dual-use" theory (Boisvert 2008, 170; see also Campbell 2007, 336; and Strandberg 2012, 88).

The label 'hybrid expressivism' is sometimes used to cover all theories which subscribe to the key idea that moral utterances express both beliefs and desires.[4] However, in accordance with what I take to be the most widespread use of the term, I will confine it to theories that develop this key idea in a distinctively *expressivist* manner and, accordingly, refer to the more general approach by the less specific term 'hybrid theory'. Other common labels for the more general approach are "mixed theory"[5] or "dual-use"[6] theory.

The task of providing an appropriate characterization of expressivism is obviously further complicated by the existence of such hybrid theories. In particular, it is not clear that they can be subsumed under the standard definition on which I have so far relied. As long as we stick to the standard definition of expressivism, it might seem that the metaethical naturalist or the metaethical non-naturalist could just as legitimately claim the ecumenical position sketched above to be a variant of naturalism or non-naturalism, which raises the question of whether the definition allows us to capture examples of hybrid expressivism, or to capture what is expressivist about them. In my view, the standard definition, as given above, is ultimately spacious enough to accommodate hybrid expressivist views and to separate them from non-expressivist hybrid theories. However, the way in which it can do so requires further clarification.

What seems clear, and what is widely accepted in the current debate, is that we can only treat a hybrid position as an example of expressivism (rather than of naturalism or non-naturalism) if the position treats the cognitive and the non-cognitive elements of the mental state expressed by moral utterances as asymmetrical and gives some kind of precedence to the latter. However, how exactly we should conceive of this kind of precedence is by no means uncontroversial. As a result, although there is much agreement with regard to the question of who is to be counted among the proponents of metaethical hybridism, there is far less agreement with regard to the question of who is to be counted among the proponents of hybrid *expressivism*.

Authors routinely cited as proponents of hybridism are David Copp, Daniel Boisvert, Stephen Barker and Michael Ridge.[7] Other authors who have been, or can be, interpreted in this way are David Alm, Richmond Campbell, James Dreier, Paul Edwards, John Eriksson, Stephen Finlay, Oliver Hallich, Frank Jackson, Richard Joyce, Nico Scarano and Jon Tresan. When it comes to locating these au-

---

4 See, for example, Toppinen 2013, 253; see also Schroeder 2009.
5 Sinnott-Armstrong 1993, 298. See also Gibbard 1993b, 316; Joyce 2009, 55.
6 Boisvert 2008, 170. See also Campbell 2007, 336; and Strandberg 2012, 88.
7 See, for example, Boisvert 2008, 170; Schroeder 2008c, 87; Copp 2009, 171; Eriksson 2009, 12f.; Schroeder 2009, 258; Sinclair 2009, 138; Kauppinen 2014b, 36f.; and Ridge 2014, 82–86.

thors among the expressivist/non-expressivist divide, however, quite different views are being forwarded. Ridge, who discusses these issues in most detail, classifies the approaches of Copp, Boisvert and Barker as cognitivist rather than expressivist. However, Copp and Boisvert themselves consider their positions to be examples of expressivism, and Sinclair takes Barker's position to be expressivist, but neither Copp's nor Boisvert's.[8]

In my view, we can set up one further general constraint which any characterization of the differences between expressivist and non-expressivist hybrid theories should satisfy. An appropriate definition of hybrid expressivism (as opposed to hybrid naturalism or hybrid non-naturalism) should preserve as much as possible of the dialectic of the previous debate over expressivism. In particular, the advantages which expressivism has traditionally been taken to have over naturalism and non-naturalism (and which have by no means been acknowledged by expressivists only) should preferably be ones that the hybrid expressivist can claim as well. As we will see, the whole point of the hybrid move is to make *some* of the arguments in favour of expressivism equally accessible to the naturalist and the non-naturalist, most notably the argument from motivation (and, arguably, the open question argument). However, there are other classic arguments in favour of expressivism which are not relevantly associated with the hybrid move, and these arguments, such as the epistemological objections to non-naturalism, ought not to simply become unavailable in virtue of the way in which hybrid expressivism is defined.

Consequently, I think that we should not classify positions as examples of hybrid expressivism that take the belief expressed by moral utterances to be a genuine moral belief, that is, a belief the content of which is explained in terms of genuine moral propositions. One of the main motivations of expressivism is provided by the view that there is no way to make sense of such propositions or, for that matter, of those supposedly moral states of affairs to which the propositions refer, if not on an expressivist basis. Allowing the label 'hybrid expressivism' to encompass views that simply postulate such propositions or states of affairs and introduce desire-like attitudes merely in order to be able to deal with the problem of motivation, therefore, would seem to violate the general constraint I have formulated above.

There are, then, two general aspects by which we can characterize hybrid expressivism. The first is that the hybrid expressivist acknowledges a certain asymmetry between the beliefs and the desire-like attitudes expressed by moral utterances and somehow privileges the latter. The second is that he conceives of the

---

8 See Sinclair 2009, 138.

beliefs expressed by moral utterances as non-moral beliefs (or beliefs with a non-moral descriptive content). The latter aspect provides a safe criterion for distinguishing hybrid expressivism from hybrid non-naturalism. It is not fully clear, however, whether it also allows us to separate the hybrid expressivist from the hybrid *naturalist* in the way suggested by Sinclair.[9] While on one reading, the naturalist explains moral utterances in terms of moral beliefs, on another reading he does not, because he identifies the content of moral beliefs with ordinary non-moral content, for example, with the fact that a certain action provides more pleasure than pain. Unless we want to impose quite a specific terminology on the naturalist, therefore, it seems that we need to rely on the first criterion as well and should hence try to cash out the asymmetry idea in more specific systematic terms.

As far as I can see, the only relevant proposal has been made by Michael Ridge who defines hybrid expressivism by way of the claim that the non-moral belief that is being expressed by moral utterances is not guaranteed to provide the truth conditions of the utterance. While some authors have taken up Ridge's idea that, unlike the hybrid naturalist or hybrid non-naturalist, the hybrid expressivist necessarily rejects the claim "that a moral utterance is guaranteed to be true just in case the belief(s) it expresses is (are) true"[10], others have been more hesitant. One reason for this might be that, given the long way expressivism has come since Ayer, there is now a slight unease towards building the notion of truth or truth conditions in *any* definition of expressivism. As far as I can see, most authors therefore prefer to cash out the asymmetry between the belief-element and the desire-element of moral utterances in more general terms which provide far less of an explanation but are at least relatively uncontroversial. Applying terminology already to be found in Hare, David Alm, for instance, has argued that the distinguishing feature of hybrid expressivism is that the hybrid expressivist takes the expression of the desire-like attitude to constitute the *"primary* meaning"[11] of moral utterances and the expression of the non-moral belief to constitute only its secondary meaning. Moreover, in a more recent publication, Sinclair resorts to such a more general criterion as well, claiming that we should distinguish hybrid expressivism on the one hand and hybrid naturalism or non-naturalism on the other by asking which of the relevant mental states is conceived of as making moral utterances "distinctive"[12].

---

9 See Sinclair 2007, 343 f.
10 Ridge 2006a, 307 f. See also Ridge 2004, 302; Ridge 2006b, 501; Ridge 2006d, 54; and Ridge 2009, 197. For similar characterizations of hybrid expressivism, see Strandberg 2012, 90.
11 Alm 2000, 357.
12 Sinclair 2009, 138.

Although such characterizations may seem somewhat unsatisfactory, they provide a sufficient basis for the purposes of the subsequent discussion. Rather than arguing for a more specific way of drawing the line between expressivist and non-expressivist hybrid theories, I will therefore confine myself to the two general criteria developed above and refrain from trying to classify each and every hybrid theorist as a proponent of either an expressivist or a non-expressivist position. I take the two criteria to be sufficient for denying that Campbell's hybrid account is expressivist in the relevant sense because he conceives of the moral belief expressed by moral utterances as inherently normative,[13] and a similar claim can be made with regard to some versions of Copp's 'realist-expressivism'.[14] Yet, the criteria do not seem to provide a sound basis for ultimately settling the status of Barker, Boisvert, Alm or Hallich. In what follows, I will simply presuppose that we *may* view the latter authors as proponents of hybrid expressivism and will therefore group them with authors such as Ridge and John Eriksson whose expressivist status seems less controversial.

A further consequence of the reliance on a more general way of distinguishing between hybrid expressivism and hybrid naturalism and non-naturalism is that the standard definition of expressivism requires no revisions. At least, this much is true as long as we interpret the word "rather" in the phrase "expresses desire-like attitudes rather than beliefs" in terms of the appeal to the 'distinctive' or 'primary' meaning of moral utterances and keep in mind that the expression of certain beliefs, namely genuine moral beliefs, is ruled out *tout court*.

2 Hybrid expressivism and the 'Frege-Geach problem'

The reason why hybrid theories have become popular in the past is that they seem to provide the 'best of both worlds', combining the respective virtues of expressivism on the one hand and naturalism or non-naturalism on the other. As we have already seen, one of the main arguments forwarded in support of ex-

---

13 See Campbell 2007, 339.
14 The qualification is necessary because Copp uses 'realist-expressivism' as a more general term designating a family of quite different hybrid theories (see Copp 2015, 55). The particular version of realist-expressivism defended by Copp himself conceives of the "moral belief" (Copp 2001, 1) expressed by moral utterances, and the "moral states of affairs" (Copp 2009, 168) represented by these beliefs, in purely naturalistic terms (see Copp 2015, 55), which means that we should conceive of his account either as an example of hybrid naturalism or as an example of hybrid expressivism.

pressivist analyses of moral language is that expressivism allows us to explain the intimate connection between moral judgement and motivation. Unlike the pure naturalist or non-naturalist who conceives of moral utterances as expressions of beliefs only, the hybrid theorist can give such an explanation without having to unsubscribe to the Humean view on motivation. If a person making a moral utterance not only expresses certain beliefs, but also certain desires or attitudes, then we may explain why we typically ascribe to her the motivation to act in a particular way by appealing to these desires or attitudes. Similarly, while the pure expressivist needs to provide an elaborate reconstruction of the propositional surface of moral discourse, the hybrid theorist seems to be in a much better position. In particular, he seems to be able to rely on additional resources when it comes to providing a solution for what is commonly considered to be the main obstacle for expressivist analyses of moral language: the so-called 'Frege-Geach problem'.

The term 'Frege-Geach problem' now usually refers to the general problem of accounting for the uses of moral predicates in embedded or unasserted contexts. While it seems intuitively plausible to many metaethicists that atomic moral utterances such as 'Tormenting cats is wrong!' express desire-like states or negative attitudes, it does not seem as plausible that more complex moral utterances, such as 'If tormenting cats is wrong, then tormenting dogs is wrong', do so, too. The expressivist, therefore, needs to come up with a plausible expressivist interpretation of the meaning of moral predicates in embedded or unasserted contexts, and this interpretation also needs to be able to explain why atomic and embedded uses of moral predicates can enter into logical relations, such as in *modus ponens* arguments of the following kind:

P1 Abortion is wrong

P2 If abortion is wrong, then in-vitro fertilisation is wrong.

C In-vitro fertilisation is wrong.

The challenge to expressivism posed by this example of moral *modus ponens* has several parts. The first task, which has already been indicated above, is to make plausible that P2 (or its components) conventionally expresses a desire-like attitude at all. The second, and related, task is to make plausible that P2 (or its components) expresses *the same* desire-like attitude that is expressed by P1.

The reason why it is not enough to simply demonstrate that P2 can be taken to express *some* kind of desire-like attitude is that the expressivist subscribes to a general mentalist account of linguistic meaning. He must therefore explain the meaning of *both* P1 and P2 in terms of the mental states they express. To concede that P1 and P2, or their respective uses of the predicate 'wrong', express different desire-like states of mind would hence commit him to the claim that 'wrong' has a different meaning in P1 and P2 and *a fortiori* to the implausible claim that the above inference is invalid.

However, these two tasks, which take centre stage in Peter Geach's original critique of emotivism (to which the 'Frege-Geach problem' owes part of its name),[15] are by no means the only ones the expressivist needs to cope with. In addition to identifying a single desire-like mental state we can plausibly take to be expressed by both P1 and P2, the expressivist owes us an explanation for why accepting P1 and P2 logically commits us to also accepting conclusion C. The least the expressivist seems to require in order to meet this third requirement is a theory that can explain why it is logically inconsistent to hold certain sets of desire-like attitudes.

The 'Frege-Geach problem' has clearly received the most attention in the debate over expressivism so far, and both Blackburn and Gibbard have made repeated attempts to demonstrate that and how the expressivist can solve it.[16] It seems fair to say, however, that most authors who have criticized expressivism along the lines of 'Frege-Geach' have not been persuaded by these attempts.[17] The popularity of hybrid versions of expressivism, or of hybrid theories in general, is to a large extent due to such worries concerning the solutions offered by Blackburn and Gibbard. The 'Frege-Geach problem' can therefore be said to have served as a motor for the more recent historical development of expressivism: it not only importantly motivates the 'quasi-realism' of the 1980s and 1990s, but also the hybrid movement of the 2000s. What is equally important to note, however, is that, in making their move, modern hybrid theorists return to ideas that already figured largely in earlier versions of expressivism, a fact I will discuss in more detail in section 3.

The view that hybrid theories allow for a decidedly different and more successful solution to the 'Frege-Geach problem' than the pure expressivist theories

---

15 See Geach 1960, 222 ff.; and Geach 1965, 461 ff. Note, however, that Geach discusses the issue not in terms of the linguistic expression of mental states but in terms of speech acts.
16 See Blackburn 1984, 189 ff.; Blackburn 1998, 70 ff.; Gibbard 1990a, 92 ff.; and Gibbard 2003, 41 ff. See also Blackburn 1993a; Blackburn 1993d; Blackburn 1993e; Blackburn 1996; Gibbard 1992b; and Gibbard 1993a.
17 For critical discussions of the 'Frege-Geach problem', see Wright 1985; Hale 1986; Schueler 1988; Brighouse 1990; Zangwill 1992; Hale 1993; Horwich 1993; Wright 1993; Dreier 1996; van Roojen 1996; Kölbel 1997; Dreier 1999; Unwin 1999; Unwin 2001; Hale 2002; Dreier 2006; Schroeder 2008a; and Schroeder 2008b. See also Miller 2003, 40 ff., 58 ff. and 96 ff.; Radtke 2008, 75 ff.; Schroeder 2010, 51 ff., 105 ff. and 128 ff.; and Schulte 2010, 245 ff.

of Blackburn and Gibbard is one we also find among authors who do not themselves subscribe to any version of hybridism. The general idea behind the supposed solution is that the logical relations of simple and complex moral sentences, as they provide the basis for *modus ponens* arguments like the one introduced above, can be explained by appealing to the relations of the *beliefs* expressed by these sentences. The particular solutions offered by hybrid theorists such as Ridge, Boisvert or Barker all work in roughly the same way. According to these authors, we should interpret our *modus ponens* argument as follows:

P1 Abortion has property K; boo to actions with property K

P2 If abortion has property K, then in-vitro fertilisation has property K; boo to actions with property K.

C In-vitro fertilisation has property K; boo to actions with property K.

The main advantage of analysing moral *modus ponens* arguments in this way is that doing so helps us to explain why there is something wrong with simultaneously accepting P1 and P2 but rejecting C. Since the belief expressed by C is logically implied by the beliefs expressed by P1 and P2, it is inconsistent to hold the two latter beliefs without also holding the former. Moreover, in order for this explanation to be available, one need not embrace any 'logic of attitudes', that is, assume that the notion of logical inconsistency can be extended to desire-like attitudes.

Although a detailed discussion of the 'Frege-Geach problem' and hybrid expressivism's ability to deal with it is beyond the scope of this book, it ought to be noted that it is less clear whether the hybrid move provides much help in also satisfying the other requirements described above. As has been stressed by Mark Schroeder, in order to successfully account for moral *modus ponens*, hybrid theorists not only need to give an explanation for why holding P1, P2 and C at the same time is inconsistent, something Schroeder refers to as the "inconsistency property"[18] of *modus ponens*. They also need to explain why holding P1 and P2 commits one to holding C, something Schroeder refers to as the "inference-licensing property"[19] of *modus ponens*. Given that C not only expresses a belief, namely the belief that in-vitro fertilisation has property K, but also a certain desire-like attitude, this further property of moral *modus ponens* cannot be explained by exclusively appealing to the beliefs expressed by P1, P2 and C. It re-

---

18 Schroeder 2009, 265.
19 Schroeder 2009, 266.

quires important further commitments in the way in which the desire-like attitudes expressed by moral utterances are conceived of.

Schroeder concedes that these further problems can be resolved as long as the hybrid theorist takes the desire-like attitude expressed by moral utterances to relate, not to the particular action or person that is being evaluated, but to actions or persons as being of a certain *kind*.[20] As the above sketch of their renditions of moral *modus ponens* indicates, this condition is equally satisfied by the accounts of Ridge, Barker and Boisvert. Conceiving of P1, P2 and the conclusion as expressions of desire-like attitudes towards the same general property K allows them to claim that any person who accepts P1 and P2 *has* already expressed the very desire-like attitude that is expressed by the conclusion. However, a person who endorses this desire-like attitude and additionally commits himself to the belief-element of the conclusion by accepting the belief-elements of P1 and P2 cannot but accept the conclusion. In contrast, if the belief and the attitudes expressed by P1, P2 and the conclusion refer not to some general property K, but specifically to abortion or in-vitro fertilisation, this explanation becomes unavailable. It is then not clear why a person accepting P1 and P2 should endorse a negative attitude towards in-vitro fertilisation. Moreover, the person does not commit herself to this negative attitude in virtue of accepting the belief-elements of P1 and P2, either.

The second point that needs to be emphasized is that the above hybrid interpretation of moral *modus ponens* does not, by itself, do anything to assuage Geach's original worry that conditionals, such as P2, do not seem to express any desire-like attitude at all. In order for his solution to the 'Frege-Geach problem' to get off the ground, the hybrid theorist needs to provide us with an independent argument for why we should conceive of conditionals including moral predicates as expressions of desire-like mental states to begin with. The strategy employed by most hybrid theorists at this point is to compare moral predicates to pejoratives, such as 'kraut', and to suggest that, like the latter, moral predicates retain some kind of attitudinal 'colouring' even when they are used in conditionals or other unasserted contexts.[21] It is far from clear, however, whether this analogy between moral predicates and pejoratives really holds and whether it can be defended with any kind of systematic argument. Yet, simply biting the bullet and conceding that, unlike P1 and C, P2 does not express any desire-like state at all,

---

20 See Schroeder 2009, 276–78. See, however, Caj Strandberg's recent critical discussion according to which even versions of hybrid expressivism that satisfy Schroeder's criterion fail to provide a solution for the 'Frege-Geach problem' (see Strandberg 2015).
21 See, for example, Copp 2001, 14 ff.; and Boisvert 2008, 180 ff. See also Joyce 2008, 393; and Schroeder 2013, 286.

just does not seem to be an option for the hybrid theorist, given that this introduces the problem of equivocation and might raise additional problems for explaining the inference-licensing property. Although the hybrid move certainly provides *some* further resources for solving the 'Frege-Geach problem', therefore, it is not obvious that, in trying to devise a solution to this problem, the hybrid theorist can fully dispense with the strategies developed by pure expressivists such as Blackburn and Gibbard.

3 Hybridism in Stevenson and Hare

Another reason for thinking that the recent move to hybridism has not entirely 'transformed' the previous debate over expressivism (something that has been suggested by Michael Ridge)[22] is that the key idea according to which moral utterances express both desire-like states and beliefs is by no means a novel one. Rather, modern versions of hybrid expressivism seem to have simply re-invented the idea that moral utterances or moral terms have descriptive and evaluative meaning which, as we have seen, is defended by both Stevenson and Hare.

In fact, given the remarks in his introduction to the second edition of *Language, truth and logic* to which I have already referred above, there even seems to be a basis for including Ayer among the proponents of hybrid expressivism. Ayer emphasizes that some applications of ethical predicates amount to nothing more than "a factual classification of an action as belonging to some class of actions by which a certain moral attitude on the part of the speaker is habitually aroused"[23], and he concedes that many ethical statements "contain, as a factual element, some description of the action, or the situation, to which the ethical term in question is being applied"[24]. There are even some traces of hybridism in the first edition of Ayer's work, given that he takes the sentence 'You acted wrong in stealing that money' to simply amount to an expression of the ordinary descriptive belief that 'you stole that money' with "a particular tone of horror"[25].

I think it would nevertheless be false to view Ayer as a hybrid expressivist. The reason is that Ayer not only emphasizes that more general ethical statements, such as 'Stealing is wrong', have "no factual meaning"[26], but uses the in-

---

22 See Ridge 2006a, 205.
23 Ayer 1936/1967, 21.
24 Ayer 1936/1967, 21.
25 Ayer 1936/1967, 107.
26 Ayer 1936/1967, 107.

troduction to the second edition of *Language, truth and logic* to explicitly restrict the application of his emotive theory to such statements, that is, to statements in which ethical terms are used "in a purely normative way"[27]. To be sure, some modern hybrid expressivists who claim to have gone beyond Stevenson and Hare provide explicit arguments for why we should not view the two as hybrid expressivists, either. On closer inspection, however, these arguments turn out to be problematic. The reason why Ridge, for example, does not want to include Hare among the hybrid expressivists is that he takes Hare's account to make descriptive meaning a contingent feature of moral utterances.[28] Yet, this simply does not seem to be an appropriate take on Hare's theory.

The argumentative basis for Hare's claim that moral utterances or moral terms have descriptive meaning is provided by the phenomenon of supervenience or, as the Hare of *Freedom and Reason* and the later works prefers to say, by the "universalizability"[29] of moral utterances. As Hare repeatedly emphasizes, our moral judgements are usually made for "reasons"[30] in the sense that they are based on certain *descriptive* "properties"[31] of the object we evaluate. Hare also refers to those properties as the "qualities"[32] which a speaker commends by calling something 'good', or as the "virtues or good-making characteristics"[33] in virtue of which the speaker evaluates the object in the way he does. In a more general way, Hare also describes the reasons for our evaluative judgements as "facts about the situation"[34] or *"something about* the subject of the judgement"[35]. The tale of the missionary and the cannibal, to which I have already referred above, provides an idea what kind of properties Hare is thinking of. According to his description, the missionary's use of 'good', when applied to persons, might be taken to refer, among other things, to the descriptive quality of 'not murdering people', while the cannibal's use of 'good' might be taken to refer to the quality of 'collecting many scalps'.[36]

As Hare further claims, the fact that the objects we evaluate have these or other descriptive properties (or that we at least take them to have them) is con-

---

27 Ayer 1936/1967, 21.
28 See Ridge 2006a, 309 f.
29 Hare 1963, 10. See also Hare 1981, 42; and Hare 1999a, 21.
30 Hare 1952, 118.
31 Hare 1981, 88.
32 Hare 1952, 148.
33 Hare 1952, 145.
34 Hare 1999a, 12.
35 Hare 1999a, 21.
36 See Hare 1952, 148 f.

veyed by our moral utterances and hence part of their *meaning*. He also claims in this context that the descriptive meaning of a moral statement is the same thing as the "semantics of the statement"[37] or as the "application conditions"[38] of the words contained in it, or as the statement's "truth conditions, plus the requirement, laid on a moral statement by having the illocutionary force of a statement, that it has to have truth conditions in order to have meaning"[39]. I will not delve into the question of whether these various characterizations of descriptive meaning really amount to the same thing, which is clearly Hare's own take on the issue.[40] What is more important at this point is to note that Hare does not seem to allow for any moral utterances that do *not* have this kind of meaning. Hare concedes that moral utterances may be devoid of *evaluative* meaning, as when we employ predicates such as 'wrong' in an 'inverted commas' sense and use it to merely refer to the moral convictions of our larger community or other groups of people. Yet, he nowhere explicitly acknowledges that moral predicates may be devoid of *descriptive* meaning. Moreover, there are quite a few statements that point in the opposite direction, as when Hare claims that the judgement 'St Francis was a good man' is *logically dependent* on the judgement that St Francis has certain descriptive qualities,[41] when he opposes moral judgements with ordinary imperations and claims that, unlike the latter, moral judgements "*have to* be made for reasons"[42], or when he refers to the "inescapable factuality or descriptivity of moral principles"[43]. It seems hard to deny, then, that Hare presents descriptive meaning as a *necessary* element of moral sentences.

It has to be admitted, however, that the position of Stevenson is much more ambiguous, something I already indicated in passing above. On the one hand, Stevenson explicitly claims that "there is always *some* element of description in ethical judgments"[44] and emphasizes, *pace* Ayer, that there is "no occasion for saying that the meaning of ethical terms is purely emotive"[45]. This suggests

---

37 Hare 1999a, 52.
38 Hare 1999a, 138.
39 Hare 1999a, 52.
40 See Hare 1999a, 138: "It should be evident by now that the same animal is here appearing in different metamorphoses. It does not make any difference whether we speak of criteria of application for a moral word (for example, 'wrong'), or about the word's descriptive meaning, or about the truth conditions of statements containing it, or about a moral standard or universal principle."
41 See Hare 1952, 145.
42 Hare 1999a, 12. (my emphasis)
43 Hare 1999a, 20.
44 Stevenson 1963c, 16.
45 Stevenson 1963b, 9.

that he holds exactly the view I have just ascribed to Hare. Moreover, Stevenson distinguishes between "emotively active and emotively inactive uses"[46] of ethical terms and thus seems to also share Hare's further view that, on certain occasions at least, moral utterances can be devoid of any emotive or evaluative meaning. On the other hand, however, and unlike Hare, Stevenson at times suggests that there are moral utterances in which the ethical predicate *is* indeed *"purely* emotive"[47]. Therefore, even if one might want to argue that Ridge's criterion does not provide a basis for denying Hare the status of hybrid expressivist, it might at least provide such a basis in Stevenson's case.

Moreover, even if Ridge's claim that Hare takes descriptive meaning to be a contingent feature of moral utterances is false, his subsequent worry that Hare's analysis in terms of descriptive and evaluative meaning only applies to *typical* uses of moral predicates still has a basis, if for other reasons than Ridge himself argues. Once we admit that we should only view an author as a proponent of hybrid expressivism if he takes descriptive and evaluative meaning to be a feature of any moral utterance whatsoever, as Ridge seems to suggest, then the fact Hare allows for moral utterances that do not have *evaluative* meaning would be sufficient to exclude Hare – and likewise Stevenson – from the group of hybrid expressivists. In fact, it should then lead us to not conceive of them as expressivists at all.

Yet, the requirement implicitly suggested by Ridge surely sets the bar too high. As we have seen, all classic expressivists acknowledge certain variations in our usage of moral terms and, as a result, restrict their analysis to something like the typical uses of moral utterances or the moral utterances of the majority of speakers on the majority of occasions. Therefore, if allowing for certain atypical or borderline cases were sufficient to deny an author his expressivist or hybrid expressivist status, it seems that none of the classic expressivists would pass the test, either. Moreover, it seems that all modern defenders of hybrid expressivism have good reasons for restricting their analysis in a similar way, given that, for the reasons already discussed, it seems generally impossible for them to make good on the radical claim that their analysis applies to all actual uses of moral terms whatsoever. That Hare's and Stevenson's core account of moral language in terms of both descriptive and evaluative meaning is only applicable to typical cases of moral utterances, therefore, should be fully compatible with the view that they are proponents of hybrid expressivism.

---

46 Stevenson 1944, 84.
47 Stevenson 1944, 267.

A final reason why modern authors are somewhat hesitant to refer to Stevenson and Hare, not only as forefathers of hybrid expressivism, but as hybrid expressivists themselves may be that they harbour doubts as to whether we may legitimately attribute to Stevenson or Hare the kind of general mentalist framework that is characteristic of modern expressivism, both in its pure and in its hybrid form.[48] However, as I have tried to show in chapter 3, there are in fact good enough reasons to interpret or reconstruct Stevenson's and Hare's theories in mentalist terms. Moreover, if we think that the possibility of reconstructing Stevenson and Hare in mentalist terms is not by itself a sufficient basis for viewing them as hybrid expressivists, then we should better conclude that we should not view them as expressivists at all, and this is a conclusion which far less authors seem willing to accept.

There is one last problem with straightforwardly classifying Hare as a hybrid expressivist, however, which has not previously been noticed and which has to do with the criteria for distinguishing hybrid expressivism from non-expressivist hybrid theories. In contrast to what has been suggested by Ridge,[49] Hare does *not* take evaluative meaning to be the primary meaning of *all* moral terms or predicates, not even in their typical uses. According to Hare, the primacy of evaluative meaning is a characteristic feature of thin moral concepts, such as 'good', 'ought' or 'wrong'. What distinguishes them from thick moral concepts, such as 'courageous', is exactly that in the case of the latter, the evaluative meaning is secondary to the descriptive meaning.[50] If we rely on the distinction between primary and secondary meaning in order to mark off hybrid expressivism from hybrid naturalism and hybrid non-naturalism, therefore, it seems that we have to conclude that Hare is a hybrid expressivist about thin moral concepts, but not an expressivist (hybrid or otherwise) about thick moral concepts. While this interpretation may appear somewhat peculiar and has, as far as I can see, not previously been endorsed by any commentators, it does seem to be the one most sympathetic to Hare's statements, at least in the absence of a more systematic explanation of what 'primacy' of meaning exactly amounts to.

---

48 This point is raised by Eriksson who, however, does not ultimately consider it as an obstacle to viewing Hare as a hybrid expressivist (see Eriksson 2009, 19).
49 See Ridge 2009, 190.
50 See Hare 1952, 118 ff.; and Hare 1963, 23 ff.

4 Speaker-relative accounts of descriptive meaning

The main challenge that has been raised for hybrid expressivism in the past is to determine the descriptive content of moral utterances, that is, to identify the descriptive beliefs that are conventionally being expressed by these utterances. The question most often discussed in this regard is whether the hybrid expressivist should conceive of this descriptive content in speaker-relative or non-speaker-relative terms. Hybrid expressivists who choose the first option are Barker, Ridge and Eriksson as well as the classic expressivists Stevenson and Hare. In contrast, accounts that conceive of the descriptive content of moral utterances as non-speaker-relative have been suggested by Boisvert and Hallich.

There are quite a few reasons why the latter strategy seems the more promising one. To begin with, if the belief expressed by moral utterances can vary from speaker to speaker (and perhaps from one occasion of utterance to another), then it is not clear why we can legitimately conceive of the supposed descriptive aspect of moral utterances as part of their linguistic *meaning* at all. It seems that, in order for certain descriptive properties of the evaluated object to be part of the meaning of a moral utterance, there should be some established linguistic conventions that link the utterance with these properties rather than others. However, to conceive of the descriptive properties as ones that vary from speaker to speaker seems to amount to denying the basis for such a convention. This means that it would even be unjustified to claim that moral utterances *express* descriptive beliefs, given that this is widely taken to mean that the utterances express these beliefs *by way of linguistic convention*.

There are two sides to this problem, which we may bring out by respectively focusing on the speaker and the audience of a moral utterance. If we take the belief expressed by moral utterances to be speaker-relative, then it seems that we must concede that, on many occasions at least, the audience will not share or even know the descriptive standard by which the speaker is judging. In fact, many hybrid expressivists who opt for the strategy in question explicitly concede as much. For example, Stevenson not only claims that, as far as descriptive meaning is concerned, moral terms have "*no* precise sense"[51] but are used somewhat vaguely. He also admits that speakers engaging in a conversation about the goodness of something may be talking past each other because the descriptive qualities the hearer takes to be relevant may differ from the ones the speaker actually has in mind.[52] Similarly, although Hare emphasizes that on

---

[51] Stevenson 1944, 86.
[52] See Stevenson 1944, 87f. See also Stevenson 1963b, 9.

many occasions, the standard by which a speaker is judging may be well known to his audience (as when a parson describes somebody as a 'good girl'),[53] he leaves no doubt that there will also be situations in which this is not the case. However, this concession does not seem to sit well with our ordinary understanding of linguistic meaning which refers to what a speaker *conveys* to his audience. If the descriptive standard by which the speaker is judging is unknown to her audience, why can the speaker be said to convey to her audience something about the descriptive properties of the evaluated object?

Now one way to deal with this problem would be to limit the hybrid expressivist analysis to speaker meaning. Yet, recent work in moral psychology strongly suggests that the exact standard by which a speaker is judging an action or a person is often unknown even to himself. In their empirical studies on moral reasoning, Jonathan Haidt and his co-researchers presented American undergraduate students with stories of deviant sexual behaviour and pressed the participants on their instant moral judgements, finding that they strongly clung to those initial judgements and often resorted to saying things like 'I don't know, I can't explain it, I just know it's wrong' or 'I know it's wrong, but I just can't come up with a reason why'.[54] While I consider the far-reaching anti-rationalist conclusions Haidt derives from these findings to be unwarranted, the least they suggest is that the possibility of a speaker's standards being unknown to himself is a general constraint that any plausible expressivist theory of the meaning of moral utterances needs to satisfy. Moreover, most hybrid expressivists who defend a speaker-relative account seem to in fact allow for this latter possibility.[55] Yet, if, on certain occasions, neither the speaker nor his audience know about the descriptive properties to which the attitude expressed by a given moral utterance relates, then it seems simply false to say that the utterance expresses *both* the attitude *and* the belief that certain descriptive properties obtain.

Worries of the above kind have been raised quite early against the accounts of Stevenson and Hare.[56] They also seem to straightforwardly apply to those modern versions of hybrid expressivism that follow in Stevenson's and Hare's footsteps and provide similar, unrestrained analyses of the speaker-relative descriptive content of moral utterances, such as John Eriksson's version that is explicitly modelled on Hare's theory of moral language. In fairness, it ought to be

---

53 See Hare 1952, 146. See also Hare 1999a, 20 f.
54 See Haidt/Björklund/Murphy 2000; and Haidt 2001.
55 See, for instance, Hare 1952, 58 f.; Barker 2000, 277; Ridge 2006a, 313 and 315; and Eriksson 2009, 18.
56 See, for instance, Brandt 1959, 231; and Urmson 1968, 72 ff. For a critique of Hare and Stevenson along similar lines, see also Hallich 2008.

noted that Hare somewhat anticipates these worries and makes an attempt to respond to them. Stressing his partial analogy between descriptive and evaluative terms, Hare claims that the looseness or vagueness we encounter in the descriptive meaning of moral predicates such as 'good' is something we find in exactly the same way in purely descriptive predicates such as 'red'. In both cases, Hare argues, we usually share a certain understanding of the relevant descriptive characteristics, even though, in both cases, there may be occasions where we do not know the exact standards of a speaker or are mistaken about them:

> It is important to notice that the exactness or looseness of their criteria does absolutely nothing to distinguish words like 'good' from words like 'red'. Words in both classes may be descriptively loose or exact, according to how rigidly the criteria have been laid down by custom or convention. It is certainly not true that value-words are distinguished from descriptive words in that the former are looser, descriptively, than the latter. There are loose and rigid examples of both sorts of word.[57]

For Hare, therefore, the indeterminacy of the descriptive meaning of moral predicates does not provide any good reasons not to refer to it as a form of meaning, unless we also want to conclude that ordinary descriptive predicates such as 'red' have no descriptive meaning, either.

However, Hare clearly overstates the similarity between ordinary descriptive and evaluative predicates at this point. While it may be true that our understanding of what makes a thing red is somewhat vague and that the views of different speakers may vary, these variations seem quite different from the variations which, if we follow Hare, we have to acknowledge with regard to moral utterances, where the descriptive meaning of different speakers' uses of 'wrong' may range from 'causes more pain than pleasure' to 'is incompatible with the categorical imperative' as from 'is forbidden by the norms of my community' to 'causes a feeling of disgust in me' or 'is forbidden by the Bible'. Something like this also seems to be the idea of Urmson who argues that, on Stevenson's related account, ethical predicates turn out to be, not only vague (as both Stevenson and Hare claim), but in fact downright ambiguous.[58]

Moreover, Hare's analogy between descriptive and evaluative predicates, if fully convincing, would ultimately prove too much. Even if we were to grant that there is far-reaching agreement among different people concerning the descriptive properties that make actions morally good, we would surely have to admit that we find at least as much agreement in the *attitudes* different people

---

57 Hare 1952, 115.
58 See Urmson 1968, 76.

hold with regard to certain objects. We find such an agreement in attitude not only with regard to forms of behaviour which can plausibly be cited as the descriptive element of thick evaluative concepts such as 'cruel' or 'courageous'. We also find it with regard to objects for which no such interpretation is plausible, such as strawberries (to use one of Hare's own examples). If the fact that most people agree about the descriptive qualities that make an action 'right' or a person 'good' were enough to justify the claim that 'right' or 'good' have descriptive meaning, why then does the fact that most people enjoy the taste of strawberries not likewise justify the idea that the term 'strawberry' has evaluative meaning? Once we accept Hare's analogy between descriptive and evaluative terms, therefore, it seems that we can no longer restrict the notion of evaluative meaning to those established examples of thin and thick evaluative concepts to which Hare himself wants to have it restricted.

By putting little constraints on the descriptive content of moral utterances and allowing it to vary from speaker to speaker, then, hybrid expressivists seem to forfeit the basis on which they can legitimately claim that moral utterances have both evaluative and descriptive meaning or conventionally express both desires and beliefs. Partly in response to the problems discussed above, some modern hybrid expressivist, most notably Ridge and Barker, have forwarded interpretations of the descriptive content of moral utterances that conceive of it as speaker-relative but nevertheless constant. On Ridge's version of hybrid expressivism, the belief expressed by the utterance is invariantly characterized by the fact that it makes anaphoric reference to the kind of property to which the attitude being expressed relates. According to the simpler of Ridge's two hybrid expressivist accounts, to which he refers as the "plain vanilla"[59] account, claims such as 'there is moral reason to X' are thus taken to express (a) an attitude of approval of a certain kind toward actions insofar as they have a certain property and (b) a belief that X has that property. The same structure is presupposed by Ridge's more sophisticated "ideal advisor"[60] account. On this account, 'there is moral reason to X' expresses (a) an attitude of approval of a certain kind toward actions insofar as they would garner approval from a certain sort of advisor and (b) a belief that X would garner approval from that sort of advisor. Similarly, according to Barker's analysis, utterances such as 'X is good' express (a) the belief that X instantiates the kind of general property the speaker approves of, and (b) the speaker's approval of this kind of general property.[61]

---

59 Ridge 2006d, 57.
60 Ridge 2006d, 57.
61 See Barker 2000, 271.

The important advantage that these versions of hybrid expressivism have over the simpler versions of Stevenson, Hare and Eriksson is that they identify one constant belief which we can quite safely attribute to any person uttering sentences of the type 'there is a moral reason to X' or 'X is good'. In order to highlight the contrast between this belief and the kinds of belief appealed to by Stevenson, Hare and Eriksson, we may describe it as a *de dicto* belief, where this is taken to refer to a belief that implies no substantial commitments regarding the property that it attributes to the object of evaluation. Although we may not know, Ridge and Barker argue, what the exact property is of which the speaker approves, we know at least that there *is* such a property and that the speaker believes the particular object of his evaluation to have it. On this basis, Ridge and Barker claim that moral utterances express at least *some* belief by way of linguistic convention, and they further claim that this fact is sufficient to allow for a hybrid expressivist analysis of moral utterances and to solve the 'Frege-Geach problem' in a way that is unavailable to the pure expressivist.

It ought to be noted that we also find a similarly invariant interpretation of the descriptive meaning of moral utterances in Stevenson's work. Stevenson explicitly provides two different patterns of analysis, and while the second pattern puts no constraints on what may serve as the descriptive component of utterances such as 'X is wrong',[62] the first takes the descriptive meaning of 'X is wrong' to consist in the self-descriptive claim 'I disapprove of X'.[63] As in the case of Ridge and Barker, this interpretation avoids the problem of unknown speaker standards because it makes descriptive meaning of moral utterances constant and thus expressible by way of linguistic convention.

However, some important objections to speaker-relative versions of hybrid expressivism apply even to the above accounts of descriptive meaning. The first objection, which has been raised by Boisvert and Schroeder, is that speaker-relative versions of hybrid expression incur serious problems with so-called 'attitude ascriptions'. To use the characterization used by Boisvert, attitude ascriptions are made with the help of attitude attribution verbs such as 'believes that', 'fears that' or 'wonders whether' which are used to attribute to other people "psychological states (belief, fear, wonderment, etc.) whose contents are given by the sentences used in their complements"[64]. The problem with attitude ascriptions results from the fact that the belief to which Ridge's and Barker's analyses appeal (and likewise Stevenson's first pattern of analysis) is still speak-

---

62 See Stevenson 1944, 207.
63 See Stevenson 1944, 21.
64 Boisvert 2008, 189.

er-relative. Though it is conceived of as having a fixed and known content, it is not, after all, the same belief for all speakers, given that its content cannot be described without the use of indexicals. To take Ridge's ideal advisor analysis: the belief expressed by 'there is moral reason to X' is not the belief that 'X would garner approval from some sort of advisor' but the belief that 'X would garner the approval of the sort of advisor that I (the speaker) approve of', and it is only in virtue of this fact that the belief makes anaphoric reference to the attitude expressed by 'there is moral reason to X' in the way Ridge claims.

We can illustrate the problem resulting from this fact with the help of the sentence 'John believes that abortion is wrong'. If the content of the belief is allowed to vary across speakers, then a speaker uttering the sentence 'John believes that abortion is wrong', for example Robert, need not express the same belief by using the phrase 'abortion is wrong' as the speaker to whom he ascribes it. As a result, it becomes impossible to provide a plausible analysis of Robert's utterance 'John believes that abortion is wrong' in hybrid terms at all. The belief which, according to Ridge's analysis, we must attribute to John if he utters the sentence 'abortion is wrong' is the belief that 'abortion would garner disapproval from the sort of advisor whom I (John) approve of'. Given that Robert's utterance 'John believes that abortion is wrong' is meant to report something about John's moral outlook and not about his own, it seems that the above belief should somehow be expressed by Robert's utterance as well. However, since 'John believes that abortion is wrong' is not being uttered by John himself but by Robert, it does not make sense to claim that the utterance expresses the belief 'abortion would garner disapproval from the sort of advisor whom I (John) approve of', and the same goes for the belief that 'John believes that abortion would garner disapproval from the sort of advisor whom I (John) approve of'. However, neither would it make sense to claim that the belief expressed by Robert is the belief that 'abortion would garner disapproval from the sort of advisor whom I (Robert) approve of' or the belief that 'John believes that abortion would garner disapproval from the sort of advisor whom I (Robert) approve of', since the former would attribute to Robert a belief he need not have and the latter would get the descriptive content of John's belief wrong.

The same difficulty arises if we rely on Stevenson's first pattern of analysis. According to Stevenson's working model, the sentence 'abortion is wrong', when uttered by John, expresses the descriptive belief that 'I (John) disapprove of abortion'. However, if we want to formulate the descriptive content of Robert's utterance 'John believes that abortion is wrong', we have to choose one of the following four candidates which are all inappropriate:

*1. I (John) disapprove of abortion,
*2. John believes that I (John) disapprove of abortion
*3. I (Robert) disapprove of abortion
*4. John believes that I (Robert) disapprove of abortion

It is tempting, of course, to try to resolve this problem by simply claiming that the belief expressed by Robert's utterance is the belief that 'John believes that abortion would garner disapproval from the sort of advisor he (John) approves of' or, if we argue within Stevenson's framework, the belief that 'John believes that he (John) disapproves of abortion'. However, once we interpret the utterance in this way, we become unfaithful to Ridge's and Stevenson's own formulations. Moreover, we get into trouble when it comes to explaining the inference-licensing property. The reason is that we may easily construct a *modus ponens* argument which mixes atomic moral claims, conditionals and attitude ascriptions. Take the following example which we may, again, attribute to our speaker Robert:

P1 John believes that abortion is wrong.

P2 If John believes that abortion is wrong, then abortion is wrong.

Conclusion Abortion is wrong.

If we allow that P1 expresses the belief that 'John believes that abortion would garner disapproval from the sort of advisor he (John) approves of', then we must interpret the desire-like attitude expressed by P1 as an attitude towards the sort of advisor *John* approves of. Otherwise, the belief and the attitude would not be related in the sense presupposed by Ridge's analysis and, in fact, by any hybrid solution to the 'Frege-Geach problem'. This requirement seems to raise certain problems on its own, given that it is not clear why Robert should express this kind of approval. What makes the interpretation even less viable is that the conclusion, when uttered by Robert, clearly expresses approval towards the sort of advisor that *Robert* approves of, which means that the desire-like attitudes expressed by P1 and the conclusion would have different objects. Yet, if P1 and the conclusion ultimately express different desire-like attitudes, we are unable to explain why somebody accepting P1 and P2 is logically committed to holding both the belief- and the desire-element of the conclusion.

The second, less discussed objection is that the speaker-relative versions of hybrid expressivism forwarded by Ridge and Barker cannot give a convincing account of moral agreement and disagreement.[65] As already indicated, one of the

---

65 A similar worry has, however, recently been raised by Eriksson (see Eriksson 2015b, 45 ff.).

purported virtues of expressivism is that it explains moral disagreement in terms of disagreement in attitude rather than disagreement in belief: unlike the defenders of naturalist or non-naturalist approaches to moral language, the expressivist can allow that two individuals having a moral disagreement may agree about all the relevant facts and hence have the same descriptive beliefs, because, unlike the former, he can still argue that the individuals disagree in that they hold diverging attitudes towards these facts. However, it seems that this advantage of expressivism gets lost once we embrace either Ridge's or Barker's hybrid analysis. The problem is not so much that, according to these analyses, two speakers disagreeing about the moral status of certain actions will not, after all, have the same descriptive beliefs. The problem is that many cases of moral disagreement will turn out not to be cases of disagreement at all, at least not in any substantial sense of the word.

As has already been indicated, both Barker and Ridge claim that the object of the desire-like attitude expressed by moral utterances is not the particular action or person that is being evaluated, but a more general property which is instantiated by the action or person in question. In fact, this is also Hare's view who makes heavy use of the idea of a general 'standard' and emphasizes that the evaluative meaning of ethical terms relates to actions or persons *insofar as they are of a certain kind*.[66] Moreover, as stressed above, it is only in virtue of conceiving of the desire-like attitude in this way that hybrid approaches seem to be able to explain the inference-licensing property of moral *modus ponens*. On Ridge's and Barker's approach, therefore, different speakers not only express different beliefs when they make a moral utterance, but the desire-like attitudes they express may relate to quite different general properties. However, if the opposing attitudes expressed, for example, by John's utterance 'abortion is wrong' and Peter's utterance 'abortion is not wrong' do not relate to the same general property, then we do not seem have a case of proper moral disagreement at all, because John and Peter might just be talking about different general properties that are equally instantiated by abortion. In this case, John and Peter might, after all, possess an absolutely identical set of belief-attitude pairs. The speaker-relative interpretations of Ridge, Barker and Hare simply fail to rule out the possibility that John expresses the belief that abortion has property K and expresses his disapproval of property K, while Peter expresses the belief that abortion has property J and expresses his approval of property J. Neither do they rule out the possibility that John believes that abortion has property J and disapproves of property J, too, and that Peter believes that abortion has property K and disap-

---

66 See Hare 1952, 129, 135 f. and 145 f.; and Hare 1981, 216 ff.

proves of property K, too. Pretty much the same seems to apply for cases of moral agreement. If the respective beliefs and attitudes expressed by two speakers uttering the sentence 'abortion is wrong' may have different objects, then it seems that, strictly speaking, the two speakers might disapprove of different things and might therefore not really agree with one another at all, or might do so only in a very weak sense of that word. It seems, then, that a speaker-relativist variant of hybrid expressivism faces problems with moral agreement and moral disagreement which are not dissimilar to the problems faced by speaker subjectivism.

To put it, again, in terms of Ridge's ideal advisor analysis: the desire-like attitude and belief we may attribute to John, if he thinks that abortion is wrong, are (a) an attitude of disapproval toward actions insofar as they would garner disapproval from a certain sort of advisor, let us call him M, and (b) the belief that abortion would garner disapproval from M; in contrast, what we may attribute to Peter, if he thinks that abortion is not wrong, are a) an attitude of approval toward actions insofar as they would garner approval from a certain sort of advisor, N, and (b) the belief that abortion would garner approval from N. Yet, if these are the mental states we must attribute to John and Peter, then it is not clear how we can appropriately capture the fact that they disagree with each other. While John and Peter can be said to have somewhat adverse desire-like attitudes, namely approval and disapproval, these attitudes are not necessarily in conflict with one another. That John disapproves of actions that are disapproved of by M does not imply that he must disapprove of whatever actions are approved of by N. In fact, he can emphatically share Peter's approval of actions that are approved of by N, just as Peter can share John's disapproval of whatever actions are disapproved of by M. However, the beliefs held by John and Peter respectively do not seem to be in conflict with each other, either. That John believes that M would disapprove of abortion does not commit him to believing that N would also disapprove of abortion, just as Peter's belief that N would approve of abortion fails to commit him to believing that M would also approve of abortion. If this is correct, however, then it seems that Ridge's, Barker's and Hare's analyses cannot provide an appropriate account of moral disagreement because they neither reconstruct it in terms of contradictory beliefs nor in terms of contradictory attitudes.

One might argue that, in setting up the problem, I have not paid sufficient attention to the fact that moral judgements of the form 'X is wrong' are all-things-considered judgements. Once we acknowledge this much, it seems that we must concede that a speaker uttering 'abortion is wrong' not only expresses the belief that 'abortion has some general property' and his disapproval of this general property, but also assigns a particular weight to his disapproval that ultimately rules out abortion as a legitimate form of behaviour. We may also put this by saying that the speaker places the general property in virtue of which he disapproves of abortion above all the other properties of abortion in virtue of which he might approve of it. If this is what lies behind the utterance 'abortion is wrong', it seems that we may no longer claim that John and Peter could share all their beliefs and desire-like attitudes, because they would at least differ with regard to the weight they assign to the views of the two advisors, M and N.

However, there are some problems with this response. First, it is not entirely clear whether all thin moral predicates to which hybrid expressivists usually apply their analyses are exclusively, or even typically, used for making all-things-considered judgements. For example, one might argue that evaluative predicates such as 'good' and 'bad' on the one hand and normative terms such as 'right' and 'wrong' or 'ought' and 'ought not' on the other differ in just this respect. It seems intuitively strange to say things like 'abortion is right and wrong at the same time', or 'something about abortion is right and something about abortion is wrong', and it seems even stranger to say 'you ought not to perform abortions in some respects, but you ought to perform abortions in other respects'. It seems far less strange, though, to say 'abortion is good and bad at the same time' or 'something about abortion is good and something about abortion is bad' or 'performing abortions is good in some respects, but bad in others'. Secondly, even if this were false, or if hybrid expressivists were to respond to the problem by explicitly restricting their analyses to what I have just referred to as normative rather than evaluative terms, they still need to explicitly address this aspect in the framework of their analyses and to provide a hybrid expressivist interpretation of it. Yet, hybrid expressivists, and expressivists in general, have not paid much attention to the all-things-considered nature of moral judgements at all, and one might think that doing so would raise further problems for expressivism.

If the meaning of moral utterances, and their action-guiding force or practical nature in particular, is essentially explained in terms of the desire-like attitudes these utterances express, then it seems that the most natural way to explain the all-things-considered nature of moral utterances would be to claim that the desire-like attitudes expressed by such utterances *override* all other desire-like attitudes of the speaker. This, however, seems to commit the expressivist to the view that we *necessarily act* on our all-things-considered moral judgements, and although Hare is sometimes thought to have endorse this extremely strong version of motivational internalism,[67] it is equally rejected by virtually all modern expressivists and non-expressivists.

It is not easy to see what other explanation of the all-things-considered nature of moral utterances is available to the expressivist, though. An alternative strategy might be to argue that all-thing-considered judgements consist of the belief and the desire-like attitude identified by Ridge and Barker and, in addition, of some separate normative judgement to the effect that the first judgement has a certain weight or authority. The obvious problem with this strategy, however, is that this separate judgement can only fulfil its function if it is itself an all-things-considered normative judgement. Yet, if it has this status, it requires a hybrid analysis as well – which means that the strategy leads into some kind of infinite regress. Far from providing an account of moral agreement and disagreement that is superior to the one provided by naturalist or non-naturalist analyses, therefore, the hybrid theories forwarded by Barker and Ridge are either unable to make room for this phenomenon at all or able to accommodate it only at considerable expenses.

5 Non-speaker-relative accounts of descriptive meaning

Given the various problems of speaker-relative versions of hybrid expressivism, there are strong reasons for thinking that hybrid expressivism presents a viable option only if expressivists manage to specify the descriptive belief expressed by moral utterances in a *non-speaker-relative* way, something that has also been claimed by Boisvert and Schroeder. However, although Boisvert himself defends a non-speaker-relative version of hybrid expressivism as his general position, he has not yet provided such a specification of the descriptive content of moral utterances. Indeed, the requirement to identify a non-speaker-relative belief that is conventionally expressed by all moral utterances, or at least by all moral utterances of the same type, seems an enormous task and one in virtue of which the

---

[67] See, for example, Brink who refers to a passage in Hare's *Moral Thinking* where Hare is concerned with the overridingness of moral judgements (Brink 1989, 42; cf. Hare 1981, 60 f.). The strong version of motivational internalism might also seem to be suggested by some of Hare's remarks in *The Language of Morals* (see, in particular, Hare 1952, 143 and 169). Note, however, that in *Freedom and Reason*, Hare explicitly refers to those latter passages and explains them in a way that suggests a weaker internalist thesis (see Hare 1963, 79). In accordance with this, in the paper *Internalism and Externalism in Ethics*, Hare explicitly describes his view on the matter in terms of the weaker internalist claim (see Hare 1999b, 96 f.).

hybrid expressivist loses a considerable part of his leverage against ordinary naturalist analyses of moral terms.

As we have seen, one of the main arguments against such analyses, employed by expressivists and non-naturalists alike, is Moore's open question argument and the related objection that all naturalist definitions of terms such as 'wrong' seem somewhat arbitrary. While many metaethicists seem willing to admit that certain natural properties, such as 'causing more pain than pleasure' or 'eliciting negative emotional responses from normal observers' or 'being desired by fully rational individuals', might in some way be connected to what makes actions morally wrong, they nevertheless reject the idea that any such natural property provides the *meaning* of the term 'wrong'. Yet, it seems that the hybrid expressivist must expect similar reactions with regard to any specification of the belief-element of moral utterances he puts forward as part of his non-speaker-relative version of hybrid expressivism. Therefore, while non-speaker-relative versions of hybrid expressivism may not encounter the kind of problems encountered by speaker-relative versions, they lose a good deal of this advantage by having problems in identifying a particular descriptive belief which we may legitimately attribute to all users of a certain moral predicate.

One attempt to provide a non-speaker-relative interpretation of the descriptive content of moral utterances has recently been made by Hallich. Hallich explicitly restricts his analysis to "Sollenssätze"[68], the German equivalent of ought sentences. According to Hallich's account, utterances such as 'Du sollst deine Versprechen halten' ('you ought to keep your promises') express the belief that 'es ist (von dir) gefordert, deine Versprechen zu halten', which can be translated as 'it is required (of you) to keep your promises'.[69] While Hallich admits that 'is required' is often used normatively, he emphasizes that there is also a purely descriptive use of the predicate and that 'it is required' can be uttered by somebody who does not himself assent to the requirement and does not think that what is being required ought to be done.[70] On this reading, what characterizes ought sentences, such as 'you ought to keep your promises', is that a desire-like attitude of approval is added to the descriptive claim 'it is required (of you) to keep your promises'. Moral utterances that make use of 'ought' are therefore conceived of as expressions of both the descriptive belief that a certain way of

---

[68] Hallich 2008, 209.
[69] I will proceed on the (defeasible) assumption that 'is required' is equivalent to 'ist gefordert' with regard to the aspects which are relevant here and therefore present Hallich's view as pertaining to the English predicate rather than to the German.
[70] See Hallich 2008, 199f.

behaviour is required and a desire-like attitude of the speaker which underwrites the requirement in question.

It ought to be noted that Hallich himself does not explicitly describe his position as an example of expressivism, but – following Hare's terminology – as a species of 'nondescriptivism'.[71] As a result, Hallich does not employ the typical terminology of (hybrid) expressivists, either: rather than talking about descriptive beliefs being expressed by ought sentences, Hallich prefers to talk about the descriptive content or the descriptive meaning of ought sentences. It also needs to be emphasized that Hallich distinguishes four different modal predicates with which we can identify the descriptive content of various types of ought sentences, namely 'ist gefordert', 'ist erlaubt', 'ist geboten' and 'ist verboten' ('is required', 'is permitted', 'is demanded' and 'is forbidden'). However, since he believes that the three other predicates can all either be defined in terms of 'ist gefordert' or are equivalent to it,[72] he restricts his argument to the latter predicate, which is why I will subsequently do so as well.

Now it is certainly true that there is a descriptive use of 'is required', even though the normative use seems to be the more common one. It is important to point out, however, that, unlike the normative use, of which one might conceive as genuinely impersonal, the descriptive use seems to be a personal use in disguise. In its descriptive understanding, 'it is required of you to keep your promises' is not only elliptical in the sense that what is being required must always be required *by somebody* or *something*. It seems that we should ultimately discard of the latter possibility: though we can say, for example, that the bible or a particular moral or legal code requires a certain way of behaviour, this way of speaking is clearly metaphorical. In its purely descriptive use, 'requiring' refers to a speech act, and speech acts can only be performed by persons.[73] It seems, then, that we need to give the full meaning of the statement 'it is required (of you) to keep your promises' as 'it is required (of you) by somebody to keep your promises'.

The belief which Hallich must take to be expressed by ought sentences, therefore, is the belief that somebody requires that one act in a certain way. A further thing to be emphasized is that the requirement to which the belief refers cannot simply be a requirement or demand made *eo ipso* by the speaker himself. If this were how Hallich conceived of the descriptive content of ought sentences,

---

71 See Hallich 2008, 118.
72 See Hallich 2008, 198.
73 This is not say, however, that these persons must necessarily be *natural* persons: there seem to be at least some legal persons, such as political governments or the *Royal Society*, about whom we can make similar claims.

his position would obviously collapse into a variant of Stevenson's first pattern of analysis and inherit its problems. In fact, Hallich himself suggests that he does *not* conceive of his position in this way. Thus, he explicitly emphasizes that uttering an ought sentence does not necessarily coincide with raising a demand of one's own.[74] Moreover, while he allows that the requirement to which an ought sentence refers may have been put into the world by the speaker himself,[75] as this is arguably the case with the divine 'Thou shalt have no other gods before me', Hallich does not understand this requirement as one that is made *by* uttering the ought sentence but as one that has already been raised beforehand.[76] The belief which, according to Hallich, is expressed by the sentence 'you ought to keep your promises' must therefore ultimately be given as the belief that 'it has previously been required (of you) by some other person to keep your promises'.

Once we specify the belief in this way, however, there seem to be good reason for doubting that it is indeed conventionally expressed by the former sentence and that something like that holds for all moral ought sentences. The main problem is that, as it stands, Hallich's analysis cannot allow for what we may describe as 'original moral claims'. Although the question of whether there is such a thing as moral progress is controversial, it seems obvious that there is at least such a thing as moral *change*, that is, a development in the moral views of a community or culture (or even of mankind in general) across generations. Yet, once we accept Hallich's interpretation, we seem to commit ourselves to a claim that is hardly compatible with a plausible understanding of moral change: the claim that whenever a particular moral ought claim, such as 'women ought to have the right to vote' or 'same sex marriage ought to be legal' or 'incest between consenting adult siblings ought not to be punished by the state', was being uttered for the first time in human history (as they all certainly were at some point), the speaker making this first utterance did not think of his view as original but took himself to be already following in other people's footsteps. It also commits us to the view that none of the speakers who subsequently made the same claim and were not, in fact, the first ones to raise the requirements mistakenly *thought* themselves to be original.

One might want to defend Hallich's proposal at this point by arguing that the acts of 'requiring something' to which his analysis appeals need not be understood as moral claims themselves, but can be understood as speech acts in virtue

---

74 See Hallich 2008, 214 f. and 365.
75 See Hallich 2008, 211.
76 See Hallich 2008, 366 f.

of which somebody, for example a person negatively affected by some kind of legal norm, expresses her wish that this norm be abolished. Thus one might think that it is sufficient for Hallich's proposal to work if, for example, we can argue that any speaker sincerely uttering the sentence 'incest between consenting adult siblings ought not to be punished by the state' must believe that some adult siblings have in the past raised the concern to have a sexual relationship with one another, where the raising of this concern is not itself conceived of as a full-blown moral utterance. However, this idea is problematic for the following reasons. It is obvious that social pressure with regard to some socially unwanted practice, sexual or otherwise, can be so great that even the individuals suffering from the prohibition of this practice will not publicly ask for is abolishment. In fact, we can even imagine that the social pressure involves a process of indoctrination which is so successful that the persons concerned will not even consciously *wish* the abolishment of the norm. However, it is simply implausible to infer that, in such a social scenario, it is impossible to sincerely utter the ought sentence in question.

The only claim we could plausibly defend is the claim that any speaker sincerely uttering the sentence 'incest between consenting adult siblings ought not to be punished by the state' must have the belief that not-punishing incest between consenting adult siblings would satisfy the (potentially unconscious) desires or preferences of certain persons. However, if we conceive of the descriptive belief expressed by moral utterances in this way, we have not only moved away quite a bit from Hallich's original analysis. We have also committed ourselves to quite substantial and controversial assumptions about what morality is all about. On account of the analysis in question, we would need to conclude that certain deontological or theonomous theories of morality which do not appeal to human preference satisfaction at all are not only inappropriate as normative theories about what makes actions right or wrong, but that their proponents fundamentally misunderstand the linguistic meaning of moral utterances and talk about something quite different. As far as I can see, there is wide agreement in the metaethical debate that a plausible analysis of the meaning of moral language should not have in tow any such commitments, and Hallich's statements concerning the neutrality of metaethics suggest that he shares this view.[77] Therefore, even if the above strategy would allow us to salvage Hallich's view that ought sentences have a constant non-speaker-relative content, it is one that he himself would probably not want to pursue.

---

77 See Hallich 2008, 57.

Hallich does not explicitly address the problems concerning 'original moral claims'. However, he provides four systematic arguments in support of his analysis which I shall briefly take up in order to demonstrate that they do not vindicate his proposal. Hallich's four arguments presuppose that the moral use of 'one ought to X' is equivalent to saying 'it is morally required to X'.[78] The four arguments are then meant to demonstrate that 'is morally required' has a constant descriptive content that is given by the descriptive 'is required' and and, *a fortiori*, that 'ought' has this descriptive content as well. While I do not want to quarrel with the idea that the moral 'ought' and the predicate 'is morally required' are roughly synonymous, I think that the four arguments intended to establish Hallich's further conclusion are not compelling.

One of these arguments is that it is possible to *partially* understand the meaning of 'is morally required' and that such a partial understanding can only be explained by acknowledging that 'is morally required' has descriptive content.[79] Hallich illustrates this point with the help of a thought experiment. He asks us to imagine a person who does not yet know any moral vocabulary and therefore neither has the moral 'ought' nor the concept 'is morally required' at her disposal. Hallich argues that if we try to explain to this person the meaning of the moral 'ought' and try to do so by saying "'one ought to do X' means 'doing X is morally required'", this person would necessarily be unable to fully grasp the meaning of 'one ought to do X'. However, she would at least *partially* understand its meaning because she would understand that our explanation refers to some kind of requirement (in the descriptive sense of that word). As Hallich points out, this would not be the case if we had tried to explain to her the meaning of 'one ought to do X' in a completely foreign language. According to Hallich, this difference between partially understanding what 'one ought to X' means and not understanding anything at all can only be explained with the help of the assumption that the phrase to which our explanation appealed, namely 'is morally required', has the descriptive content 'is required' which can be isolated from the full meaning of 'is morally required' and be understood even by somebody who does not understand any moral vocabulary.

In my view, this argument is an obvious case of *petitio principii*. It seems plausible to assume that a person with no knowledge of moral vocabulary who is familiar with the descriptive use of 'is required' and is then taught the meaning of 'one ought to do X' in the way Hallich describes will come to *think* that 'it is morally required' refers to some kind of requirement raised by

---

78 Hallich 2008, 201.
79 For the following, see Hallich 2008, 202f.

a particular person. The reason for assuming this is that the same linguistic expression ('required') occurs in both sentences and that we can expect a person with no information to the contrary to presume that the expression means the same thing in different contexts (or that the two uses of the expression are at least intimately related to one another). However, it simply does not follow that a person who regards the phrase 'it is morally required' in this way acquires a partial *understanding* of it. Obviously, 'to understand' and 'understanding' are success words. A partial understanding in Hallich's sense is therefore only given if the person *rightly* thinks what she thinks, and this is only the case if 'it is morally required' actually has the descriptive content the person takes it to have. Yet, this is just the issue that Hallich's argument is meant to resolve. Thus, rather than providing an independent argument in favour of his analysis, Hallich's appeal to the supposed partial understanding of 'it is morally required' pre-decides the issue in an illegitimate way. Somebody who does not yet accept Hallich's claim that the meaning of the moral 'ought' and of 'it is morally required' is partly constituted by the descriptive 'is required' will simply deny that the person described by Hallich acquires a partial understanding of the two phrases, and he will be right to do so even from a neutral perspective, given that Hallich's argument simply begs the question.

Something similar holds for Hallich's second argument.[80] The second argument appeals to the consideration that it is self-contradictory to apply the predicate 'is morally required' to an object without also applying the purely descriptive predicate 'is required' to this object. According to Hallich, it would be self-contradictory to say such things as 'Keeping one's promises is morally required, but there is nothing/nobody which/who requires that we keep our promises'. In such a case, it would be unclear what the speaker means by 'is morally required' because, as Hallich urges, how can anything be morally required if there is nobody who requires it? Now this latter question, which is intended by Hallich as a rhetorical question, has the same character as the argument reviewed before: if we agreed that nothing can be forbidden, morally or otherwise, if nobody forbids it, or that nothing can be required, morally or otherwise, if nobody required it, then we would have good reason to accept Hallich's analysis. In this case, however, there would be no need for any additional argument in the first place because, by agreeing about this much, we would already have reached an agreement about the descriptive meaning of 'it is morally required'.

Whether the second set of considerations provides us with any independent argument, then, hinges on whether the sentences offered by Hallich are in fact

---

80 See Hallich 2008, 203 f.

5 Non-speaker-relative accounts of descriptive meaning — 131

self-contradictory, and it seems that they are not. That there is the appearance of a contradiction is mostly due to the fact that, in introducing the descriptive use of 'is required' in the latter half of the sentence, Hallich does not restrict himself to the personal use of 'is required' and also fails to explicitly rule out the possibility that the person 'requiring' promise-keeping might be the speaker himself. However, once we eliminate the 'nothing ... which', replace 'nobody' by 'no other person' and add a temporal dimension, the sentence does not seem self-contradictory any more: 'Keeping one's promises is morally required, but there is no other person who has so far required that we keep our promises'. This suggests that the appearance of contradiction surrounding Hallich's original formulation is simply be due to the fact that we tend to give the second 'require' a normative reading as well – in which case there would clearly be a contradiction. If, in contrast, we remain fully aware of the descriptive meaning of 'require' in the second half of the sentence, as the revised formulation forces us to be, it is not clear why the sentence should be self-contradictory at all.

In fact, the example of 'original moral claims' already discussed not only shows that such statements are possible and well-formed, but even gives us an idea of how they can turn out to be actually true. A radical moral reformer who fundamentally rejects the moral standards of his community, and of all other communities he is aware of, can certainly say that certain ways of behaviour that are commonly regarded with indifference or even deemed impermissible are morally required and then admit that nobody has so far required them. In fact, we can expect him to say this in a tone of moral indignation and to criticize all other individuals for not having raised the requirement in the way he now does. Far from providing conclusive support for his analysis, therefore, Hallich's second argument rather casts doubt on it.

Hallich's third argument is that we can always respond to somebody's 'doing X is morally required' by asking 'who requires that?'.[81] According to Hallich, if utterances of the type 'doing X is morally required' did not express the belief that somebody requires that we do X, this question should not be open at all but clearly violate linguistic conventions – because there would be no reason why the moral requirement to do X should have any author into whose nature we may inquire in the first place.

Now although the considerations underlying the third argument are perhaps the ones that put most pressure of the critic of Hallich's analysis of ought sentences, his way of putting the point appears somewhat misguided because the openness of the question employed by Hallich simply fails to refute the critic's

---

[81] See Hallich 2008, 201f.

position. To say that a question is 'closed' (rather than 'open') is to claim that the answer to the question is already known or has already been given. Hallich is surely right to claim that the question 'who requires that?', imagined as a response to somebody's 'doing X is morally required', is not closed in this sense. However, the critic of Hallich's analysis can happily accept this because it does not show that 'is morally required' has 'is required by somebody' as its descriptive content at all. What the critic has to claim in order to refute Hallich's analysis is not that what is morally required *cannot* have been required by some other person, but only that it *need not* have been required by some other person. The question 'who requires that?' would only be closed in the relevant sense if it were *impossible* that some person should have previously required what the first speaker takes to be morally required. Only in this case would the answer to the question 'who required that?' be one that has already been given because in saying 'doing X is morally required', the speaker would have implied that there is no person who has required X. That the question 'who requires that?' is still open is equally compatible with the view that 'doing X is morally required' *necessarily implies* that somebody has required X as with the view that it *merely permits* that somebody has required X.

What needs to be shown in order to prove Hallich's point, therefore, is not that 'who required that?' is an *open* question, but that 'has anybody required that?' is a *closed* question to which the first speaker could respond by saying something like 'well, I just told you, didn't I?'. Once we put the point this way, however, Hallich's third argument turns out to be the second argument in disguise. Just as we could argue that it is not self-contradictory to say 'Keeping one's promises is morally required, but there is no other person who has so far required that we keep our promises', we can argue that the question 'has anybody required that?' is an open question because it might be the case that what is morally required has not yet been required by any person at all or at least not by any person other than the speaker. The true argumentative import of Hallich's further considerations can be brought out if we slightly revise Hallich's question so as to actively suggest that 'doing X is morally required' implies what Hallich's analysis takes it to imply. Thus, if we formulate the question as 'so who has so far required it then?' (rather than 'who requires that?'), we are left with a question that should, in fact, seem somewhat misguided or surprising if Hallich's analysis were incorrect, and one might want to argue that the question is not misguided or surprising in the relevant sense.

Yet, there are certainly different phenomena that can explain the appearance of meaningfulness here and the most important one is equivocation. The critic of Hallich's analysis does not deny that there is a descriptive variant of 'is required', he only claims that it is not part of the meaning of 'is morally required'. Neither does the critic deny that both phrases make use of the same word and are therefore, at least in a superficial sense, related to one another. The basis provided by these assumptions, however, is sufficient to explain the appearance of meaningfulness which 'so who has so far required it then?' bears as a response to 'doing X is morally required'. Thus we may argue that it is exactly because 'required' is ambiguous that the question is not obviously nonsensical but retains an air of legitimacy. In fact, it does not seem too hard to come up with examples in which equivocation is obviously occurring, but where the ultimately illegitimate response seems *prima facie* intelligible. Take, for instance, the case of somebody who responds to 'the food is spoiled' by saying 'who spoiled it then?' The response is misleading and will be taken to be intended as a joke. However, the response does not seem to violate relevant linguistic conventions to such a degree that we would not understand what the person is talking about. The identity of the expressions being used even seems to lure us into intuitively thinking that the response might be an adequate one.

In view of this, it seems that the appropriate test is not so much whether the question 'so who has so far required it then?' immediately *sounds* illegitimate, but rather whether we can answer the question in a way that resolves the confusion and proves the question to be illegitimate. Thus, in the latter example, we can say something like 'Well, nobody has spoiled the food. It has just gone bad because it was exposed to the sun for so long', thereby making clear that something can spoil without being spoiled by somebody. The question, then, is whether there is a way to respond in a similar manner to the question 'so who has so far required it then?'. On Hallich's view, it should be impossible to respond to the question by saying 'well, nobody has so far explicitly required that' and to thereby point out the illegitimacy of the question. However, I have already demonstrated that this *is* indeed a possible reply, as long as we keep in mind the restriction that it must be some person other than the speaker who has raised the requirement in question. There is no reason why we should not respond to 'so who has so far required it then?' by saying 'Well, no other person has so far required it. But, in my opinion, doing X is exactly what is morally required'.

The final argument has the character of a plausibility check.[82] According to Hallich, assuming that 'is morally required' is some kind of thick moral concept with a fixed descriptive content is ultimately more plausible than assuming otherwise. The reason is that, in Hallich's view, if it is at least *possible* to conceive of a concept in this way, this provides *prima facie* evidence for doing so. Until some-

---

82 See Hallich 2008, 204.

body has conclusively proven the falsity of the view in question, we should therefore stick to it and accept that 'is morally required' has a constant descriptive content that is given by 'is required' and that the same is true, *a fortiori*, of 'ought'.

Given that the same linguistic expression appears in 'is morally required' and 'is required by some person', Hallich seems to be right that the burden of proof rather lies with those who want to *deny* that the descriptive 'is required' is part of the meaning of 'is morally required'. However, Hallich sets the bar far too high by suggesting that the burden of proof can only be discharged by conclusively and irrefutably proving that the descriptive 'is required' *cannot* be part of the meaning of 'is morally required'. In order to discharge the burden of proof, it seems sufficient to explain why it is more *plausible* to assume that 'is required' is *not* part of the meaning of 'is morally required' than to assume that it *is* part of this meaning. Such reasons may consist in considerations that directly speak against the view that 'is required' is part of the meaning of 'is morally required', but also in considerations that provide an alternative explanation for why the same linguistic expression is used in both cases.

Hallich not only emphasizes that the relevant considerations have not been forwarded in the metaethical debate so far, but also suggests that no such considerations are available. In my view, however, the possibility of 'original moral claims' represents a consideration of the former kind, and this consideration weighs heavily against Hallich's analysis in light of the fact that the three counter-arguments provided by Hallich are not compelling. Moreover, it seems that we can indeed give an alternative explanation for why the same expression appears in 'is morally required' and 'is required by some person', an explanation which relies on a very common idea about the history of moral language. As is widely recognized, Western morality is a morality with a distinctive background, provided by Judeo-Christian religion. In accordance with this, our moral language has been strongly shaped by certain religious assumptions and their implications. One of these assumptions or implications is the idea that moral requirements are ultimately requirements raised by a person, namely by God. That the moral 'ought' is roughly equivalent to 'it is morally required', and that 'requiring' is something that is typically done by persons, can therefore plausibly be traced back to the religious origin of Western morality.

To conceive of the history of moral language in this way, however, by no means commits us to thinking that today's meaning of 'is morally required' cannot but be explained in terms of requirements raised by persons. As I have already emphasized with regard to preference utilitarianism, an important and widely accepted general constraint on metaethical analyses is that they should not commit us to substantial normative-ethical positions. In modern pluralist societies, moral predicates, such as 'is morally required', are used by speakers with a variety of religious views, including both atheist and agnosticist views. In light of this fact, analysing the meaning of moral language in a way that has all sincere users of moral language presupposing God's existence would seem even more problematic than analysing it in terms of human and non-human preferences. Yet, we would certainly commit us to such a theonomous view on morality if we analysed our actual use of 'Doing X is morally required' as implying that God requires us to do X. The same would be true if we were to forward the slightly weaker claim that 'Doing X is morally required' implies that *some* person requires us to do X *and* to admit that, in some cases (such as in the cases of 'original moral claims'), this person can only be God.

Therefore, rather than trying to salvage Hallich's central claim at any cost and presupposing a theonomous understanding of morality by way of linguistic analysis, we should admit that 'is morally required' may once have had the descriptive meaning Hallich attributes to it (or, in fact, an even more specific descriptive meaning, given by the predicate 'is required by God'), but argue that, due to secularisation processes and the emergence of modern pluralist societies, it has lost this part of its meaning and must hence be analysed differently. In this manner, we could explain why we use the same linguistic expression when saying that X is morally required and when saying that some person requires X. At the same time, however, we could do justice to the possibility of 'original moral claims' and the fact that we can (now) say things like 'No other person has so far required that we do X. But, in my opinion, doing X is exactly what is morally required'.

In order to complete our discussion of Hallich's version of hybrid expressivism, it needs to be pointed out that, in later passages of his book, Hallich subjects his initial analysis to certain qualifications which might be taken to render it immune to the criticism I have just developed. After having introduced and extensively justified his analysis of moral ought sentences, Hallich concedes in passing that the requirement to which speakers uttering such sentences refer might not yet have been raised and might even never be explicitly raised at all. In these cases, according to Hallich, we have to conceive of the requirements as merely hypothetical ones.[83]

From my point of view, it is hard to see this concession as anything other than an *ad hoc* epicycle meant to overcome the fundamental problems of the initial analysis. In the end, however, it does not really strengthen the analysis but sacrifices it. The problem with the qualification or extension consists in the fact

---

[83] See Hallich 2008, 240f.

that it is no longer clear what the descriptive content of a given token ought sentence really is, or how the belief expressed by such a sentence is to be characterized. It is surely possibly to claim, as Hallich does in a deliberately vague manner, that ought sentences refer to "Forderungssachverhalte"[84] (propositions about requirements). However, what we should demand from a semantic analysis is that it enables us to precisely determine the descriptive content of the sentences that are being analysed, and in its qualified form, Hallich's analysis is unable to satisfy this demand.

Hallich, therefore, misses the target he has explicitly set for himself, namely to identify a constant descriptive content of moral ought sentences and to thereby overcome the indeterminacy of the accounts of Stevenson and Hare. If we take Hallich's qualification seriously, then a person uttering the sentence 'one ought to keep one's promises' says *either* that somebody has required in the past that we keep our promises, *or* that somebody will require in the future that we keep our promises, *or* that somebody could perhaps require that we keep our promises. We are not then left with any constant descriptive content that is safely identifiable by the speaker's audience, and it is not clear whether, in this form, Hallich's analysis is immune to the objections that Urmson and others have raised against Hare and Stevenson.

Yet, it would not be of any help if we made the analysis slightly more definite and gave the descriptive content as the disjunctive belief that 'somebody has required in the past that we keep our promises, somebody will require in the future that we keep our promises or somebody could perhaps require that we keep our promises' (or *exclusively* as the latter belief, i.e. as the belief that 'somebody could perhaps require that we keep our promises'). The problem with this supposed solution is that the analysis would cease to be convincing as a specific analysis of the meaning of moral ought sentences. Both the disjunctive belief and the more limited belief that 'somebody could perhaps require that we keep our promises' are beliefs that a sincere speaker of the sentence 'one ought to keep one's promises' could hardly reject. However, very much the same goes for a speaker uttering the sentence 'it is good to keep one's promises' and even for a speaker uttering a purely descriptive sentence such as 'keeping one's promises facilitates lasting social cooperation': Since keeping one's promises is a type of action, and since all actions can in principle be required by somebody at some point, there is no compelling reason why we should conceive of the belief as one that we can attribute *qua* linguistic convention to those

---

[84] Hallich 2008, 211.

speakers *and only those* speakers who render keeping promises the object of a moral ought sentence.

It would seem far more convincing, therefore, to solely integrate the requirement aspect into the definition of the *attitude* that is being expressed and to translate the sentence 'one ought to keep one's promises' as 'hurrah to any actual/possible requirement to keep one's promises'. Such an analysis, however, would stand in similar need of further justification, since it is not supported by Hallich's systematic arguments which are obviously designed to support a quite different claim. Moreover, if Hallich were to analyse moral ought sentences in the above manner, his account would no longer be a version of hybrid expressivism at all, but merely a specific variant of pure expressivism. What would distinguish it from accounts such as Ayer's would only be that, instead of directly relating the attitude that is being expressed to the type of action under consideration, it takes some kind of detour and adds the idea of a requirement as a further element, giving the meaning of 'one ought to keep one's promises' as 'hurrah to any actual/possible requirement to keep one's promises' rather than 'hurrah to keeping one's promises'. Yet, it is hard to see how integrating the idea of a requirement into what is at heart a pure expressivist analysis should provide any help in trying to salvage the rationality and justifiability of moral discourse – which is what, in explicit opposition to Ayer, Hallich formulates as his overall objective.

With regard to the debate over hybrid expressivism, then, our final conclusion must be that Hallich does not succeed in identifying a constant non-speaker-relative descriptive content of moral ought statements based on a common understanding of semantic meaning. As intuitively plausible as the idea that moral ought sentences 'have something to do with requirements' may be: it cannot be turned into an adequate hybrid analysis of ought statements and solve hybrid expressivism's crucial problems.

6 Descriptive meaning and *de dicto* beliefs

Is there, then, any non-speaker-relative descriptive belief that we can plausibly take to be expressed by moral ought statements (or moral statements of another type) – a belief which hearers may attribute to the speaker in virtue of linguistic conventions even when they are ignorant of the actual reasons that led the speaker to make the statement? In my view, the only further candidate worthy of consideration is a *de dicto* belief that expresses the supervenience of moral utterances in some sort of general, non-speaker-relative way. As we have seen, the reason why Hare, for example, thinks that moral utterances have descriptive in addition to evaluative meaning is that our moral judgements must always be related to the descriptive properties of the evaluated objects and, in some sense of that word, *follow* from those properties. As we have also seen, neither the audience nor the speaker himself need to be absolutely clear about what these properties are. However, the least the audience knows about the speaker, and the speaker knows about himself (as long as he uses moral language in accordance with the idea that the moral supervenes on the non-moral), is that he believes that there are *some* such properties, that is, some properties that make what he claims to be morally right right and what he claims to be morally wrong wrong. Accordingly, it seems that we may not sensibly respond to a speaker uttering 'abortion is morally wrong' by saying 'I understand that you commend not to allow abortions, but do you also think that abortion has any descriptive properties in virtue of which you are commending this?'.

It seems, then, that we can identify at least one belief that we may safely attribute to a speaker using moral predicates such as 'good', 'right' or 'ought'. This belief is what we may describe as a *de dicto* belief: it is not the substantial belief that the evaluated object, i.e. a particular action, has certain specified properties, but only a kind of summary belief to the effect that the descriptive properties which the object possesses (and which are left unspecified) warrant a certain reaction. The possibility of interpreting the belief conventionally expressed by moral utterances along these lines is pointed out by Eriksson who suggests it as a possible way of escaping the problems resulting from unknown speaker standards but does not further discuss the prospects of the strategy.[85] However, given the way in which the *de dicto* belief can be said to express the very idea of supervenience or universalizability, it seems that it might be the strategy that actually conforms best with the spirit of Hare's original approach to which Eriksson is so obviously indebted. In fact, in a paper published in 2001, Michael Smith has suggested that we should read Hare's account of moral language in something like these terms and argued that, in virtue of the fact that beliefs of the type in question are plausibly expressed by all moral utterances, pure expressivism is not a stable position but necessarily collapses into this form of Harean hybrid expressivism.[86] Finally, some remarks made by Boisvert in the course of criticizing speaker-relative accounts seem to suggest a similar interpretation of the descriptive content of moral sentences. Boisvert emphasizes that the descriptive properties picked out by the predicates 'right' and 'wrong' are not specific

---

[85] See Eriksson 2009, 29.
[86] See Smith 2001, 95–98.

properties but the more general properties of rightness and wrongness,[87] and one way of interpreting this claim is to read it as saying that 'right' and 'wrong' pick out the descriptive properties that make an action wrong, whatever those properties happen to be.[88]

Yet, neither of the three authors provides a precise formulation of the belief in question, and once we try to do so, we see that there are serious problems in defending a hybrid expressivist position on the basis of the above proposal. The initial problem, which is not sufficiently addressed by either Smith or Boisvert, is how to specify the content of the belief without invoking normative terms. The most natural way to describe the content of the *de dicto* belief expressed by 'abortion is wrong' is perhaps to describe it as the belief that abortion has certain wrong-making characteristics – which, as a matter of fact, would be very much in line with one of Hare's characterization of descriptive meaning. However, the obvious problem with this analysis is that 'wrong' – the moral predicate for which we want to provide a hybrid expressivist analysis – appears as part of the content of the belief, which means that the belief is not, after all, a purely descriptive belief, even though the 'characteristics' to which it refers may be instantiated by descriptive properties. However, we seem to run into a similar kind of problem if we try to specify the content of the *de dicto* belief in question without using the term 'wrong', such as when we describe it as the belief that the descriptive properties of abortion provide *reasons* for having a negative attitude towards it or *warrant* disapproval. While these specifications may strip the belief of any obvious moral content, they fall short of turning it into a proper descriptive belief.

One idea of how to get rid of the normative content would be to think of the relationship between the belief and the simultaneously expressed attitude, not in terms of 'warrant' or in some other normative terms, but in *explanatory* or *causal* terms. According to this idea, the *de dicto* belief expressed by 'abortion is wrong' is not the belief that 'certain descriptive properties of abortion warrant a negative desire-like attitude towards it', but the belief that 'certain descriptive properties of abortion *explain* or *cause* a negative desire-like attitude towards it'. It seems, however, that we may legitimately attribute such a belief to a speaker judging that abortion is wrong only in virtue of the fact that *he himself* expresses such a negative desire-like attitude towards abortion. Otherwise, we would run into the same kinds of problem faced by Hallich's proposal. However, if the

---

[87] See Boisvert 2008, 178.
[88] Note, however, that in a later passage, Boisvert himself introduces a more specific property, namely 'maximizing general welfare', as a possible candidate for the descriptive property denoted by the term 'right' (see Boisvert 2008, 185).

true descriptive content of the 'abortion is wrong' is given by the belief that 'certain descriptive properties of abortion explain or caused *my* (the speaker's) negative desire-like attitude towards it', then we are again left with a speaker-relative content after all. We may surely attribute the belief in question to everybody uttering the sentence 'abortion is wrong', even to a speaker who does not know exactly why he disapproves of abortion. Thus, it seems strange to imagine a speaker who disapproves of abortion, but who does not believe that there is an explanation for this fact which appeals, in some way or the other, to the properties of abortion. Similarly, it seems strange to imagine that a speaker disapproving of abortion would not believe that his disapproval is caused by something in the object he disapproves of. However, the crucial question is whether the above proposal has any advantages over Ridge's and Barker's accounts when it comes to attitude ascription and moral disagreement.

The answer is that the proposal may have some such advantages when it comes to explaining moral disagreement, but that it has the same problem with attitude ascriptions. Moreover, the very same feature that makes the analysis immune to the problems with moral disagreement renders it incompatible with the solution to the 'Frege-Geach problem' that made Ridge's and Barker's accounts attractive in the first place. To begin with attitude ascription: if we return to our example of Robert uttering 'John believes that abortion is wrong', we quickly see that there is no way to accommodate the descriptive content which the proposal under consideration forces us conceive of as part of John's belief. Thus, the following four options all seem inappropriate:

*1. Certain properties of abortion explain or caused my (John's) negative desire-like attitude towards it.
*2. John believes that certain properties of abortion explain or caused my (John's) negative desire-like attitude towards it.
*3. Certain properties of abortion explain or caused my (Robert's) negative desire-like attitude towards it.
*4. John believes that certain properties of abortion explain or caused my (Robert's) negative desire-like attitude towards it.

As before, *1 and *2 are beliefs that Robert simply cannot express when uttering 'John believes that abortion is wrong' because they contain indexical references to John, while *3 is a belief that Robert need not have and *4 does not correctly describe what John believes.

The reason why the above proposal has less of a problem with moral disagreement is that it conceives of the desire-like attitude expressed by 'abortion is wrong' as relating to abortion rather than to the descriptive properties which cause or explain the attitude. Once we grant that this is a psychologically plausible view, we avoid the problem that, when respectively uttering 'abortion is wrong' and 'abortion is not wrong', John and Peter cannot be taken to disagree with each other because they might have both the same beliefs and the same desire-like attitudes: while John need not deny that there are both properties in abortion that explain why he, John, disapproves of abortion, and properties that explain why Peter approves of it, John and Peter necessarily disagree with each other insofar as John disapproves of abortion while Peter approves of it. The problem with the proposal, however, is that this general interpretation of the desire-like attitudes expressed by moral utterances undermines the explanation of the inference licensing-property I have sketched above. In fact, if we interpret the descriptive belief expressed by 'abortion is wrong' in terms of the *de dicto* belief in question, the *modus ponens* argument does not even get off the ground:

> P1 Certain properties of abortion explain my (the speaker's) negative desire-like attitude towards it; boo to abortion.
>
> P2* If certain properties of abortion explain my negative desire-like attitude towards it, then certain properties of in-vitro fertilisation explain my negative desire-like attitude towards it; boo to abortion/in-vitro fertilisation.
>
> K Certain properties of in-vitro fertilisation explain my negative desire-like attitude towards it; boo to in-vitro fertilisation.

The proposed interpretation of the *de dicto* belief creates severe problems for rendering the conditional of the argument. For one thing, it is not clear whether we should think of the attitude expressed by the conditional as an attitude towards abortion (as in the first premise), or as an attitude towards in-vitro fertilisation (as in the conclusion), or as an attitude towards both abortion and in-vitro fertilisation. The problem with the two latter options is that the whole idea of the above *modus ponens* argument seems to be to allow for the possibility that someone who does not yet think that in-vitro fertilisation is wrong may come to think of it in this way *in virtue of the argument*. However, this means that it should be possible to assent to the conditional without having the attitude described by 'boo to in-vitro fertilisation'. Yet, the first of the three options does not provide much help, either. If the attitude expressed by both premises were 'boo to abortion', then it would not be true to say that somebody who assents to both premises must have the attitude expressed by the conclusion, namely a negative attitude towards in-vitro fertilisation.

A second problem following from the nature of the *de dicto* belief is that we also encounter problems in trying to formulate the *belief* expressed by the conditional of the argument. As it stands, our formulation is somewhat ambiguous because the second "it" might refer either to 'abortion' or to 'in-vitro fertilisation'. However, it seems that there is no legitimate way of resolving this ambiguity. If we take the first option and formulate the belief expressed by the conditional as the belief that 'If certain properties of abortion explain my negative desire-like attitude towards abortion, then certain properties of in-vitro fertilisation explain my negative desire-like attitude towards abortion', we are left with a belief whose content seems self-contradictory. However, the same holds if we interpret the belief as the belief that 'If certain properties of abortion explain my negative desire-like attitude towards in-vitro fertilisation, then certain properties of in-vitro fertilisation explain my negative attitude towards in-vitro fertilisation'.

An additional problem is that under this interpretation, the content of the belief presupposes that the speaker already has a negative desire-like attitude towards in-vitro fertilisation which presupposition, as I have already emphasized, is not warranted. It is for this latter reason that it would provide no help to interpret the "it" differently in the antecedent and the consequent of the conditional, either. The belief that 'If certain properties of abortion explain my negative desire-like attitude towards in-vitro fertilisation, then certain properties of in-vitro fertilisation explain my negative attitude towards in-vitro fertilisation' is a belief which we may not legitimately ascribe to every person uttering 'If abortion is wrong, then in-vitro fertilisation is wrong'. The reason is that the person making the utterance need not have any negative attitude towards in-vitro fertilisation to begin with in which case there would be no foundation for any conditional belief about what properties might explain the existence of this attitude.

For this reason, it would not even help us if we followed Eriksson into rejecting the common hybrid solution to the 'Frege-Geach problem'. According to Eriksson, the expressivist can concede that in certain contexts, such as in the conditional of a moral *modus ponens* argument, moral predicates such as 'wrong' do not express any attitudes at all. Eriksson's crucial idea is that the expressivist is not thereby forced to also concede that this changes the meaning of 'wrong', which means that he might escape the problem of equivocation.[89] If this were true, the expressivist could happily accept that, on the *de dicto* interpretation, the two premises and the conclusion of a moral *modus ponens* argument express different attitudes or attitudes towards different objects. However, in order for this alternative solution to the Frege-Geach problem to work, it must still be the case that the two premises and the conclusion express descriptive beliefs which, taken together, form a valid argument. Yet, as I have just shown, the

---

89 See Eriksson 2009, 10f.

de dicto interpretation under consideration is unable to make good on this requirement.

Appealing to *de dicto* beliefs expressing the supervenience of the moral on the non-moral, then, is not a fruitful strategy for identifying an uncontroversial and non-speaker-relative descriptive content of moral utterances, especially if such a strategy is meant to preserve hybrid expressivism's additional resources for solving the 'Frege-Geach problem'. Though one might argue that there is indeed some non-speaker-relative *de dicto* belief that is conventionally expressed by moral utterances, this belief fails to play any systematic role because it does not provide any reasons for the expressed desire-like attitude and does not, for instance, help to secure the possibility of rational argument or explain moral *modus ponens*.

This leaves us with the question of whether Smith is right in claiming that, on any plausible interpretation of moral utterances, pure expressivism collapses into hybrid expressivism. As we have seen above, if we do not want the *de dicto* belief expressing the idea of supervenience to be a normative belief that demands a hybrid analysis in its own right, we must ultimately conceive of it as a belief that fails to play any systematic role when it comes to explaining how moral sentences enter into logical relations with other moral or non-moral sentences. It is then on par with quite a few other beliefs that we could legitimately attribute to a speaker uttering a moral sentence, such as the belief that 'it is me who is talking just now' or the belief that 'somebody is listening just now'. However, if this much is true, then it would seem misleading to draw the conclusion that pure expressivism collapses into hybrid expressivism in virtue of the *de dicto* belief in question, given that we would hardly want to make this claim on the basis of the fact that utterances of the sentence 'abortion is wrong' can be said to conventionally express the belief that 'it is me (the speaker) who is talking just now'. As long as a metaethical position does not acknowledge the expression of any further, non-trivial beliefs which possess some systematic importance with regard to moral argument and moral deliberation, therefore, it seems 'pure' enough to be described as a variant of pure expressivism.

7 Does pure expressivism collapse into a hybrid variant of speaker subjectivism?

Even if we accept the above conclusion, the issue of whether pure expressivism is an internally stable theoretical position is not fully settled yet. That pure expressivism might collapse into another metaethical view has also been argued on the basis of slightly different considerations, and in order to assess the stability of pure expressivism, we need to take up these considerations as well. Thus, in their 1998 paper *A problem for expressivism*, Frank Jackson and Philip Pettit claimed that expressivism cannot avoid collapsing into a variant of speaker subjectivism because expressivists must ultimately concede that utterances such as 'X is wrong' conventionally express the belief that the speaker himself has a negative attitude towards X.[90]

Jackson and Pettit define expressivism as a bipartite theory which holds (a) that ethical sentences lack truth conditions, are not truth-apt, truth assessable etc., and (b) that ethical sentences "express certain distinctive pro and con *attitudes*, and express them without in any sense reporting them: without even reporting them in the broad sense in which 'The present King of France is bald' reports the existence of the King as well as his baldness"[91]. They then develop their crucial idea that expressivism cannot plausibly explain how ethical sentences can express attitudes without also reporting them on the basis of general considerations concerning linguistic meaning.

According to Jackson and Pettit, theories of linguistic meaning, in particular those following in the Lockean tradition, need to acknowledge that our ending up with certain linguistic conventions is to be understood in terms of our explicitly or implicitly entering into agreements for the use of particular words for particular things. Entering into such agreements, however, requires that we *know* that this is what we are using the words for.[92] For example, an explanation for why the word 'square' refers to the property of being square must acknowledge that the agreement establishing the meaning of 'square' is grounded in the shared knowledge of our using 'square' in order to signify the property of being square. In Jackson and Pettit's view, however, we can explain this further fact only by presupposing that our convention is based on the fact that we sometimes take something to be square and recognize that we do so: in order to know that we and other speakers use 'square' in order to signify the property of being square, we must have reason to attribute to a speaker using the word the belief that the object he describes by the help of the term 'square' has the property of being square.

Yet, if this general line of thought is correct, then it seems that in order for words such as 'good' to serve as linguistic expressions of desire-like attitudes, we must also presuppose that speakers using these words usually have these attitudes and recognize that they do so. For, as Jackson and Pettit emphasize,

---

90 See Jackson/Pettit 1998. See also Jackson/Pettit 2003; and Jackson 2001.
91 Jackson/Pettit 1998, 239.
92 See Jackson/Pettit 1998, 241.

"we could hardly have agreed to use the word for an attitude we did not recognize and failed to believe we had, since that would be to use the word for 'we know not what'"[93]. Or, as Jackson and Pettit also put it, we could not have learned to express positive desire-like attitudes towards certain things by calling these things 'good' if we had not learned to use 'good' when we have the relevant attitudes. 'Good' could not have acquired its positive expressive meaning if we had learned to use 'good' when we have no idea what our attitudes are or believe them to be negative attitudes towards the object in question.[94] However, if, as Jackson and Pettit conclude from this, the expressivist must allow that we sincerely use the word 'good' only when we believe that we have a certain kind of attitude, it seems difficult to deny that we express this belief by using the word 'good' and that the sentence in which the word figures has genuine truth conditions, namely those of that very belief. Yet, without such a denial, Jackson and Pettit argue, expressivism simply becomes a variant of speaker subjectivism.

There have been quite a few attempts to defend expressivism against Jackson and Pettit's challenge.[95] Two things about these attempts are surprising. The first is that most commentators focus on trying to show how expressivists can ultimately deny that moral sentences have truth conditions, or to show that they can at least deny that moral sentences have 'ordinary' or 'logical' as opposed to 'Lockean' truth conditions.[96] As we have seen in chapter 2, however, the expressivist position is not taken to characteristically include a denial of the truth assessability of ethical sentences anymore. It is not clear, therefore, why this part of Jackson and Pettit's challenge should be of primary importance. In my view, a discussion of the challenge ought rather to focus on the second part and examine whether expressivists need to acknowledge that moral utterances express self-descriptive beliefs reporting the speaker's attitudes and whether their position thereby collapses into a hybrid form of speaker subjectivism.

The main thing to be asked here is whether we should accept Jackson and Pettit's quite demanding characterization of the expressivist thesis. According to Jackson and Pettit, expressivists not only claim that moral utterances express desire-like states of mind rather than beliefs (as the standard definition of expressivism has it), but also that moral utterances do not, in addition to this, re-

---

[93] Jackson/Pettit 1998, 242.
[94] See Jackson/Pettit 2003, 86.
[95] See, for example, Barker 2000, 269 ff.; Smith/Stoljar 2003, 69 ff.; Dreier 2004b, 86 ff.; Ridge 2006b, 504 ff.; and Schroeder 2014, 281.
[96] See Barker 2000; and Smith/Stoljar 2003. For the latter, more qualified claim, see Dreier 2004b; and Schulte 2010.

port these attitudes, not even in a broad sense of that word. The second surprising aspect of the previous discussion of Jackson and Pettit's challenge is that most critics of the challenge accept this characterization without further explanation. In my view, there are good reasons to question and ultimately reject it, and it seems that the force of many of the arguments provided by previous critics of Jackson and Pettit depends on doing so.

To begin with, while it may be true that some classic expressivists have suggested the above understanding of the expressivist claim, it is obviously incompatible with the theories of other classic expressivists. An example of the former kind is Ayer. Ayer elaborates on the distinction between expressivism and speaker subjectivism by emphasizing that "the expression of a feeling assuredly does not involve the assertion that one has it"[97]. While Ayer is happy to concede that expressing and reporting feelings can go together and even concedes that "the assertion that one has a certain feeling *always* involves the expression of that feeling"[98], he is adamant that the reverse does not hold. As an example, he cites the feeling of boredom which we can express merely by tone and gestures, that is, without uttering any words at all.

In a similar way, Blackburn suggests at times that the difference between expressivism and speaker subjectivism is secured by the fact that, according to expressivism, a person making a moral utterance *only* expresses a desire-like attitude without, simultaneously, saying that she has the attitude.[99] Jackson and Pettit explicitly refer to these examples, and their reply to Ayer's challenge is to admit that one can express attitudes without reporting them, but to claim that this is not what happens in the case of moral utterances: expressions of boredom, or ejaculations such as 'Boo' and 'Hurrah', are not governed by the sort of fine-grained and clear-cut linguistic conventions regulating the making of moral utterances; accordingly, they do not report the speaker's attitudes in the way moral utterances do, but at best *suggest* them.[100]

However, as should already be clear from the previous discussion, Stevenson's view is quite different from the one I have just attributed to Ayer and, provisionally, to Blackburn. Stevenson not only claims that moral utterances express both desire-like attitudes and truth-conditional beliefs. According to his first pattern of analysis, these beliefs are just the kind of reporting beliefs the speaker subjectivist analysis appeals to. Yet, Stevenson obviously thinks that his analysis still remains sufficiently distinct from subjectivist analyses, and the main reason

---

[97] Ayer 1936/1967, 109.
[98] Ayer 1936/1967, 109. (my emphasis)
[99] See Blackburn 1984, 169.
[100] See Jackson/Pettit 1998, 244 ff. See also Jackson/Pettit 2003, 87.

why he thinks so is that he takes his hybrid analysis to be able to account for moral disagreement in a way speaker subjectivism cannot. If Stevenson does not shy away from the concession that moral utterances express reporting beliefs, why should other expressivists be worried by this supposed implication of their views and not simply bite the bullet?

It seems that a natural response to Stevenson's position would be for Jackson and Pettit to positively incorporate the distinction between pure expressivism and hybrid expressivism and confine their argument to the former. While Stevenson's example shows that the hybrid expressivist need not be bothered by the fact that moral utterances cannot express desire-like attitudes without reporting them, the position of the pure expressivist would still be undermined by this concession. In my view, however, even this much is doubtful. As I have argued above, the pure expressivist can allow that *some* beliefs are conventionally expressed by moral utterances, as long as he can avoid attributing any systematic importance to these beliefs. Yet, it is not clear why something like this should not also hold for beliefs which report the speaker's desire-like attitudes. As long as the pure expressivist can plausibly argue that the status of the attitude-expression differs significantly from the status of the belief-expression and that, because of this, the expression of the attitude is more essential to the moral utterance than the expression of the belief, it seems that he can maintain a distinctive and non-subjectivist position.

Possible strategies for making such an argument could be to appeal to the inferential relations of moral utterances. In fact, it is at this very point that Jackson and Pettit seem to simply misrepresent Blackburn's position. In the section from *Spreading the word* to which Jackson and Pettit refer, Blackburn explicitly takes up the possibility that utterances or terms, such as the pejorative 'kraut', combine evaluative content with truth-conditional descriptive content, and he emphasizes that the expressivist need not subscribe to the idea that the terms he describes as expressions of desire-like attitudes cannot also be conceived of as expressions of descriptive beliefs. Blackburn's reason for making this claim is not that he wants to advance a hybrid version of expressivism or distinguish between thin and thick moral predicates. The point he wants to make is rather that the crucial question is not whether an utterance expresses beliefs or desire-like attitudes in some sense of that word, but which one of the expressed states of mind "gives the role of the saying"[101]. In accordance with these considerations, Blackburn considers it to be sufficient for the expressivist

---

[101] Blackburn 1984, 170.

if he can argue that desire-like attitudes provide the "*distinctive* meaning"[102] of moral utterances.

Certain remarks made in direct response to Jackson suggest that something like this is still Blackburn's view. According to Blackburn's reply to Jackson, the expressivist can maintain a distinctive position by relying on the "distinctive inferential role"[103] that we accord to moral utterances. We do not, for example, think that somebody who utters the sentence 'Hitler was a good thing' is right simply in virtue of the fact that he himself has a positive attitude towards Hitler – which is what we should be doing if the meaning of the utterance essentially consisted in the report of this attitude. However, if this is the main point behind Blackburn's expressivism, then it seems that Jackson and Pettit attribute to Blackburn a more restrictive position regarding the expression of descriptive beliefs than he actually embraces.

There is also a problem with the way in which Jackson and Pettit reply to Ayer's claim that we can express feelings without reporting them. As we have seen, Jackson and Pettit basically concede this point, but argue that what may be a correct description of ejaculations or exclamations such as 'boo' or 'hooray' is not a correct description of moral utterances. The problem is that, in claiming that exclamations do not report attitudes but merely suggest them, Jackson and Pettit seem to become unfaithful to their own broad understanding of what it is to report an attitude. If 'suggesting' that one has an attitude does not count as reporting it (in the sense Jackson and Pettit consider damaging to expressivism), then it is not clear why the expressivist should not be able to escape Jackson and Pettit's challenge by employing their own distinction and arguing that moral utterances may *suggest* that the speaker has certain attitudes (by implicature or by some other kind of linguistic convention) but not *report* them.

The reason why Jackson and Pettit do not further consider this possibility is that they treat 'suggesting an attitude' as a weaker form of *expressing* an attitude, not as a weaker form of reporting an attitude. Thus they claim that in order to rely on the exclamation analogue, expressivists have to take the view that moral utterances "serve only in a very loose fashion to signal the presence of the attitudes they express"[104]. However, if this is what is meant by saying that words 'suggest' certain attitudes of the speaker, then Jackson and Pettit's previous claim that exclamations such as 'boo' or 'hooray' merely suggest attitudes seems to seriously understate the role of desire-like attitudes with regard to

---

[102] Blackburn 1984, 170.
[103] Blackburn 2001b, 30.
[104] Jackson/Pettit 1998, 247.

such exclamations. To use Jackson and Pettit's own example, 'boo' and 'hooray' do not seem to merely 'signal the presence of certain attitudes in a very loose fashion'. They seem to express them in a way that makes it appropriate to think that expressing these attitudes is what the linguistic meaning of 'boo' and 'hooray' is all about. Accordingly, it is far from being clear that Jackson and Pettit are right to claim that there are no clear-cut linguistic conventions governing the use of such exclamation words. However, if this is not the right way of drawing a line between exclamations and moral utterances, why should the pure expressivist admit that the crucial point of Ayer's analogy is mistaken?

If the somewhat subtler understanding of the role of desire and belief developed in presenting Blackburn's position is the right way to conceive of pure expressivism, then the question to be answered in response to Jackson and Pettit's challenge is not whether the pure expressivist can deny that moral utterances report the attitudes of the speaker in a broad sense of that word. It rather is whether the pure expressivist has a sound basis for claiming that moral utterances, even if they may *both* express desire-like attitudes *and* reporting beliefs, are *primarily* expressions of desire-like attitudes such that a speaker subjectivist analysis of these utterances is inappropriate.

The problem of speaker subjectivist analyses to which Blackburn alludes in his response to Jackson is, of course, the classic problem of accounting for moral agreement and disagreement and, as I have already indicated, the same issue provides Stevenson with his reasons for thinking that his hybrid analysis of moral utterances is distinct from, and superior to, speaker subjectivism.[105] It needs to be emphasized, however, that Jackson and Pettit explicitly confront this issue and argue that expressivism does *not* have any advantages over speaker subjectivism when it comes to explaining moral agreement and disagreement because the speaker subjectivist can ultimately rely on all the resources the expressivist relies on. Moreover, even some critics of Jackson and Pettit, most notably James Dreier, have conceded that Jackson and Pettit's defence of this particular idea is plausible.[106] In order to see whether the argument from moral agreement and disagreement provides a sound basis for defending the distinctiveness and superiority of pure expressivism, or whether other arguments are required, we should, therefore, assess Jackson and Pettit's idea of how even the speaker subjectivist can plausibly account for moral agreement and disagreement.

---

[105] That speaker subjectivism cannot make sense of moral disagreement is also the view of many non-expressivists. See, for example, already Ross 1930/2002, 83.

[106] See Dreier 2004b, 90. For a recent systematic discussion of the nature of moral disagreement and the constraints it imposes on plausible analyses of moral language, see Padel 2020.

In my view, there are actually two different ideas at work here, one of which is suggested rather than fully developed by Jackson and Pettit. Their more explicit argument amounts to the claim that the speaker subjectivist can explain moral agreement and disagreement by locating it, not so much in the linguistic expression of desire-like attitudes, but in the psychological fact that these attitudes are present in two speakers who, for instance, are discussing the moral status of abortion. Thus, to take the example of moral disagreement, Jackson and Pettit claim that once we admit that there is such a thing as 'disagreement in attitude', then the speaker subjectivist approach can make use of this idea as well because there can be no doubt that two speakers uttering 'abortion is wrong' and 'abortion is not wrong', or even their speaker subjectivist translations 'I disapprove of abortion' and 'I do not disapprove of abortion', have different attitudes with regard to abortion. Moreover, these adverse attitudes not only account for the initial disagreement of the two speakers but also explain why, as Stevenson emphasizes, their disagreement can persist even if the speakers come to fully agree in their descriptive beliefs about abortion.

However, in contrast to Dreier, I do not think that this speaker subjectivist way of accounting for moral disagreement is plausible after all. As Jackson and Pettit explicitly emphasize, their argument commits us to the view that moral disagreement is "a psychological phenomenon"[107]. On this interpretation, the production of sentences makes our disagreement public, but "it does not create them"[108]. Even if we accept the latter point and concede that *some* kind of disagreement must have already been present before two speaker can expound different views on abortion by way of an explicit argument, it seems that their discussion creates a new kind of disagreement or takes their disagreement to another level rather than just making it public. Our ordinary understanding of verbal disputes is that the linguistic statements made by the parties are incompatible with one another and that, as a bystander, we may subscribe to the statements of one of the parties, but cannot subscribe to both statements at the same time.

Moreover, if Jackson and Pettit's psychological account of disagreement were correct, we would have to conclude that two people who have never expressed their views on abortion to one another, and perhaps never even met one another, disagree *in the same way* as people who are having an explicit argument about abortion. The only difference between the two cases Jackson and Pettit's account can allow for is that the two people having an explicit argument

---

[107] Jackson/Pettit 1998, 251.
[108] Jackson/Pettit 1998, 251.

know that they have different attitudes towards abortion whereas people who never had such an argument with one another can only speculate about this. However, this seems to defy our ordinary experience of explicit moral disagreement which is not simply one of two individuals exposing their previously held attitudes, but rather one of different statements or speech-acts colliding with one another.

There is, however, a second strategy for arguing that the speaker subjectivist can mimic the expressivist's appeal to disagreement in attitude, and this strategy is at least suggested by Jackson and Pettit as well. The crucial idea is to argue that we cannot report our attitudes (in the way the speaker subjectivist analysis has it) without expressing it at the same time. As we have seen, this is a concession made by Ayer, and Jackson and Pettit explicitly subscribe to Ayer's view.[109] However, if every report of one's attitude regarding abortion *a fortiori* counts as expressing this attitude, then two speakers uttering 'abortion is wrong' and 'abortion is not wrong' would not only *have* different attitudes towards abortion, but would linguistically *express* these attitudes even on the speaker subjectivist reading. Moreover, as long as the speaker subjectivist can make good on the idea that the reports 'I disapprove of abortion' and 'I do not disapprove of abortion' provide the primary semantic meaning of the relevant utterances, he might be able to claim that his analysis, though employing of the expressivist machinery, remains a speaker subjectivist analysis after all.

In my view, this is clearly the more promising strategy for the speaker subjectivist to pursue because it can accommodate the way in which we take the disagreement of two parties explicitly arguing with one another to be essentially constituted by what they say (rather than what they feel). However, it is not clear whether the central claim – i.e., that it is impossible to report an attitude without expressing it – withstands scrutiny. We may think, for example, of cases in which speakers report their attitudes in some kind of distanced or detached manner. A penitent sitting in a confessional box, self-consciously and guilt-ridden confessing to the priest that he desires his neighbours wife and asking for absolution, or an objectophile telling his psychiatrist that he likes having sex with his hammond organ, but doing so out of the desperate wish that the psychiatrist can somehow cure him from this strange desire. In both cases, it is clear that the speakers report their desire-like attitudes, but far less clear whether they also express them in the relevant way. In accordance with this, it is not clear whether two speakers that report adverse attitudes must necessarily disagree in the way presupposed by the second argumentative strategy. If one person

---

[109] See Jackson/Pettit 1998, 243.

reports one of her attitudes in a kind of detached manner, saying, for example, 'I like cheese with nutella!' in a self-conscious way, and a second person responds to this by saying, 'Well, fortunately, I do not like that', it seems doubtful whether we should conceive of this as a case of genuine disagreement. Not only can the two sentences be true at the same time. The speakers even seem to agree that liking cheese with nutella is a preference or desire that one should better not have.

The important point with regard to moral utterances is that we cannot imagine a speaker sincerely uttering the sentence 'abortion is wrong' to have a similar distanced or detached stance towards what he says. As pure expressivists such as Blackburn and Gibbard have repeatedly emphasized, an important feature of moral utterances is the feature of *endorsement*, the fact that the speaker identifies with what he says, and it seems that this feature is not well-preserved in a subjectivist analysis which primarily conceives of moral utterances as reports. Accordingly, the case of moral disagreement seems to crucially differ from the nutella and cheese-example. Even if we assume that two speakers uttering 'abortion is wrong' and 'abortion is not wrong' are on friendly terms with one another and agree that the moral status of abortion is a very complex and tricky business where no easy answers are to be had, the fact remains that their ultimate evaluations are opposed to one another and are underwritten by the two speakers in a way that any plausible metaethical analysis needs to account for.

There are two options for the pure expressivist who wants to accommodate the connection between moral utterances and endorsement and put pressure on the speaker subjectivist at this point. The first option is to define the expression relation in a narrow way and to argue that we only express desire-like attitudes with an utterance if we endorse or underwrite these attitudes by making our utterance. According to this view, self-conscious reports of the kind 'I like cheese with nutella!' would describe an attitude, but not express it.

It is important to note here that the expressivist would not thereby become unfaithful to his general mentalist framework or argue in contradiction to the parity thesis. He can still allow that reports of the above kind are expressions of *belief* because the relevant endorsement would pertain to belief as well, and while a person saying 'I like cheese with nutella!' may not underwrite her positive attitude towards cheese with nutella, she certainly underwrites the belief that she has this attitude. In order to account for the endorsement we find in moral disagreement, the speaker subjectivist would then have to concede that two speakers uttering 'abortion is wrong' and 'abortion is not wrong' do not express attitudes *simply in virtue of* reporting them and to claim that we have independent reasons for seeing them as underwriting their attitudes towards abortion by making their utterances. However, it seems that, in order to be able to make this claim, the speaker subjectivist needs to give up his subjectivist analysis of the primary meaning of the two sentences.

The second option for the pure expressivist would be to admit that even reports of the above self-conscious kind are expressions of desire-like attitudes, but to emphasize that the desire-like attitudes they express are significantly different from the attitudes expressed by moral utterances. A natural idea, which we find in both Blackburn and Gibbard, is that the desire-like attitudes expressed by moral utterances are higher-order attitudes (or complexes of attitudes that involve such higher-order attitudes). Once we conceive of the attitudes expressed by 'abortion is wrong' and 'abortion is not wrong' along these lines, it seems that we can plausibly explain why moral utterances work differently than mere attitude-reports. The question to be asked, however, is whether the speaker subjectivist can employ this strategy as well. The ordinary speaker subjectivist analysis does not put any restrictions on the attitudes reported by the speaker and, as a result, cannot account for moral disagreement in the above manner. Yet, a more sophisticated speaker subjectivist analysis could consist in the claim that the attitude reported by a speaker making a moral utterance is not just any old attitude, but a higher-order attitude (or a complex of attitudes including higher-order attitudes). Once the meaning of 'abortion is wrong' is taken to be something like 'I have a negative higher-order attitude towards abortion' or 'I disapprove of abortion (which means that I have a negative attitude towards abortion which I approve of)', the subjectivist might be able to explain moral disagreement in a way that leaves the speaker subjectivist status of his analysis intact.

For this reason, it seems that the pure expressivist, if he wants to stick to the view that expressivists can explain moral disagreement in a way the subjectivist cannot, should rather choose the first of the two options, and in the following section, I will return to the question of whether the presupposed interpretation of the expression relation is a viable one. Yet, apart from moral agreement and disagreement, there are other aspects of moral utterances and their inferential relations to which the pure expressivist may appeal in order to argue that the distinctive meaning of moral utterances is only preserved in an expressivist and not in a speaker subjectivist analysis. For example, as we have already seen, hybrid theories that conceive of the descriptive content of moral utterances as speaker-relative not only tend to have certain problems with moral disagreement, but also with attitude ascriptions, and it seems that something like this should also hold for the non-hybrid, speaker-relative account provided by ordinary speaker subjectivism.

Also, it has been argued that, on Jackson and Pettit's view, certain inferences come out as valid inferences that should not do so, such as the following inference provided by Dreier:

Abortion Argument

Abortion is wrong.
Therefore, I have at least one moral attitude.[110]

Another argument provided by Dreier is that the speaker subjectivist analysis paints a false picture of the evidence to which we may appeal in support of our moral utterances. If 'abortion is wrong' primarily meant 'I disapprove of abortion', then it seems that I should be able to cite something like 'I was brought up Catholic' as evidence for my claim that abortion is wrong. As Dreier rightly emphasizes, however, my Catholic upbringing simply seems to be the wrong kind of evidence for the claim I am making.[111]

The reason for thinking that some such argument against Jackson and Pettit (or a combination of arguments) must be successful is that Jackson and Pettit's challenge, if correct, would prove too much and ultimately lead into some implausible kind of global speaker subjectivism. As Jackson and Pettit themselves argue, accepting their Lockean explanation of meaning not only leads to the concession that moral utterances report certain beliefs of the speaker, but to the concession that commands, such as 'Shut the door!', do so as well. If we accept Jackson and Pettit's general line of argument, there seems to be no way to deny that speakers have learned to use 'Shut the door!' only when they believe that they have the desire that the door be shut, and that they express this belief whenever they use the sentence. We can add that the argument can also be extended to questions: can we deny that, in learning how to ask questions, we have learned to ask a question regarding a certain issue only when we believe to be in a particular mental state with regard to the issue, namely a state of ignorance, doubt or uncertainty? If not, doesn't this mean that questions express beliefs, namely the belief that I, the speaker, am in a state of ignorance, doubt or uncertainty with regard to the object of my question?

If we follow Jackson and Pettit's argument all the way through, the above considerations commit us to the claim that commands and questions have truth conditions (which many critics have found implausible enough to reject Jackson and Pettit's analysis straightaway). They also commit us to viewing com-

---

110 Dreier 2004b, 91.
111 See Dreier 2004b, 90.

mands and questions as reports and therefore to being speaker subjectivists about commands and questions. However, this just seems inappropriate because we would thereby even out crucial differences in the meaning and the communicative function of commands, questions and ordinary assertions. It seems that Jackson and Pettit's argument would ultimately force us to conclude that, in using language, we would never do anything other than report our mental states to each other. This, however, seems to make the communicative behaviour of human beings self-referential in an inadmissible way. Yet, if these problems justify interpreting commands and question in a non-subjectivist manner in order to salvage their primary meaning or their primary communicative role, then it is not clear why such an interpretation should be unavailable for moral utterances and why the expressivist should not be in a position to employ it in order to defend his distinctive position against the speaker subjectivist.

I conclude, therefore, that the concession that moral utterances may, in some sense of that word, express reporting beliefs of the speaker does not let pure expressivism collapse into speaker subjectivism or into a version of hybrid expressivism. Of course, whether pure expressivists can ultimately defend the view that moral utterances only express beliefs which are devoid of any systematic importance is still an open question. However, the burden of proof clearly lies with the hybrid expressivist who wants to embrace the positive claim that such beliefs are in fact expressed by moral utterances and who thereby incurs the responsibility of providing a specification of those beliefs which allows us to critically assess his position.

8 Relational expressivism and neo-expressivism

There are two further variants of expressivism which have recently been forwarded as a result of the debate over hybrid expressivism and which I want to briefly address in order to conclude my overview of the most important variations on the basic expressivist theme. The emergence of the first position, *relational expressivism*, can directly be traced back to the problems encountered by hybrid expressivists in trying to identify the descriptive content of moral utterances. Proponents of relational expressivism include Ridge, who has recently given up his hybrid approach to moral utterances in favour of a relationalist account, and Teemu Toppinen.[112] The possible virtues of relational expressivism have also

---

[112] See Toppinen 2013; and Ridge 2014, 7 f.

been emphasized by Mark Schroeder.[113] The crucial idea of relational expressivism is to conceive of the mental states conventionally expressed by moral utterances neither as beliefs nor as desires nor as hybrid states constituted by a belief *and* a desire, but as *relational* states: as relations, that is, between a descriptive belief and a desire-like attitude. According to this idea, moral utterances presuppose, by way of conventional meaning, that the speaker has both a relevant belief and a relevant desire which are suitably related to one another. However, the meaning is not constituted by the *content* of these beliefs and desires, but by the more general relation between the two.

The obvious advantage of this approach in comparison to ordinary hybrid expressivism is that there is no need to specify any constant non-speaker-relative content of the descriptive belief. Relational expressivists can allow that the standards employed by different speakers using moral terms may vary because they do not claim that the content of the speakers' beliefs are typically conveyed by the speakers' utterances. What is being conveyed is only that the speakers are in a relational state of mind with regard to the object they evaluate, and that this relational state has some descriptive belief and some kind of pro- or con-attitude as its *relata*. Since this relational state can be instantiated by quite different beliefs and desire-like attitudes, the relational expressivist can dispense with an identification of *the* descriptive content of moral utterances and hence solve the problems discussed above by avoiding them in the first place.

It should be noted, however, that this solution is not so much achieved *within* the hybrid framework but rather at the expense of it. By conceiving of the mental state expressed by moral sentences as one relational state, the relational expressivist gives up on the central idea of hybrid theories and introduces a new paradigm. Moreover, it seems that, in order not to collapse into either pure expressivism or naturalism, relational expressivism must not conceive of the relational state expressed by moral utterances as either desire-like or belief-like. However, if the relational mental state expressed by moral utterances is neither a belief nor a desire-like attitude itself, then it seems that the standard definition of expressivism cannot straightforwardly be applied to relational expressivist accounts. Moreover, an idea which we could still attribute to the hybrid expressivist, namely that there is a crucial asymmetry between the belief-element and the desire-element of moral utterances in favour of the latter, does not seem to be one we can easily attribute to an account that conceives of the distinctive meaning of moral utterances in terms of a relation between two such elements. However, if there is no way within the relationalist framework to reconstruct the dis-

---

[113] See Schroeder 2013.

tinctive meaning of moral utterances in terms of desire-like attitudes *rather* than descriptive beliefs, then it is not clear why we should think of the relational approach as an example of expressivism rather than an example of naturalism.

Moreover, although relational expressivism may appear like a natural advancement of hybrid expressivism and the solution to all its problems, it faces problems of its own. The main question to be asked here is how exactly we should conceive of relational mental states in psychological terms and whether any such states will figure in our best overall theory of human psychology. Moreover, once we allow that, for any two mental states that stand in a relevant relation with one another, we may simply postulate an additional relational mental state over and above these two mental states, it seems that we can quite easily multiply the relational states that we may attribute to a speaker uttering a moral sentence. Not only does our picture of the human mind then become quite a crowded one. The question also becomes: why should we view moral sentences as expressions of a relation that holds between an ordinary descriptive belief and a pro- or con-attitude and not, for example, as expressions of a more complex relation that holds between two relational states, or between relational and non-relational states?

It might be argued that the relational expressivist can avoid at least some of these problems by restricting his relationalist analysis to moral *utterances:* while moral utterances express relational states rather than ordinary beliefs and desires, the relational expressivist might argue, moral thinking is constituted, not by relational mental states, but by the relevant beliefs and desires themselves. The problem with this idea, however, is that expressivism is now usually understood as a theory about *both* moral language *and* moral thought.[114] In fact, as Schroeder himself emphasizes, to provide a plausible account of moral thought that coheres with the proposed account of moral language and allows for a crucial continuity between private moral judgements and public moral utterances is something we should expect from any plausible theory of moral language. Therefore, once the relational expressivist drives a wedge between these two aspects of our moral practice and forwards a psychologistic semantics that interprets moral utterances as expressions of mental states *different* from the ones that actually constitute moral thinking, expressivism seems to lose much of its attractiveness.

The task for relational expressivists, then, is to show that their idea of a relational mental state is more than just an *ad hoc* epicycle meant to solve the linguistic problems of hybrid expressivism and that it can form an integral part of a

---

114 See Schroeder 2008a, 4 and 151f.

more comprehensive theory of moral judgement that is both psychologically and semantically adequate. It seems fair to say that relational expressivists are still working on this task, even though one can hardly avoid the impression that the psychological side of things is being neglected. Without further entering into the discussion of the existing accounts, we can at least conclude that the view that is sometimes suggested by proponents of relational expressivism, namely that the move to relationalism comes at no cost at all because relational expressivism offers all the virtues of hybrid expressivism without any of its vices, is misleading. The appeal to relational mental states clearly imposes burdens on the expressivist that might ultimately outweigh its benefits.

The second position that has more recently emerged from the debate over expressivism is *neo-expressivism* as endorsed by Dorit Bar-On, Matthew Chrisman and James Sias.[115] The reason why neo-expressivism appears even less to be an example of expressivism is that neo-expressivists reject a mentalist approach to linguistic meaning and claim that we should conceive of the meaning of moral utterances in more conservative terms, namely in terms of propositions.[116]

The key idea of neo-expressivism is that we need to distinguish between two kinds of expression, 'a-expression' and 's-expression'. While neo-expressivists concede that we might want to conceive of the *act* of making a moral utterance as an expression of a mental state, they reject the idea that we should conceive of the semantic meaning of the *sentences* being uttered in terms of the expression of mental states.[117] Therefore, while neo-expressivists allow that moral discourse has a distinctive expressive function, they claim that moral sentences have propositions as their semantic content. Moreover, in a more recent publication, Bar-On, Chrisman and Sias explicitly claim that neo-expressivism is itself neutral on the question of whether or not the mental states a-expressed by moral utterances are belief-like or desire-like and suggest that their view is independent of Humean accounts of motivation.[118] While particular variants of neo-expressivism might share the fundamental psychological assumptions defended by expressivists such as Blackburn, then, they might also not. Moreover, even those versions of neo-expressivism which do share the assumptions, would not thereby come to embrace the traditional expressivist approach to *meaning*. Thus, unless we want to distance ourselves from the traditional idea that, as a metaethical position, expressivism is first and foremost a position concerning

---

115 See Bar-On/Chrisman 2009; and Bar-On/Chrisman/Sias 2015.
116 See, in particular, Bar-On/Chrisman/Sias 2015, 224 f.
117 See Bar-On/Chrisman 2009, 136 f.
118 Bar-On/Chrisman/Sias 2015, 244 f.

the meaning of moral utterances or moral terms, there do not seem to be many reasons for conceiving of neo-expressivism as a genuinely expressivist position and to include it as such a position in what follows.

9 Summary

The purpose of this chapter was to thoroughly examine an idea which has dominated most of the more recent discussion of expressivism, namely that moral utterances express *both* beliefs *and* desires. The existence of such 'hybrid' analyses of moral utterances raises the question of how to analytically distinguish between hybrid variants of expressivism on the one hand and hybrid variants of naturalism and non-naturalism on the other. It also raises the question of whether the standard definition of expressivism introduced in chapter 2 is spacious enough to accommodate the former.

The aim of section 1 was to address these two questions. I argued that hybrid theories deserve to be classified as examples of hybrid expressivism only if they (a) postulate a certain asymmetry between the belief and the desire expressed by a moral utterance and somehow privilege the latter, and (b) conceive of the belief in question as a non-moral belief or belief with a non-moral descriptive content. Moreover, I claimed that, once we draw the distinction between hybrid expressivism and non-expressivist hybrid theories in this way, the standard definition of expressivism is still applicable since we can draw upon condition (a) in order to claim that, even for the hybrid expressivist, moral utterances express desires "rather" than beliefs.

In the second section, I introduced what has traditionally been taken to present the main obstacle to expressivist analyses of moral language: the problem of accounting for uses of moral predicates in embedded or unasserted contexts standardly referred to as the 'Frege-Geach problem'. After describing the additional resources for dealing with this problem made available by the hybrid move, I pointed out that the hybrid solution to the 'Frege-Geach problem' is dependent upon further conditions. As has been shown by Mark Schroeder, the solution depends on the fact that the desire-like attitude expressed by moral utterances is taken to relate to a more general descriptive property rather than to the particular object that is being evaluated. Finally, I emphasized that even for versions of hybrid expressivism satisfying this condition a residual challenge remains, namely to explain why we may legitimately take conditional and other unasserted uses of to express non-cognitive attitudes at all, and I expressed doubts as to whether the analogy between moral predicates and pejoratives typically appealed to in this context can provide such an explanation.

In section 3, I made clear that hybrid expressivism is not a recent invention but something we already find in Stevenson and Hare. In defending this view, I demonstrated that arguments for not including the two among the hybrid expressivists, like the ones provided by Michael Ridge, fail to do justice to Stevenson's and Hare's relevant statements. In contrast to what is claimed by Ridge, Hare could be shown to conceive of descriptive meaning as a necessary element of typical moral utterances, which is why it would be misleading to classify him as a proponent of pure rather than expressivism. Answering the question of whether Stevenson ought to be classified as hybrid expressivist was hindered by the fact that he is ambiguous on the issue of descriptive meaning, claiming both that there are, and that there are not, instances in which moral language is used in a purely emotive fashion, that is, without any descriptive meaning whatsoever. As in the case of Hare, however, it seemed impossible to deny that Stevenson embraces hybrid expressivism at least with regard to some key uses of ethical terms.

Both Hare and Stevenson conceive of the descriptive element of moral utterances as speaker-relative, and the aim of section 4 was to describe the serious problems that arise for such versions of hybrid expressivism. Simpler speaker-relative accounts, like the ones of Hare and Stevenson but also the one recently suggested by John Eriksson, give rise to the question of why we may conceive of the descriptive properties to which a speaker's non-cognitive attitude refers as part of the meaning of his utterance at all, given that these properties may be unknown to his audience and are not conveyed in any way but what he says. More sophisticated accounts, like the ones forwarded by Ridge and Barker, try to overcome this problem by conceiving of the descriptive belief as speaker-relative but nevertheless constant belief, something to which I referred as a *de dicto* belief. However, since the beliefs in question contain indexical references to the speaker, the accounts could be shown to incur serious problems of their own, and the same could was true of Stevenson's 'first pattern of analysis' according to which the meaning of 'This is wrong' can be given as 'I disapprove of X; do so as well!'. All three accounts turned out to be unable to deal with so-called 'attitude ascriptions' and, as a result, cannot provide a satisfactory account of certain forms of moral *modus ponens*. Moreover, both Barker's and Ridge's approach face the problem of adequately accounting for cases of moral disagreement. In this latter context, I also addressed the fact that many moral utterances express all-things-considered judgements and pointed to certain problems which potentially arise from this fact for both hybrid and pure variants of expressivism.

The upshot of section 4, then, was that the hybrid strategy can only successfully be pursued if the expressivist manages to identify a non-speaker-relative belief that is conventionally expressed by moral utterances. After arguing that subscribing to a non-speaker-relative account deprives the expressivist of much of his leverage against the naturalist, I critically reviewed the only fully-fleshed out non-speaker-relative account that has so far been forwarded, namely Oliver Hallich's analysis of ought sentences. I argued that the systematic arguments provided in support of the Hallich's proposal tend to beg the question and that the analysis cannot account for the possibility of 'original moral claims', or can do so only at the expense of ultimately collapsing into a version of pure expressivism.

In section 6, I revisited the idea that the descriptive belief expressed by moral utterances could be a *de dicto* belief and discussed whether we may conceive of the supposed descriptive meaning in terms of a general supervenience claim, something that has been suggested by Michael Smith and John Eriksson. The initial problem with this strategy was to specify the relevant belief without invoking any normative concepts. Once we did so, however, and conceived of the relationship between belief and desire, not in terms of 'warrant' or 'reasons', but in explanatory or causal terms, we were again left with a speaker-relative belief which could not serve the crucial functions the hybrid expressivist wants to assign to it: though the resulting account had less of a problem with moral disagreement than the accounts of Barker and Ridge, it encountered the same problems with attitude ascriptions and incurred even further difficulties with solving the 'Frege-Geach problem'.

The conclusion of my review of the existing speaker-relative and non-speaker-relative accounts was, therefore, that there are indeed some descriptive beliefs which we legitimately ascribe to somebody making a moral utterance. Yet, these beliefs cannot give the hybrid expressivist what he is after since they cannot be claimed to play any systematic role in moral argument and moral deliberation. It was for this very reason, however, that Smith's further objection according to which the supervenience of the moral on the non-moral has every plausible version pure expressivism collapse a form of hybrid expressivism could be rejected.

The rejection of Smith's objection led over to the discussion of a similar worry raised by Frank Jackson and Philip Pettit, namely that expressivism must necessarily collapse into a hybrid variant of speaker subjectivism. According to Jackson and Pettit, moral language could only have acquired the function the expressivist assigns to it if speakers learned to use the predicates supposedly expressive of the relevant non-cognitive states when they are actually in those states and recognize that they are. If, however, the linguistic expression of the relevant attitudes is so closely associated with recognizing that one has them, then it is hard to avoid the conclusion that, in addition to expressing the attitude, a speaker making a moral utterance also expresses the belief that he has it – or so Jackson and Pettit argue.

My critical discussion focused on the question of whether the expressivist needs to avoid the latter conclusion to begin with or whether he can actually concede that speakers uttering a moral sentence express both a desire and a reporting belief, without thereby becoming unfaithful to their expressivist approach. Drawing on the ideas of the former section, I argued that the expressivist can indeed maintain a distinctive, non-subjectivist position as long as he avoids attributing any systematic importance to the belief in question. By once more looking at the works of Ayer, Stevenson and Blackburn, it could be shown that this understanding is in fact suggested by some of the classic expressivists themselves, whose relevant statements Jackson and Pettit tend to neglect or misrepresent. Moreover, apart from the fact that Jackson and Pettit's argument fails to do justice to the views of some leading proponents of expressivism, it could also be shown to suffer from incoherences and to ultimately lead into an implausible form of global speaker subjectivism, according to which we must not only view moral utterances as self-reports but likewise questions and commands.

The conclusion emerging from sections 1 to 7, therefore, was that hybrid expressivism is a failed enterprise because the beliefs we may plausibly be taken to be conventionally expressed by moral utterances are ones which fail to give the hybrid expressivist what he really wants. In the final section, I looked at two approaches that have recently been forwarded as alternatives to the previously reviewed versions of hybrid expressivism: relational expressivism, as endorsed by Teemu Toppinen and Michael Ridge, and neo-expressivism, as endorsed by Dorit Bar-On, Matthew Chrisman and James Sias.

I argued that these alternative approaches cannot help the hybrid expressivist out of his predicament, or can do so only by forcing him to abandon his expressivism. This was particularly clear in the case of neo-expressivism, since neo-expressivists reject the mentalist approach to semantic meaning. However, even in the case of relational expressivism, which is the view that the mental state conventionally expressed by moral utterances is a relational state that holds between a non-cognitive attitude and an (unspecified) descriptive belief, it was not at all obvious why to conceive of the proposal as a version of hybrid expressivism rather than a specific version of pure expressivism or even naturalism. In addition, I argued that the proposal faces challenges of its own, most importantly the challenge of making sense of relational mental states in more robust psychological terms and the challenge of accounting for the continuity between moral thought and moral utterances.

The overall conclusion of chapter 5, then, was expressivists should resist the hybrid move and that the possible value and superiority of the expressivist analysis hinges on whether pure expressivism can ultimately been made to work. This conclusion tends to reinforce the importance of psychological questions emphasized in previous chapters. If hybrid expressivism presented a viable option, one would certainly expect the expressivist to provide the kind of robust distinction between beliefs and desires demanded at the end of chapter 4 and one would also expect him to provide a specification of the particular desire-like state expressed by moral utterances. However, since it is the descriptive belief that does most of the work (like, for example, explaining moral *modus ponens*) and since the belief provides a propositional content in terms of which the desire-like state can be specified, the relevant task might not be so demanding after all. If, however, pure expressivism is the only viable option, then the question about the exact nature of the expressed mental state retains its full force.

The moral attitude problem and the expression relation

Any overview of the previous debate over expressivism would be incomplete if it failed to include a brief survey of the main challenges which, apart from the 'Frege-Geach problem', have been raised against expressivism in the past. One such challenge, which owes its prominent standing in the more recent debate to Mark Schroeder, is to provide an appropriate account of the so-called 'expression relation'. Having a clear grasp of this challenge and the attempts to deal with it is not only important for understanding the current state of the debate over expressivism. It will also prepare the discussion of the psychological implications of expressivism that follows in the next chapter because it will help us to see why the expressivist incurs important commitments in the philosophy of mind, even if his initial aim may be to provide an analysis of the meaning of moral utterances.

The second objection I will discuss in the present chapter, and which is usually referred to as the 'moral attitude problem', is even more closely related to the psychological aspects of expressivism. The reason for addressing this objection first is that it poses such a fundamental challenge that expressivism would not even get off the ground if there were no way to get around the objection. Discussing the problem, therefore, seems important in order to dispel the impression that the expressivist relies on notions of which he cannot possibly make sufficient sense.

1 The specification challenge and the open question argument

The 'moral attitude problem', christened by Alexander Miller,[1] comes in a weaker and a stronger form. In its weaker form, the objection simply amounts to the claim that expressivists have not, so far, provided an appropriate specification of the non-cognitive mental state that is supposedly being expressed by moral utterances and, in fact, not even tried sufficiently hard to tackle the issue. Proponents of this view include, for instance, David Merli and Russ Shafer-Landau.[2]

---

[1] See Miller 2003, 43 ff.
[2] See Shafer-Landau 2003, 154 f.; and Merli 2008, 30. See also Schroeder who at least claims that expressivists have not provided specifications of the mental state expressed by logically complex moral sentences (see Schroeder 2008a, 8 f.).

1 The specification challenge and the open question argument

In its strong form, the objection amounts to the claim that expressivists must *necessarily* fail with their attempts to provide an appropriate specification of the non-cognitive state in question because they face some kind of dilemma. Either, the objection goes, the expressivist characterizes the non-cognitive state in wholly non-moral terms, for instance as a particular non-moral feeling or emotion. Then the non-cognitive state will not be one that is necessarily linked to moral utterances in the way needed for the expressivist analysis to work. Or, he partly characterizes the mental state in question in moral terms, for instance as a feeling of moral approval or a moral sentiment. Then, however, his specification will either be circular and uninformative or amount to postulating a mysterious *sui generis* state of mind. Apart from Miller himself, proponents of this stronger and potentially more damaging objection include Thomas Baldwin, Michael Smith, Christoph Halbig, Gerhard Ernst and Manfred Harth.[3]

Let us start with the weaker claim. On the face of it, the criticism that expressivists have done too little to specify the non-cognitive state of mind they take to be expressed by moral utterances appears unjustified. There is no lack of descriptions of the state in question in the works of the classic expressivists. If anything, expressivists can be said to have provided us with *too many* specifications and to have thereby ultimately obscured the issue. Ayer simultaneously refers to the non-cognitive state as a 'feeling', an 'emotion', a 'sentiment' and a state of 'approval'.[4] Stevenson predominantly describes it as an 'attitude', but suggests that this more general term is meant to equally cover 'feelings', 'emotions', 'desires', 'wishes' and 'approval' or 'disapproval' or, to be more precise, to refer to the *disposition* to be in all these kinds of mental states.[5]

Hare primarily provides his specifications for the non-cognitive state in his later works. In *The language of morals*, Hare mostly discusses the *problems* associated with further specifying the state in question and highlights certain difficulties with the terms 'approval', 'attitude', 'desire', 'feeling' or 'wish'.[6] In *Moral thinking*, he seems slightly more optimistic that there is a way to informatively describe the non-cognitive state and refers to it as a 'preference' or 'desire',

---

[3] See Baldwin 2001, 9; Smith 2001, 107 ff.; Smith 2002, 157 ff.; Halbig 2007, 234 f.; Ernst 2008, 88 ff.; and Harth 2008, 51 ff. For similar worries concerning expressivism's ability to meet the "specification challenge" (Merli 2008, 30), see d'Arms/Jacobson 1994, 739 f.; Rosen 1998, 389; and Merli 2008, 43. Note, moreover, that the point is already raised by Hare himself (see Hare 1952, 10 ff.) and taken up by Brandt (see Brandt 1959, 222 ff.).
[4] See Ayer 1936/1967, 21, 103, 107 f. and 112.
[5] See Stevenson 1944, 59 f. and 90; Stevenson 1963b, 1 f.; and Stevenson 1963a, 59.
[6] See Hare 1952, 10 ff.

and, more specifically, as a 'universal preference'.[7] Moreover, in *Sorting out ethics*, Hare appears less hostile than before to calling the state an 'attitude of approval' and suggests that we might adopt Stevenson's idea that this attitude is a disposition to have certain feelings and desires.[8]

Blackburn's usage is even more clearly indebted to Stevenson. Blackburn mostly refers to the non-cognitive mental state as an 'attitude' (or 'stance'), but suggests that we might also want to describe the particular instantiations of the relevant mental states by calling them 'feelings', 'sentiments', 'emotions', 'desires', 'appetites' or 'sensibilities'.[9] In fact, in his most extensive discussion of the issue in *Ruling passions*, Blackburn develops the idea of a "staircase of practical and emotional ascent"[10], a "spiral of emotional identifications and demands"[11], that leads from simple likes and dislikes at the bottom of the emotional scale to complex higher-order attitudes at the top, and he suggests, citing Gilbert Ryle, that any appropriate picture of ethics needs to equally include "tempers, habits, dispositions, moods, inclinations, impulses, sentiments, feelings, affections, thoughts, reflections, opinions, principles, prejudices, imaginations and fancies"[12].

In Gibbard's theory, the issue is introduced at two different stages. Since Gibbard's theory is primarily a theory about claims of rationality, the specification challenge first occurs with regard to the non-cognitive mental state that is expressed by non-moral normative utterances of the type 'it is rational to do X' or 'X is the thing to do'. According to Gibbard's original account, we should conceive of this state of mind as a state of 'norm-acceptance' or, more specifically, as a state of accepting a system of norms that permit X.[13] Gibbard also refers to the state of mind as a state of "normative governance"[14] or simply as a "normative judgment"[15]. In the years preceding the publication of *Thinking how to live*, Gibbard has come to describe the non-cognitive states expressed by normative utterances as 'plans' or "states of contingency planning"[16]. However, Gibbard empha-

---

7 See Hare 1981, 107, 185, and 219f.
8 See Hare 1999a, 106f.
9 See Blackburn 1981, 177; Blackburn 1984, 167; Blackburn 1986, 122; Blackburn 1993d, 184f.; Blackburn 1993a, 365; Blackburn 1996, 83; Blackburn 1998, 5 and 68; Blackburn 2001b, 28; Blackburn 2002, 125; Blackburn 2005a, 146; and Blackburn 2006, 149.
10 Blackburn 1998, 9.
11 Blackburn 1998, 9.
12 Blackburn 1998, 13.
13 See Gibbard 1990a, 7 and 86; Gibbard 1990b, 791; and Gibbard 1992a, 202.
14 Gibbard 1993a, 72.
15 Gibbard 1993b, 316.
16 Gibbard 2003, 180.

1 The specification challenge and the open question argument —— 167

sizes that the shift of terminology does not signal a shift of position but merely one of "expository purpose"[17], and in one of his most recent publications, he has reactivated the terminology of 'norm-acceptance'.[18]

The second stage at which the specification of mental states becomes an issue is in the attempt to distinguish moral utterances from other kinds of rationality judgements. According to Gibbard's view, what is distinctive about moral utterances is that they express the acceptance of norms with a specific moral content. Moral utterances express judgements about what moral feelings it is rational to have, and the moral feelings that Gibbard takes to be of prime importance here are guilt and resentment.[19] The norms whose acceptance we express with our moral utterances are therefore conceived of as norms that prescribe guilt and resentment for certain situations (or types of situations).

There has been, then, an abundance of attempts to meet the specification challenge and to describe the non-cognitive mental state expressed by moral utterances with the help of a more specific psychological vocabulary. However, that the objection still has a point is due to two related problems. The first problem is that expressivists have often qualified their specifications. Thus, both Hare and Blackburn, who, as we have seen, describe the non-cognitive attitude expressed by moral utterances as a 'desire', emphasize that they use 'desire' only in a wide sense of that term and that a speaker sincerely uttering a positive moral evaluation of a particular action need not have any desire more narrowly construed to perform the action in question.[20] Similarly, Gibbard, who in his later works predominantly describes the non-cognitive state expressed by normative utterances as a 'plan', has repeatedly emphasized that he is using the term in a somewhat artificial sense that differs from ordinary usage.[21] At least some of the specifications that have been provided in the past, therefore, may seem more informative than they really are because they appeal to established terms of folk psychology but do not use these in accordance with their ordinary meaning. Moreover, one might think that by discharging of their duties in this way, expressivists are really stealing away from it.

We already find worries of this kind in Stephen Toulmin's early critical discussion of emotivism to which Toulmin himself refers as the 'imperative approach'. According to Toulmin, the main mistake of proponents of the imperative approach, such as Ayer, lies in the kind of generalization they try to defend:

---

17 Gibbard 2003, 181.
18 See Gibbard 2015.
19 See, for instance, Gibbard 1990a, 6.
20 See Hare 1981, 185; Blackburn 2001b, 28; and Blackburn 2006, 150.
21 See Gibbard 2006a, 730f.; Gibbard 2011, 35; and Gibbard 2014, 169 and 174ff.

while moral utterances may, on certain occasions, work like exclamations, ejaculations or commands and express feelings or desires, they do not always, or even typically, work this way. Taken literally, therefore, the central thesis of the imperative approach seems false. As Toulmin suggests, however, if the analysis is not literally correct, then we should rather give it up than trying to salvage it by introducing dubious qualifications. In the following passage, which deserves to be quoted at length, Toulmin equally blames all the three approaches he is discussing, namely the 'objectivist', the 'subjectivist' and the 'imperative' approach, for this kind of mistake and suggests that the qualifications employed by their defenders do not really improve their accounts but make them vague and philosophically unsatisfactory:

> Each approach, if taken literally, misrepresents our ethical concepts in a way which cannot be ignored. And in each case, being in a false position to start with, the theorist spends the greater part of his time trying to redeem his initial failure by *ad hoc* modifications [...]. But this is like trying to overcome a mistake in natural history by saying, 'Of course a ram is no *ordinary* bull', instead of admitting that it is not a bull at all and starting afresh. All they can do is elaborate their terminology, in the double hope of hiding their initial mistakes, and of getting their theories to fit our ideas of goodness and rightness in spite of these mistakes. And, in so doing, they make their arguments vague beyond redemption.[22]

The second problem with the available responses to the specification challenge results from the fact that expressivists have typically specified the non-cognitive state of mind with the help of multiple and quite different terms. As we have seen, Ayer, Stevenson and Blackburn all allow for certain variations in the ways in which the non-cognitive 'attitude' expressed by moral utterances is instantiated. As a result, it becomes quite uncertain what kind of particular mental state we may legitimately attribute to a person uttering a sentence like 'abortion is wrong'. However, since it is in virtue of the mental state that, according to expressivism, moral utterances acquire their meaning, it is unclear how we can grasp the full meaning of 'abortion is wrong' (as opposed to 'abortion is good' or 'I find the idea of having an abortion disgusting') if the only thing we know about a speaker uttering this sentence is that he expresses some of the many possible examples of a non-cognitive attitude.

The same problem arises from the fact that some expressivists, most notably Blackburn and Gibbard, conceive of the state of mind expressed by moral utterances as a *complex* of non-cognitive mental states, a complex which characteristically involves higher-order attitudes, or attitudes regarding the attitudes of *others*, such as the desire that other individuals have the same kind of attitude

---

22 Toulmin 1970, 61 f.

we have, or even the disposition to express hostility at those who do not concur in our attitudes.[23] The idea that the attitudes associated with moral utterances are partly directed at the behaviour of others is already an integral part of Stevenson's first pattern of analysis which gives the meaning of 'This is wrong' as 'I disapprove of this; do so as well!'.[24] Moreover, Stevenson anticipates Blackburn's and Gibbard's explicit appeal to higher-order attitudes by suggesting that moral attitudes are typically ones we identify with or which we approve of.[25] Yet, while these higher-order and other-regarding attitudes might help to explain why 'abortion is wrong' differs from 'I find the idea of having an abortion disgusting', it seems that we cannot legitimately attribute all elements of such a complex mental state to all speakers sincerely uttering a sentence like 'abortion is wrong'.

For example, it seems a common occurrence today that people making moral utterances shy away from the social-regulatory aspects of morality. It is not unusual nowadays that individuals forward their moral views as if they were a wholly private affair: as something that they hold for themselves but that they would not, of course, expect others to comply with as well. Accordingly, the idea that, say, our moral convictions concerning marital fidelity not only require *us* to abide by certain principles of truthfulness towards our spouses but also entitle or even require us to socially sanction the unfaithfulness of *others* has somewhat fallen in disfavour. There is a high probability that a person showing the latter kind of behaviour would be regarded as a meddler. It is far from clear, therefore, whether the kind of higher-order mental states that Blackburn and Gibbard appeal to in order to capture the claim to objectivity included in moral utterances are ones that we may typically attribute to ordinary speakers. The most we seem entitled to say is that a speaker *ought* to be in this state, where this 'ought', however, is itself a moral or perhaps a rational 'ought' rather than the 'ought' of linguistic convention. Again, then, the accounts provided by expressivists such as Blackburn and Gibbard allow for variations in the states of mind of sincere speakers, which raises the question of how we can explain that moral utterances, such as 'abortion is wrong', have such a fixed and clear-cut meaning.

The underlying reasons for the problems just described are arguably provided by what Miller and other advocates of the 'moral attitude problem' describe as

---

[23] See, for example, Blackburn 1996, 83; Blackburn 1998, 9f. and 68; Blackburn 2001b, 28; Blackburn 2002, 125; ; Blackburn 2006, 150; Gibbard 1990a, 155 and 168ff.; and Gibbard 1992c, 35.
[24] See Stevenson 1944, 21; see also Ayer 1936/1967, 108.
[25] See Stevenson 1963c, 25; and Stevenson 1963a, 59.

the first horn of the expressivist's dilemma: any unambiguous and unqualified specification of the non-cognitive mental state that is supposedly being expressed by moral utterances seems to be vulnerable to counter examples. One of the more recent critiques of expressivism along these lines comes from Michael Smith, who, however, discusses not only moral utterances but normative utterances more generally.[26] As Smith emphasizes, the task of specifying the non-cognitive mental state expressed by normative utterances is complicated by the fact that there is often good reason not to attribute certain desires or aversions to a speaker making a normative utterance. We may easily imagine, for instance, an unwilling addict who claims that it is undesirable to take drugs – and does so in spite of his strong desire to take them. In addition to his desire to take drugs, we can expect the unwilling addict to also have positive feelings or emotions towards taking drugs, for example because he vividly remembers states of happiness caused by his previous drug use. The task for the expressivist, then, becomes the task of making plausible the idea that, despite of these positive desires, emotions and feelings towards taking drugs, the drug addict's normative claim can be said to express his negative desires, emotions or feelings towards taking drugs. In particular, he needs to tell us how these supposedly negative desires, emotions and feelings relate to the addict's positive ones and how the two groups of mental states can coexist with one another.

    The most natural idea is to think that the negative desires, emotions or feelings are higher-order desires, emotions or feelings. However, as we have seen, it is not clear that speakers uttering typical normative sentences always need to have higher-order attitudes that align with their assessment of a particular course of action. In accordance with this, we might want to argue that we can conceive of the unwilling drug addict as not having a higher-order attitude of the appropriate kind. Moreover, appeals to higher-order attitudes notoriously face regress problems. Even if the unwilling addict may have a negative second-order desire, emotion or feeling towards his positive first-order desire, emotion or feeling: can we rule out that he has even higher-order desires, emotions and feelings that, again, speak in favour of taking drugs – and perhaps partly explain his inability to stay sober? Or, if we explicitly concede the possibility of such third- or fourth-order desires, emotions and feelings, can we give good reasons for why his normative utterance expresses his second-order but not his third- or fourth-order desires, emotions and feelings? In a similar vein, Smith argues that a person may stand in some kind of distanced or even critical relationship to her higher-order desires as well, for example because she be-

---

26 For the following, see Smith 2002, 157 ff. See also Smith 2001, 107 ff.

lieves them to be the result of social pressure or indoctrination. In this case, she might think that there really are no good reasons to do or desire what her higher-order desires ask her to do or desire and she might not subscribe to any normative utterance prescribing the behaviour in question. Higher-order desires, emotions or feelings, therefore, seem to be neither necessary nor sufficient for sincerely making moral utterances (or normative utterances in general), which suggests that the appeal to such higher-order mental states will not guarantee that the expressivist can successfully answer the specification challenge.

The vagueness of the standard definition of expressivism, which describes the non-cognitive states of mind expressed by moral utterances as 'desires' or 'desire-like', is not only due to the fact that the term 'expressivism' refers to a family of metaethical theories and is meant to equally apply to the accounts of different authors. It is also due to the fact that even with regard to one single author, there simply is no unambiguous and unqualified specification of the mental state a definition could draw upon. The question is, however, whether such a general, qualified or vague characterization in non-moral terms is sufficient to turn expressivism into an acceptable theory about the meaning of moral language. As I have already emphasized, there are several moral predicates or terms – 'good', 'right', 'ought' – which seem to work quite differently. In the above vague form, expressivism does not provide us with a criterion that would allow us to capture these differences in the meaning of the key moral terms. Instead, it uniformly analyses them as expressions of some kind of non-cognitive desire-like attitude which may, or may not, be a desire, an emotion or a feeling and which may, or may not, include higher-order states of mind, and this seems significantly less than what we should expect of a satisfactory account of linguistic meaning.

The problems with identifying ordinary non-cognitive mental states that can, at the same time, provide moral utterances with their distinctive meaning may be the reason why some expressivists tend to employ, at times at least, overt moral terminology in describing the distinctive states of mind expressed by moral utterances. Thus Ayer refers to the mental states in question as "moral approval or disapproval"[27], as an "ethical feeling"[28] and as "moral sentiments"[29]. Stevenson describes the attitudes expressed by moral utterances as "peculiarly moral"[30] and suggests that the attitudinal dispositions in question manifest themselves in moral sentiments such as guilt, remorse and indignation. Blackburn refers

---

27 Ayer 1936/1967, 21.
28 Ayer 1936/1967, 108.
29 Ayer 1936/1967, 107.
30 Stevenson 1963a, 59. See also Stevenson 1944, 90 ff.

to the relevant 'sensibility' or 'commitment' as an "ethical sensibility"[31] or "ethical commitment"[32]. And Gibbard, as we have already seen, describes the non-cognitive state expressed by normative utterances as a state of norm-acceptance or a "normative judgment"[33]. What needs to be asked, therefore, is whether this can be a legitimate way of securing the distinctiveness of moral meaning or whether, as Miller and other advocates of the 'moral attitude problem' suggest, any appeal to distinctively moral attitudes will have the expressivist impaled on the second horn of a dilemma.

In order to answer this question, we need to strictly distinguish between a couple of different ideas which the advocates of the 'moral attitude problem' tend to run together. The first idea is that, by postulating specific moral attitudes, the expressivist gives up on his metaphysical naturalism and allows for non-natural entities that are all as mysterious as the robust moral properties or facts to which the classic non-naturalist appeals.[34] If this is the idea behind the claim that expressivism faces a dilemma, it seems to me that expressivists need not worry too much about it. Although the mental states postulated by the expressivist in question are specifically moral or *sui generis*, they still are conceived of *as mental states* and hence as ordinary natural facts. Unlike the classic non-naturalist, therefore, the expressivist does not extend the world to any properties or qualities of a different general kind, but simply suggests that some of the psychological phenomena that are part of the natural world deserve to be distinguished from others and categorized in a different way.

However, it has to be admitted that merely emphasizing the psychological and empirical reality of *sui generis* mental states *as* mental states will not completely get the expressivist off the hook. A second idea fuelling the worries of the advocates of the 'moral attitude problem' is the idea that there is no way to mark off these *sui generis* mental states from their non-moral cousins without inadmissibly appealing to specifically moral contents. While one might concede that moral attitudes or moral sentiments, such as guilt or resentment, can themselves be conceived of as straightforward psychological facts or events, one might still worry that we cannot explain the nature of these sentiments without relying on genuinely ethical propositions or robust moral facts or properties. It is a common idea, for example, that the feeling of guilt involves thinking that one has done something wrong, just as the feeling of resentment towards some other person involves thinking that this other person has done something wrong. However,

---

[31] Blackburn 1998, 5.
[32] Backburn 1998, 9.
[33] Gibbard 1993b, 316.
[34] See, d'Arms/Jacobson 1994, 740. See also Baldwin 2001, 9.

if, following the expressivist strategy, we want to explain 'wrongness' in terms of guilt and resentment rather in terms of robust natural or non-natural properties, we seem to get caught up in some kind of vicious circle.

Yet, it is far from clear that the only way to explain the nature of specific moral attitudes is to describe them as attitudes towards moral rightness and wrongness or, for that matter, towards moral goodness or ought-to-be-doneness. To begin with, as I have already pointed out in my discussion of Hare's critique of emotivism, theoretically describing a mental state with the help of certain moral concepts does not imply that a person in this mental state must have these concepts at her disposal as well. In order to feel pain or fear, one does not need to be able to understand the words 'pain' or 'fear' nor to have any sophisticated ideas about what pain and fear are or how they are being caused. Why, then, should the ability to experience particular feelings, which we may want to theoretically describe as 'moral', necessarily presuppose that one possesses the concept 'moral' or the concepts of 'wrongness' or 'ought-to-be-doneness'?

Moreover, even at a more theoretical level, the appeal to specific moral attitudes does not seem to commit us to an acknowledgement of genuine ethical propositions or *sui generis* moral properties or facts. Thus, one might think that the nature of such attitudes can be explained, not by appealing to specific propositional contents, but by appealing to certain *functional* roles these attitudes play within the social life of human beings. In fact, this is just what Gibbard is trying to do when he attempts to justify the idea of a distinctive state of 'norm-acceptance' or 'normative governance' by placing it within a speculative evolutionary story.[35] Moreover, Peter Schulte has recently suggested that we may explain the specific nature of *sui generis* moral attitudes by appealing to formal aspects, such as the fact that these attitudes are universalizable and can be logically combined with other attitudes and embedded in complexes of higher-order attitudes.[36] Finally, Sebastian Köhler in his recent discussion of the 'moral attitude problem' has argued that the expressivist might make use of the kind of network analysis employed by naturalists such as Jackson and Pettit,[37] and identify *sui generis* moral attitudes with the help of folk platitudes surrounding our concept of moral utterance.[38]

It seems, therefore, that the expressivist may resort to the notion of *sui generis* mental states without becoming unfaithful to his own naturalistic enterprise.

---

[35] See Gibbard 1990a, 55 ff.
[36] See Schulte 2010, 168 ff.
[37] See, for example, Jackson/Pettit 2004. See also Jackson 1998, 28 ff.; and Smith 1994a, 36 ff.
[38] See Köhler 2013, 495 ff.

The true import of the 'moral attitude problem', therefore, is neither to be found in the idea that moral attitudes are theoretically mysterious nor in the idea that any conception of such attitudes will necessarily introduce some kind of vicious circularity. Rather, it lies in the fact that the appeal to *sui generis* moral attitudes places the expressivist under the burden of providing a functionalistic theory that can meet two related demands: first, it needs to make *sui generis* moral states of mind conceptually intelligible and provide a sufficient basis for the assumption that these states of mind do in fact exist; and secondly, it needs to demonstrate that explaining the functions in question in terms of non-cognitive attitudes is ultimately more plausible than explaining them in a different way, as, for example, in terms of genuine moral beliefs.

That this latter task might be quite a demanding one is not only implicitly suggested by Köhler who confines himself to the relatively modest assumption that there is some "license for optimism"[39] with regard to the idea that the best psychological theory of moral thinking will ultimately identify the *sui generis* moral states of mind as desire-like attitudes. It is also suggested by Schulte's attempt to account for the nature of moral attitudes in formal terms, given that the aspects to which Schulte crucially appeals, such as universalizability and logical embeddability, are traditionally associated with beliefs rather than desires.

In a similar manner, the expressivist may argue that the first horn of the supposed dilemma does not present him with any insurmountable obstacle, either. What the problems discussed above reveal is not that no explanation of the relevant non-cognitive state in non-moral terms can ever be successful. Rather, it is that an expressivist employing this strategy loses much of his leverage against naturalist analyses of moral utterances: for any non-moral attitude (or complex of non-moral attitudes) that the expressivist appeals to, we may legitimately ask whether a person making a moral utterance necessarily expresses it, which suggests that expressivist analyses that take the specification challenge seriously and provide determinate descriptions of the state of mind expressed by moral utterances might in the end seem no less arbitrary than those naturalist analyses which the expressivist strives to avoid. Yet, if the expressivist refuses to provide any determinate description, he places himself under the burden of having to come up with another explanation for the differences in the meaning of different

---

39 Köhler 2013, 505. It should be noted that Köhler is concerned with the mental states that constitute moral thinking rather than with their linguistic expression. However, the strategy outlined by him can easily be extended to this latter aspect.

moral terms – or would else have failed in trying to provide an appropriate account of the meaning of moral language.

Köhler explicitly defends the prospects of expressivism along these lines, too, suggesting that the expressivist can provide a reductive specification of moral attitudes in non-moral terms by simply piggy-backing on the specification of moral beliefs that is provided by the metaethical naturalist.[40] The underlying idea is that the supposed dilemma set up by the advocates of the 'moral attitude problem' is one that any non-expressivist who wants to explain moral utterances in terms of beliefs faces in about the same way: either, the non-expressivist specifies the beliefs in question in genuinely moral or *sui generis* terms, like the classic non-naturalist who awards these beliefs non-naturalistic moral content; or, he attempts to provide a specification in non-moral terms, then he faces variants of the open question challenge. As Köhler notes, however, naturalists have come up with explanatory strategies in the past in virtue of which this latter challenge is not considered to be as fatal as it previously was taken to be.

One of these strategies is the network style analysis already mentioned. According to this approach, we can specify the nature of moral beliefs by first summarizing, via folk platitudes, how competent speakers use and conceive of moral utterances. We then try to fit the relevant platitudes into a coherent and systematic framework and use this framework in order to provide an analysis of the concept of moral utterance in terms of a different, but equally naturalistic concept. Since the equivalence of the two concepts need not be obvious to ordinary speakers, the fact that the analysis allows for the open question challenge does not suffice to show that it is false.

Another strategy is the one employed by 'Cornell realists' such as Richard Boyd and David Brink.[41] The general idea of this approach, which is usually developed within the framework of Kripke-Putnam style semantics, is that two terms which apparently refer to different properties, such as 'wrong' and 'causes more pain than pleasure', may refer to the same naturalistic property as a matter of synthetic *a posteriori* fact.[42] The example usually appealed to is the example of 'water' and 'H_2O': although both terms refer to the same naturalistic property,

---

[40] For the following, see Köhler 2013, 487 ff.
[41] See Boyd 1988; and Brink 1989. See also Schaber 1997.
[42] It should be noted that the main purpose of the Cornell realist approach is to show that our moral concepts are concepts of natural properties, or that moral properties are identical to natural properties, not that moral concepts are necessarily *reducible* to non-moral concepts. For this distinction, see Sturgeon 2006, 98 f., who points out that we may not have non-moral terms for all the natural properties there are. In this case, using a moral term might be the only way to refer to the natural property the term signifies.

this is not something competent speakers knew all along. Accordingly, the question 'This is water, but is it also H₂O?' might have been considered to be an open question. If, however, this fact is insufficient to show that 'water' and 'H₂O' refer to different properties, then why should the fact that competent speakers consider the question 'This is wrong, but does it also cause more pain than pleasure?' to be an open question prove that 'wrong' and 'causes more pain than pleasure' signify different properties?

Köhler's point is not so much that we should subscribe to any of these two prominent approaches to conceptual analysis and semantic meaning. In fact, at least the Cornell realist approach seems to commit us to quite a demanding, non-standard view on linguistic meaning. The point is rather that any naturalist who wants to fend off the open question argument needs to subscribe to *some* such kind of approach, and once he does so, he is no longer in a position to turn the open question argument against an expressivist who is willing to make use of the same theoretical machinery.

While I fully agree with this part of Köhler's argument, it is important not to overstate what is achieved by it. What Köhler's analysis helps to establish is what I have already suggested above, namely that expressivists do not find themselves in any dilemma in the strong sense of the word because they have certain strategies for providing a specification of the attitudes expressed by moral utterances in wholly non-moral terms – strategies that are all as viable as the ones open to the naturalist. However, what is equally important is that the expressivist is not in *any better position* than the naturalist with regard to the relevant variant of the open question challenge. The need to emphasize this derives from the fact that, as we have seen, one of the key moves in the history of expressivism has been to argue that metaethical naturalism is damaged by the open question argument in a way that expressivism is *not*. Even if Köhler's analysis is correct and there is a way for the expressivist to overcome the first horn of the dilemma, the relevant considerations suggest that this kind of superiority claim is simply false.

One might want to argue that, while the expressivist might not be in a better position than the naturalist, he at least remains in a better position than the *non-naturalist* because, unlike him, the latter is committed to the idea of mysterious non-natural properties. However, the discussion of the 'moral attitude problems' reveals that this is not the case, either, because the general idea underlying the strategies employed by defenders of the expressivist program, such as Gibbard, Schulte and Köhler, backfires on the expressivist. Just as the expressivist taking the first horn of the dilemma can piggy-back on the explanations of the nature of moral beliefs provided by the naturalist, the non-naturalist can piggy-back on the explanations of the nature of *sui generis* moral attitudes provided by those expressivists who take the second horn of the dilemma: if the expressivist can specify *sui generis* moral attitudes in functionalist terms rather than in terms of specifically non-natural contents, why should the non-naturalist not be able to specify *sui generis* moral *beliefs* in functionalist terms, without any appeal to the kind of robust non-natural properties which has earned classic non-naturalism the reputation of mysteriousness?

We may conclude, then, that the considerations surrounding the 'moral attitude problem' fail to show that expressivism is a non-starter, something which has been suggested by quite a few of those authors who have sketched the problem in the past. However, the considerations nevertheless tend to seriously affect the strength of the expressivist position in that they deprive the expressivist of some of his dialectical advantages over the metaethical naturalist and the metaethical non-naturalist. As far as his rejection of naturalism is concerned, it seems that appeals to the open question argument will not get the expressivist anywhere, while as far as the non-naturalist is concerned, it seems that appeals to the mysteriousness of non-natural properties will not get the expressivist anywhere. The expressivist, therefore, is well-advised to look for ammunition against these rival metaethical positions elsewhere.

2 The expression relation (I): The causal account and its place in classic expressivism

The debate over the expression relation is not directly related to the psychological aspects of expressivism but concerns questions that are first and foremost linguistic in nature: what does it mean to say that an utterance, moral or otherwise, *expresses* a certain state of mind, and is there a way for the expressivist to characterize the linguistic convention linking moral utterances to non-cognitive mental states in a manner that lends overall plausibility to his approach?

Yet, as both the present and the subsequent section will show, though primarily concerned with linguistic issues, the discussion of the expression relation provides further grounds for the view that the expressivist must make substantial claims in moral psychology in order to maintain a stable metaethical position. The discussion will even reveal that the problem of providing an appropriate account of the expression relation and the 'moral attitude problem' are intimately related: whether the expressivist can plausibly argue that certain mental states, such as the higher-order states to which Blackburn and Gibbard appeal, provide moral utterances with their typical meaning in spite of the fact that these mental states are often not present in a speaker making such an utterance (and are perhaps even *known* not to be present in him) very much depends on how the expressivist conceives of the expression relation.

Unlike the objections appealing to the 'moral attitude problem', the challenges appealing to the expression relation do not take the form of a dilemma and, consequently, do not amount to the idea that any plausible account of the expression relation must fail or prove to be incompatible with the fundamental expressivist idea. The point is the more modest one we also encountered within the context of the 'moral attitude problem', namely (a) that expressivists have said far too little about what should really be a crucial element of their theories, (b) that those accounts of the expression relation that *have* been provided (or at least suggested) by leading expressivists face serious problems, and (c) that any plausible account of the expression relation comes at a certain cost because it introduces unwanted theoretical commitments or deprives expressivism of some of its supposed advantages over rival metaethical views.

The criticism that expressivists have not shown an appropriate interest in developing the crucial notion of linguistically expressing a mental state has most forcefully been articulated by Mark Schroeder,[43] even though the idea that the notion of expression requires more in the way of clarification and justification is already suggested by early critics of emotivism, such as Richard Brandt and James Urmson.[44] In comparison, Schroeder's critique seems much more justified than the claim that expressivists have failed to provide specifications of the 'moral attitude' (which, by the way, is a claim Schroeder explicitly does *not* subscribe to).[45] Prior to Schroeder's discussion, the only explicit discussion of how to systematically cash out the idea of linguistically expressing mental states is provided in Gibbard's *Wise choices, apt feelings*, where Gibbard defends the idea that expressing a state of mind consists in uttering words conventionally intended to get somebody to think that one is in this state of mind by means of that somebody's recognizing this intention.[46] Apart from Gibbard's discussion, what we find in the classic expressivists are only more or less implicit suggestions on how to understand the idea of expression, suggestions which leave important questions unanswered. The two strategies employed in this context are (a) the explicit opposition of *expressing* a mental state and *reporting* it (which virtually

---

43 See Schroeder 2008a, 7 and 16; and Schroeder 2008c, 86 f.
44 See Brandt 1959, 204 and 209; and Urmson 1968, 30 ff..
45 See Schroeder 2008c, 86: "A great deal of ink has been spilled over what *kind* of non-cognitive attitude various normative judgments express, and over various problems raised for this kind of view. But very little has been said about what *expression* is, in the first place."
46 See Gibbard 1990a, 85. See also Gibbard 2003, 75 ff., where Gibbard partly retreats from his earlier account. More recent attempts to elaborate on the expression relation and respond to Schroeder's challenge can be found in Schulte 2010, 178 ff.; and Ridge 2014, 108 ff. Moreover, Blackburn takes up the issue in his unpublished paper *Social and individual expression*.

all classic expressivists invoke in order to distance themselves from speaker subjectivism),[47] and (b) the attempt to paraphrase the relevant sense of 'express' by using such verbs as 'to evince'[48], 'to give vent'[49], 'to voice'[50] or 'to avow'[51].

One reason why the classic expressivists have paid so little attention to the expression relation may be that talk of 'expression' is so ubiquitous in linguistic contexts that the idea of linguistic expression might appear to be trivial and unproblematic. However, as we have seen in the discussion of the expressivist status of Ayer and Hare in chapter 3, the problem with the widespread use of 'express' and 'expression' is that it is heterogeneous because quite different phenomena, linguistic as well as non-linguistic, are being invoked as the *relata* of the expression relation. While the idea that linguistic signs 'express' other linguistic entities, such as propositions or speech acts, might indeed be somewhat trivial, the idea that linguistic signs 'express' non-linguistic entities such as mental states is clearly not as trivial and requires much more in the way of explanation and justification. Therefore, as long as we take 'judgement' to refer to a mental event (rather than a public utterance), it is not at all clear whether we should subscribe to Gibbard's relaxed view according to which the claim that words express judgements will be accepted "by almost anyone"[52]. Moreover, even if one is willing to admit that certain words can express judgements (or other mental events or mental states) *on certain occasions*, this concession falls short of the idea Gibbard and other expressivists are really after, namely that words *generally* express mental states and acquire their linguistic meaning in virtue of this very fact.

The second part of the challenge, i.e. that the accounts of the expression relation that *have* been forwarded or at least suggested by expressivists in the past are inappropriate, asks for a much more nuanced assessment. What is certainly true and widely acknowledged within the metaethical debate is that any purely *causal* understanding of the expression relation needs to be rejected.[53] According to the causal understanding, saying that utterances 'express' a certain mental

---

47 See Ayer 1936/1967, 109 f.; Stevenson 1944, 33; Stevenson 1963c, 23; Hare 1981, 58; Blackburn 1984, 169; Blackburn 1998, 50; Gibbard 1990a, 84; and Gibbard 2003, 76.
48 See Ayer 1936/1967, 107 and 109; Blackburn 1984, 167 and 169; and Gibbard 1990a, 172. Note that Hare rejects this way of paraphrasing the relevant sense of 'express' (see Hare 1952, 10; and Hare 1999a, 105).
49 See Stevenson 1944, 38.
50 See Blackburn 1986, 122; and Blackburn 1998, 50.
51 See Blackburn 1998, 68; Gibbard 1986a, 474; and Gibbard 1990a, 73.
52 Gibbard 1990a, 84.
53 See, for instance, Joyce 2008, 375; Schroeder 2008a, 25 f.; Schroeder 2008c, 98 ff.; Joyce 2009, 32; Schulte 2010, 149; and Eriksson 2015a, 154. See also Ridge 2014, 196.

state (or type of mental state) means that the utterance is *caused* by the mental state (or type of mental state): uttering the sentence 'abortion is wrong' expresses a non-cognitive attitude towards abortion, on this view, because the speaker has such an attitude towards abortion which causes him to utter the sentence 'abortion is wrong'. Such causal interpretations of 'expression' might be suggestive when they are being applied to unintentional bodily reactions, such as gasping or blushing, which can be said to express states of mind such as admiration or embarrassment in just this sense. However, they clearly do not work for linguistic utterances, such as 'I was home before midnight' or 'Your new dress is so beautiful!' or even 'Booh!'.

The obvious problem with the causal interpretation is that such utterances can be insincere without this affecting their linguistic meaning. Even if a teenage daughter utters 'I was home before midnight' merely in order not to be told off or punished by her parents, her 'I was home before midnight' still means the same thing, and it is only in virtue of this fact that her lie can fulfil its desired function in the first place. A purely causal interpretation of the expression relation simply cannot account for this consistency in meaning. If the sentence acquires its meaning in virtue of the mental state, in this case a belief, that causes the speaker to make the utterance, its meaning would have to differ once it is being uttered by the insincere daughter because she obviously does not actually believe that she was home before midnight but knows quite well that she came home much later than that.

It is clear, then, that a purely causal understanding of the expression relation fails to satisfy a general constraint that any plausible account of the expression relation needs to satisfy, namely to allow that the meaning of utterances such as 'I was home before midnight' or, for that matter, 'abortion is wrong', is somewhat independent of the mental states that cause a particular speaker to make them. Or, to put things differently, any plausible account of the expression relation needs to allow for utterances to express a mental state the speaker is not actually in.

Yet, what is far less clear is whether any of the classic expressivists makes the fundamental (and quite obvious) mistake of relying on a purely causal understanding of the expression relation to begin with. It is frequently claimed that Ayer, though indicating rather than fully developing his understanding of the expression relation, endorses a causal interpretation of expression. As already argued in chapter 3, it is just because Ayer's key paraphrase 'to evince' suggests such a causal interpretation of 'to express' that Hare rejects Ayer's analysis as misleading, and similar claims have been made by Schroeder and Schulte.[54] Evidence that Ayer might indeed have thought of the relevant kind of expression in purely causal terms is also provided by the fact that he compares moral utterances with cries of pain and with gestures signalling boredom,[55] and that he likens the utterance 'You acted wrongly in stealing that money' to saying 'You stole that money' in a tone of horror and then elaborates on the latter example by claiming that the tone serves to show that the utterance "is attended by certain feelings in the speaker"[56].

The second classic expressivist (dis)credited with a causal understanding of the expression relation is Stevenson.[57] There are two main pieces of evidence which indicate that Stevenson might have endorsed a causal interpretation of 'expression'. The first consists in the fact that Stevenson describes the expressive aspect of emotive meaning by paraphrasing 'to express' with 'to give vent', thereby suggesting that the attitude expressed by a moral utterance acts like some sort of causal drive pushing the speaker to make his utterance.[58] Moreover, in an early version of his definition of emotive meaning, Stevenson phrases his later claim that emotive words 'express' attitudes as the claim that emotive words "result from"[59] affective responses in people. The second piece of evidence consists in Stevenson's overall theory of meaning, which, as we have already seen, is decidedly psychologistic and causalistic. The general idea behind Stevenson's theory of meaning is that we should explain the meaning of utterances in terms of the psychological states that cause such utterances as well as in terms of the psychological processes which the utterances cause in the hearer. Stevenson's reconstruction of linguistic meaning, then, seems to appeal to a simple and straightforward causal chain in which states of mind function as causes and bring about linguistic utterances as their effects which, again, function as causes and bring about affective responses in the hearer, and it may not be easy to see how this causalistic view on linguistic meaning should allow for any non-causal understanding of the expression relation.

Finally, Schroeder has argued that there are traces of a causal understanding of 'expression' even in Blackburn's work, in spite of the fact that Blackburn officially rejects this understanding.[60] The key evidence to which Schroeder ap-

---

54 See Schroeder 2008a, 25; Schroeder 2008c, 98 f.; and Schulte 2010, 149.
55 See Ayer 1936/1967, 108 f.
56 Ayer 1936/1967, 107.
57 See Schulte 2010, 149.
58 See Stevenson 1944, 38 f.
59 Stevenson 1963c, 21.
60 See Schroeder 2008a, 25; and Schroeder 2008c, 98 f.

peals is the fact that Blackburn paraphrases the idea of utterances expressing states of mind by saying that the utterances are used to 'voice' states of mind, the presupposition obviously being that one cannot *voice* a state of mind one is not actually in. Basically the same point can be made by reminding ourselves of the fact that Blackburn explicitly takes up Ayer's paraphrase for 'expressing an attitude', namely the phrase 'evincing an attitude'. A further, though so far overlooked, piece of evidence is provided by Blackburn's curious claim that Mackie, though not a quasi-realist, was nevertheless an expressivist,[61] which claim seems plausible only if we presuppose a causal understanding of expression. While Mackie appears to have thought that what *causes* moral utterances are usually the subjective desires, feelings or attitudes of the speaker, he clearly conceived of the conventional meaning of these utterances in terms of *beliefs* and, more specifically, in terms of beliefs that are systematically false because they presuppose the existence of objective moral values.

What needs to be emphasized, however, is that there is also strong evidence that *neither* of these three classic expressivists wants to defend a purely causal understanding of the expression or happens to overlook the fact that utterances count as expressions of states of mind in spite of the fact that the person making them is not actually in this state. As Schroeder himself points out, the clearest example is Blackburn. In his 1995 paper *The flight to reality*, Blackburn explicitly rejects an individualistic Lockean model of meaning which attempts to explain the meaning of utterances solely in terms of the subjective states which the speaker experiences at the time of utterance, and he emphasizes the connection between linguistic meaning and public convention.[62] Moreover, in quite a few of the passages in which Blackburn paraphrases 'expressing an attitude' as 'voicing an attitude' or 'evincing an attitude', he indicates that we may only expect the speaker to actually have the attitude if his utterance is sincere.[63] In fact, in a passage from *Ruling passions*, to which Schroeder also refers, Blackburn suggests that insincerity is not the only case in which a speaker expresses a mental state he is not actually in, by pointing to the possibility that the speaker may simply be deceived about his own state of mind.[64] This point is taken up again in Blackburn's 2006 paper on *Antirealist expressivism and quasi-realism*, where Blackburn explicitly subscribes to the more general *dictum* that "one can express attitudes one does not oneself hold"[65]. Finally, in his yet unpublish-

---

61 See Blackburn 2006, 154.
62 See Blackburn 1995, 49f.
63 See Blackburn 1984, 169; and Blackburn 1998, 50f.
64 See Blackburn 1998, 69.
65 Blackburn 2006, 151.

ed paper *Social and individual expression*, Blackburn displays a certain unease at restricting the relevant cases to examples of either insincerity or self-deception, suggesting that the best way to conceive of expression may not be in terms of the externalization of attitudes, but in terms of "putting 'something' in the public domain for acceptance and guidance, where the 'something' put there may or may not have a personal psychological identity in the mentality of the speaker"[66].

Yet, what is equally important to emphasize is that, contrary to what Schroeder suggests, we find evidence that speaks against a purely causal understanding of the expression relation in the works of Ayer and Stevenson as well. The first thing to be noted about Ayer's position is that the pieces of evidence speaking in favour of the causal understanding are by no means unambiguous. Though he at one point compares moral utterances with cries of pain, the commonality Ayer is after is not so much that they are both caused by certain psychological states or events. Rather, it is that they are both unverifiable because they do not express genuine propositions. Secondly, although Ayer likens moral utterances to descriptive sentences uttered with a tone of horror, this does not yet help to establish that he conceives of expression in causal terms, because even a tone of horror can be faked and can actually be caused by something other than a feeling of horror. Thirdly, the claim that the tone of horror "serves to show" that the expression of the sentence "is attended by certain feelings in the speaker" is compatible with the idea that, though the speaker actually *has* certain feelings and indicates this with his utterance, these feelings do not *cause* his utterance. Since at least some usages of the verb 'to show' do not imply that what is being shown must actually exist, it is even compatible with the idea that the speaker may be deceiving his audience about the feelings he actually has.

There is also some positive evidence that Ayer is unwilling to accept a straightforward causal interpretation of 'expression'. The main evidence comes from passages in which Ayer emphasizes the connection between linguistic meaning and social convention in a way not dissimilar to Blackburn. Thus, Ayer somewhat qualifies the role he awards to the feelings of the speaker by claiming that we may define the meaning of the various moral words in terms of "the different feelings they are *ordinarily taken to express*"[67]. Moreover, in comparing the expression of feeling he takes to be characteristic of the utterance 'Stealing money is wrong' to the use of double exclamation marks in the written 'Stealing money!!', Ayer emphasizes that the exclamation marks can count as an

---

66 Blackburn, *Social and individual expression*, 9.
67 Ayer 1936/1967, 108. (my emphasis)

expression of feeling only when there is a "suitable convention"[68] to this effect. If the mere fact that a writer's negative feelings towards stealing caused him to put two exclamation marks behind 'Stealing money' does not warrant the claim that the exclamation marks 'express' his negative feelings towards stealing, however, why should the mere fact that some negative feelings towards stealing caused a speaker to say 'Stealing money is wrong' warrant the claim that the speaker has expressed negative feelings towards stealing, as the purely causal account of expression has it?

The last piece of evidence is provided by a passage in Ayer's *On the analysis of moral judgements* in which he rejects his earlier view that moral utterances are merely expressive of feelings of approval or disapproval as an "oversimplification"[69]. According to Ayer's restatement of his view,

> [t]he fact is rather than what may be described as moral attitudes consists in certain patterns of behaviour, and that the expression of a moral judgement is an element in the pattern. The moral judgement expresses the attitude in the sense that it contributes to defining it.[70]

It has to be admitted that Ayer's claim is somewhat cryptic and that characterizing the expression relation is not his main concern. However, the way in which the last sentence makes the moral attitude depend on the moral judgement rather than *vice versa* speaks against a naïve causal understanding of 'expression' and seems to suggest that a speaker may express an attitude he does not (yet) have.

There are important non-causalistic strands in Stevenson's account as well. The reason why we should not attribute to Stevenson a simple causal understanding of the expression relation is that Stevenson is keen to qualify the connection between the meaning of linguistic utterances on the one hand and the actual psychological states of speaker and hearer on the other. Thus Stevenson emphasizes that we should not straightforwardly identify meaning with "all the psychological causes and effects that attend a word's utterance"[71] but only with those causes and effects that the word's utterance has a *tendency* to be connected with. As Stevenson further emphasizes, this tendency must be one that exists for all speakers of the language, persistently clings to the word's utterance and is realizable independently of the individual circumstances of the particular utter-

---

[68] Ayer 1936/1967, 107.
[69] Ayer 1949/1954, 239.
[70] Ayer 1949/1954, 239.
[71] Stevenson 1963c, 20. See also Stevenson 1944, 54.

ance.⁷² Stevenson's reason for qualifying the connection between meaning and the psychological states of speaker and hearer in this way is exactly the one pointed out by modern critics of the naïve causal understanding of expression, namely the fact that linguistic meaning is "relatively unchanging"⁷³ and cannot be cancelled unilaterally,⁷⁴ a fact of which an unqualified causal theory of meaning cannot really make any sense.

In accordance with these considerations, Stevenson's definitions of meaning in general, and descriptive and emotive meaning in particular, all appeal to the idea that words have a *tendency* or *disposition* to cause, or be caused, by (cognitive or non-cognitive) psychological processes.⁷⁵ Moreover, Stevenson tries to single out the relevant tendencies or dispositions by applying the term 'meaning' only to those tendencies or dispositions of a word that have "been caused by, and would not have developed without, an elaborate process of conditioning which has attended the sign's use in communication"⁷⁶. Stevenson's strategy in trying to account for the persistence of meaning, then, is to appeal to social conventions by which words acquire the power or dispositions to cause and be caused by psychological states of speaker and hearer in the first place.

The crucial role of convention is also indicated by Stevenson's related claims that the relevant tendencies of an emotive word arise "through the history of its usage"⁷⁷ or "on account of its history in emotional situations"⁷⁸ or that the tendencies of emotive words derive "from the habits that have been formed throughout the course of their use in emotional situations"⁷⁹. The relevant kind of history is clearly a social history, just as forming linguistic habits on the basis of prior situations of use is essentially a social phenomenon. Moreover, Stevenson explicitly appeals to the idea of linguistic conventions in explaining the differences between the linguistic *expression* of emotions and attitudes and the natural manifestations of emotions and attitudes we find in laughs, sighs or groans.⁸⁰

What deserves to be noted in this context is also that, in most of his characterizations of meaning in general or emotive meaning in particular, Stevenson avoids the claim that the attitudes expressed by emotive words are attitudes of

---

72 See Stevenson 1963c, 21.
73 Stevenson 1944, 44.
74 See Stevenson 1944, 40.
75 See Stevenson 1944, 33, 54, 57, 62 and 70; Stevenson 1963c, 21; and Stevenson 1963a, 63 f.
76 Stevenson 1944, 57.
77 Stevenson 1963c, 21.
78 Stevenson 1944, 33.
79 Stevenson 1944, 41.
80 See Stevenson 1944, 37 ff.

the speaker himself. Thus, Stevenson usually speaks unspecifically of the psychological causes and effects or psychological processes that attend a word's utterance or are connected with it,[81] and defines emotive meaning as resulting from affective responses "in people"[82] or, even more generally, as 'expressions of attitudes' without specifying at all whose attitudes he is talking about.[83] Moreover, in a passage where Stevenson *does* refer to the speaker as the very person whose attitudes are being expressed, Stevenson confines himself to saying that emotive words are "fitted"[84] to express the attitudes of the speaker, thereby allowing for the theoretical possibility that emotive words may also express other people's attitudes or perhaps attitudes that are not instantiated in any individual persons at all. However, it would be false to infer from this that Stevenson does not conceive of the expressive aspect of emotive meaning as a result of psychological processes in the speaker. In his discussion of the passive disposition of a sign to be used in a certain way, Stevenson makes it quite clear that the disposition in question is constituted by "a correlation between some range of a person's psychological processes and *his* use of a sign"[85] and that the relevant causal stimuli are provided by psychological processes in the speaker.

The problem with Stevenson's account, therefore, is not that he unflinchingly defends a purely causal account of the expression relation. It is rather that the causalistic elements and the conventionalistic elements of Stevenson's theory of meaning do not fit together as neatly as Stevenson suggests. In particular, it is not clear how we should make sense of the idea which is crucial for Stevenson's account of speaker meaning: the idea that words have a "passive"[86] disposition or tendency *to be used* in a certain way. While the actual use of a word in a given situation can in principle be explained causally by appealing to some occurrent mental state of the speaker using it, it appears that the *tendency* of the word to be used in such a situation cannot be explained in this way. If one wants to stick to Stevenson's overall causalistic framework, however, it seems that one must somehow locate this tendency itself within a causal network and identify its prior causes, at least in a general way.

Stevenson conventionalism suggest that these causes are provided by the speaker's communicative experiences and the reactions of his past audiences. Yet, once we concede that the passive disposition constituting the meaning of

---

81 See Stevenson 1963c, 20; and Stevenson 1944, 54f.
82 Stevenson 1963c, 21.
83 See Stevenson 1944, 33; and Stevenson 1963a, 63f.
84 Stevenson 1944, 41.
85 Stevenson 1944, 57. (my emphasis)
86 Stevenson 1944, 57.

a word has been caused by an essentially *social* process, then it seems that, if anything, the word should be expressive of this *process*, not of some individual speaker's state of mind. While this way of trying to make sense of the passive disposition of words may be compatible with Stevenson's general causalistic approach, it seems to undermine the individualistic psychological aspects of Stevenson's theory, in particular the suggestion that words have emotive meaning in so far as they express non-cognitive states of mind of the speaker. Alternatively, one might try to defend this latter claim by interpreting the passive disposition of emotive words merely in terms of the hearer's tendency to *attribute* to speaker speaker using them certain attitudes. In this case, however, one seems to have sacrificed the part of Stevenson's causalistic theory of meaning that is concerned with the causal history of utterances, given that the subsequent attributions made by the hearer are certainly not what has *caused* the word's utterance.

However, it would be premature to conclude from this that Stevenson's appeal to social conventions cannot be reconciled with his causalistic theory of meaning and his understanding of the expressive aspects of emotive meaning. In fact, it seems that we may interpret Stevenson's theory in a way that allows us to reject the premise I have so far left unchallenged, namely that a causalistic theory of meaning commits Stevenson, in one way or the other, to a simple causal understanding of the expression relation. While it is true that, according to Stevenson, the passive disposition of words to be used in a certain way is to some extent the result of a social process, it does not follow that the states of mind of individual speakers play no role in this process. On the contrary, any plausible story of the way in which words historically acquire a disposition to cause certain responses in hearers and to be used in certain ways by speakers needs to acknowledge that past communicative experiences will affect the mental states of those involved in it.

For example, if a person experiences that 'good' is often being used by people who otherwise reveal that they have a favourable attitude towards what they call 'good', we can expect her to acquire the belief that people who use 'good' often have favourable attitudes towards what they describe as 'good' and perhaps even the belief that 'good' can be used, in some way or the other, to indicate such an attitude. Likewise, a person who experiences usages of 'good' to often cause certain reactions in other people can be expected to acquire the belief that she herself may cause such reactions by using 'good', too. However, if this is correct, it seems that we may at least partly locate the causes of the passive tendency of words to be used in a certain way within the speaker who uses them. That the word 'good', for instance, has the passive disposition to be used in order to get people to pursue certain objects or activities can at least partially be explained by appealing to the psychological state of a speaker using 'good' because we can expect this speaker to have, for example, the belief that using this word will actually get other people to pursue the objects or activities in question.

The conventional nature of meaning emphasized by Stevenson, then, seems compatible both with the overall causalistic framework and the idea that the states of mind of a speaker essentially contribute to what her utterances mean. Moreover, once we recognize that the tendency of a word to be used in a certain way may depend on quite *different* states of mind on part of the speaker, some of which are cognitive (such as the belief that hearers will react in certain ways) and some of which are non-cognitive (such as the pro- or con-attitude towards the object to which the speaker applies the word), we might have even found a way to successfully distance ourselves from the naïve causal understanding of 'expression' within Stevenson's framework. While the above account does not allow us to say that an insincere use of 'good' was caused by one of the speaker's pro-attitudes, it at least allows us to say that the insincere use of 'good' was caused by the speaker's states of mind, one of which may have been the belief that 'good' can be used to induce certain responses. It would be compatible then with Stevenson's account, on this reading, to say that the utterance was invested with its meaning by the speaker's states of mind.

What is of crucial importance in this context is that, in describing the passive disposition of words to be used in a certain way, Stevenson himself characterizes this disposition as "a correlation between some *range* of a person's psychological processes and his use of a sign"[87], thereby explicitly providing some leeway with regard to the states of mind that constitute the expressive meaning of a word. The idea suggested by this remark is one of a *complex* of mental states or events (rather than of one single state or kind of state) that provides a word with its passive tendency to express attitudes and hence with its emotive meaning, and this idea seems to allow that the expressive function and the emotive meaning of a word remain constant even when one element of the relevant complex of psychological processes is absent. Stevenson's claim that the meaning of a sign is constituted, not by the actual causes and effects that adhere to its use, but by those psychological processes which *tend* to adhere to its use, then, might in the end allow us to claim that positive speaker-attitudes contribute to the meaning of the word 'good', or are being expressed by it, even if, on some occasions, a speaker uttering the word may not actually have such an attitude.

---

[87] Stevenson 1944, 57. (my emphasis)

It may very well be possible, therefore, to satisfy the constraints set up by the critics of the naïve causal understanding of 'expression' within the framework of Stevenson's causalistic theory of meaning. Be that as it may, the more important conclusion to be drawn from all this is that we fail to do justice to Ayer and Stevenson as well as Blackburn and misdiagnose the problems of their accounts if we attribute to them a straightforward and simple causal understanding of 'expression'. The problem with these accounts is not that Ayer, Stevenson and Blackburn ignore the conventional aspects of meaning and the fact that speakers who are insincere or deceived about their own states of mind use terms like 'good' or 'wrong' with the same meaning. It is rather that Ayer, Stevenson and Blackburn do not pay enough attention to what follows from this fact and fail to turn their relatively vague references to linguistic conventions into a comprehensive and consistent account of the expression relation.

However, something like this also seems to be true of many modern authors who explicitly take up the issue of how to define the expression relation. A strategy that is quite common among the contributors to the more recent debate is to characterize the relevant sense of 'expression' by simply qualifying the causal understanding in the required way and to explicitly allow for insincere utterances, or for utterances made under self-deception, to retain their ordinary meaning. For example, in some of his earlier publications, Ridge essentially confines his discussion of the expression relation to the claim that an utterance can express an attitude the speaker does not actually have and supports this claim by pointing to the general role of conventions and citing insincerity and self-deception as relevant examples.[88] Similarly, Boisvert defines the sense of 'expression' to which expressivists should appeal by the simple principle (E):

> (E): If a speaker utters$_{(CL)}$ an ethical sentence, then the speaker performs a direct illocutionary act whose sincerity condition requires the speaker to have a pro- or con-attitude.[89]

Finally, Caj Strandberg has recently forwarded an equally simple characterization of the expression relation that appeals to the idea of 'conventional semantic meaning'. According to this characterization, a sentence can be understood "to express the minimal mental state that a person has to be in, in order for it to be consistent with the conventional meaning of the sentence to assert or accept it"[90]. As should have become clear, these moves are ones we already find in

---

[88] See Ridge 2004, 314; Ridge 2006b, 502 and 504; and Ridge 2009, 198.
[89] Boisvert 2008, 179. Note that "utters$_{(CL)}$" stands for "correctly and literally utters" (Boisvert 2008, 177).
[90] Strandberg 2012, 90.

Ayer and Stevenson as well as in Blackburn's earlier discussion of the matter, and there are related suggestions in some of Hare's works and in Gibbard's earliest publications on expressivism.[91]

What is lacking both in these classic expressivists and in most of their modern commentators is a positive account of the expression relation which further explains the mechanism by which signs continue to express certain mental states even where they are not being caused by these mental states. We find such a positive account of 'expression' only in a handful of authors, most notably in Gibbard, Schroeder and Schulte, and we may also include Blackburn whose more recent considerations on the topic are explicitly motivated by the aim of going beyond the mere exclusion of insincerity and self-deception. The questions to be asked next, then, are: Do these authors succeed in their attempts to provide a plausible and more comprehensive account of the 'expression relation'? And do the relevant accounts commit the expressivist to giving up on some of the features that made his position attractive and provided him with advantages over naturalism and non-naturalism?

3 The expression relation (II): Alternatives to the causal account

As already noted above, Gibbard is the only classic expressivist who attempts to provide a positive characterization of what expressivists mean, or should mean, by 'expression'. The account forwarded by Gibbard is clearly indebted to Grice's theory of meaning in that it awards a central role to the speaker's intentions. Gibbard develops his account of 'expression' with the help of an example of Caesar and Cleopatra conversing about both matters of fact and matters of rationality and irrationality. According to Gibbard's example, when Caesar tells Cleopatra 'I was captured by pirates in my youth', we can assume (a) that he wants her to know about his capture by pirates, (b) that he thinks she lacks a true belief about the subject, (c) that he believes that she thinks him sincere and (d) that she thinks him an authority on events of his youth. The crucial role of Caesar's intentions is then brought out by Gibbard in the following passage:

> Caesar thus intends to get Cleopatra to believe that he was captured by pirates in his youth, and to do so in the following manner. He utters words that conventionally purport to express, on the part of any speaker, a belief that he was captured by pirates in his youth. He intends her to come to accept that he has this belief, and to do so in virtue of her rec-

---

[91] See Hare 1999a, 17 f.; and Gibbard 1983, 211.

ognition of his intention. Since she takes him to be sincere, she has reason to accept, upon hearing his words, that he does believe that he was captured by pirates in his youth. Since she thinks him an authority on his youth, she concludes from his believing it that he indeed was captured by pirates in his youth.[92]

The important point about this proposal is that, though Caesar's sincerity is a relevant issue, the meaning of his utterance does not depend on the fact that Caesar *is* indeed sincere, but merely on the fact that Cleopatra *believes* him to be so. Therefore, Caesar does not need to have the belief that he was captured by pirates in his youth for his utterance to communicate this belief to Cleopatra. In fact, it does not even seem necessary that Cleopatra *believes* Caesar to be sincere in order for his utterance to communicate this belief on Caesar's behalf: as long as Cleopatra believes that Caesar's *intention* is to get her to believe that he has the belief in question, Gibbard's analysis can provide an explanation for why 'I was captured by pirates in my youth' means what it does. The sincerity condition is only necessary to explain how the more general convention to which Gibbard's analysis appeals could ever have been established: if hearers would not, routinely, imply that a speaker who wants to get them to attribute to him a certain belief actually has this belief, it would be difficult to see how utterances such as 'I was captured by pirates in my youth' could have ever come to serve the communicative function they serve.

In Gibbard's view, a similar rationale can be given for normative utterances, such as when Caesar tells Cleopatra 'It makes best sense to divide the command of your army'. According to the account of *Wise choices*, we should see Caesar as expressing his acceptance of a system of norms that tell Cleopatra to divide the command of her army, and, as with factual belief, expressing this state of mind consists in Caesar's uttering words conventionally intended to get Cleopatra to think that he is in this state of mind, where Cleopatra's recognition of this intention is the means by which this change in Cleopatra's beliefs is meant to be achieved.[93] In fact, Gibbard claims that the parallels with belief extend even farther than this and allow for the claim that Caesar's 'It makes best sense to divide the command of your army' gives Cleopatra *some* reason to divide her army, just as Caesar's 'I was captured by pirates in my youth' gives her reason to believe that Caesar was captured by pirates in his youth.[94] The crucial point is whether Cleopatra will consider Caesar to be an authority on how to successfully command an

---

[92] Gibbard 1990a, 84f.
[93] See Gibbard 1990a, 85f.
[94] See Gibbard 1990a, 86.

army in something like the sense in which she considers him to be an authority on events of his youth.

However, it is exactly because of the crucial role played by the speaker's intentions that Gibbard's Gricean account of the expression relation is widely rejected. This rejection is based on a variety of considerations. To begin with, as Schroeder points out, Gibbard's account of 'expression' inherits something like the 'Frege-Geach problem': if the meaning of 'abortion is wrong' is explained by the fact that a speaker uttering this sentence intends to convey to the listener that he has a negative desire-like attitude towards abortion, then it seems that the meaning of 'If abortion is wrong, then in vitro-fertilisation is wrong' must at least partially be explained by the fact that a speaker uttering this sentence – and uttering the antecedent in particular – intends to convey to the listener that he has a negative desire-like attitude towards abortion. However, it seems that speakers uttering the sentence in question usually do not have this intention at all.

More generally, it seems that speakers uttering moral or non-moral sentences may pursue all kinds of intentions in making their utterance, intentions that cannot all safely be connected to the meaning of the sentences in the way Gibbard's analysis presupposes. In fact, in *Spreading the word*, Blackburn expresses just these two worries with regard to Gricean accounts of meaning, pointing out (a) that the phrase 'the cat is in the garden', if being uttered as part of the conditional 'if the cat is in the garden, you will not see any birds', is not usually uttered with the intention of inducing the belief that the cat is in the garden, and (b) that, on occasion, a speaker may assert something even though he knows quite well that his audience already has the belief he thereby expresses or, alternatively, has reason to think that they will never come to share his belief in spite of his utterance.[95]

We find similar considerations in other critics of Gricean accounts of meaning such as Ridge and Schulte. Ridge simply emphasizes that "some sentences are characteristically uttered with no audience at all – or with no audience to whom we intend to convey our intentions"[96]. In a similar vein, Schulte claims that the utterance 'you are lying' is rarely intended to get the listener to believe that he is lying, just as the sentence 'the second world war ended in 1945', when written in a class essay, is not intended to get the teacher to believe that the second world war ended in 1945, because in both cases, the speaker or writer knows

---

95 See Blackburn 1984, 123.
96 Ridge 2014, 108.

full well that his audience already possesses the relevant beliefs.[97] Moreover, Schulte points to empirical psychological findings emerging from so-called 'false-belief tasks' which suggest that three-year old children, though able to utter well-formed sentences and to mean something with these sentences, are yet incapable of forming the complex Gricean intentions to which Gibbard's account appeals.[98]

In support of Gibbard, Schroeder explicitly emphasizes that, according to the full account of *Wise choices*, "not *just any* intentions of a speaker to convey information about her mental states to her audience will make the speaker count as expressing those mental states"[99], but only those intentions that "take advantage of *already existing linguistic conventions*"[100]. However, as Schroeder plausibly argues, this restriction makes Gibbard's position somewhat unstable, because it is not clear how to define the relevant linguistic conventions if not in terms of propositional contents or other related notions. Yet, any reliance on such notions tends to threaten the overall expressivist enterprise because the notions seem to be able to explain semantic meaning in their own right and thus make the appeal to the crucial idea of utterances expressing mental states seem dispensable.[101] In Schroeder's view, Gibbard can only maintain his position if he can argue that those contents which explain the relevant linguistic conventions (or make them viable) are not suited to figure in a more basic or more direct explanation of semantic meaning, and it seems that there is reason to doubt that this will actually be true of any possible "*ur*-contents"[102] with which the expressivist might come up.

According to Schroeder's critique, then, the reason why Gibbard's account is unstable is basically identical with why the simplest interpretation of the expression relation, to which Schroeder refers as the "*same content* account"[103], fails. The idea of the same content account is to explain the relevant sense of 'expression' by appealing to the content of the mental states that are being expressed.

---

97 See Schulte 2010, 188.
98 See Schulte 2010, 191. In support of his claim, Schulte refers to Heinz Wimmer and Josef Perner's study *Beliefs about beliefs: Representation and constraining of wrong beliefs in young children's understanding of deception*, conducted in the early 1980s (see Wimmer/Perner 1983). Perner has since then defended the relevant claims in a series of publications. The objection that Gricean accounts cannot sufficiently accommodate young children's linguistic capacities is also raised by Ruth Millikan (see Millikan 1984, 69; and Millikan 2005, 95).
99 Schroeder 2008c, 105.
100 Schroeder 2008c, 105.
101 See Schroeder 2008c, 106 f.
102 Schroeder 2008c, 106.
103 Schroeder 2008c, 97. See also Schroeder 2008a, 24 f.

That an utterance expresses a mental state simply means, on this reading, that it has the same propositional content as the mental state in question. Thus, the utterance 'the cat is in the garden' expresses the belief that 'the cat is in the garden' just because its shares the content of this belief. However, the problem with this way of accounting for the expression relation is that the key idea of expressivism is to initially explain the meaning of utterances (and the meaning of moral utterances in particular), not in terms of propositional contents, but in terms of the expression of mental states, in order to then, and on this basis, *earn* the notion of an ethical proposition or moral propositional content. The same content account, therefore, is incompatible with the expressivist order of explanation because it makes the 'expression' of mental states depend on propositional contents rather than *vice versa*, and something similar seems to ultimately be true of Gibbard's Gricean account the expression relation.

Schroeder and Schulte have both forwarded positive proposals for how to characterize the expression relation without relying on the speaker's intentions in the way Gibbard's account does. The crucial idea of Schroeder's proposal, which he refers to under the heading "assertability expressivism", is to retain Gibbard's idea that a sentence expresses a mental state by being associated with the proposition that a speaker uttering the sentence is in the mental state in question, but to detach this idea from what the speaker does or intends and view it instead as a semantic property of the sentence.[104] As Schroeder argues, we may think of this property in terms of the "assertability conditions"[105] or "semantic correctness conditions"[106] of the sentence, that is, in terms of linguistic rules that lay down when it is permissible to assert the sentence in question.[107] According to Schroeder's specific account, the relevant conditions are not provided by the truth-conditions of the sentence, but by the presence of certain mental states in the speaker: just as it is permissible to assert 'the cat is in the garden' only if you believe that 'the cat is in the garden', the assertability expressivist will argue that it is permissible to assert 'abortion is wrong' only if you have a negative desire-like attitude towards abortion.[108]

In Schroeder's view, assertability expressivism satisfies all the constraints that a plausible account of the expression relation needs to satisfy because it can easily accommodate insincerity and other examples where speakers express

---

104 See Schroeder 2008a, 28.
105 Schroeder 2008a, 29.
106 Schroeder 2008a, 30.
107 See Schroeder 2008a, 29.
108 A similar view on 'expression' has also been forwarded by Eriksson (see Eriksson 2009, 17f.).

a mental state they are not actually in. Yet, one worry one might have with regard to Schroeder's account is whether this account allows us to sufficiently discriminate between those different cases. As we have seen, Schroeder takes the assertability condition of an utterance such as 'abortion is wrong' to consist in the fact that the speaker *has* a negative desire-like attitude towards abortion, not in the fact that the speaker himself *believes* to have this kind of attitude. On this reading, the person who deliberately lies about what she thinks about abortion and the person who is deluded about her true attitude towards abortion equally violate the assertability conditions of 'abortion is wrong' and make a specifically linguistic mistake. However, while it is quite plausible to make the latter claim about the insincere person, it seems less plausible to make it about the person suffering from self-deception.

Moreover, even if we accept that both speakers do make linguistic mistakes (if perhaps with unequal culpability), the question remains how to contrast the two cases within Schroeder's framework. Of course, we can always draw a psychological distinction by pointing out that the latter person has a belief the former person does not have, namely the belief to have a negative desire-like attitude towards abortion. Yet, it seems that this difference does not allow us to fully capture what distinguishes the two utterances *as speech acts*. While the first utterance is a deliberate lie whose primary communicative intention is to induce a false belief in the hearer, the second utterance is not. Whereas Gibbard's Gricean account with its emphasis on the speaker's intentions can accommodate this difference as a *linguistic* rather than merely psychological one, it seems that Schroeder's account cannot.[109]

However, it would obviously be of no help to the expressivist to give the assertability condition of 'abortion is wrong' as the condition that the speaker himself *believes* to have a negative desire-like attitude towards abortion because this move would deprive the expressivist of the ability to deal with the challenge of Jackson and Pettit I have discussed above. Under this interpretation, we can certainly contrast the liar with the deluded person because only the liar violates the relevant linguistic rules whereas the utterance of the deluded person comes out as linguistically correct. Moreover, the interpretation would allow us to sufficiently distinguish the case of the sincere but deluded person from the case of the sincere and undeluded person because this distinction is, arguably, merely a psychological one: what distinguishes the two persons is not that they have

---

[109] Schroeder's discussion suggests that this is because he would not accept the premise that speakers can be deluded about their own states of mind. Thus, Schroeder partly justifies his general approach to assertability conditions by claiming that mental states are something to which speakers have access (see Schroeder 2008c, 110).

different communicative intentions or put language to a different use, but simply that the one has a false belief about his own mental states that the other one has not. The problem, however, is that the interpretation awards the wrong kind of meaning to utterances such as 'abortion is wrong': since the assertability condition is meant to characterize 'expression' and to thereby explain the primary meaning of linguistic utterances, we must conclude from the above revised definition of the assertability conditions that the mental state expressed by 'abortion is wrong' is not any negative desire-like attitude towards abortion, but the belief that 'I (the speaker) have a negative desire-like attitude towards abortion'. Yet, this just means that the above version of assertability expressivism must primarily conceive of moral utterances as reports of the speaker's attitudes and is therefore unable to ward off Jackson and Pettit's challenge.

It seems, then, that assertability expressivism has to be set up in just the way it is set up by Schroeder if it is to provide the expressivist with a plausible and stable analysis of the expression relation. Moreover, it is not clear whether the fact that Schroeder fails to provide us with any explicit resources for accommodating the difference between insincerity and self-deception as a specifically linguistic difference significantly affects the value of his proposal. After all, the linguistic conventions to which Schroeder appeals are explicitly characterized by him as *semantic* correctness conditions, and this seems to leave the possibility that the assertability expressivist might explain the difference between insincerity and self-deception in terms of further, perhaps *pragmatic* correctness conditions – which conditions are arguably satisfied by the deluded person but not by the liar. In addition, one might think that there is a way to characterize the relevant assertability conditions which does not suggest as strongly that the deluded person makes a linguistic mistake. For example, the account recently forwarded by Michael Ridge, though clearly related to Schroeder's proposal, seems to fare slightly better in this regard because it focuses less on the side of the speaker and more on the side of his listeners and their reactions. Ridge's definition of the relevant sense of 'expression' is as follows:

> Accountability Expression: A declarative sentence 'p' in sense S in a natural language N used with assertive force in the context of utterance C expresses a state of mind M if and only if conventions which partially constitute N dictate that someone who says 'p' in sense S in C with assertive force is thereby *liable* for being in state M.[110]

---

[110] Ridge 2014, 109.

As Ridge emphasizes,[111] the notion of liability (or accountability) to which his definition appeals is not understood as a normative but as a purely conventional notion. That a speaker uttering 'p' with assertive force is *liable* for being in state M does not mean, on this understanding, that he has misbehaved, or violated duties or obligations, if he utters 'p' without being in state M. Rather, it means that his listeners will *de facto* take him to be in state M. Therefore, while Ridge's definition asks us to put the insincere and the deluded speaker into the same category, there is less of a suggestion that they make the same kind of mistake or use language to the same purpose.

According to Schroeder himself, there are other reasons why actual expressivists should be somewhat hesitant to embrace his version of assertability expressivism, even though it promises to solve their problems with the expression relation. These reasons have to do with the fact that the adoption of assertability expressivism commits the expressivist to "a highly controversial view about the semantic content of ordinary, non-normative language"[112], which seems to also be true of Schulte's alternative proposal which crucially appeals to Ruth Millikan's teleofunctionalist theory of semantic meaning.[113]

According to Schulte's rendition of Millikan's notion of a function, an entity can be said to have the function to φ if and only if the entity exists (and exists in the way it does) because its ancestors have performed φ with a sufficient frequency.[114] As Schulte emphasizes, this notion of a function cannot only be applied to living beings, but also to words and other linguistic devices, given that such devices can be reproduced by speakers.[115] On Millikan's original account, we can explain, for instance, the distinctive meaning of ordinary indicative sentences and imperatives by appealing to the following functions: while indicatives have the function to produce true beliefs, imperatives have the function to produce actions and, in particular, to produce compliance.[116] Schulte argues that we should describe the functions of indicatives and imperatives in a slightly different way, though, by relying on the idea that the fundamental function of the devices in question is to transfer states of mind: while their 'wide' function may be to produce true beliefs, the 'narrow' and most relevant function of indicatives is to transfer opinions; and while the 'wide' function of imperatives may

---

111 See Ridge 2014, 109.
112 Schroeder 2008c, 112.
113 For the following, see Schulte 2010, 192 ff.
114 For Millikan's original definition, see Millikan 1984, 26–28.
115 See also Millikan 1984, 22 and 29 ff.
116 See Millikan 1984, 53 f. See also Millikan 2005, 94.

be to produce actions, their 'narrow' and most relevant function is to transfer intentions.

In Schulte's view, the above teleofunctionalist approach to language allows us to provide an alternative account of the expression relation. According to Schulte's proposal, an utterance of type U expresses a mental state M if and only if utterances of type U have the function to transfer mental state M. Schulte argues that this account has none of the problems of Gibbard's Gricean account of the expression relation. Thus, the teleofunctionalist can allow that sentences are sometimes uttered with no audience at all (or to listeners that already share the relevant beliefs or attitudes of the speaker) because he need not presuppose that utterances (or types of utterances) fulfil their specific function on every occasion, as long as he can plausibly argue that they fulfil it (or have fulfilled it) in a sufficiently large number of cases.[117]

Moreover, that the utterance of a sentence *has* a certain function is not dependent on the fact that the speaker *intends* to utter the sentence with this function.[118] The teleofunctionalist, therefore, need not presuppose that all speakers capable of forming well-formed and meaningful sentences, including young children, are also capable of forming complex intentions. As Schulte points out, the account can nevertheless appeal to such intentions in order to explain cases in which words are used so as to not perform their ordinary function, as in cases of insincerity or irony: the reason why the appeal to Gricean intentions is unproblematic here, according to Schulte, is that very young children are not only incapable of forming Gricean intentions, but equally incapable of performing speech acts of this kind.

One minor problem with Schulte's account is that the latter claim does not seem to hold up against the existing empirical evidence. While it may be correct that very young children are incapable of being ironical and perhaps, to use another of Schulte's examples, incapable of using words metaphorically, there is strong evidence that they are capable of lying. According to a recent study by Angela Evans and Kang Lee, a considerable number of two-year old children lies frequently, and the same conclusion emerges from a study published by Anne

---

[117] This point is also emphasized by Millikan: "The standardizing and stabilizing function of a language device should be thought of not as an invariable function or as an average function but as a function that accords with a critical mass of cases of actual use, forming a center of gravity to which wayward speakers and hearers tend to return after departures." (Millikan 1984, 4) See also Millikan 1984, 31f.

[118] Again, this point is already emphasized by Millikan, who explicitly distinguishes between the 'proper' functions of language devices on the one hand and their 'actual' or 'intended' functions on the other (see Millikan 1984, 1f.; and Millikan 2005, 95).

Wilson, Melissa Smith and Hildy Ross in 2003.[119] Moreover, in their 2000 paper entitled *Children's everyday deception and performance on false-belief tasks*, the developmental psychologists Paul Newton, Vasudevi Reddy and Ray Bull not only report lies in two-year olds but specifically argue that young children's ability to lie (or to deceive by linguistic means) correlates in no relevant way with their abilities to correctly attribute false beliefs to others.[120] Alan Polak and Paul Harris, who present a much more ambiguous picture in their related 1999 study, at least agree that "even among children who perform poorly on standard false-belief tasks, there is a tendency to deny a minor misdemeanor"[121]. It seems therefore, that by appealing to Gricean functions in order to explain the speech act of lying, Schulte becomes vulnerable to the same kind of objection he levels against Grice. As in the case of Schroeder, however, this does not appear to be a significant weakness of his account of the expression relation but rather something that can be straightened out by some kind of complementary argument.

The more important issues arising for Schulte's account concern the question of whether the underlying teleofunctionalist explanation of semantic meaning is plausible. The least to be said here is that the explanation raises questions that require a more detailed discussion. One of these questions is whether the teleofunctional explanation of semantic meaning is faced with a kind of circularity problem. According to Schulte's understanding of 'functions', our words have functions in virtue of the fact that they exist (in the way they do) because previous speakers have transferred their mental states with a certain frequency. The obvious question, then, is how these previous speaker transferred their mental states? One answer would be that they have used other words or no words at all. If so, it is not clear why this process should have led to the establishment of the words with whose meaning we are concerned. Another answer is that previous speakers have transferred their mental states with the help of those very words or their direct ancestors, and this is also what is suggested by Millikan's original account.[122] However, the question then becomes: what was it about those words that allowed previous speakers to thereby successfully transfer their mental states – if not the words' meaning? It seems that the least Schulte needs to concede at this point is that there is some way for words to acquire a basic and unrefined meaning which allows for the transfer of mental states and which is not, itself, to be explained in terms of the function which the words acquire by way of frequent reproduction.

---

119 See Evans/Lee 2013; and Wilson et al. 2003.
120 See Newton et al. 2000.
121 Polak/Harris 1999, 567.
122 See, for example, Millikan 1984, 26 and 28.

The second question, then, is how exactly to conceive of the process by which words acquire their initial unrefined meaning. Why are some words chosen as the basic vehicles for transferring mental states of the speaker, but not others? What makes a word a more or less suitable means for transferring mental states of the speaker? It seems that any plausible answer to these questions will eventually have to introduce at least one rival explanation of meaning. This suggests that the teleofunctionalist approach might better be conceived of as a *hybrid* approach to semantic meaning: as an approach that explains the meaning of our modern, well-refined language in terms of reproductively generated functions, but also relies on a quite different explanation of meaning that is applied more locally to the earlier stages of our linguistic development.

In fact, Millikan seems to concede something like this, by suggesting that linguistic signs originally emerge from natural signs and by allowing that the way in which language devices initially acquire proper functions is "derived directly from speakers' purposes in using them"[123]. Moreover, while it seems that, say, picture theories or onomatopoetic theories might be well suited to account for certain forms of propositional content, they seem less suited to explain the phenomenon to which Schulte's account crucially appeals, namely the linguistic transfer of mental states, and in particular the transfer of desire-like attitudes. It seems much more intuitive to think that the initial ability of words to transfer such attitudes must somehow be grounded in a *causal* connection between these words and the attitudes of the speaker, which means that Schulte's teleofunctionalist theory of semantic meaning might, in some sense, depend on a causalistic theory of meaning or on a causal interpretation of the linguistic expression of mental states. However, if this were true, then it would not be clear whether Schulte's account is really as different from Stevenson's qualified causalistic theory of meaning as Schulte himself claims. The advantage of Schulte's account would then seem to consist, not in the fact that it can completely dispense with any causalistic explanation of semantic meaning whatsoever, but rather in the fact that it provides a positive specification of those conventional aspects of semantic meaning to which Stevenson alludes but which he fails to adequately capture in his theory.

A further question raised by Schulte's ultimate characterization of the expression relation is: what additional function is performed by moral utterances over and above the function of ordinary imperatives? As we have seen, Schulte takes the function of *imperatives* to consist in the transfer of intentions or conative attitudes in general. However, in order to retain the distinctive feature of

---

[123] Millikan 2004, 107. See also Millikan 2004, 103.

expressivism, Schulte needs to argue that moral utterances transfer conative attitudes as well. In order to explain how moral utterances have acquired this function, Schulte needs to identify a specific function that is performed by moral utterances but not, in an equal way, by ordinary imperatives. According to Schulte's discussion of this point, the need for an additional type of utterance derives from the existence of specific types of conative states. The particular function performed by moral utterances, on this reading, is that they transfer desire-like attitudes that crucially differ from the attitudes transferred by ordinary imperatives because they possess features which the latter lack, such as universalizability and logical embeddability. As I have already indicated, however, this specification of the particular mental states expressed by moral utterances puts them in close proximity to cognitive mental states, namely to beliefs. The obvious question to ask, therefore, is whether it is really less plausible to postulate the existence of genuinely moral or other normative beliefs than to postulate the existence of a *sui generis* sub-category of belief-like non-belief attitudes, and one of the main challenges for Schulte's account is to demonstrate why this is so.

In order to conclude our discussion of the more recent attempts to provide a plausible account of the expression relation, I would like to return to Blackburn's recent proposal which I have already mentioned above. To recall, the main idea forwarded by Blackburn is that we should not conceive of the linguistic 'expression' of attitudes in terms of their externalization, but in terms of "putting 'something' in the public domain for acceptance and guidance, where the 'something' put there may or may not have a personal psychological identity in the mentality of the speaker". The background for this proposal is provided by the story of Magnus, the wine taster, who has lost every pleasure in drinking wine but is still a first-rate wine critic, retaining his memory and his "powers of discrimination"[124], but finding his subjective enjoyment slipping away.

As Blackburn emphasizes, the case of Magnus sets a challenge to an expressivist interpretation of aesthetic utterances because Magnus is neither insincere nor deluded but continues to make straightforward evaluative utterances, yet the way in which Magnus expresses feelings of pleasure or other relevant attitudes is clearly not one to be conceived of in terms of externalization. The problem with the proposal meant to deal with such cases is that Blackburn is merely offering something akin to a metaphor after all and that this metaphor seems equally acceptable to expressivists and non-expressivists. As long as we allow that the 'something' that is being put in the public domain may not be a desire-like atti-

---

[124] Blackburn, *Social and individual expression*, 8.

tude at all, then it is not clear why the proposal should be an expressivist proposal in the first place, since virtually all kinds of naturalists and non-naturalists can, in some way or the other, try to make sense of the publicity condition and the idea that moral utterances are somehow concerned with the acceptance of certain views and the guidance of human behaviour. The least we should assume, therefore, is that what is being put in the public domain is a desire-like attitude, even if not necessarily one the speaker himself possesses, and this view is also suggested by some related statements in Blackburn's *Antirealist expressivism and quasi-realism*.[125]

Yet, it seems that this still leaves the idea which is meant to shed light on the expression relation underspecified. If the only relevant constraint is that moral utterances are about attitudes that are put in the public domain for acceptance or guidance, then it seems that some important rivals of expressivism would still remain in the picture. Even defenders of a simple speaker subjectivist view that translates 'abortion is wrong' as 'I disapprove of abortion' seem to be in a position to allow that by making a moral utterance, a speaker puts an attitude in the public domain. In order to rule out a speaker subjectivist interpretation of expression, therefore, the expressivist needs to place a certain emphasis on the element of acceptance and guidance contained in Blackburn's characterization. In fact, it seems that this leads us back to the idea sketched in the discussion of Jackson and Pettit's challenge to expressivism, namely the idea that the expressivist should tie the notion of 'expression' to the notion of endorsement. Drawing on this idea, the expressivist might claim that one is only putting an attitude forward in the relevant sense if one not only reports it or introduces it as an object of discussion but also endorses it in some way.

However, this does not bring the difficulties to an end. First, such a proposal obviously raises the question of how to cash out the idea of endorsement in systematic terms, and the most natural way of doing so is debarred for the expressivist: if he argues that one only endorses an attitude if one actually has a positive higher-order attitude towards it, then he is left with a variant of the causal understanding of the expression relation after all. All he would have achieved is to replace one type of causally efficient attitude with another. The strategy suggested by Blackburn, therefore, provides an alternative to the causal understanding of expression only if there is a non-causalistic strategy for reconstructing the endorsement of attitudes.

Secondly, even if there is such a strategy, it is still not clear whether the expressivist will be able to thereby ensure the distinctiveness of his position. The

---

125 See Blackburn 2006, 151.

reason is that some rivals of expressivism seem to be able to satisfy even this qualified condition. Thus, 'fitting attitude' accounts,[126] which analyse the utterance 'abortion is wrong' as the claim that certain negative attitudes are 'fitting' (or 'adequate' or 'warranted') responses to abortion, seem to be able to account for the idea that a speaker making a moral utterance thereby puts a desire-like attitude in the public domain and endorses it in some relevant sense, and the same seems to be true of dispositional theories of value which give the meaning of 'X is good' as 'I would desire X if I were fully rational'.[127] It seems, therefore, that Blackburn needs to embrace a more demanding notion of 'expression', or, for that matter, of 'endorsement', in order to retain a distinctive expressivist position, and, as in the case of Schulte, it is not clear whether he can make sense of this notion without appealing to some kind of causal connection between moral attitude and linguistic utterance.

There is reason to believe, then, that the most promising strategy for explaining the crucial notion of 'expression' is to follow Schroeder's and Ridge's lead and to think of the expression relation in terms of assertability conditions or in terms of the linguistic accountability of the speaker. In fairness to Schulte, however, it should be emphasized that Schroeder and Ridge do not provide accounts that positively explain how the relevant linguistic conventions developed in the first place. Once a defender of assertability expressivism or accountability expression commits himself to a particular story about why sentences have the kind of semantic correctness conditions he claims them to have, or why speakers are liable in the way he takes them to be, he might face problems not unlike those faced by the teleofunctionalistic explanation complementing Schulte's characterization of the expression relation. Yet, since there are quite different ways of explaining the development of linguistic conventions, one might still think that proponents of Schroeder's or Ridge's approach will not necessarily run the risk of having to rely on a causal account of meaning after all.

However, this does not mean that Schroeder's or Ridge's approach, or in fact *any* plausible account of the expression relation, can do without postulating *some* kind of causal connection between linguistic utterances and the actual mental states of the speaker. While it is hard to see how the causal history of individual utterances should ever account for their meaning or fully explain the linguistic conventions that help to determine this meaning, it is equally hard to see how linguistic conventions that demand a speaker to be in a certain

---

[126] See Jacobson 2011 for an overview.
[127] The most influential recent proponent of such a dispositional theory is Michael Smith (see, in particular, Smith 1994a). However, see already Brandt 1979.

type of mental state when making an utterance could ever have evolved if speakers making utterances of this type – or some rudimentary variant of it – had not often or typically been in the very type of mental state. This, I take it, is the fundamental truth in Jackson and Pettit's Lockean account of language. Moreover, if we as current speakers were not typically in those mental states the assertability conditions of our utterances demand us to be in, then we would permanently be violating the semantic correctness conditions of our language and permanently be talking past each other. In other words, to accept Schroeder's or Ridge's account of the expression relation but to simultaneously deny that there is any interesting causal connection between utterances and the types of mental states that are part of their assertability conditions (or part of speaker's liability conditions), would amount to the wildly implausible claim that our linguistic conventions are based on a terrific mistake because they have us constantly ascribe mental states to our communicative partners which are not really instantiated. The reason why this claim would be wildly implausible is that we would then have quite a hard time explaining why language can so successfully fulfil its social functions, one of which consists in social coordination.

With regard to the subsequent discussion of the psychological implications of expressivism, therefore, the most important conclusion to be drawn from the debate over the expression relation is that the contributors to this debate tend to somewhat overstate the distinction between the hopelessly defective causal interpretation of 'expression' on the one hand and some supposedly appropriate non-causal interpretation on the other. Neither are the accounts provided by classic expressivists such as Ayer, Stevenson and Blackburn as completely wedded to a naïve causal understanding of 'expression' as critics tend to suggest, nor are the accounts forwarded by Schroeder, Ridge and Schulte as independent of the idea that desire-like attitudes actually cause moral utterances as some anti-causalists seem to think. The critical examination of the debate over the 'expression relation' suggests that expressivists must allow for a frequent causal connection between moral utterances and a particular type of mental state and that they thereby incur substantial commitments, not only in the philosophy of language, but also in the philosophy of mind. That the expressivist may, and should in fact, reject a naïve causal understanding of the expression relation does not mean that he can thereby avoid having to deal with the psychology of speakers making moral utterances.

4 Summary

The purpose of this chapter was to take a closer look at two of the main challenges that have been raised against expressivism in the past and to see what a thorough discussion of these challenges can contribute to the analysis of the psychological implications of expressivism, which is the object of the final chapter of this book. According to the first of these challenges, usually referred to under the name 'moral attitude problem', expressivists have not only failed to provide a satisfactory specification of the desire or non-cognitive state supposedly expressed by moral utterances so far, but might in fact be unable to ever do so because they face the dilemma of either identifying the attitude in question with a non-moral attitude, whose link with moral utterances must then be precarious, or illegitimately describing it by invoking straightforward normative vocabulary. According to the second challenge, expressivists need to say much more about what it actually means to 'express' a mental state by way of linguistic convention because the existing accounts of the 'expression relation', in particular the naïve causal account suggested by both Ayer and Stevenson, fail.

With regard to the 'moral attitude problem', I conceded that the weaker version of the objection is justified since the existing attempts to specify the attitude in question indeed remain unsatisfactory. However, I argued that there is no real dilemma for the expressivist here, which is why the stronger version of the version seems unjustified. The problem for the expressivist is not that there is no way for him to consistently specify the desire-like state expressed by moral utterances, but that any such specification comes at a certain cost because the expressivist is bound to lose some of his dialectic advantage over either the naturalist or the non-naturalist. Another conclusion to be drawn from the discussion was that, the possibility of providing a functionalist analysis of the attitude in question notwithstanding, the specification challenge can hardly be answered satisfactorily without engaging in genuine psychological theorizing and developing robust conceptions of the moral attitude and of beliefs and desires in general.

With regard to the expression relation, the overall result of my discussion was that the differences between causal and non-causal conceptions have been greatly exaggerated in the recent debate. At the very least, the extent to which this distinction bears on the evaluation of the existing attempts to describe what the relevant kind of 'expression' is have seriously been overstated. Thus, it could be shown in section 2 that none of the classic expressivists, not even Ayer, endorses the causal interpretation of the expression relation in its pure form. Even the early expressivists crucially appeal to linguistic conventions in trying to make further sense of the notion of expression, and they all equally accept the basic idea that one can express a mental state without actually being in this state. Moreover, as was shown in section 3, the more recent conceptions of the expression relation provided by Schroeder, Ridge, Schulte and Blackburn are by no means as independent of causal aspects as they are sometimes taken to be. In order to be able to explain how the relevant linguistic conventions could have ever come to be established, all three accounts, and in fact *any* plausible account of the expression relation, must allow for a frequent causal connection between moral utterances and the states of mind they conventionally express. Not only may we conclude, then, that the oft-berated naïve causal understanding of the expression relation is something of a red herring in the debate over expressivism: the general relevance of causal aspects provides further reasons for thinking that the basic expressivist idea cannot wholly be disentangled from psychological assumptions about the mental states speakers actually find themselves in when making moral utterances.

Against independence: Expressivism and (empirical) moral psychology

The results of the previous chapters provide a basis from which we can now attempt to answer the question that was raised at the beginning of this book, namely whether the expressivist commits himself to any substantial claims in moral psychology and, in particular, whether he needs to embrace the thesis I have referred to as *sentimentalism about moral judgement*. The purpose of answering this question has guided the previous examination of several systematic aspects of expressivism and especially the preceding discussion of the expression relation. In this final chapter, I want to address the issue head-on and discuss it in a more comprehensive and systematic way.

In order to do so, I will, first, provide a more detailed account of the 'independence thesis' forwarded by Richard Joyce, according to which genuinely psychological issues have no bearing on the evaluation of metaethical expressivism. I will then, secondly, look at the way in which the classic expressivists have explicitly commented upon the underlying question, as well as at the views on the matter that can be derived from their key claims and argumentative strategies. Thirdly, I will enter into a free-standing systematic discussion of the reasons for why psychological issues are relevant to the expressivist approach and identify the kind of psychological claim the expressivist needs to embrace. Finally, in section 4, I will address some more general methodological questions concerning the relationship of metaethical approaches to moral psychology on the one hand and straightforward empirical approaches on the other.

1 The independence thesis

The thesis that metaethical expressivism is independent of any substantial claims in moral psychology is a thesis to which I will subsequently refer to as the *independence thesis*. It has most forcefully been advocated by Richard Joyce. Joyce develops his view in critical discussion of the idea that recent empirical data from neuroscience and social psychology undermine moral rationalism and support 'emotivism', which term Joyce uses interchangeably with the term 'expressivism'. According to Joyce, something like this is suggested by social psychologists like Jonathan Haidt, but also by philosophers like Shaun Nichols or Jesse Prinz who employ empirical methods themselves or crucially rely on the empirical findings of others.

In Joyce's view, the idea simply results from some kind of terminological confusion: since metaethical emotivism is a theory about moral language and "most clearly construed as concerning the *function* of public moral utterances"[1], psychological studies which reveal what goes on in the head of somebody making a moral utterance are generally irrelevant to the truth of emotivism or expressivism, even if they managed to conclusively show that moral utterances are caused by desire-like attitudes, a position Joyce refers to as "psychological emotivism"[2].

The argument Joyce provides in support of the independence thesis very much focuses on the meaning of 'expression' and builds on an emphatic rejection of the naïve causal understanding of the expression relation. Joyce emphasizes that, although 'expression' is sometimes used to denote a causal relation, as when we say that, by kicking her little brother, Emily expressed her anger, it is often *not* used in this sense. One such example is provided by when we say of Emily's subsequent apology that Emily expressed her regret, which can be true even if her apology was insincere and she did not actually feel an ounce of regret and hence was not moved to apologize by the relevant kind of feeling.[3] According to Joyce, the claim made by emotivists and modern expressivists is concerned with this latter kind of expression and hence logically independent of the question of which states of mind speakers are actually in when they make a moral utterance.[4] For Joyce, the only way to decide whether or not emotivism or expressivism are true is "to investigate directly the nature of linguistic conventions surrounding our moral discourse, not the nature of neurological etiology"[5]. Joyce concedes that uncovering these linguistic conventions might be

---

[1] Joyce 2008, 373. (my emphasis)
[2] Joyce 2009, 34. It should be noted that some of Joyce's statements suggest that he is only concerned with making a weaker claim, namely that empirical psychological evidence cannot prove the truth of metaethical emotivism because metaethical emotivism adds a linguistic claim to 'psychological egoism' and therefore goes significantly beyond it (see, for instance, Joyce 2008, 375; and Joyce 2009, 34). However, this weaker claim does not warrant Joyce's general dismissive attitude towards the appeal to empirical psychological evidence in metaethics, which is explicitly directed at the idea that the relevant data "support" (Joyce 2008, 372) emotivism. Obviously, this idea could be true even if further, genuinely linguistic evidence were required as well. Moreover, the weaker thesis does not sit well with Joyce's explicit claims that metaethical emotivism is logically *independent* of 'psychological emotivism' (see Joyce 2009, 34) and that metaethical emotivism *neither* implies motivational internalism *nor* is implied by it (see Joyce 2009, 32f.).
[3] See Joyce 2008, 375.
[4] See also Joyce 2009, 32.
[5] Joyce 2008, 376.

"in substantial part"[6] an empirical inquiry. He emphasizes, however, that the empirical evidence relevant to this kind of sociolinguistic enterprise is quite different from the one produced by neuroscience or social psychology and that the appeal to the former kind of evidence "is fairly pervasive in metaethics, and indeed in philosophy in general"[7].

Now one problem with Joyce's argument is that one might want to question this latter view on metaethics and argue that, despite the recent rise of experimental philosophy, empirical investigations into how competent speakers actually use moral terms do not play the role in metaethics and moral philosophy one should expect them to play. However, the more important problem is that, as we have seen, the inadequacy of a naïve causal understanding of the expression relation is by no means sufficient for rejecting empirical psychological evidence as irrelevant to the proper assessment of emotivism or expressivism.

Even if we conclude from cases of insincerity or self-deception that the meaning of a token utterance does not depend on its being caused by a certain mental state of the speaker, it does not follow that such causal relations do not contribute to the utterance's meaning at all, especially if we consider it as an utterance of a certain type. In fact, the case of insincerity very much acts like a case in point here. The whole point of an insincere apology is to make the hearer *think* that we are in a certain kind of mental state where we are actually not. If the considerations of the preceding section are correct, then the fact that we can successfully mislead a hearer in this way is only intelligible if speakers uttering apologies actually *are* in a state of regret in a critical number of cases. In other words, while the case of a speaker who purports to be in a mental state he is not actually in may be a common occurrence, it is clearly parasitic on the case of a speaker who *is* in the kind of mental state his utterance expresses. The fact that expressivists do not, or at least should not, conceive of the expression relation in terms of a naïve causal understanding, therefore, does not suffice to demonstrate that they are not, or need not be, concerned with matters of psychological fact.

The question of whether expressivists commit themselves to substantial psychological claims and have reason to pay attention to the findings of empirical psychology, then, is one that clearly requires a more detailed discussion than Joyce allows it. In what follows, I will address this question with the purpose of rejecting Joyce's independence thesis. There are two strategies for refuting Joyce's thesis which I will both pursue. The first and simpler strategy is to show that, as a matter of fact, leading expressivists *do* subscribe to substantial psycho-

---

6 Joyce 2008, 376.
7 Joyce 2008, 377.

logical claims and explicitly discuss psychological theories or empirical findings in order to support and defend their positions. The second and more demanding strategy is to show that this is not merely a contingent aspect of their theories but that, on any plausible understanding of the expressivist thesis, expressivists are committed to making this kind of appeal to moral psychology. The first strategy will be the subject of the subsequent section, while the second will be my main concern in section 3.

2 Modern expressivists and the psychology of moral judgement

In my previous discussion, I have repeatedly emphasized that expressivism is first and foremost a linguistic thesis. In fact, it was for this very reason that I criticized commentators who build a psychological claim into the very definition of expressivism and postponed the discussion of the psychological implications of expressivism until the main questions surrounding expressivism's linguistic claim had been addressed. Although Joyce is certainly right therefore to stress the characteristic linguistic concern of expressivists, he nevertheless paints a distorted picture of the nature of modern expressivism. Joyce explicitly takes up the question of whether one might not also define expressivism in terms of the psychological thesis that moral judgements, understood not as public utterances but as mental states or events, are desires or desire-like attitudes. However, he rejects this "mentalistic construal"[8] of expressivism as being "unconventional"[9] and unfaithful to the understanding of those theorists who put expressivism on the metaethical map, namely Ogden and Richards, Ayer, Carnap and Stevenson. Yet, while it may be true that these early expressivists did not bother much with moral thought as opposed to moral language, it is clearly false to say that the mentalist interpretation of expressivism is unconventional. The reason why this is false is that those expressivists who had the biggest impact on the modern debate over expressivism but are not mentioned by Joyce, namely Blackburn, Gibbard and even Hare, are clearly interested in *both* moral thought *and* moral language.

As we have already seen in chapter 2, Blackburn is not only concerned with the meaning of moral utterances, but also with the question of what constitutes moral thinking. In fact, this even seems to be Blackburn's main concern and the

---

8 Joyce 2009, 39.
9 Joyce 2009, 39.

one that forms the core of his theory about morality. This emphasis is often overlooked because one of the earliest of Blackburn's publications on expressivism, the book *Spreading the word*, is generally concerned with issues in the philosophy of language. However, even in *Spreading the word*, expressivism is initially introduced by Blackburn as a thesis about the "practice of judging"[10] and about the kind of "commitment"[11] that constitutes judging something to be good or bad, of which commitment, according to Blackburn's characterization, the expressivist conceives not as a belief but as an attitude.[12] While Blackburn is, therefore, clearly interested in the meaning and function of moral utterances, this interest is just as clearly derived from a more general interest in the "practice of moralizing"[13], of which making moral utterances is but one element.

If anything, Blackburn's concern with moral psychology has become even more prominent and visible after the publication of *Spreading the word*. As is indicated by numerous statements we find in publications from the late 1980s and early 1990s, the true object of Blackburn's expressivist argument is what the "essence of ethics"[14] is or "what ethics, as a socially going concern, actually consists in"[15], and the psychological characterization of the states of mind we are in when we are doing ethics always lies at the heart of Blackburn's discussion.[16] In *Ruling passions*, published in 1998, the linguistic analysis of our moral practice is then quite explicitly relegated to the background, with claims about the nature of moral thinking and valuing taking centre stage throughout most of the book.[17] Moreover, in the introduction to his recent collection of essays, entitled *Practical tortoise raising*, Blackburn admits to very much having lost interest in the semantics of moral language and to being much more interested in those wider explanatory questions on which he takes the semantics of moral utterances to ultimately depend, including questions in the philosophy of mind.[18]

Though we do not find the same preoccupation with moral psychology in Gibbard, especially not in his more recent work, there can be no doubt that the latter conceives of expressivism as a theory about both moral thought and

---

10 Blackburn 1984, 167.
11 Blackburn 1984, 167.
12 See Blackburn 1984, 167.
13 Blackburn 1984, 169.
14 Blackburn 1996, 85.
15 Blackburn 1995, 50.
16 See also Blackburn 1991, 39f.; and Blackburn 1992, 295.
17 See, for instance, Blackburn 1998, 49f. See also Blackburn's own characterization of the book in Blackburn 2001a, 1.
18 See Blackburn 2010b, 2.

moral language as well. One of the earliest sketches of Gibbard's expressivism is devoted to the psychological propensities that are involved in a sense of justice, paying only little attention to the language by which we express these propensities.[19] And while the linguistic question of what it means to call something 'rational' may become more and more important in the publications leading up the *Wise choices* and in the book itself, Gibbard's interest is always in the psychological question of what constitutes the psychological state of regarding something as rational as well.[20] Moreover, even in Gibbard's more recent publications, which, as we have seen, are mostly devoted to a possibility proof for some kind of expressivist normative language, Gibbard tends to present his theory as a theory that is also concerned with normative thought.[21]

Finally, we may note that even Hare's writings, whose theory is usually understood as a linguistic theory about the meaning and the logical behaviour of moral terms, display a clear tendency towards the discussion of moral thinking and moral reasoning. While there is hardly any mention of these aspects in *The language of morals*, they are explicitly introduced in *Freedom and reason* and become the main focus in *Moral thinking*.[22] Therefore, even though one might want to argue that Hare's distinctive take on moral thinking and moral reasoning is logical rather than psychological, it would seem inadequate to say that his version of expressivism is strictly confined to linguistic issues and incurious about speakers' mentalities.

It is important to note that this emphasis on both moral thinking and moral language is clearly reflected in the more recent literature on expressivism. Characterizations of expressivism as a thesis about either the semantics of moral utterances or the psychology of moral judgement (or both) have become quite common,[23] and some commentators, most notably Mark Schroeder, have even gone as far as to suggest that modern expressivism is *primarily* a theory about moral thought and that this is exactly what distinguishes modern expressivist theories from the "speech act theories"[24] of Ayer, Stevenson and Hare.[25] Given Hare's pro-

---

19 See Gibbard 1982, 33.
20 See Gibbard 1985b, 11; Gibbard 1986a, 474; Gibbard 1986b, 218; and Gibbard 1990a, 7 and 55.
21 See, for instance, Gibbard 1993b, 315; Gibbard 2003, 180 f.; Gibbard 2011, 35 f.; and Gibbard 2014, VIII.
22 See Hare 1963, 86 ff.; and Hare 1981.
23 See, for instance, Horwich 1993, 67 f.; O'Leary-Hawthorne/Price 1996, 276; Ridge 2003, 563; Copp 2004, 24; d'Arms/Jacobson 2006, 192; Ridge 2014, 5; and Dreier 2015, 155 f. Note that some of these characterizations are applied to non-cognitivism (rather than expressivism), which is, however, conceived of as either equivalent to expressivism or as a more general metaethical category under which expressivism can be subsumed.
24 Schroeder 2008c, 74.

ven interest in moral thinking and given the fact that at least some modern proponents of expressivism, such as Boisvert, continue to appeal to speech act terminology in setting up their theories, this may appear to be a bit of an overstatement. If nothing else, however, Schroeder's claim suffices to show that the more comprehensive nature of Blackburn's and Gibbard's expressivist agenda has not been lost on commentators. Joyce's claim that the mentalistic characterization of expressivism is unconventional, therefore, does not withstand scrutiny. Accordingly, the fact that the argument in support of his independence thesis exclusively appeals to public moral utterances casts serious doubts on it.

A further reason why Joyce's picture of the expressivism debate is a distorted one is that he does not sufficiently acknowledge that both Blackburn and Gibbard present psychological or other empirical evidence as relevant to their argument and explicitly engage with it in order to defend their views against objections. In Blackburn's work, we not only find an affirmative discussion of 18th century philosophy of mind, as exemplified by Hume and Adam Smith.[26] We also find arguments appealing to recent neuroscientific evidence, such as the evidence from psychopaths or sociopaths gathered by Antonio Damasio and his collaborators,[27] and to studies in evolutionary biology.[28] Moreover, these references to empirical research on human nature and the human mind are by no means restricted to *Ruling passions*, where Blackburn's purpose is to develop an overall sentimentalist theory of human morality. They can equally be found in publications that deal with the expressivist thesis more narrowly construed.[29]

Pretty much the same can be said about Gibbard. One core element of the expressivist theory laid out in *Wise choices* is an (admittedly speculative) evolutionary story about how and why the peculiar mental state of norm-acceptance has evolved in humans.[30] In addition, Gibbard explicitly considers psychological evidence forwarded by researchers such as Elliot Turiel or Jonathan Haidt and points out that certain features of his theory are supported by recent 'dual-process' theories in empirical psychology.[31] Furthermore, he explicitly takes up chal-

---

25 See Schroeder 2008a, 3f. and 151f. See also Schroeder 2008c, 74f. Similar views have been suggested by Campbell, Schulte and Horgan/Timmons (see Campbell 2007, 321; Schulte 2010, 156; and Horgan/Timmons 2015, 206).
26 See Blackburn 1998, 97ff.
27 See Blackburn 1998, 125ff.
28 See Blackburn 1998, 144ff.
29 See, for example, Blackburn 1993c, 168; Blackburn 1995, 51; and Blackburn 1996, 85.
30 See Gibbard 1990a, 55ff. See also Gibbard 1982, 33ff.; Gibbard 1985b, 15; Gibbard 1986a, 474f.; Gibbard 1994, 98f.
31 See Gibbard 2006b, 198ff.; Gibbard 2011, 35f.; and Gibbard 2015, 177ff.

lenges based on such empirical findings, like the one raised by Shaun Nichols who argues that the meaning of moral utterances should not be explained in terms of warranted guilt or resentment because young children, though capable of making moral utterances, are yet incapable of understanding the concept of guilt.[32]

The implicit acknowledgement that empirical psychological evidence bears on the appropriateness of the expressivist analysis of moral language is something we even find in early expressivists, such as Stevenson. Given Stevenson's causalistic definition of linguistic meaning and the way in which he ties emotive meaning to the dynamic use of language, there is hardly a way for him to argue that his semantic analysis is independent of claims about human psychology, and Stevenson seems to willingly concede as much even though he does not himself enter into any detailed psychological discussion.[33]

The only way to defend Joyce's independence thesis, then, is to claim that modern expressivists are misled in confronting empirical psychological or biological evidence and make unnecessary concessions to researchers examining the psychological or biological reality of moral judgement. In what follows, I will reject this claim and try to demonstrate that expressivists have good reasons for extending their theory about the meaning of moral utterances to claims about the nature of moral judgement and for caring about whether existing empirical research supports these claims. This demonstration will give me the opportunity to tie together the relevant results of the previous chapters.

3 Why expressivists ought to be sentimentalists about moral judgement

We may begin by emphasizing that neither Blackburn nor Gibbard seem to conceive of their appeal to empirical psychology or evolutionary biology as a merely contingent aspect of their arguments, as a kind of unforced concession to the recent interest in moral judgement and moral reasoning shown by empirical researchers of various strands. Quite to the contrary, both Blackburn and Gibbard introduce their discussions of empirical evidence and evolutionary considerations as something to which, as expressivists, they are reasonably committed.

This is especially clear in Gibbard's case. Gibbard motivates his evolutionary speculations in *Wise choices* by explicitly claiming that his account of normative

---

32 See Gibbard 2006b. For Nichols' challenge, see Nichols 2004, 83 ff.
33 See, for instance, Stevenson 1944, 7.

language requires him to enter into psychology and to make plausible that the mental state of norm-acceptance to which his analysis appeals actually exists.[34] In a similar manner, Blackburn suggests that the 'essence of ethics' lies, not in the network of propositions people are asserting, but "in the underlying contours of their sensibility: the contours of attitude and emotion that drive them in their actions and their relations to others"[35]. He then explicitly emphasizes that the psychological and the semantic enterprise "will need to go hand in hand"[36] and "that it is hard to see how an investigation into the moral proposition could get very far without saying something of what we ourselves are up to when we judge such propositions to be true or false or verified or beyond debate or open to doubt"[37]. Both authors suggest, therefore, that there are systematic reasons why the expressivist cannot do without genuinely psychological considerations, and the purpose of the subsequent discussion is to get a clearer picture of what these reasons are.

Let us start the systematic discussion of the independence thesis with the quite radical idea that the concepts of belief and desire to which the expressivist analysis appeals to are not really psychological concepts at all, but can wholly be reconstructed in linguistic terms. As we have seen, some contributors to the debate have suggested that a belief is simply what is expressed by a declarative sentence. A defender of Joyce's independence thesis might resort to this understanding of 'belief' in order to argue that the properties of 'being a belief' and 'not being a belief' relevant to expressivism are *linguistic* properties, so that any discussion of genuinely psychological conceptions of belief and desire is uncalled for and, in fact, misguided.

The obvious problem with this way of defending the independence thesis is that, once we understand the expressivist theory in this sense, it does not even get off the ground. As is acknowledged by all contributors to the debate, moral utterances often take the form of declarative sentences. Moreover, it is quite common to refer to one's moral judgements as a matter of belief, as when we say 'I believe that abortion is wrong' rather than just 'Abortion is wrong' or ask another person whether or not she believes that abortion is wrong. In fact, Joyce's himself emphasizes that any attempt to make a moral claim but to simultaneously deny that one believes its content results in a 'Moore-paradoxical' sentence,

---

34 See Gibbard 1990a, 25 f.: "I myself need to look at human psychology for another reason: an expressivistic analysis like mine requires it."
35 Blackburn 1996, 85.
36 Blackburn, *Social and individual expression* (ms), 2.
37 Blackburn, *Social and individual expression* (ms), 2.

such as 'Hitler was evil, but I don't believe that'.[38] If we restrict the notion of belief such as to denote a wholly linguistic phenomenon, therefore, we cannot but conclude that moral utterances do in fact express beliefs, which means that a purely linguistic variant of the expressivist thesis, though in principle possible, is impossible to defend.

We can make basically the same point by emphasizing that the linguistic side of things, i.e. what we have referred to as the propositional surface of moral discourse, is not what *supports* the expressivist idea but instead what presents the most important *obstacle* to it. The reason why Blackburn and Gibbard devote so much attention to linguistic matters and, for example, put so much effort into solving the 'Frege-Geach problem', is not that evidence from our ordinary linguistic practices helps them to build their positive case for expressivism. It is that, only if this evidence can satisfactorily be accommodated, expressivism becomes a serious metaethical contender in the first place.

It is important here to recall that both Blackburn and Gibbard view the question of whether or not expressivism provides the best account of moral language as one which cannot be decided in the linguistics arena and conceive of the considerations that help us to adjudicate between expressivism and its rivals as non-linguistic ones. In accordance with this, most of the arguments which have traditionally been forwarded in support of expressivism, and which have been reviewed in chapter 4, are not linguistic arguments at all: they appeal to epistemological, metaphysical and psychological considerations. Moreover, those arguments which we might not want to assign to any of these categories – such as the open question argument and perhaps the argument from supervenience – either fail to lend distinctive support to expressivism (because they speak against naturalism but not against non-naturalism or vice versa), or confront the naturalist or non-naturalist with problems that a plausibly refined version of expressivism faces in about the same way (as shown by our discussion of hybrid expressivism and the 'moral attitude problem' in chapters 5 and 6).

If we draw the strict line between linguistic and non-linguistic claims suggested by Joyce's discussion, it is not clear why any of the epistemological, metaphysical and psychological arguments forwarded in favour of expressivism should be relevant at all. That they are taken to be relevant is the result of the fact that metaethicists are not usually concerned with ordinary speakers' transparent understanding of how moral terms and utterances are being used, but with the philosophical question of how to sensibly reconstruct the meaning of those terms and utterances in a systematic and coherent manner. If this were

---

38 See Joyce 2009, 41 f.

3 Why expressivists ought to be sentimentalists about moral judgement — 217

not the overall interest behind most, if not all, of modern metaethics, it would not be clear why metaethics would not just be a part of empirical sociolinguistics. However, once we concede that there is more to metaethics than sociolinguistics, we seem to also have to concede that non-linguistic considerations pertaining to our common moral practice provide an important input for metaethics, and that psychological or other considerations may be exactly what tips the balance in favour of one systematic reconstruction of moral language as opposed to another.

Of course, this still leaves the possibility that the expressivist might not need to enter into any kind of psychological discussion because the appeal to epistemology or metaphysics is already sufficient for him to make his case. However, even if this were true, and even if there were a way to draw a clear line between moral psychology on the one hand and the relevant epistemological aspects on the other, Joyce's argument for the irrelevance of psychological evidence would still be inadequate because it proceeds by way of the quite general suggestion that psychological evidence cannot bear on metaethical analyses because it is *non-linguistic* evidence.

Moreover, there are actually good reasons for doubting that the appeal to metaphysics or to non-psychological aspects of epistemology allows the expressivist to already rest his case. As we have seen in chapter 4, the key argument in most defences of expressivism is the motivation argument. Yet, this argument seems to rest on a certain understanding of the psychology of moral thought rather than on an understanding of moral semantics, moral epistemology or moral metaphysics. Since what motivates a person is not the mental state she expresses by way of linguistic expression, but the mental state she is actually in, the expressivist can only exploit the supposed connection between sincere moral utterances and motivation if he is willing to embrace the idea that moral judgements are constituted by desire-like mental states and that a person making a sincere moral utterance typically is in such state.

Apart from the role of the motivation argument as a crucial motivation for expressivist analyses of moral language, there are also more general reasons to think that expressivism should be a thesis about both moral language and thought. It is quite natural to think that these two elements are just two sides of the same coin. As already emphasized, there is no way to deny that moral utterances can be insincere or deluded so that a speaker uttering 'Abortion is wrong' need not necessarily *think* that abortion is wrong. In turn, we might also want to resist the idea that moral thinking is some kind of inner monologue that is necessarily carried out in linguistic form. Yet, these two caveats notwithstanding, it seems that any plausible metaethical theory needs to acknowledge a characteristic continuity between moral thought and moral language and to allow that what people standardly do when they make moral utterances is to simply transfer their moral thoughts to the public sphere and make them known to others. This idea, which I will subsequently refer to as the *continuity thesis*, provides strong reasons for thinking that a version of expressivism that claims (a) that public moral utterances express desire-like states of mind rather than beliefs, and (b) that private moral thoughts or judgements are constituted by beliefs rather than desire-like states of mind must be, if not downright incoherent, then at least seriously unstable.

The continuity thesis also tends to put pressure on metaethical positions that either exclusively agree with the expressivist interpretation of moral utterances or exclusively agree with the sentimentalist interpretation of moral judgement. An example of the former kind is provided by hybrid theories according to which moral utterances express desire-like attitudes by implicature, which are often motivated by the motivation argument as well. Such theories must explain why *private* moral judgements are crucially associated with motivation for action, too, and it seems that the appeal to implicature does not itself provide a basis for such an explanation.[39] An example of the latter kind is provided by speaker subjectivism, at least on the reading suggested by Joyce himself. Joyce indicates that the mentalist version of expressivism (or expressivism as a psychological thesis) is simply identical to the mentalist version of speaker subjectivism (or speaker subjectivism as a psychological thesis).[40] However, it seems doubtful whether speaker subjectivism, if we conceive of its psychological implications in this way, can account for the continuity of moral thought and moral thinking in an appropriate way. The speaker subjectivist would then have to postulate that moral thoughts and moral utterances have different intentional objects: while the object of a person's moral judgement is the action that is being evaluated (or a more general property to which the person's pro- or con-attitude relates), the object of a person's moral utterance is his own psychological state which he describes or reports.

A further consideration supporting the view that the expressivist ought to avoid an asymmetrical analysis of moral language and moral thought is that such an analysis will rob him of the dialectical advantages he might have over rival metaethical theories.[41] If, for example, the reason to resist naturalist or

---

39 See also Fletcher 2015, 192; and Schroeder 2015, 283f. See also Copp who tries to defend his version of an implicature view against such charges (see Copp 2015, 56ff.).
40 See Joyce 2009, 34 and 39. See also Jackson who likewise suggests that, according to speaker subjectivism, a moral thought is not constituted by the thinker's belief that he has a certain desire-like attitude, but by the attitude itself (see Jackson 2001, 11).
41 See also Schroeder 2008a, 151f.; and Schroeder 2010, 75.

non-naturalist analyses of moral language is that we cannot initially make sense of the idea of a moral proposition or of robust moral properties, then it seems that the very same reason should speak against conceiving of moral thinking in terms of moral beliefs because it is not clear how to make sense of such beliefs if not in terms of moral propositions or robust moral properties. In turn, *if* there is a way to conceive of moral beliefs without relying on moral propositions or robust moral properties, for example by conceiving of them in purely functionalist terms, then it is not clear why the functionalist analysis should not also allow us to provide a naturalist or non-naturalist analysis of moral language. Whatever the epistemological, metaphysical or psychological considerations motivating expressivist analyses of moral language are, therefore, it seems that the expressivist can take full advantage of those considerations only if he extends his analysis to moral thought and embraces a symmetrical interpretation of these two key elements of our moral practice.

Finally, as repeatedly emphasized, it is difficult to give a plausible explanation for why moral utterances have come to express certain mental states by linguistic convention if there is no systematic connection between those mental states and the mental states speakers are actually in when they are making moral utterances. The only way to argue that moral utterances express desire-like states of mind while simultaneously denying that these states of mind are instantiated in speakers in a critical number of cases is to suggest that there *was* such a connection between the meaning of moral words and the psychology of speakers when moral words initially acquired their meaning, but that this connection has since been disrupted. However, it is far from clear why this kind of disruption should have occurred and, what is more, it is not clear how moral language could have continued to fulfil its social function if it now failed to provide us with any reliable evidence of the actual mental states of the people we converse with and, in particular, of their motivations.

The upshot of all this, then, is that on any plausible understanding of the overall expressivist approach, expressivism makes *both* a claim about the meaning of moral utterances *and* a psychological claim about the nature of moral judgement. While Joyce is certainly right that the linguistic claim is not identical to the psychological claim and that psychological evidence alone is insufficient to prove the truth of expressivism as a linguistic-*cum*-psychological thesis, it seems undeniable that a purely linguistic version of expressivism is unstable and that psychological evidence bears on the truth of expressivism just as linguistic evidence does. The exact psychological claim to which the expressivist reasonably commits himself can be formulated as follows:

Sentimentalism about moral judgement: Moral judgements are constituted by desires or desire-like states of mind rather than beliefs.

There are three further comments I would like to make with regard to the way in which I have just phrased the psychological commitment of expressivism. First, though the term 'judgement' may not have figured largely in this chapter so far, I have tried to consistently use it to refer to a psychological or mental phenomenon rather than a linguistic one. It ought to be noted, however, that we find both usages in the current metaethical debate. While most contributors to the debate use 'judgement' in the psychological sense,[42] it has also become quite common to use it as a synonym for linguistic terms such as 'utterance' or 'speech act'.[43] One way to deal with the ambiguity of the term would be to distinguish between 'private judgements' and 'public judgements'.[44] However, I think that a clearer terminological distinction is desirable. I have therefore chosen to use term 'utterance' when referring to the public, linguistic side of things and to restrict the term 'judgement' to moral thinking. Yet, I did not adopt the even more restrictive understanding of 'judgement' according to which judgements are constituted by *beliefs*, since this would obviously make the claim referred to as *sentimentalism about moral judgement* incoherent. Though the 'classic' narrow understanding of 'judgement' is sometimes still employed or suggested by contributors to the modern metaethical debate,[45] it has clearly been superseded by a broader understanding of the term according to which 'judgement' denotes a more general psychological category that equally allows for judgements that are constituted by beliefs as for judgements that are constituted by desires or desire-like states.

---

42 See, for example, Brighouse 1990, 225; Dancy 1993, 3; Scanlon 1998, 33f.; Horgan/Timmons 2000, 121f.; Gibbard 2003, 76; Ridge 2003, 563f.; Campbell 2007, 321; Wedgwood 2007, 4; Merli 2008, 25; Kauppinen 2010, 236f.; Strandberg 2012, 90; Kauppinen 2014b, 20f.; Ridge 2014, 4f.; Fletcher 2015, 175; Hay 2015, 76; Prinz 2015, 70; Ridge 2015, 135 and 142; and Toppinen 2015a, 150.
43 See, for instance, Copp 2001, 7; Unwin 2001, 60; Joyce 2002, 336; Sinclair 2007, 343; Sinclair 2008, 265; Joyce 2009, 31; and Van Roojen 2014, 4. In addition, there are quite a few authors who do not explicitly elaborate on their use of the term 'judgement', but seem to apply it both to the mental and to the linguistic phenomenon. Commentators who explicitly note the ambiguity of the term 'judgement' include Scarano, Campbell and Kauppinen (see Scarano 2001, 13; Campbell 2007, 321; Kauppinen 2010, 253; and Kauppinen 2014b, 20).
44 This strategy is suggested by Joyce's use of the phrase "public moral judgement" (Joyce 2009, 31). Something like this is also suggested by Railton's use of the term 'judgement' (see Railton 2008, 44).
45 See, for instance, Blackburn 1981, 177f.; Blackburn 1984, 187f.; Blackburn 1995, 53; Jackson 2001, 11; Barker 2006, 299; and Döring 2010, 284;

Secondly, even those authors who conceive of moral judgements in the psychological sense sometimes employ the term 'to express' in formulating the psychological claim that complements expressivism's linguistic thesis. Thus, it is not at all uncommon to say that moral judgements, understood as mental phenomena, 'express' desire-like attitudes.[46] However, given that the expression relation needs to be understood in terms of a social linguistic convention, it is not clear how to make sense of the idea that private moral judgements or thoughts 'express' mental states. The more natural thing to say, it seems, is that these thoughts or judgements *are* mental states, or *consist* in mental states, or are *instantiated* or *constituted* by mental states. For this reason, I have confined talk of 'expression' to moral utterances and not applied it to moral judgements.

Thirdly, while the standard way of describing the relationship between moral judgements and states of mind is, indeed, to claim that moral judgements simply *are* particular states of mind (or *consist* in such states),[47] this way of talking appears to be, in one important respect, misleading because judgements are, strictly speaking, mental *events* rather than mental states.[48] The relationship between moral judgements and mental states, therefore, cannot be one of straightforward identity. Rather, it should be captured by the idea that mental states, which are plausibly understood as dispositional states, manifest themselves in moral judgements, and my (perhaps unsatisfactory) way of trying to bring out this somewhat looser connection is to resort to the claim that moral judgements are *constituted* by mental states.[49]

4 Philosophical moral psychology, empirical moral psychology and experimental philosophy: A note on methodology

There is one final claim one might possibly resort to in trying to (at least partially) defend Joyce's position, and in order to complete our discussion of the independence thesis, we need to address this claim as well. The claim is based on a

---

46 See, for example, Brighouse 1990, 225; Dancy 1993, 3; Ridge 2003, 563; and Campbell 2007, 321.
47 See, for example, Dancy 1993, 3; Campbell 2007, 321; Wedgwood 2007, 4; Joyce 2009, 39; Kauppinen 2010, 236 and 253; Strandberg 2012, 90; Kauppinen 2014b, 20; Ridge 2014, 4f.; Fletcher 2015, 175; Prinz 2015, 70; Ridge 2015, 135; and Toppinen 2015a, 150.
48 I am grateful to Markus Stepanians for pressing me on this point. The point has also recently been conceded by Michael Ridge (see Ridge 2014, 128).
49 For a similar terminology, see Ridge 2003, 563f.; Merli 2008, 25; and Ridge 2015, 142

distinction between what we may refer to as "philosophical moral psychology"[50] on the one hand and empirical moral psychology on the other. The idea is to concede that the expressivist commits himself to a non-linguistic claim that crucially appeals to certain concepts of folk psychology, such as 'desire' or 'belief', or perhaps to philosophically refined versions of those concepts, but to nevertheless argue that the expressivist does not thereby commit himself to any substantial claims in *empirical* psychology.

According to this line of thinking, the expressivist faces the task of providing a symmetrical and coherent account of moral thought and moral language in terms of fundamental psychological concepts and of showing that these concepts are suitably linked to how we conceive of our ordinary moral practice. However, whether these concepts correctly describe the reality of moral thinking as a matter of psychological empirical fact is a question the expressivist need not bother with, which means that, despite his commitment to *sentimentalism about moral judgement*, he can ignore the findings of social psychology, neuroscience or other empirical disciplines.

In response to this challenge, it first needs to be admitted that we find the theoretical distinction between philosophical psychology on the one hand and empirical psychology on the other in both Gibbard and Blackburn. Gibbard emphasizes that the purpose of his speculative discussion of normative psychology is mainly to develop an appropriate conceptual framework and that his chief interest is not in the literature on experimental psychology.[51] Similarly, Blackburn, in his discussion of motivational internalism, emphasizes that his thesis about the connection between moral judgement and motivation for action is a conceptual, not a causal one.[52]

However, although Gibbard and Blackburn may both put much more emphasis on the discussion of psychological *concepts* than on the discussion of empirical psychological evidence, they *do* engage with the latter kind of evidence and thereby implicitly suggest that the philosophical discussion cannot (or should not) be wholly disentangled from the scientific one. Moreover, Gibbard explicitly concedes that "the tests of a normative psychology must, in the end, be empirical"[53] and, more generally, that one of the main tasks of philosophy is to deal with new findings in science and to make sense of "the scientific image"[54] of ourselves as human beings.

---

50 Kauppinen 2010, 25.
51 See Gibbard 1990a, 26.
52 See Blackburn 2002, 123f.
53 Gibbard 1986a, 475.
54 Gibbard 2002c, 51.

Again, there are good reasons for adopting this view of the relationship of conceptual analysis and empirical science. The view that empirical psychological evidence, as well as other kind of empirical evidence, is directly relevant to any satisfactory analysis of the concepts of folk psychology has implicitly or explicitly been endorsed by a variety of philosophical and non-philosophical authors in the past. The claim in question can be read as an attack on any strict *a priori/a posteriori* distinction as well as on the traditional idea that, being an *a priori* enterprise, conceptual analysis must consist in a kind of armchair philosophy.

The defence of Joyce's rejection of empirical psychological evidence sketched above is meant to only rule out empirical psychological evidence as irrelevant, not the kind of empirical linguistic evidence to which many recent advocates of experimental philosophy appeal. Since the defence is, therefore, in principle consistent with rejecting a form of a armchair philosophy that takes no kind of empirical evidence to be relevant whatsoever, it hinges on the narrower question of whether there is any basis for philosophers interested in the nature of our psychological concepts to specifically reject empirical *psychological* evidence. It nevertheless seems helpful at this point to address the issue more generally and to see, first, whether the philosophical analyst can do without any empirical linguistic evidence in order to then, secondly, turn to the question of whether psychological evidence is relevant to the philosophical analysis of psychological concepts.

Let us begin, therefore, with a rough summary of the way in which experimental philosophers have argued for the relevance of empirical linguistic evidence in the past. The main idea is that philosophical conceptual analysis is, initially at least, concerned with our ordinary concepts and that these concepts are either empirical facts themselves or at least intimately related to such facts, in particular to facts about our own linguistic behaviour. What a particular ordinary concept is or amounts to, on this view, is revealed by the use that ordinary speakers make of certain relevant terms. The right way to do conceptual analysis, therefore, must be to do empirical linguistics or at least to let empirical linguistics support one's non-empirical philosophical considerations.

In my view, the two most radical positions one could adopt in this debate are equally implausible. Neither can the gathering of empirical linguistic evidence simply replace traditional philosophical analysis and make it superfluous, nor is there any good justification for completely ignoring such evidence where it can be had and for exclusively relying on one's own intuitions or the (often inconsistent) intuitions of fellow philosophers. The position I want to argue for in what follows, therefore, is some kind of intermediate position according to which empirical linguistic evidence is in principle relevant and admissible, but philosophical analysis is more, and needs to be more, than just collecting data about ordinary speakers' uses of relevant terms.

One problem with a more radical defence of armchair philosophy is that the wholesale rejection of empirical investigation into ordinary linguistic practice seems somewhat arbitrary since a strict *a priori/a posteriori* distinction is not very convincing. Trivially, the linguistic intuitions of the armchair philosopher have been formed by a gradual learning process and his experience of how other speakers actually use certain words. If this is true, however, then philosophers would draw an arbitrary line if they took the appeal to this kind of internalized linguistic experience to leave the *a priori* character of conceptual analysis unaffected, while taking the appeal to surveys that explicitly record other speakers' linguistic habits to introduce an illegitimate *a posteriori* element. Both of these appeals are appeals to empirical evidence, if perhaps of a different kind.

This is not to say that the *a priori/a posteriori* distinction might not be helpful and appropriate in certain contexts. If, for example, the concept in question is one for which a generally accepted definition or perhaps a stipulated technical definition exists, and if the aim of the analysis is to bring out the logical consequences or implications of this definition, then it seems that we may legitimately refer to this enterprise as *a priori*. Yet, while a mathematical investigation into the properties of triangles may adequately be captured by the above characterization, the metaethical investigation into the meaning and implications of ordinary moral terms is most clearly not.

Of course, this all leaves the radical armchair philosopher with the chance to simply drop the *a priori/a posteriori* terminology and to argue that it is exactly because of the differences between the two kinds of empirical or *a posteriori* evidence that the conceptual analyst should exclusively rely on the former and disregard the latter. One point that is often made in this context is that what we are really interested in when we are doing conceptual analysis is not how ordinary speakers use certain terms or employ certain concepts, but how *competent* speakers use them when they use them *correctly*. However, the problem with this defence of the privileged status of armchair philosophy, which we find, for example, in Antti Kauppinen's recent discussion of the issue,[55] is that it seems to be based on the presupposition that, where concepts are concerned, there exists an entirely speaker-independent truth of the matter, a truth which some speakers happen to grasp while others do not. Yet, it is not at all clear how there could be any such speaker-independent truth of the matter or how

---

55 See Kauppinen 2007, 101 ff. See also Kauppinen 2014a, 282 f.

it should itself be conceptualized. Moreover, even if there were such a truth of the matter, it is not clear why philosophers should belong to those speakers who have grasped it and should be able to unbiasedly rely on the relevant knowledge when doing armchair philosophy.

However, if a speaker's incompetence with regard to the meaning or the application of a particular concept does not consist in the failure to grasp some wholly speaker-independent truth of what our concepts really mean or refer to, what does it instead consist in? Surely, we would not want to commit us to the view that all speakers employ concepts correctly or that the idea of competence cannot be applied to how speakers use linguistic terms at all. It seems, therefore, that we need some conception of what makes a speaker more competent than others.

In my view, the incompetence of incompetent speakers can be taken to primarily consist in two things. First, it can be taken to consist in incoherencies or inconsistencies in their usage of relevant terms. We already discussed this aspect in chapter 4 where we saw that any plausible metaethical analysis of our actual usage of moral language will have to compensate for certain errors made by ordinary speakers and that all the classic expressivists conceive of their philosophical enterprise along these lines. Yet, in accordance with this, we may argue that the first aspect of incompetence is already sufficiently accounted for if philosophers critically review and systematically unify empirical linguistic evidence, not only if they completely ignore it.

Critics of experimental philosophy, such as Kauppinen, are certainly right to emphasize that the usage of questionnaires does not provide a universal remedy for the problems of armchair philosophy, since the results will always call for some kind of dialogic interpretation and yield a unified and coherent picture only after partial revision. However, while all this may show that a possible contribution of linguistic surveys and other empirical methods to metaethics (or other areas of conceptual analysis) ultimately depends on philosophical reflection and interpretation, it does not show that philosophers can do, or should do, without any such empirical input whatsoever.

Secondly, the incompetence of ordinary speakers might consist in the fact that they use terms or employ concepts in disregard of relevant pieces of information or knowledge. However, what is suggested by this very point is exactly that non-linguistic empirical findings cannot be entirely excluded from conceptual analysis understood as a philosophical enterprise, either. In order to decide what element of the ordinary understanding or ordinary usage of relevant terms needs to be given up, the philosopher has to rely on true or reliable information about the world, as it is provided by the empirical sciences. The purpose of an informed philosophical conceptual analysis, then, cannot be to simply appeal to crucial aspects of our ordinary linguistic practice in order to provide a coherent account of a local, circumscribed area. Ideally, it should also be in reflective equilibrium with our empirical knowledge about the world. Yet, such a wider reflective equilibrium can only be attained if the findings of the natural and social sciences are taken into account by the philosophical analyst. The way in which Blackburn and Gibbard appeal to empirical evidence and incorporate evolutionary models into their argument suggests that modern expressivists generally acknowledge this relevance of empirical research.

As already indicated, however, the extreme view that conceptual analysis is nothing more than empirical evidence properly acknowledged and does not depend on the contribution of any kind of armchair philosophy is as implausible as the radical armchair philosophy position I have just rejected. In my view, there are two main reasons why this is so. The first trivial point, which is nevertheless often overlooked by non-philosophers, is that we can only empirically investigate the nature of, say, the human will or moral reasoning if we already possess a certain conception of the will or of moral reasoning, and, ideally, an informed or critically reflected conception. Without such a conception, we would not be able to identify what we want to investigate, or to identify the kind of evidence that is relevant to the inquiry in question. Empirical evidence, therefore, is not independent of philosophical conceptual analysis but actually presupposes it. An appropriate form of conceptual analysis, then, cannot consist in some kind of pure empirical research or in philosophers simply reading off the implications of existing empirical research. It can only result from an interplay of armchair philosophy, empirical linguistic research and other forms of empirical research, in which all these three elements affect one another and are reconciled with each other in the sense of a wider reflective equilibrium.

The second and possibly more contentious reason is that it cannot be completely ruled out that we need to cling to certain concepts, or to a certain understanding of these concepts, even against relevant empirical evidence because this evidence tends to undermine the entire project of reflectively understanding ourselves as acting and thinking individuals. To give one example: even if findings in empirical psychology would compellingly suggest that human beings do not have a free will, there might be philosophical reasons for maintaining the idea of human beings as being equipped with such a will, be it because we cannot but conceive of ourselves as free or because the sincere acknowledgement of the lack of free will would entirely undermine our practical orientation towards the world and towards our fellow human beings.

A second possible example, which is more relevant to the discussion of expressivism and moral sentimentalism, is the following one: even if empirical research into human reasoning were to strongly suggest that the reasons in virtue of which we act are merely *ex post* rationalizations, there could be good philosophical considerations in favour of clinging to the idea of human beings as agents who respond to reasons. Again, these considerations might consist in the fact that we simply cannot conceive of ourselves differently or in the fact that, in giving up the conception in question, we would not really be coherent. Thus, one might think that giving up the conception of ourselves as beings that respond to reasons would ultimately undermine our deliberative and argumentative practice and with it any empirically based argument in favour of giving up our conception in the first place, since any such argument must, at some point, (implicitly) appeal to reasons and our responsiveness to them.

Of course, when acknowledging the relevance of both armchair philosophy and empirical research, we need to strictly distinguish two different questions. The first question is whether empirical findings are *in principle* relevant to the philosophical enterprise because they provide a *kind* of evidence or input that is apt to further this enterprise; the second question is whether the existing empirical evidence does, in fact, provide us with a basis for deciding or settling the concrete philosophical issues because they are sufficient to tip the scale in one direction rather than the other.

The point of the previous discussion was to answer the first question, and to answer it in the affirmative. It is fully compatible with this answer, however, to think that empirical findings pertaining to a certain philosophical issue, such as Jonathan Haidt's findings concerning the nature of moral reasoning, are not as significant as their advocates take them to be. Again, this seems to be exactly the kind of view endorsed by Gibbard who doubts that psychologists have settled the question of whether psychopaths make genuine moral judgements (or, as a matter of fact, can settle this question all by themselves), but explicitly emphasizes that the philosopher, whose distinctive contribution consists in this kind of interpretative task, should fully appreciate what empirical psychologists have to say about the issue. The distinction between the potential and the actual contributions of empirical psychology is sometimes neglected by Kauppinen who demonstrates that we should be sceptical as to whether empirical psychological evidence allows us to decide the specific debate between internalists and externalists about moral motivation, but thereby wants to rule out empirical psychological evidence as fundamentally irrelevant to the whole of metaethics.

I conclude, then, that what philosophers should aim for in philosophical moral psychology (and conceptual analysis more generally) is some kind of reflective equilibrium between (a) philosophers' reflected intuitions about the relevant concepts or terms, (b) people's actual usage of these concepts or terms, and (c) non-linguistic empirical research pertaining to the concepts and terms. This envisaged reflective equilibrium not only concerns single terms or concepts, but also the way in which they are related to terms or concepts in their vicinity. For example, the best philosophical theory of moral judgement not only needs to strive for a reflective equilibrium with regard to philosophers' intuitions, people's actual linguistic usage and non-linguistic empirical research about 'moral judgement'. It also needs to put the analysis of 'moral judgement' in equilibrium with conceptualizations of 'action', 'moral motivation', 'moral reasoning' or 'moral disagreement'. In virtue of these manifold connections, the best overall philosophical theory of moral judgement might ultimately discard linguistic or non-linguistic evidence concerning some single term or concept altogether. However, to say that, in extreme cases, we may end up wholly discarding the empirical psychological literature on, say, psychopathy or moral motivation, or the most widespread uses of, say, the term 'desire', is quite different from saying that, as moral philosophers, we need not pay any attention to this kind of evidence in the first place.

To get back to the more specific case of metaethical expressivism: in view of the fact that, as we have seen above, the expressivist commits himself to a substantial psychological claim about the nature of moral judgement and thereby incurs the task of at least acknowledging the existing empirical psychological research on this issue, it needs to be criticized that the emphasis of the previous debate over expressivism has clearly been on linguistic matters, such as on the 'Frege-Geach problem', the recent psychological turn in metaethics notwithstanding. Even authors such as Schroeder who explicitly admit the crucial relevance of moral thinking and hence of issues within the philosophy of mind have done little to actually discuss the psychological aspects of expressivism. The only exception is, arguably, provided by the debate over moral motivation which has generally been conducted with an eye on the motivation argument for expressivism. Apart from the adherence to a more general methodological division between purely conceptual and purely empirical questions, which I have just rejected as inappropriate, a possible reason for this neglect of the psychological issues might consist in a certain scepticism with regard to the explanatory power or reliability of existing empirical studies. However, as I have just argued, this scepticism asks for critically engaging with the studies in question rather than for turning a blind eye to them.

Schroeder justifies his exclusive focus on the semantic issues surrounding expressivism in a different way. According to Schroeder, any attempt to attack expressivism from outside the semantic field is misguided because it is impossible to identify the non-semantic commitments of expressivism without having fully developed its semantic program.⁵⁶ Schroeder may certainly be right that more sophisticated applications of expressivism in epistemology or the philosophy of mind, such as Hartry Field's expressivism about the *a priori*, Chrisman's expressivism about knowledge, or David Velleman and Nishi Shah's expressivism about beliefs, very much depend on the semantic program being successfully carried out.⁵⁷ However, given the general mentalist starting point and the fact that the fundamental thesis of expressivism depends on certain psychological distinctions and even on a substantial psychological claim, it seems undeniable that the viability and plausibility of the semantic program itself hinges on whether the expressivist has a plausible psychological theory to begin with. Moreover, while it may be impossible to specify all psychological commitments of expressivism from the outset, it seems possible to identify at least the most fundamental of these commitments, such as the distinction between beliefs and desires and the idea that moral judgements are constituted by some kind of desire or desire-like state of mind. The natural order of the discussion of expressivism, therefore, should be to first examine these fundamental claims in the philosophy of mind in order to then turn to the semantic question of whether we can, and should, explain the meaning of moral language in terms of this philosophy of mind, not vice versa.

5 Summary

The purpose of this chapter was to systematically engage with Richard Joyce's 'independence thesis', according to which the primary linguistic thesis defended by the expressivist can wholly be disentangled from inquiries into the psychological nature of moral judgement. After sketching Joyce's argument and the way in which it appeals to the rejection of a naïve causal understanding of the expression relation, I first demonstrated that Joyce's characterization of the expressivist enterprise does not do justice to how leading expressivists conceive of their approaches. Blackburn, Gibbard and even Hare present their theories as theories about both moral language and moral thought, and something similar could be said about Stevenson. Moreover, Blackburn and Gibbard explicitly engage with empirical psychological research and view this kind of engagement, not as a contingent aspect of their discussion, but as something to which the expressivist is reasonably committed.

---

56 See Schroeder 2008a, XII.
57 See Schroeder 2008a, 6f.

In section 3, I approached the relationship between expressivism and moral psychology from a more systematic perspective, attempting to show that and why this latter view is indeed correct. Drawing on the discussion of 'creeping minimalism' in chapter 4, I first emphasized that the distinction between beliefs and desires, on which the basic expressivist thesis crucially relies, cannot be reconstructed in wholly linguistic terms because, given the propositional surface of moral language, this would render the thesis manifestly false. The expressivist needs to make sense of this distinction in robust psychological terms and, as shown by the discussion of the 'moral attitude problem' in chapter 6, needs to provide a further specification of the particular non-cognitive attitude supposedly expressed by moral utterances in doing so.

Secondly, and relatedly, I revisited the methodological considerations of the classic expressivists discussed in chapter 4, subscribing to Blackburn's and Gibbard's claim that the only way to justify the expressivist approach and to prove its superiority over rival metaethical approaches is to appeal to *non-linguistic* evidence. Moreover, I cast doubt on the view that a restricted appeal to epistemological and/or metaphysical considerations would already allow the expressivist to rest his case, pointing to the prominence of motivational considerations in the previous debate.

Thirdly, I forwarded the 'continuity thesis' according to which we typically conceive of the act of making a moral utterance as the act of making our moral thoughts known to others and argued that theories which conceive of the two aspects of morality in fundamentally different psychological terms cannot sufficiently account for this kind of continuity. Fourthly, drawing upon the discussion of the 'expression relation' in chapter 6, I argued that the expressivist can only provide a plausible explanation for how moral utterances have come to conventionally express desire-like states if he subscribes to the claim that the very states are actually instantiated in speakers in a critical number of cases. My overall conclusion, therefore, was that the expressivist ultimately commits himself to a substantial thesis in the philosophy of mind, namely to the claim that moral judgements are constituted by desires or desire-like states of mind rather than beliefs, which claim I introduced as *sentimentalism about moral judgement*.

I further defended this conclusion by rejecting a qualified version of the independence thesis according to which the expressivist approach is dependent on substantial claims in 'conceptual' or 'philosophical' psychology but nevertheless independent of any empirical psychological data. In challenging this more qualified view, I entered into more general methodological considerations concerning the relationship of metaethics, philosophical philosophy and empirical science and characterized the aim of metaethics, and conceptual analysis in general, as that of achieving a form of reflective equilibrium between (a) philosophers' reflected intuitions about the relevant concepts or terms, (b) people's actual usage of these concepts and terms, and (c) non-linguistic empirical research pertaining to them.

Conclusion

The aim of this book was inquire into the psychological commitments of metaethical expressivism and to critically examine the 'independence thesis' according to which the enterprise of providing an adequate analysis of the meaning of moral utterances and the enterprise of determining the nature of moral judgements are wholly independent of one another. A secondary but equally important aim was to use the discussion of the 'independence thesis' in order to address a number of issues that have been neglected in the previous debate over expressivism and to thereby contribute to a better overall understanding of what expressivism is all about.

My ultimate conclusion is that the 'independence thesis' must be rejected. According to the argument developed in this book, and in chapter 7 in particular, the success of articulating and defending a genuinely expressivist analysis of moral language depends upon a number of more substantial psychological assumptions. In order to achieve a determinate and stable overall position and allow for the continuity of moral thought and moral utterances, the expressivist not only has to rely on a robust psychological distinction between beliefs and desires and provide a concrete specification of the desire-like mental states actually expressed by moral utterances, but also to embrace a particular view on the nature of moral judgements, which view I have introduced as *sentimentalism about moral judgement*.

The upshot of my discussion, therefore, was that any plausible version of expressivism will subscribe to the following three claims (or to suitably refined versions of it):

> *Mentalism:* The meaning of linguistic utterances is to be explained in terms of the mental states they express.
>
> *Sentimentalism about moral expression:* Moral utterances express desires or desire-like states of mind rather than beliefs.
>
> *Sentimentalism about moral judgement:* Moral judgements are constituted by desires or desire-like states of mind rather than beliefs.

While the two former claims constitute the primary linguistic analysis as reflected in the standard definition of expressivism, the third claim represents a commitment the expressivist incurs in the course of making further sense of the primary analysis and justifying it in a way that proves it to be superior to rival metaethical approaches.

Another main lesson to the drawn from the previous discussion is that there is a greater continuity between the 'classic' expressivists than is usually acknowledged. Given the striking similarities in the ways in which Ayer, Stevenson, Hare, Blackburn and Gibbard subscribe to the basic expressivist idea, conceive of the status of their metaethical enterprise, defend their theories against rival approaches and elaborate on the crucial idea of 'expression', there is neither a sound basis for excluding any of these writers from the expressivist camp nor for drawing a hard-and-fast line between the emotivism of Ayer and Stevenson and the prescriptivism of Richard Hare or between early non-quasi-realist expressivism and the theories of Blackburn and Gibbard. The orthodox view, according to which the early 'emotivists' Ayer and Stevenson provide crude and unrefined versions of the expressivist approach and it is only with the approaches of Blackburn and Gibbard that expressivism becomes a respectable and reasonably conservative metaethical doctrine in the first place, then, needs be taken with a pinch of salt.

Although I have addressed possible strengths and weaknesses of metaethical expressivism throughout this book, my intention was not to pass final judgement on whether the expressivist approach is a viable one after all and whether it is indeed superior to naturalist and non-naturalist analyses of moral language. One main reason for this reservation was that one cannot really decide this question without entering into the debate about the psychological nature of moral judgement, which, in turn, forces us to pay attention to empirical evidence gathered by social and developmental psychologists and neuroscientists. Just because the 'independence thesis' is false, we can expect both conceptual psychological considerations and empirical evidence to bear on the assessment of expressivism on the one hand and naturalism and non-naturalism on the other. At the same time, we can expect the previous discussion of expressivism, and the linguistic and non-linguistic considerations forwarded by Blackburn, Gibbard and others, to bear on the assessment of moral sentimentalism and moral rationalism as on the evaluation of the empirical evidence provided in support of either of these approaches to moral judgement. Any respectable assessment of either expressivism, naturalism and non-naturalism or moral sentimentalism and moral rationalism, then, needs to be embedded within a more comprehensive argument about how we use moral language and how we make moral judgements.

References

Alm, David (2000): "Moral conditionals, non-cognitivism and meaning". In: *The Southern Journal of Philosophy*. 38. pp. 355–77.
Altham, J. E. J. (1986): "The legacy of emotivism". In: Macdonald, G./Wright, C. (Eds.): *Fact, science and morality. Essays on A. J. Ayer's Language, truth and logic*. Oxford: Blackwell. pp. 275–288.
Anscombe, G. E. M. (1957): *Intention*. Oxford: Blackwell.
Árdal, Páll S. (1966): *Passion and value in Hume's Treatise*. Edinburgh: Edinburgh University Press.
Árdal, Páll S. (1977): "Another look at Hume's account of moral evaluation". In: *Journal of the History of Philosophy*. 15. pp. 405–421.
Audi, Robert (2004): *The good in the right. A theory of intuition and intrinsic value*. Princeton, NJ: Princeton University Press.
Ayer, Alfred J. (1935): "The criterion of truth". In: *Analysis*. 3. pp. 28–32.
Ayer, Alfred J. (1936/1967): *Language, truth and logic*. London: Victor Gollancz.
Ayer, Alfred J. (1954): "On the analysis of moral judgements". In: Ayer, Alfred J.: *Philosophical Essays*. London: Macmillan. pp. 231–249.
Ayer, Alfred J. (2000): *Hume. A very short introduction*. Oxford: Oxford University Press.
Baldwin, Thomas (2001): "Expressing feelings and synthesising truths". In: *Philosophical Books*. 42. pp. 3–9.
Bar-On, Dorit/Chrisman, Matthew (2009): "Ethical neo-expressivism". In: Shafer-Landau, R. (Ed.): *Oxford studies in metaethics*. Vol. 4. Oxford: Oxford University Press. pp. 133–165.
Bar-On, Dorit/Chrisman, Matthew/Sias, James (2015): "(How) Is ethical neo-expressivism a hybrid view?" In: Ridge, M./Fletcher, G. (Eds.): *Having it both ways: Hybrid theories and modern metaethics*. Oxford: Oxford University Press. pp. 223–247.
Barker, Stephen J. (2000): "Is value content a component of conventional implicature?" In: *Analysis*. 60. pp. 268–279.
Barker, Stephen J. (2006): "Truth and the expressing in expressivism". In: Horgan, T./Timmons, M. (Eds.): *Metaethics after Moore*. Oxford: Clarendon Press. pp. 299–317.
Barnes, W. H. F. (1934): "A suggestion about value". In: *Analysis*. 1. pp. 45–46.
Blackburn, Simon (1981): "Reply: Rule-following and moral realism". In: Holtzman, S./Leich, C. M. (Eds.): *Wittgenstein: To follow a rule*. Abingdon: Routledge. pp. 163–187.
Blackburn, Simon (1984): *Spreading the word. Groundings in the philosophy of language*. Oxford: Oxford University Press.
Blackburn, Simon (1986): "Morals and modals". In: Macdonald, G./Wright, C. (Eds.): *Fact, science and morality. Essays on A. J. Ayer's Language, truth and logic*. Oxford: Blackwell. pp. 119–141.
Blackburn, Simon (1991): "Reply to Sturgeon". In: *Philosophical Studies*. 61. pp. 39–42.
Blackburn, Simon (1992): "Through thick and thin". In: *Proceedings of the Aristotelian Society*. Suppl. Vol. 66. pp. 285–299.
Blackburn, Simon (1993a): "Realism, quasi, or queasy?" In: Haldane, J./Wright, C. (Eds.): *Reality, representation, and projection*. Oxford: Oxford University Press. pp. 365–383.
Blackburn, Simon (1993b): "Errors and the phenomenology of value". In: Blackburn, Simon: *Essays in quasi-realism*. New York: Oxford University Press. pp. 149–165.

Blackburn, Simon (1993c): "How to be an ethical antirealist". In: Blackburn, Simon: *Essays in quasi-realism*. New York: Oxford University Press. pp. 166–181.
Blackburn, Simon (1993d): "Attitudes and contents". In: Blackburn, Simon: *Essays in quasi-realism*. New York: Oxford University Press. pp. 182–197.
Blackburn, Simon (1993e): "Moral realism". In: Blackburn, Simon: *Essays in quasi-realism*. New York: Oxford University Press. pp. 111–129.
Blackburn, Simon (1993f): "Circles, finks, smells, and biconditionals". In: *Philosophical Perspectives. 7: Language and Logic*. pp. 259–279.
Blackburn, Simon (1995): "The flight to reality". In: Hursthouse, R./Lawrence, G./Quinn, W. (Eds.): *Virtues and reasons: Philippa Foot and moral theory. Essays in honour of Philippa Foot*. Oxford: Clarendon Press. pp. 35–56.
Blackburn, Simon (1996): "Securing the nots: Moral epistemology for the quasi-realist". In: Sinnott-Armstrong, W./Timmons, M. (Eds.): *Moral knowledge? New readings in moral epistemology*. Oxford: Oxford University Press. pp. 82–100.
Blackburn, Simon (1998): *Ruling passions. A theory of practical reasoning*. Oxford: Clarendon Press.
Blackburn, Simon (2001a): "Summary of *Ruling passions*". In: *Philosophical Books*. 42. pp. 1–2.
Blackburn, Simon (2001b): "Reply to Baldwin, Jackson and Svavarsdóttir". In: *Philosophical Books*. 42. pp.
Blackburn, Simon (2002): "Précis of *Ruling passions*". In: *Philosophy and Phenomenological Research*. 65. pp. 122–135.
Blackburn, Simon (2005a): "Must we weep for sentimentalism?" In: Dreier, J. (Ed.): *Contemporary debates in moral theory*. Malden, MA: Blackwell. pp. 144–159.
Blackburn, Simon (2005b): "Quasi-realism no fictionalism". In: Kalderon, M. E. (Ed.): *Fictionalism in metaphysics*. Oxford: Clarendon Press. pp. 322–338.
Blackburn, Simon (2006): "Antirealist expressivism and quasi-realism". In: Copp, D. (Ed.): *The Oxford handbook of ethical Theory*. Oxford: Oxford University Press. pp. 146–162.
Blackburn, Simon (2010a): "The majesty of reason". In: Blackburn, Simon: *Practical tortoise raising*. Oxford: Oxford University Press. pp. 283–307.
Blackburn, Simon (2010b): "Introduction". In: Blackburn, Simon: *Practical tortoise raising*. Oxford: Oxford University Press. pp. 1–3.
Blackburn, Simon (2010c): "Truth, beauty, and goodness". In: Blackburn, Simon: *Practical tortoise raising*. Oxford: Oxford University Press. pp. 26–46.
Blackburn, Simon (unpublished manuscript): "Response to Marc Hauser's Princeton lecture, 2008".
Blackburn, Simon (unpublished manuscript): "Social and individual expression".
Blackburn, Simon/Sinclair, Neil (2006): "Comments on Gibbard's *Thinking how to live*". In: *Philosophy and Phenomenological Research*. 72. pp. 699–706.
Boisvert, Daniel R. (2008): "Expressive-Assertivism". In: *Pacific Philosophical Quarterly*. 89. pp. 169–203.
Boisvert, Daniel R. (2015): "Expressivism, nondeclaratives, and success-conditional semantics". In: Ridge, M./Fletcher, G. (Eds.): *Having it both ways: Hybrid theories and modern metaethics*. Oxford: Oxford University press. pp. 22–50.
Boyd, Richard (1988): "How to be a moral realist". In: Sayre-McCord, G. (Ed.): *Moral realism*. Ithaca: Cornell University Press. pp. 181–228.

Brandt, Richard B. (1959): *Ethical theory. The problems of normative and critical ethics.* Englewood Cliffs, NJ: Prentice-Hall.
Brandt Richard B. (1979): *A theory of the good and the right.* Oxford: Clarendon Press.
Bricke, John (1996): *Mind and morality. An examination of Hume's moral psychology.* Oxford: Oxford University Press.
Brighouse, M. (1990): "Blackburn's projectivism – an objection". In: *Philosophical Studies.* 59. pp. 225 – 235.
Brink, David O. (1989): *Moral realism and the foundations of ethics.* Cambridge: Cambridge University Press.
Brink, David O. (1997): "Moral motivation". In: *Ethics.* 108. pp. 4 – 32.
Broad, C. D. (1930/2009): *Five types of ethical theory.* Abingdon: Routledge.
Broad, C. D. (1934): "Is "goodness" a name of a simple non-natural quality?" In: *Proceedings of the Aristotelian Society.* 34. pp. 249 – 268.
Brown, Charlotte (1994): "From spectator to agent: Hume's theory of obligation". In: *Hume Studies.* 20. pp. 19 – 35.
Burgess, John P. (1983): "Why I am not a nominalist". In: *Notre Dame Journal of Formal Logic.* 24. pp. 93 – 105.
Campbell, Richmond (2007): "What is moral judgment?" In: *The Journal of Philosophy.* 104. pp. 321 – 349.
Carnap, Rudolf (1935): *Philosophy and Logical Syntax.* London: Kegan Paul.
Charlow, Nate (2014): "The problem with the Frege-Geach problem". In: *Philosophical Studies.* 167. pp. 635 – 665.
Chrisman, Matthew (2008): "Expressivism, inferentialism, and saving the debate". In: *Philosophy and Phenomenological Research.* 77. pp. 334 – 358.
Chrisman, Matthew (2012): "On the meaning of 'ought'". In: Shafer-Landau, R. (Ed.): *Oxford Studies in Metaethics.* Vol. 7. Oxford: Oxford University Press. pp. 304 – 332.
Chrisman, Matthew (2014): "Attitudinal expressivism and logical pragmatism". In: Hubbs, G./Lind, D. (Eds.): *Pragmatism, law, and language.* New York: Routledge. pp. 117 – 135.
Chrisman, Matthew (2016): *The meaning of 'ought'. Beyond descriptivism and expressivism in metaethics.* New York: Oxford University Press.
Cohon Rachel (1997): "Is Hume a noncognitivist in the motivation argument?" In: *Philosophical Studies.* 85. pp. 251 – 266.
Cohon, Rachel (2008): *Hume's morality: Feeling and fabrication.* Oxford: Oxford University Press.
Copp, David (2001): "Realist-expressivism: A neglected option for moral realism". In: *Social Philosophy and Policy.* 18. pp. 1 – 43.
Copp, David (2004): "Moral naturalism and three grades of normativity". In: Schaber, Peter (Ed.): *Normativity and naturalism.* Heusenstamm: Ontos. pp. 7 – 45.
Copp, David (2009): "Realist-expressivism and conventional implicature". In: Shafer-Landau, R. (Ed.): *Oxford studies in metaethics.* Vol. 4. Oxford: Oxford University Press. pp. 167 – 202.
Copp, David (2015): "Can a hybrid theory have it both ways? Moral thought, open questions, and moral motivation". In: Ridge, M./Fletcher, G. (Eds.): *Having it both ways: Hybrid theories and modern metaethics.* Oxford: Oxford University press. pp. 51 – 74.

Cuneo, Terence (2006): "Saying what we mean: An argument against expressivism". In: Shafer-Landau, R. (Ed.): *Oxford studies in metaethics*. Vol. 1. Oxford: Oxford University Press. pp. 35–71.
Cuneo, Terence (2013): "Properties for nothing, facts for free? Expressivism's deflationary gambit". In: Shafer-Landau, R. (Ed.): *Oxford studies in metaethics*. Vol. 8. Oxford: Oxford University Press. pp. 223–251.
Czaniera, Uwe (2001): *Gibt es moralisches Wissen? Die Kognitivismus-Debatte in der analytischen Moralphilosophie*. Paderborn: Mentis
D'Arms, Justin/Jacobson, Daniel (1994): "Expressivism, morality, and the emotions". In: *Ethics*. 104. pp. 739–763.
D'Arms, Justin/Jacobson, Daniel (2000a): "The moralistic fallacy: On the 'appropriateness' of emotions". In: *Philosophy and Phenomenological Research*. 61. pp. 65–90.
D'Arms, Justin/Jacobson, Daniel (2000b): "Sentiment and value". In: *Ethics*. 110. pp. 722–748.
D'Arms, Justin/Jacobson, Daniel (2006): "Sensibility theory and projectivism". In: Copp, D. (Ed.): *The Oxford handbook of ethical theory*. Oxford: Oxford University Press. pp. 186–218.
Dancy, Jonathan (1993): *Moral reasons*. Oxford: Blackwell.
Dancy, Jonathan (2006): "Nonnaturalism". In: Copp, D. (Ed.): *The Oxford handbook of ethical theory*. Oxford: Oxford University Press. pp. 122–145.
Davis, Wayne (2002): *Meaning, expression, and thought*. New York: Cambridge University Press.
Debes, Remy (2011): "Editor's introduction". In: *The Southern Journal of Philosophy*. 49. pp. 1–3.
Divers, John/Miller, Alexander (1994): "Why expressivists about value should not love minimalism about truth". In: *Analysis*. 54. pp. 12–19.
Divers, John/Miller, Alexander (1995): "Platitudes and attitudes: A minimalist conception of belief". In: *Analysis*. 55. pp. 37–44.
Döring, Sabine A. (2010): "Why be emotional?" In: Goldie, P. (Ed.): *The Oxford handbook of philosophy of emotion*. Oxford: Oxford University Press. pp. 283–302.
Dreier, James (1996): "Expressivist embeddings and minimalist truth". In: *Philosophical Studies*. 83. pp. 29–51.
Dreier, James (1999): "Transforming expressivism". In: *Nous*. 33. pp. 558–572.
Dreier, James (2002): "The expressivist circle: Invoking norms in the explanation of normative judgment". In: *Philosophy and Phenomenological Research*. 65. pp. 136–143.
Dreier, James (2004a): "Meta-ethics and the problem of creeping minimalism". In: *Philosophical Perspectives. 18: Ethics*. pp. 23–44.
Dreier, James (2004b): "Lockean and logical truth conditions". In: *Analysis*. 64. pp. 84–91.
Dreier, James (2006): "Negation for expressivists: A collection of problems with a suggestion for their solution". In: Shafer-Landau, R. (Ed.): *Oxford studies in metaethics*. Vol. 1. Oxford: Oxford University Press. pp. 217–233.
Dreier, James (2015): "Another world: The metaethics and metametaethics of reasons fundamentalism". In: Johnson, R. K./Smith, M. (Eds.) (2015): *Passions and projections: Themes from the philosophy of Simon Blackburn*. Oxford: Oxford University Press. pp. 155–171.

Dunaway, Billy (2010): "Minimalist semantics in meta-ethical expressivism". In: *Philosophical Studies*. 151. pp. 351–371.
Dunn, Robert (2004): "Moral psychology and expressivism". In: *European Journal for Philosophy*. 12. pp. 178–198.
Dworkin, Ronald (1996): "Objectivity and Truth: You'd better believe it". In: *Philosophy and Public Affairs*. 25. pp. 87–139.
Dworkin, Ronald (2011): *Justice for hedgehogs*. Cambridge, MA: The Belknap Press.
Enoch, David (2011): *Taking morality seriously: A defense of Robust Realism*. Oxford: Oxford University Press.
Eriksson, John (2009): "Homage to Hare: Ecumenism and the Frege-Geach problem". In: *Ethics*. 120. pp. 8–35.
Eriksson, John (2015a): "Hybrid expressivism". In: Ridge, M./Fletcher, G. (Eds.): *Having it both ways: Hybrid theories and modern metaethics*. Oxford: Oxford University press. pp. 149–170.
Eriksson, John (2015b): "Explaining disagreement: A problem for (some) versions of hybrid expressivism". In: *Pacific Philosophical Quarterly*. 96. pp. 39–56.
Ernst, Gerhard (2008): *Die Objektivität der Moral*. Paderborn: Mentis.
Evans, Angela D./Lee, Kang (2013): "Emergence of lying in very young children". In: *Developmental Psychology*. 49. pp. 1958–1963.
Falk, W. D. (1975): "Hume on practical reason". In: *Philosophical Studies*. 27. pp. 1–18.
Field, Hartry (2001): *Truth and the absence of fact*. Oxford: Oxford University Press.
Finlay, Stephen (2005): "Value and implicature". In: *Philosopher's Imprint*. 5. pp. 1–20.
Fletcher, Guy (2015): "Moral utterances, attitude expression, and implicature". In: Ridge, M./Fletcher, G. (Eds.): *Having it both ways: Hybrid theories and modern metaethics*. Oxford: Oxford University press. pp. 173–198.
Frankena, William K. (1963): *Ethics*. Englewood Cliffs, NJ: Prentice-Hall.
Frege, Gottlob (1918): *Der Gedanke. Eine logische Untersuchung*. Erfurt: Stenger.
Geach, Peter T. (1960): "Ascriptivism". In: *Philosophical Review*. 69. pp. 221–225.
Geach, Peter T. (1965): "Assertion". In: *Philosophical Review*. 74. pp. 449–465.
Gert, Joshua (2002): "Expressivism and language learning". In: *Ethics*. 112. pp. 292–314.
Gert, Joshua (2006): "Mistaken Expressions". In: *Canadian Journal of Philosophy*. 36. pp. 459–479.
Gibbard, Allan (1982): "Human evolution and the sense of justice". In: French, P. A./Uhling, T. E./Wettstein, H. K. (Eds.): *Midwest studies in philosophy*. Vol. 7. pp. 31–46.
Gibbard, Allan (1983): "A noncognitivistic analysis of rationality in action". In: *Social Theory and Practice*. 9. pp. 199–221.
Gibbard, Allan (1985a): "Normative objectivity". In: *Nous*. 19. pp. 41–51.
Gibbard, Allan (1985b): "Moral judgment and the acceptance of norms". In: *Ethics*. 96. pp. 5–21.
Gibbard, Allan (1986a): "An expressivistic theory of normative discourse". In: *Ethics*. 96. pp. 472–485.
Gibbard, Allan (1986b): "Rationality and human evolution". In: Garver, N./Hare, P. (Eds.): *Naturalism and rationality*. Buffalo: Prometheus Books. pp. 217–233.
Gibbard, Allan (1990a): *Wise choices, apt feelings. A theory of normative judgment*. Cambridge, MA: Harvard University Press.

Gibbard, Allan (1990b): "Norms, discussion, and ritual: Evolutionary puzzles". In: *Ethics*. 100. pp. 787–802.
Gibbard, Allan (1992a): "Moral concepts: Substance and sentiment". In: *Philosophical Perspectives. 6: Ethics*. pp. 199–221.
Gibbard, Allan (1992b): "Reply to Blackburn, Carson, Hill, and Railton". In: *Philosophy and Phenomenological Research*. 52. pp. 969–980.
Gibbard, Allan (1992c): "Précis of *Wise choices, apt feelings*". In: *Philosophy and Phenomenological Research*. 52. pp. 943–945.
Gibbard, Allan (1993a): "Reply to Blackburn". In: *Philosophical Issues. Vol. 4: Naturalism and Normativity*. pp. 67–73.
Gibbard, Alan (1993b): "Reply to Sinnott-Armstrong". In: *Philosophical Studies*. 69. pp. 315–327.
Gibbard, Allan (1994): "Meaning and Normativity". In: *Philosophical Issues. Vol. 5: Truth and Rationality*. pp. 95–115.
Gibbard, Allan (1996): "Projection, quasi-realism, and sophisticated realism". In: *Mind*. 105. pp. 331–335.
Gibbard, Allan (2002a): "Normative and recognitional concepts". In: *Philosophy and Phenomenological Research*. 64. pp. 151–167.
Gibbard, Allan (2002b): "Knowing what to do, seeing what to do". In: Stratton-Lake, P. (Ed.): *Ethical intuitionism: Re-evaluations*. Oxford: Clarendon Press. pp. 212–228.
Gibbard, Allan (2002c): "The reasons of a living being". In: *Proceedings and Addresses of the American Philosophical Association*. 76. pp. 49–60.
Gibbard, Allan (2003): *Thinking how to live*. Cambridge, MA: Harvard University Press.
Gibbard, Allan (2006a): "Reply to critics". In: *Philosophy and Phenomenological Research*. 72. pp. 729–744.
Gibbard, Allan (2006b): "Moral feelings and moral concepts". In: Shafer-Landau, R. (Ed.): *Oxford studies in meatethics*. Vol. 1. Oxford: Oxford University Press. pp. 195–215.
Gibbard, Allan (2006c): "Précis of *Thinking how to live*". In: *Philosophy and Phenomenological Research*. 72. pp. 687–698.
Gibbard, Allan (2011): "How much realism? Evolved thinkers and normative concepts". In: Shafer-Landau, R. (Ed.): *Oxford studies in metaethics*. Vol. 6. Oxford: Oxford University Press. pp. 33–51.
Gibbard, Allan (2014): *Meaning and normativity*. Oxford: Oxford University Press.
Gibbard, Allan (2015): "Improving sensibilities". In: Johnson, Robert K./Smith, Michael (Eds.) (2015): *Passions and projections: Themes from the philosophy of Simon Blackburn*. Oxford: Oxford University Press. pp. 172–188.
Gill, Michael B. (2008): "Metaethical variability, incoherence, and error". In: Sinnott-Armstrong, W. (Ed.): *Moral psychology*. Vol. 2. Cambridge, MA: MIT Press. pp. 387–402.
Grice, Herbert P. (1989): *Studies in the way with words*. Cambridge, MA: Harvard University Press.
Hägerström, Axel (1964): *Philosophy and religion*. Transl. by Robert T. Sandin. New York: Humanities Press.
Haidt, Jonathan (2001): "The emotional dog and its rational tail: A social intuitionist approach to moral judgment". In: *Psychological Review*. 108. pp. 814–834.
Haidt, Jonathan/Björklund, Fredrik/Murphy, Scott (2000): "Moral dumbfounding: When intuition finds no reason". Unpublished manuscript.

Halbig, Christoph (2007): *Praktische Gründe und die Realität der Moral*. Frankfurt/M.: Klostermann
Hale, Bob (1986): "The compleat projectivist". In: *The Philosophical Quarterly*. 36. pp. 65–84.
Hale, Bob (1993): "Can there be a logic of attitudes?" In: Haldane, J./Wright, C. (Eds.): *Reality, representation, and projection*. Oxford: Oxford University Press. pp. 337–63.
Hale, Bob (2002): "Can arboreal knotwork help Blackburn out of Frege's abyss?" In: *Philosophy and Phenomenological Research*. 65. pp. 144–149.
Hallich, Oliver (2000): *Richard Hares Moralphilosophie. Metaethische Grundlagen und Anwendung*. Freiburg: Alber.
Hallich, Oliver (2008): *Die Rationalität der Moral. Eine sprachanalytische Grundlegung der Ethik*. Paderborn: Mentis.
Harcourt, Edward (2005): "Quasi-realism and ethical appearances". In: *Mind*. 114. pp. 249–275.
Hare, Richard M. (1952): *The language of morals*. Oxford: Oxford University Press.
Hare, Richard M. (1963): *Freedom and reason*. Oxford: Clarendon Press.
Hare, Richard M. (1970): "Meaning and speech acts". In: *The Philosophical Review*. 79. pp. 3–24.
Hare, Richard M. (1981): *Moral thinking. Its levels, method, and point*. Oxford: Oxford Clarendon Press.
Hare, Richard M. (1995): "Off on the wrong Foot". In: *Canadian Journal of Philosophy*. 25. Suppl. 1. pp. 67–77.
Hare, Richard M. (1999a): *Sorting out ethics*. Oxford: Oxford University Press.
Hare, Richard M. (1999b): "Internalism and externalism in ethics". In: Hare, Richard M.: *Objective prescriptions and other essays*. Oxford: Clarendon Press. pp. 96–108.
Harman, Gilbert (1977): *The nature of morality. An introduction to ethics*. New York: Oxford University Press.
Harman, Gilbert (1986): *Moral agent and impartial spectator. The Lindley Lecture*. Lawrence, KS: The University of Kansas Press.
Harrison, Jonathan (1976): *Hume's moral epistemology*. Oxford: Clarendon Press.
Harth, Manfred (2008): *Werte und Wahrheit*. Paderborn: Mentis.
Hay, Ryan (2015): "Attitudinal requirements for moral thought and language". In: Ridge, M./Fletcher, G. (Eds.): *Having it both ways: Hybrid theories and modern metaethics*. Oxford: Oxford University press. pp. 75–94.
Hill, Thomas E. Jr. (1992): "Gibbard on morality and sentiment". In: *Philosophy and Phenomenological Research*. 52. pp. 957–960.
Horgan, Terry/Timmons, Mark (2000): "Nondescriptivist cognitivism: Framework for a new metaethics". In: *Philosophical Papers*. 29. pp. 121–153.
Horgan, Terry/Timmons, Mark (2006a): "Expressivism, Yes! Relativism, No!" In: Shafer-Landau, R. (Ed.): *Oxford studies in metaethics*. Vol. 1. Oxford: Oxford University Press. pp. 73–98.
Horgan, Terry/Timmons, Mark (2006b): "Cognitivist Expressivism". In: Horgan, Terry/Timmons, Mark (Eds.): *Metaethics after Moore*. Oxford: Clarendon Press. pp. 255–298.
Horgan, Terry/Timmons, Mark (2015): "Modest quasi-realism and the problem of deep moral error". In: Johnson, R. K./Smith, M. (Eds.) (2015): *Passions and projections: Themes from the philosophy of Simon Blackburn*. Oxford: Oxford University Press. pp. 190–209.

Horwich, Paul (1993): "Gibbard's theory of norms". In: *Philosophy and Public Affairs*. 22. S. 67–78.
Horwich, Paul (1994): "The essence of expressivism". In: *Analysis*. 54. pp. 19–20.
Horwich, Paul (1998): *Truth*. Second edition. Oxford: Oxford University Press.
Jackson, Frank (1998): *From metaphysics to ethics: A defence of conceptual analysis*. Oxford: Oxford University Press.
Jackson, Frank (2001): "What is Expressivism?" In: *Philosophical Books*. 42. pp. 10–17.
Jackson, Frank/Oppy, Graham/Smith, Michael (1994): "Minimalism and truth aptness". In: *Mind*. 103. pp. 287–302.
Jackson, Frank/Pettit, Philip (1998): "A problem for expressivism". In: *Analysis*. 58. pp. 239–251.
Jackson, Frank/Pettit, Philip (2003): "Locke, expressivism, conditionals". In: *Analysis*. 63. pp. 86–92.
Jackson, Frank/ Pettit, Philip (2004): "Moral functionalism and moral motivation". In: Jackson, F./Pettit, P./Smith, M.: *Mind, morality, and explanation. Selected collaborations*. Oxford: Clarendon Press. pp. 189–210.
Jacobson, Daniel (2011): "Fitting attitude theories of value". In: *Stanford Encyclopedia of Philosophy*. pp. 1–33.
Jenkins, C. S. I. (2015): "What quasi-realists can say about knowledge". In: Johnson, R. K./ Smith, M. (Eds.) (2015): *Passions and projections: Themes from the philosophy of Simon Blackburn*. Oxford: Oxford University Press. pp. 64–84.
Joyce, Richard (2001): *The myth of morality*. Cambridge: Cambridge University Press.
Joyce, Richard (2002): "Expressivism and motivation internalism". In: *Analysis*. 62. pp. 336–44.
Joyce, Richard (2005): "Moral fictionalism". In: Kalderon, M. E. (Ed.): *Fictionalism in metaphysics*. Oxford: Clarendon Press. pp. 314–321.
Joyce, Richard (2008): "What neuroscience can (and cannot) contribute to metaethics". In: Sinnott-Armstrong, W. (Ed.): *Moral psychology*. Vol. 3. Cambridge, MA: MIT Press. pp. 371–394.
Joyce, Richard (2009): "Expressivism, motivation internalism, and Hume". In: Pigden, C. (Ed.): *Hume on motivation and virtue*. Basingstoke: Palgrave. pp. 30–56.
Kauppinen, Antti (2007): "The rise and fall of experimental philosophy". In: *Philosophical Explorations*. 10. pp. 96–118.
Kauppinen, Antti (2010): "Moral judgment and volitional incapacity". In: Campbell, J. K./ O'Rourke, M./Silverstein, H. S. (Eds.): *Actions, Ethics, and Responsibility*. Cambridge, MA: The MIT Press. pp. 235–258.
Kauppinen, Antti (2014a): "Ethics and Empirical Psychology: Critical Remarks to Empirically Informed Ethics". In: Christen, M./van Schaik, C./Fischer, J./Huppenbauer, M./Tanner, C. (Eds.): *Empirically Informed Ethics: Morality between Facts and Norms*. Cham: Springer. pp. 279–305.
Kauppinen, Antti (2014b): "Moral Sentimentalism". In: *Stanford Encyclopedia of Philosophy*. pp. 1–89.
Kennett, Jeanette/ Fine, Cordelia (2008): "Internalism and the evidence from psychopaths and 'acquired sociopaths'". In: Sinnott-Armstrong, W. (Ed.): *Moral psychology*. Vol. 3. Cambridge, MA: MIT Press, pp. 173–190.

Köhler, Sebastian (2013): "Do expressivists have an attitude problem?" In: *Ethics.* 123. pp. 479–507.
Kölbel, Max (1997): "Expressivism and the syntactic uniformity of declarative sentences". In: *Critica.* 29. pp. 3–51.
Kramer, Matthew (2017): "There's nothing quasi about quasi-realism: Moral realism as a moral doctrine". In: *The Journal of Ethics.* 21. pp. 185–212.
Künne, Wolfgang (2003): *Conceptions of truth.* Oxford: Oxford University Press.
Lenman, James (2003): "Disciplined syntacticism and moral expressivism". In: *Philosophy and Phenomenological Research.* 66. pp. 32–57.
Lewis, David (1973): "Causation". In: *The Journal of Philosophy.* 70. pp. 556–567.
Lewis, David (2005): "Quasi-realism is fictionalism". In: Kalderon, M. E. (Ed.): *Fictionalism in metaphysics.* Oxford: Clarendon Press. pp. 314–321.
Locke, John (1689/1975): *An essay concerning human understanding.* Ed. with an introduction by P. H. Nidditch. Oxford: Oxford University Press.
Loeb, Don (2008): "Moral incoherentism: How to pull a metaphysical rabbit out of a semantic hat". In: Sinnott-Armstrong, W. (Ed.): *Moral psychology.* Vol. 2. Cambridge, MA: MIT Press. pp. 355–386.
Mackie, John L. (1946): "A refutation of morals". In: *Australasian Journal of Psychology and Philosophy.* 24. pp. 77–90.
Mackie, John L. (1977): *Ethics. Inventing right and wrong.* London: Penguin.
Mackie, John L. (1980): *Hume's moral theory.* London: Routledge & Kegan.
Merli, David (2008): "Expressivism and the limits of moral disagreement". In: *The Journal of Ethics.* 12. pp. 25–55.
Miller, Alexander (1998): "Emotivism and the verification principle". In: *Proceedings of the Aristotelian Society.* 98. pp. 103–124.
Miller, Alexander (2003): *An introduction to contemporary metaethics.* Cambridge: Polity Press.
Millikan, Ruth G. (1984): *Language, thought, and other biological categories. New foundations for realism.* Cambridge, MA: The MIT Press.
Millikan, Ruth G. (2004): *Varieties of meaning. The 2002 Jean Nicod Lectures.* Cambridge, MA: The MIT Press.
Millikan, Ruth G. (2005): *Language. A biological model.* Oxford: Clarendon Press.
Moore, George E. (1903/1993): *Principia Ethica.* Revised edition. With the preface to the second edition and other papers. Edited and with an introduction by T. Baldwin. Cambridge: Cambridge University Press.
Newton, Paul et al. (2000): "Children's everyday deception and performance on false-belief tasks". In: *British Journal of Developmental Psychology.* 18. pp. 297–317.
Nichols, Shaun (2004): *Sentimental rules. On the natural foundations of moral judgment.* New York: Oxford University Press.
Nichols, Shaun (2008): "Sentimentalism naturalized". In: Sinnott-Armstrong, W. (Ed.): *Moral psychology.* Vol. 2. Cambridge, MA: MIT Press. pp. 255–274.
O'Leary-Hawthorne, John/Price, Huw (1996): "How to stand up for non-cognitivists". In: *Australasian Journal of Philosophy.* 74. pp. 275–92.
Ogden, C. K./Richards, I. A. (1923/1930): *The meaning of meaning. A study of the influence of language upon thought and of the science of symbolism.* 3rd revised edition. London: Kegan Paul.

Padel, Stephan (2020): *Moral disagreement. A metaethical investigation.* Heidelberg: Synchron.
Parfit, Derek (2011): *On what matters.* Vol. 2. Oxford: Oxford University Press.
Polak, A./Harris, P. L. (1999): "Deception by young children following noncompliance". In: *Developmental Psychology.* 35. pp. 561–568.
Price, Huw (2015): "From quasi-realism to global expressivism – and back again?" In: Johnson, R. K./ Smith, M. (Eds.) (2015): *Passions and projections: Themes from the philosophy of Simon Blackburn.* Oxford: Oxford University Press. pp. 134–152.
Prinz, Jesse J. (2007): *The emotional construction of morals.* New York: Oxford University Press.
Prinz, Jesse J. (2015): "An empirical case for motivational internalism". In: Björnsson, G./ Strandberg, C./Francén Olinder, R./Eriksson, J./Björklund, F. (Eds.): *Motivational internalism.* New York: Oxford University Press. pp. 61–84.
Radtke, Burkhard (2009): *Wahrheit in der Moral. Plädoyer für einen moderaten Moralischen Realismus.* Paderborn: Mentis.
Railton, Peter (2008): "Naturalism relativized?" In: Sinnott-Armstrong, W. (Ed.): *Moral psychology.* Vol. 1. Cambridge, MA: MIT Press. pp. 37–44.
Railton, Peter (2015):" Just how *do* passions rule? The (more) compleat projectivist". In: Johnson, R. K./ Smith, M. (Eds.) (2015): *Passions and projections: Themes from the philosophy of Simon Blackburn.* Oxford: Oxford University Press. pp. 210–227.
Ramsey, Frank P. (1927): "Facts and propositions". In: *Proceedings of the Aristotelian Society.* 7. pp. 153–170.
Rawls, John (1971): *A theory of justice.* Cambridge, MA: The Belknap Press of Harvard University Press.
Ridge, Michael (2003): "Non-cognitivist pragmatics and Stevenson's 'Do so as well'". In: *Canadian Journal of Philosophy.* 33. pp. 563–574.
Ridge, Michael (2004): "How children learn the meanings of moral words: Expressivist semantics for children". In: *Ethics.* pp. 301–317.
Ridge, Michael (2006a): "Ecumenical expressivism: Finessing Frege". In: *Ethics.* 116. S. 302–336.
Ridge, Michael (2006b): "Sincerity and expressivism". In: *Philosophical Studies.* 131. S. 487–510.
Ridge, Michael (2006c): "Saving the ethical appearances". In: *Mind.* 115. pp. 633–649.
Ridge, Michael (2006d): "Ecumenical expressivism: The best of both worlds?" In: Shafer-Landau, R. (Ed.): *Oxford studies in metaethics.* Vol. 2. Oxford: Oxford University Press. pp. 51–76.
Ridge, Michael (2009): "Moral assertion for expressivists". In: *Philosophical Issues.* 19. pp. 182–204.
Ridge, Michael (2014): *Impassioned belief.* Oxford: Oxford University Press.
Ridge, Michael (2015): "Internalism: Cui bono?" In: Björnsson, G./Strandberg, C./Francén Olinder, R./Eriksson, J./Björklund, F. (Eds.): *Motivational internalism.* New York: Oxford University Press. pp. 135–149.
Rosen, Gideon (1998): "Blackburn's *Essays in Quasi-Realism*". In: *Nous.* 32. S. 386–405.
Ross, David (1930/2002): *The right and the good.* Ed. by P. Stratton-Lake. Oxford: Clarendon Press

Rüther, Markus (2013): *Objektivität und Moral. Ein problemgeschichtlich-systematischer Beitrag zur neueren Realismusdebatte in der Metaethik*. Münster: Mentis.
Russell, Bertrand (1935/1956): *Religion and Science*. Oxford: Oxford University Press.
Sauer, Hanno (2017): *Moral judgments as educated intuitions*. Cambridge, MA: The MIT Press.
Sayre-McCord, Geoffrey (1997): "The metaethical problem". In: *Ethics*. 108. pp. 55–83.
Sayre-McCord, Geoffrey (2008): "Moral semantics and empirical inquiry". In: Sinnott-Armstrong, W. (Ed.): *Moral psychology*. Vol. 2. Cambridge, MA: MIT Press. pp. 403–412.
Sayre-McCord, Geoffrey (2012): "Metaethics". In: *Stanford Encyclopedia of Philosophy*. pp. 1–33.
Scanlon, Thomas M. (1998): *What we owe to each other*. Cambridge, MA: The Belknap Press.
Scanlon, Thomas M. (2014): *Being realistic about reasons*. Oxford: Oxford University Press.
Scarano, Nico (2001): *Moralische Überzeugungen. Grundlinien einer antirealistischen Theorie der Moral*. Paderborn: Mentis.
Scarano, Nico (2006): "Metaethik – ein systematischer Überblick". In: Düwell, M./Hübenthal, C./Werner, M. (Eds.): *Handbuch Ethik*. Stuttgart: Metzler. pp. 25–35.
Schaber, Peter (1997): *Moralischer Realismus*. Freiburg: Alber.
Schaber, Peter/Wolf, Jean-Claude (1998): *Analytische Moralphilosophie*. Freiburg: Alber.
Schmidt, Thomas (2004): "Moral values and the fabric of the world". In: Schaber, P. (Ed.): *Normativity and naturalism*. Heusenstamm: Ontos. pp. 121–134.
Schmidt, Thomas (2006): "Realismus – Intuitionismus – Naturalismus". In: Düwell, M./Hübenthal, C./Werner, M. (Eds.): *Handbuch Ethik*. Stuttgart: Metzler. pp. 49–60.
Schnall, Ira M. (2004): "Philosophy of language and meta-ethics". In: *The Philosophical Quarterly*. 217. pp. 587–594.
Schroeder, Mark (2008a): *Being for. Evaluating the semantic program of expressivism*. New York: Oxford University Press.
Schroeder, Mark (2008b): "What is the Frege-Geach problem?" In: *Philosophical Compass*. 3. pp. 703–720.
Schroeder, Mark (2008c): "Expression for expressivists". In: *Philosophy and Phenomenological Research*. 76. pp. 86–116.
Schroeder, Mark (2009): "Hybrid expressivism: Virtues and vices". In: *Ethics*. 119. pp. 257–309.
Schroeder, Mark (2010): *Noncognitivism in ethics*. London; New York: Routledge.
Schroeder, Mark (2013): "Tempered expressivism". In: Shafer-Landau, R. (Ed.): *Oxford studies in metaethics*. Vol. 8. Oxford: Oxford University Press. pp. 283–314.
Schroeder, Mark (2014): "Does expressivism has subjectivist consequences?" In: *Philosophical Perspectives*. 28. pp. 278–290.
Schroeder, Mark (2015): "The truth in hybrid semantics". In: Ridge, M./Fletcher, G. (Eds.): *Having it both ways: Hybrid theories and modern metaethics*. Oxford: Oxford University Press. pp. 273–293.
Schueler, G. F. (1988): "Modus ponens and moral realism". In: *Ethics*. 98. S. 492–500.
Schulte, Peter (2010): *Zwecke und Mittel in einer natürlichen Welt. Instrumentelle Rationalität als Problem für den Naturalismus?* Paderborn: Mentis.
Sepielli, Andrew (2012): "Normative uncertainty for non-cognitivists". In: *Philosophical Studies*. 160. pp. 191–207.
Shafer-Landau, Russ (2003): *Moral Realism. A Defence*. New York: Oxford University Press.

Silk, Alex (2013): "Truth conditions and the meanings of ethical terms". In: Shafer-Landau, R. (Ed.): *Oxford Studies in Metaethics*. Vol. 8. Oxford: Oxford University Press. pp. 195–222.
Sinclair, Neil (2006): "The moral belief problem". In: *Ratio*. 19. pp. 249–260.
Sinclair, Neil (2007): "Propositional clothing and belief". In: *The Philosophical Quarterly*. 57. pp. 342–362.
Sinclair, Neil (2008): "Free thinking for expressivists". In: *Philosophical Papers*. 37. pp. 263–287.
Sinclair, Neil (2009): "Recent work in expressivism". In: *Analysis*. 69. pp. 136–147.
Sinhababu, Neil (2017): *Humean nature. How desire explains action, thought, and feeling*. Oxford: Oxford University Press.
Sinnott-Armstrong, Walter (1993): "Some problems for Gibbard's norm-expressivism". In: *Philosophical Studies*. 69. pp. 297–313.
Sinnott-Armstrong, Walter (2000): "Expressivism and embedding". In: *Philosophy and Phenomenological Research*. 61. pp. 677–693.
Skorupski, John (2010): *The domain of reasons*. Oxford; New York: Oxford University Press.
Slote, Michael (2006): "Moral sentimentalism and moral psychology". In: Copp, D. (Ed.): *The Oxford handbook of ethical theory*. Oxford: Oxford University Press. pp. 219–239.
Slote, Michael (2010): *Moral Sentimentalism*. New York: Oxford University Press.
Smith, Michael (1987): "The Humean theory of motivation". In: *Mind*. 96. pp. 36–61.
Smith, Michael (1994a): *The moral problem*. Oxford: Blackwell.
Smith, Michael (1994b): "Why expressivists about value should love minimalism about truth". In: *Analysis*. 54. pp. 1–12.
Smith, Michael (1994c): "Minimalism, truth-aptitude and belief". In: *Analysis*. 54. pp. 21–26.
Smith, Michael (1998): "Response-dependence without reduction". In: *European Review of Philosophy*. 3. pp. 85–108.
Smith, Michael (2001): "Some not-much-discussed problems for non-cognitivism in ethics". In: *Ratio*. 4. pp. 93–115.
Smith, Michael (2002): "Which passions rule?" In: *Philosophy and Phenomenological Research*. 65. pp. 157–163.
Smith, Michael (2004a): "The possibility of philosophy of action". In: Smith, M.: *Ethics and the a priori. Selected essays on moral psychology and meta-ethics*. Cambridge: Cambridge University Press. pp. 155–177.
Smith, Michael (2004b): "Moral realism". In: Smith, M.: *Ethics and the a priori. Selected essays on moral psychology and meta-ethics*. Cambridge: Cambridge University Press. pp. 181–207.
Smith, Michael (2004c): "Ethics and the a priori: A modern parable". In: Smith, M.: *Ethics and the a priori. Selected essays on moral psychology and meta-ethics*. Cambridge: Cambridge University Press. pp. 359–380.
Smith, Michael (2004d): "In defence of the moral problem. A reply to Brink, Copp, and Sayre-McCord". In: Smith, M.: *Ethics and the a priori. Selected essays on moral psychology and meta-ethics*. Cambridge: Cambridge University Press. pp. 259–296.
Smith, Michael (2004e): "Exploring the implications of the dispositional theory of value". In: Smith, M.: *Ethics and the a priori. Selected essays on moral psychology and meta-ethics*. Cambridge: Cambridge University Press. pp. 297–317.

Smith, Michael (2004 f): "Internalism's wheel". In: Smith, M.: *Ethics and the a priori. Selected essays on moral psychology and meta-ethics.* Cambridge: Cambridge University Press. pp. 318–342.
Smith, Michael (2005): "Meta-ethics". In: Jackson, F./Smith, M. (Eds.): *Oxford handbook of contemporary philosophy.* Oxford: Oxford University Press. pp. 3–30.
Smith, Michael (2010a): "Humeanism about motivation". In: O'Connor, T./Sandis, C. (Eds.): *A companion to the philosophy of action.* Chichester: Blackwell. pp. 153–158.
Smith, Michael (2010b): "Dworkin on external skepticism". In: *Boston University Law Review.* 90. pp. 509–520.
Smith, Michael/Stoljar, Daniel (2003): "Is there a Lockean argument against expressivism?" In: *Analysis.* 63. pp. 76–86.
Snare, Francis (1991): *Moral, motivation and convention. Hume's influential doctrines.* Cambridge: Cambridge University Press.
Stevenson, Charles L. (1944): *Ethics and language.* New Haven: Yale University Press.
Stevenson, Charles L. (1963a): "The emotive conception of ethics and its cognitive implications". In: Stevenson, Charles L.: *Facts and values. Studies in ethical analysis.* New Haven: Yale University Press. pp. 55–70.
Stevenson, Charles L. (1963b): "The nature of ethical disagreement". In: Stevenson, Charles L.: *Facts and values. Studies in ethical analysis.* New Haven: Yale University Press. pp. 1–9.
Stevenson, Charles L. (1963c): "The emotive meaning of ethical terms". In: Stevenson, Charles L.: *Facts and values. Studies in ethical analysis.* New Haven: Yale University Press. pp. 10–31.
Stevenson, Charles L. (1963d): "Relativism and nonrelativism in the theory of value". In: Stevenson, Charles L.: *Facts and values. Studies in ethical analysis.* New Haven: Yale University Press. pp. 71–93.
Stevenson, Charles L. (1963e): "Moore's arguments against certain forms of ethical naturalism". In: Stevenson, Charles L.: *Facts and values. Studies in ethical analysis.* New Haven: Yale University Press. pp. 117–137.
Stoljar, Daniel/Damnjanovic, Nic (2010): "The deflationary theory of truth". In: *Stanford Encyclopedia of Philosophy.* pp. 1–22.
Strandberg, Caj (2012): "A dual aspect account of moral languag"e. In: *Philosophy and Phenomenological Research.* 84. pp. 87–122.
Strandberg, Caj (2015): "Options for hybrid expressivism". In: *Ethical Theory and Moral Practice.* 18. pp. 91–111.
Sturgeon, Nicholas L. (2006): "Ethical naturalism". In: Copp, D. (Ed.): *The Oxford handbook of ethical theory.* Oxford: Oxford University Press. pp. 91–121.
Svavarsdóttir, Sigrún (2001): "On Simon Blackburn's *Ruling passions*". In: *Philosophical Books.* 42. pp. 18–26.
Sweigart, John (1964): "The distance between Hume and emotivism". In: *The Philosophical Quarterly.* 14. pp. 229–236.
Tarkian, Tatjana (2009): *Moral, Normativität und Wahrheit. Zur neueren Debatte um Grundfragen der Ethik.* Paderborn: Mentis.
Thomson, Judith Jarvis (2006): "The legacy of *Principia*". In: Horgan, T./Timmons, M. (Eds.): *Metaethics after Moore.* Oxford: Clarendon Press. pp. 233–254.

Timmons, Mark (1999): *Morality without foundations. A defense of ethical contextualism.* New York: Oxford University Press.
Toppinen, Teemu (2013): "Believing in expressivism". In: Shafer-Landau, R. (Ed.): *Oxford studies in metaethics.* Vol. 8. Oxford: Oxford University Press. pp. 252–282.
Toppinen, Teemu (2015a): "Pure expressivism and motivational internalism". In: Björnsson, G./Strandberg, C./Francén Olinder, R./Eriksson, J./Björklund, F. (Eds.): *Motivational internalism.* New York: Oxford University Press. pp. 150–166.
Toppinen, Teemu (2015b): "Relational expressivism and Moore's paradox". In: *Journal of Ethics and Social Philosophy.* 9. pp. 1–8.
Toulmin, Stephen E. (1970): *An examination of the place of reason in ethics.* Cambridge: Cambridge University Press.
Unwin, Nicholas (1999): "Quasi-realism, negation and the Frege-Geach problem". In: *The Philosophical Quarterly.* pp. 337–352.
Unwin, Nicholas (2001): "Norms and negation: A problem for Gibbard's logic". In: *The Philosophical Quarterly.* 51. pp. 60–75.
Urmson, James O. (1968): *The emotive theory of ethics.* London: Hutchinson.
Van Roojen, Mark (1996): "Expressivism and irrationality". In: *Philosophical Review.* 105. pp. 311–35.
Van Roojen, Mark (2014): "Moral cognitivism vs. non-cognitivism". In: *Stanford Encyclopedia of Philosophy.* pp. 1–88.
Wallace, R. Jay (2005): "Moral psychology". In: Jackson, F./Smith, M. (Eds.): *Oxford handbook of contemporary philosophy.* Oxford: Oxford University Press. pp. 86–113.
Wedgwood, Ralph (1997): Noncognitivism, truth and logic. In: Philosophical Studies. 86. pp. 73–91.
Wedgwood, Ralph (2007): *The Nature of Normativity.* Oxford: Clarendon Press.
Wiggins, David (1991): "Ayer's ethical theory: Emotivism or subjectivism?" In: Griffiths, A. P. (Ed.): *A. J. Ayer. Memorial essays.* Cambridge: Cambridge University Press. pp. 181–196.
Wiggins, David (1998): "In a subjectivist framework". In: Fehige, C./Wessels, U. (Eds.): *Preferences.* Berlin; New York: de Gruyter. pp. 212–232.
Wilson, Anne E. et al. (2003): "The nature and effects of young children's lies". In: *Social Development.* 12. pp. 21–45.
Wimmer, Heinz/Perner, Josef (1983): "Beliefs about beliefs: Representation and constraining of wrong beliefs in young children's understanding of deception". In: *Cognition.* 13. pp. 103–128.
Wright, Crispin (1985): "Review of Blackburn *Spreading the word*". In: *Mind.* 94. pp. 310–19.
Wright, Crispin (1993): *Realism, meaning and truth.* Second Edition. Oxford: Blackwell.
Zangwill, Nick (1992): "Moral modus ponens". In: *Ratio.* 5. pp. 177–93.

Index of names

Alm, David   30, 36, 38, 101, 103f.
Altham, J. E. J.   33
Anscombe, Elizabeth   34
Árdal, Páll S.   44f.
Audi, Robert   30
Ayer, Alfred J.   1–4, 6f., 9, 13, 16, 18f., 22–25, 27, 30–32, 37, 39, 41f., 44–54, 56, 60, 62–64, 66, 72–76, 80–83, 86, 90, 98f., 103, 109–111, 137, 146, 148f., 151, 162, 165, 167–169, 171, 179–184, 189f., 204f., 210, 212, 233

Baldwin, Thomas   30, 38, 165, 172
Bar-On, Dorit   1, 9, 23, 31, 36, 66, 100, 158, 162
Barker, Stephen J.   2, 8, 22, 41, 66, 101f., 104, 107f., 114f., 117f., 120–122, 124, 140, 145, 160f., 220
Barnes, W. H. F.   45, 62
Björklund, Fredrik   115
Blackburn, Simon   1–5, 7f., 10, 12, 14, 18–20, 22, 24–33, 37–45, 57f., 60–64, 66f., 80–82, 85f., 90f., 93–95, 97–99, 106f., 109, 146–149, 152f., 158, 162, 166–169, 171f., 177–179, 181–183, 189f., 192, 201–204, 206, 210f., 213–216, 220, 222, 226, 229f., 233
Boisvert, Daniel R.   2, 22, 30–32, 36, 100–102, 104, 107f., 114, 118, 124, 138f., 189, 213
Boyd, Richard   175
Brandt, Richard B.   17, 38, 115, 165, 178, 203
Bricke, John   45
Brighouse, M.   40, 106, 220f.
Brink, David O.   24, 36, 38, 124, 175
Broad, C. D.   44f.
Brown, Charlotte   44
Bull, Ray   199
Burgess, John P.   65

Campbell, Richmond   100f., 104, 213, 220f.

Carnap, Rudolf   45, 62, 66, 210
Charlow, Nate   36
Chrisman, Matthew   1, 9, 12, 15, 22f., 28, 30f., 33f., 36, 45, 66, 92, 96, 100, 158, 162, 229
Cohon, Rachel   44
Copp, David   1f., 22, 28, 30, 38, 101f., 104, 108, 212, 218, 220
Cuneo, Terence   2, 22, 27f., 30–32, 41, 65f.
Czaniera, Uwe   2, 14, 23, 28, 36, 41

Damasio, Antonio R.   18, 213
Damnjanovic, Nic   26
Dancy, Jonathan   37, 220f.
d'Arms, Justin   4, 22, 24, 36–40, 65f., 165, 172, 212
Davis, Wayne   31
Debes, Remy   38
Divers, John   23, 27, 92
Döring, Sabine A.   220
Dreier, James   22, 27f., 30f., 34, 61, 91–94, 101, 106, 145, 149f., 154, 212
Dunaway, Bill   30
Duncan-Jones, A. S.   45, 62
Dunn, Robert   4
Dworkin, Ronald   13f., 16, 36, 40, 65f., 91, 95

Edwards, Paul   101
Enoch, David   14
Eriksson, John   31, 100f., 104, 113–115, 118, 120, 138, 142, 160f., 179, 194
Ernst, Gerhard   12, 15, 18, 24, 30, 32, 37f., 65f., 91, 165
Evans, Angela D.   198f.

Falk, W. D.   44
Field, Hartry   26, 229
Fine, Cordelia   31, 37f.
Finlay, Stephen   36, 101
Fletcher, Guy   218, 220f.

Index of names

Frankena, William K.   17, 38, 65
Frege, Gottlob   26, 106

Geach, Peter T.   106, 108
Gert, Joshua   24, 30 f.
Gibbard, Allan   1–5, 7 f., 10, 12, 15, 18–20, 22, 24, 28–33, 36–43, 45, 57–64, 67, 82–86, 90 f., 94 f., 98–101, 106 f., 109, 152 f., 166–169, 172 f., 176–179, 190–195, 198, 210–216, 220, 222, 226 f., 229 f., 233
Gill, Michael B.   30, 38
Grice, Herbert P.   31, 190, 199

Hägerström, Axel   45, 62
Haidt, Jonathan   4, 18, 115, 207, 213, 227
Halbig, Christoph   32, 37 f., 40, 165
Hale, Bob   36, 106
Hallich, Oliver   8, 12, 15, 17, 32, 37 f., 101, 104, 114 f., 125–137, 139, 161
Harcourt, Edward   30 f., 34, 40, 61, 65, 91
Hare, Richard M.   1 f., 4, 7 f., 13, 16–18, 22, 24 f., 28–32, 37–42, 45, 51–57, 60, 62–64, 69, 76–82, 86, 90 f., 98 f., 103, 109–118, 121–124, 126, 136–139, 160, 165–167, 173, 179 f., 190, 210, 212, 229, 233
Harman, Gilbert   4, 13, 17, 20, 44
Harris, Paul   199
Harrison, Jonathan   45
Harth, Manfred   22, 24, 30, 36, 91, 165
Hay, Ryan   100, 220
Hill, Thomas E.   30, 36
Horgan, Terence   1 f., 22, 31, 38 f., 61, 93 f., 213, 220
Horwich, Paul L.   23, 26, 28, 30, 33, 106, 212
Hume, David   4, 12, 38 f., 44 f., 82, 98, 213

Jackson, Frank   8 f., 22 f., 27, 30, 35, 38, 101, 144–151, 154 f., 161 f., 173, 195 f., 202, 204, 218, 220
Jacobson, Daniel   4, 22, 24, 36–40, 65 f., 165, 172, 203, 212
Jenkins, C. S. I.   30, 40, 65

Joyce, Richard   2, 4 f., 10 f., 19 f., 22, 30, 34–38, 40 f., 44 f., 65, 100 f., 108, 179, 207–210, 213–221, 223, 229

Kauppinen, Antti   4, 15, 22, 28, 30 f., 36–38, 61, 95, 100 f., 220–222, 224 f., 227
Kennett, Jeanette   31, 37 f.
Köhler, Sebastian   9, 30, 173–176
Kölbel, Max   22, 36, 106
Kramer, Matthew   35
Kripke, Saul   175
Künne, Wolfgang   26

Lee, Kang   198 f.
Lenman, James   24, 30, 92 f.
Lewis, David   40, 66, 68 f., 71, 97
Locke, John   31
Loeb, Don   30

Mackie, John L.   3 f., 8 f., 12–14, 17, 20, 39 f., 44 f., 65, 67 f., 70 f., 80, 88 f., 97 f., 182
Merli, David   30, 164 f., 220 f.
Miller, Alexander   12, 15, 23 f., 27, 30 f., 37–39, 92, 106, 164 f., 169, 172
Millikan, Ruth G.   193, 197–200
Moore, George E.   8, 12–14, 16 f., 72, 76, 78, 82, 86, 95, 98, 125, 215
Murphy, Scott   115

Newton, Paul   199
Nichols, Shaun   4, 18, 38, 207, 214

Ogden, C. K.   45, 62, 210
O'Leary-Hawthorne, John   212
Oppy, Graham   23, 27

Padel, Stephan   149
Parfit, Derek   4, 22 f., 31, 33, 37 f., 40
Perner, Josef   193
Pettit, Philip   8 f., 22 f., 30, 144–151, 154 f., 161 f., 173, 195 f., 202, 204
Polak, A.   199
Price, Huw   1, 22, 40, 44, 65–67, 91, 212
Prinz, Jesse   4, 18, 28, 38, 207, 220 f.
Putnam, Hilary   175

Index of names

Radtke, Burkhard   14 f., 22 f., 37, 66, 91, 106
Railton, Peter   30, 33, 38, 61, 220
Ramsey, Frank P.   26
Rawls, John   44
Reddy, Vasudevi   199
Richards, I. A.   45, 62, 210
Ridge, Michael   1–3, 8–10, 22 f., 28, 31–34, 36–39, 61, 65 f., 91, 93, 99–104, 107–110, 112–115, 117–122, 124, 140, 145, 155, 160–162, 178 f., 189, 192, 196 f., 203 f., 206, 212, 220 f.
Rosen, Gideon   31, 33, 36, 65, 91, 165
Ross, David   149
Ross, Hildy   199
Russell, Bertrand   45, 62
Rüther, Markus   15, 32, 34 f., 37, 65
Ryle, Gilbert   166

Sauer, Hanno   38
Sayre-McCord, Geoff   15, 23, 30, 37 f.
Scanlon, Thomas M.   29, 37, 95, 220
Scarano, Nico   12, 15, 17, 32, 35, 37, 101, 220
Schaber, Peter   23 f., 36, 38, 175
Schmidt, Thomas   23, 37 f.
Schnall, Ira M.   23, 31
Schroeder, Mark   1, 3, 8–10, 15, 23, 30–34, 36 f., 60, 100 f., 106–108, 118, 124, 145, 156 f., 159, 164, 178 f., 181–183, 190, 192–197, 199, 203 f., 206, 212 f., 218, 228 f.
Schueler, G. F.   106
Schulte, Peter   2 f., 10, 32, 34 f., 37, 41, 106, 145, 173 f., 176, 178 f., 181, 190, 192–194, 197–201, 203 f., 206, 213
Sepielli, Aandrew   36
Shafer-Landau, Russ   22 f., 28, 37, 40, 65, 164
Shah, Nishi   229
Sias, James   9, 23, 31, 36, 66, 100, 158, 162
Silk, Alex   36
Sinclair, Neil   2, 30 f., 33, 36, 41, 94, 96, 101–103, 220
Sinhababu, Neil   38

Sinnott-Armstrong, Walter   22, 30, 33, 35, 83, 91, 100 f.
Skorupski, John   37 f.
Slote, Michael   4, 38
Smith, Adam   213
Smith, Melissa   199
Smith, Michael   12, 15, 18, 22 f., 27, 30, 33 f., 36–38, 61, 92, 138 f., 143, 145, 161, 165, 170, 173, 203
Snare, Francis   44
Stepanians, Markus   221
Stevenson, Charles L.   1 f., 6–9, 16, 18 f., 22–25, 28, 30–32, 37, 39, 41, 45, 48–53, 56, 60, 62–64, 74–76, 79–82, 86, 90, 98 f., 109–116, 118–120, 127, 136, 146 f., 149 f., 160, 162, 165 f., 168 f., 171, 179, 181, 183–190, 200, 204 f., 210, 212, 214, 229, 233
Stoljar, Daniel   26, 145
Strandberg, Caj   30, 100 f., 103, 108, 189, 220 f.
Sturgeon, Nicholas L.   175
Svavarsdóttir, Sigrún   38
Sweigart, John   44

Tarkian, Tatjana   15, 22, 31, 33, 35, 37 f., 40, 65 f.
Thomson, Judith J.   2, 41
Timmons, Mark   1 f., 22, 31, 38 f., 61, 94, 213, 220
Toppinen, Teemu   1, 9, 30, 33 f., 100 f., 155, 162, 220 f.
Toulmin, Stephen E.   45, 167 f.
Tresan, Jon   101
Turiel, Elliot   213

Unwin, Nicholas   30 f., 106, 220
Urmson, James O.   28, 66, 115 f., 136, 178

Van Roojen, Mark   22 f., 28, 31, 35–37, 40, 45, 65, 220
Velleman, David   229

Wallace, R. Jay   18
Wedgwood, Ralph   22 f., 31, 36–38, 220 f.
Wiggins, David   44
Wilson, Anne E.   199

Wimmer, Heinz   193
Wolf, Jean-Claude   23f., 36, 38
Wright, Crispin   91, 106

Zangwill, Nick   106

Index of subjects

armchair philosophy   223–227

belief   1, 3, 6–8, 10, 30–34, 38 f., 42, 47 f., 50 f., 53 f., 56–63, 67–69, 75 f., 82, 87–96, 98–105, 107–109, 114 f., 117–128, 131, 136–147, 149, 152, 154–163, 174 f., 180, 182, 187 f., 190–199, 201, 205, 211, 215 f., 218–220, 222, 229 f., 232
– descriptive belief   61, 109, 114, 119, 121, 124–126, 128, 137, 139, 141 f., 145, 147 f., 150, 156 f., 160–163
– moral belief   61, 67, 89–92, 94, 99, 102–104, 174–177, 219
– non-moral belief   75, 103, 159
– normative belief   61, 143, 201

cognitive   6, 31, 42, 48, 61, 93, 96, 100 f., 185, 188, 201
cognitivism   1 f., 14, 36, 61, 93 f., 102
conceptual analysis   17, 176, 223–227, 230
conservative   3, 7, 20, 62, 65–67, 69, 73, 75, 80 f., 86 f., 89 f., 97 f., 158, 233
continuity thesis   218, 230
convention   10, 67, 72, 77 f., 87–89, 114, 116, 118, 131, 133, 136 f., 144, 146, 148 f., 169, 177, 182–185, 187, 189, 191, 193, 196, 203–206, 208, 219, 221

descriptivism   50, 78–80, 96
desire   1, 3, 6–12, 18, 30, 32–35, 37–39, 41 f., 50, 53–57, 61, 63, 65, 67–69, 76, 78, 82, 87–90, 93, 95 f., 98–109, 117, 120–126, 128, 139–154, 156–159, 161–163, 165–168, 170 f., 174, 182, 192, 194–196, 200–205, 208, 210, 215, 217–222, 228–230, 232
– higher-order desire   153, 166, 168–171, 173, 177, 202
direction of fit   34, 93
disagreement   17, 31 f., 35, 49–51, 74 f., 79, 82, 89 f., 98, 120–122, 124, 140, 147, 149–153, 160 f., 228

ecumenical expressivism   1, 100
emotion   18, 35, 39, 46, 48, 63, 165 f., 170 f., 185, 215
emotivism   1, 6, 9, 14, 18 f., 22–24, 39, 44 f., 52, 54, 56, 62, 64, 66, 73, 75 f., 90, 106, 167, 173, 178, 207–209, 233
epistemology   4, 6 f., 15–17, 19 f., 35, 37, 39, 41, 76, 79, 81, 86, 98 f., 102, 216 f., 219, 229 f.
error theory   3, 8, 14, 17, 20, 40, 44 f., 65, 67, 70 f., 80, 85, 87–90, 97 f.
expression relation   3, 5, 9–11, 20, 34, 54, 56, 60, 64, 67, 152 f., 164, 177–181, 183 f., 186 f., 189 f., 192–194, 196–209, 221, 229 f.

feeling   24, 28, 46, 48–50, 52–56, 59, 63, 82 f., 85, 116, 146, 148, 165–168, 170–173, 178, 181–184, 201, 208
Frege-Geach problem   5 f., 8, 90, 104–109, 118, 120, 140, 142 f., 159, 161, 164, 192, 216, 228

hermeneutic   65
hybrid expressivism   1 f., 6, 8, 19, 49, 100–104, 107–109, 112–115, 117 f., 120, 122, 124 f., 135, 137 f., 143, 147, 155–163, 216

ideationalism   31
imperative   49, 116, 167 f., 197, 200 f.
imperative theory   45, 62
independence thesis   5, 10 f., 19 f., 207–209, 213–215, 221, 229 f., 232 f.
inferentialism   96
intuition   79, 81 f., 86, 223 f., 227 f., 231
intuitionism   14, 79, 98

judgement   5 f., 10, 13, 15–19, 23–30, 37, 39, 42, 46–48, 52 f., 57, 59 f., 63, 72 f., 75 f., 79, 82, 84 f., 88, 90, 95, 98 f., 105, 110 f., 115, 122–124, 138, 157 f., 160,

167, 179, 184, 210, 212, 214f., 217–222, 227–230, 232f.

linguistic   4–7, 10, 16–20, 31f., 34f., 41f., 44, 47, 51, 53–55, 57f., 63f., 66–68, 71–74, 78, 81, 85, 87–89, 92, 97–99, 105f., 114f., 118, 128, 130f., 133–137, 144, 146, 148–150, 157f., 161, 169, 171, 174, 176f., 179–185, 189, 193–197, 199–201, 203–206, 208, 210–212, 214–217, 219–233

meaning   6, 12, 16–18, 20, 24f., 29, 31–36, 39, 42, 44–48, 50–61, 63–66, 68–70, 73f., 76–79, 82f., 90, 93–97, 103–106, 109, 111–117, 121, 123, 125f., 128–130, 132, 134–138, 142, 144, 148f., 151, 153–160, 162, 164, 167–169, 171f., 174–177, 179–194, 196f., 199f., 203, 208–212, 214, 216, 219, 224f., 229, 232
– descriptive meaning   8, 24f., 49–51, 53, 56, 63, 78f., 110–114, 116–118, 124, 126, 130f., 135, 137, 139, 160f.
– emotive meaning   24, 48–50, 53, 181, 185–188, 214
– expressive meaning   145, 188
mentalism   6, 30–35, 41f., 47f., 50, 55f., 58–60, 63f., 67f., 100, 105, 113, 152, 158, 162, 210, 218, 229, 232
metaethics   1, 3–6, 11–18, 20–22, 30–34, 38f., 41f., 44f., 62, 64f., 68, 71f., 75f., 81, 83, 85f., 89, 94f., 97–101, 128, 134, 143, 152, 158, 171, 175–179, 207–210, 212, 216–218, 220, 224f., 227f., 230, 232f.
metaphysics   7, 15, 17, 81, 86, 172, 216f., 219, 230
metasemantic   35f., 38, 42, 56
methodology   7, 11, 20, 62, 68f., 72, 83, 97–99, 207, 221, 228, 230
minimalism   5, 7f., 10, 26–29, 61, 65, 84, 91–93, 99, 230
– minimalism about belief   61, 92–94, 99
– minimalism about facts   29, 84
– minimalism about properties   29, 84
– minimalism about representation   92f.
– minimalism about truth   8, 26–29, 61, 84, 91
moral attitude problem   5, 9, 164, 169, 172–178, 205, 216, 230
moral facts   6, 15, 26, 28–30, 42, 62, 67, 83, 87–89, 172
moral properties   6, 15, 28–30, 42, 62, 67, 83, 172f., 175, 219
moral truth   6, 26f., 29f., 41f., 62, 67, 83, 90
motivation   17f., 53, 63, 76, 79f., 82, 86, 98, 102, 105, 124, 158, 208, 217–219, 222, 227f., 230

naturalism   8f., 14, 25, 33, 36, 79, 81f., 86, 99, 101–105, 113, 121, 124f., 156f., 159, 161f., 172–177, 190, 202, 205, 216, 218f., 233
neo-expressivism   1, 8f., 19, 100, 155, 158f., 162
neutrality   13f., 128
non-cognitive   6, 18, 31, 35, 41f., 46, 48, 50, 59–61, 63, 81f., 92f., 96, 100f., 159–162, 164–168, 170–172, 174, 177f., 180, 185, 187f., 205, 230
non-cognitivism   14, 23, 212
non-descriptivism   25, 29
non-naturalism   3, 9, 14, 17, 25, 33, 36, 76, 79, 81f., 86, 94–96, 98f., 101–105, 113, 121, 124f., 159, 172, 175–177, 190, 202, 205, 216, 219, 233
non-quasi-realism   6–8, 87, 89f., 98f., 233

ontology   4, 6, 14f., 17–20, 29, 35, 88, 99
open question argument   8f., 72, 76, 82, 86, 98, 102, 125, 164, 176f., 216

parity thesis   32, 60, 63, 152
pejorative   108, 147, 159
pragmatic   35f., 42, 196
prescriptivism   1, 14, 18, 22, 25, 39, 45, 52, 57, 62, 69, 233
projection   39f.
projectivism   7, 22, 39f., 42, 57, 67, 88
proposition   5, 7, 10, 16, 24, 27, 35, 40, 43, 45–48, 62, 65, 67, 80f., 94, 99, 102,

105, 136, 158, 163, 172 f., 179, 183, 193 f., 200, 215 f., 219, 230
psychologistic semantics   31, 157
psychology   4–8, 10 f., 15, 17–21, 34–37, 39, 41–44, 47, 51, 53, 55–57, 64, 81, 88, 90, 92–96, 99, 115, 118, 150, 157 f., 162–164, 167, 172, 174, 177, 181, 183–188, 193, 195, 201, 204–223, 226–230, 232 f.
pure expressivism   1, 9, 100, 137 f., 143 f., 147, 149, 155 f., 161–163

quasi-realism   1–3, 5–8, 11, 14, 18–20, 26, 40–42, 45, 60, 62, 65–69, 80–85, 87–92, 94–96, 98–100, 106, 182, 202

rationalism   39, 61, 88, 90, 98 f., 115, 207, 233
realism   1, 14, 25 f., 81, 84, 91, 104, 175 f.
reflective equilibrium   226–228, 231
relational expressivism   1, 8 f., 19, 100, 155–158, 162
representation   92 f., 193
revisionary   3, 7, 20, 45, 62, 65 f., 72, 74, 77, 80, 86 f., 89 f., 97 f.

semantic   14–17, 19, 29, 31, 35 f., 38 f., 42, 56, 111, 136 f., 151, 157 f., 162, 175 f., 189, 193 f., 196 f., 199 f., 203 f., 211 f., 214 f., 217, 228 f.
sentiment   39, 46, 48, 165 f., 171 f.
sentimentalism   4–6, 11, 38 f., 42, 63, 89 f., 98 f., 213 f., 218, 226, 233
– sentimentalism about moral expression   6, 30 f., 34–36, 42, 46, 50, 60, 63, 67 f., 100, 232
– sentimentalism about moral judgement   19, 39, 88, 207, 220, 222, 230, 232
specification challenge   164–168, 171, 174, 205
standard definition   1, 6, 8, 30–32, 38, 41 f., 46–48, 53, 55–57, 59 f., 62–65, 67, 72, 80, 91–93, 99–101, 104, 145, 156, 159, 171, 232
subjectivism   9, 14, 44, 66, 72 f., 75, 122, 143–147, 149–155, 161 f., 168, 179, 202, 218
supervenience   74, 78, 81, 98, 110, 137 f., 143, 161, 216

www.ingramcontent.com/pod-product-compliance
Lightning Source LLC
Chambersburg PA
CBHW020751160426
43192CB00006B/297